1996

COMPUTER FACIAL
ANIMATION

COMPUTER FACIAL ANIMATION

Frederic I. Parke
Keith Waters

A K PETERS
Wellesley, Massachusetts

Editorial, Sales, and Customer Service Office

A K Peters, Ltd.
289 Linden Street
Wellesley, MA 02181

Front cover images: Reprinted with permission of Steve DiPaola.

Library of Congress Cataloging-in-Publication Data

Parke, Frederic I.
      Computer facial animation / Frederic I. Parke, Keith Waters.
            p. cm.
      Includes bibliographical references and index.
      ISBN 1-56881-014-8
      1. Computer animation. 2. Face. I. Waters, Keith. II. Title.
TR897.7.P37   1996
006.6—dc20   96-25110
                                                                                CIP

Printed in the United States of America
00 99 98 97 96   10 9 8 7 6 5 4 3 2 1

Contents

Preface

This book is about computer facial models, computer generated facial images, and facial animation. In particular it addresses the principles of creating face models and the manipulation or control of computer generated facial attributes. In addition, various sections in the book describe and explain the development of specific computer facial animation techniques over the past 20 years, as well as those expected in the near future.

In recent years there has been considerable interest in computer-based three-dimensional character animation. Part of this interest is a strong fascination in the development and use of facial animation. There is no single reason for this burst of activity, but it has certainly been fueled by both an emerging computer animation film production industry and the games industry. There has also been a rapid growth of interest within the scientific community. In this context, it has been desirable to develop simulations of surgical procedures, careful and precise observations of computer facial animation, and the production of detailed visualizations of human anatomy.

The first SIGGRAPH tutorials on the *State of the Art in Facial Animation* in 1989 and 1990 provided a vital vehicle to collect and present material from a variety of face-related disciplines. The success of these two courses and the material presented therein prompted the development of this book. Therefore the text covers much of the material presented in those tutorials plus a number of topics that originally were not included.

This book was written to meet the perceived need for a text which pulls together, explains, and documents the diverse developments in facial animation. Since the information on computer facial animation is currently quite fragmented, we wish to make this technology much more accessible to a wide range of readers, spanning the spectrum from the merely curious, to serious users of computer animation systems, to system implementers, and to researchers. As a result the book contains enough depth necessary for serious animators, provides valuable reference for researchers, and still remains accessible to those with little or no sophistication in this area. Our expectation is that this book be used as a text, or as a case-study reference, for courses in computer animation.

Acknowledgments

We would like to thank Brad deGraf, Steve DiPaola, Matt Elson, Jeff Kleiser, Steve Pieper, Bill Reeves, Lance Williams, and Brian Wyvill, who participated in the 1989 and 1990 SIGGRAPH Facial Animation tutorials and who presented much of the material which formed the initial basis for this book.

We would also like to thank the many others who assisted us in the development of this book.

Authors

Frederic I. Parke joined IBM in 1991 where he is a senior member of the Visual Systems Architecture group of the IBM RISC System/6000 Division in Austin, TX. Prior to joining IBM, Dr. Parke was Professor of Computer Science and Director of the Computer Graphics Laboratory at the New York Institute of Technology. Dr. Parke has been active in the development of facial animation since 1971. He received his Ph.D. in 1974 from the University of Utah. He is the author of a number of technical papers on facial animation and has lectured widely on the subject. He organized and chaired the SIGGRAPH *Introduction to Computer Animation* tutorials in 1983, 1984, and 1985. In 1989 and 1990 he organized and chaired the SIGGRAPH tutorials *State of the Art in Facial Animation.*

Current Address:

Visual Systems, 4506
IBM, RISC System/6000 Division
11400 Burnet Road
Austin, TX 78758
Internet: fparke@austin.ibm.com

Keith Waters joined Digital Equipment in 1991 where he is a consulting engineer at the Cambridge Research Laboratory in Boston, MA. Keith received his Ph.D. from Middlesex University in 1988 and prior to joining Digital he was a member of the research staff at Schlumberger's Laboratory for Computer Science in Austin, TX. Dr. Waters' Ph.D. research resulted in the development of *muscle-based* models for facial animation. To date Dr. Waters has published a number of technical papers on facial animation, including physically based models for animation and medical applications. In 1989 and 1990 he was a principal contributor to the SIGGRAPH tutorials on the *State of the Art in Facial Animation*.

Current Address:

Cambridge Research Laboratory
Digital Equipment Corporation
One Kendall Square, Bldg 700
Cambridge, MA 02139
Internet: waters@crl.dec.com

1

Introduction

1.1. Introduction

In recent years there has been considerable interest in computer-based three-dimensional facial character animation. This is not a new endeavor; initial efforts to represent and animate faces using computers go back more than 20 years. However, a recent flurry of activity in character animation has promoted a concurrent interest in facial animation. Our intent is to present the principles of facial animation to enable animators to develop their own systems and environments.

The human face is interesting and challenging because of its familiarity. Essentially, the face is the part of the body we use to recognize individuals; we can recognize a face from vast universe of similar faces and are able to detect very subtle changes in facial expression. These skills are learned early in life, and they rapidly develop into a major channel of communication. Small wonder, then, that character animators pay a great deal of attention to the face.

Human facial expression has been the subject of much investigation by the scientific community. In particular the issues of universality of facial expression across cultures and the derivation of a small number of principal facial expressions have consumed considerable attention. *The Expression of the Emotions in Man and Animals*, published by Charles Darwin [Dar72] in 1872, dealt precisely with these issues and sowed the seeds for a subsequent

1

century to research, clarify, and validate his original theories. The value of this body of work, and of others in this field, requires no explanation in the context of facial animation.

The ability to model the human face and then animate the subtle nuances of facial expression remains a significant challenge in computer graphics. Despite a heavy reliance on traditional computer graphics algorithms such as modeling and rendering, facial animation has been poorly defined, without well-understood solutions. Facial animations often are developed with *ad-hoc* techniques that are nonextendible and rapidly become brittle. Therefore, this book presents a structured approach, by describing the anatomy of the face, working though the fundamentals of facial modeling and animation, and describing some state-of-the-art techniques.

1.2.   About This Book

The purpose of this book is to provide a source for readers interested in the many aspects of computer-based facial animation. In this book we have tried to capture the basic requirements for anyone wanting to animate the human face, from key framing to physically based modeling. The nature of the subject requires some knowledge of computer graphics, although a novice to the subject also can find the book an interesting resource about the face.

Clearly the field of computer-generated facial animation is rapidly changing; every year new advances are reported, making it difficult to capture the state of the art. However, it is clear that facial animation is a field whose time has come. The growth of increasingly complex computer-generated characters demands expressive, articulate faces. What is interesting is that most of the techniques employed today involve principles developed in the research community several years ago — in some instances, more than a couple of decades.

So why this sudden surge of interest in computer-generated facial animation? There is no single reason, although we can point to several key influences. Perhaps the most interesting is forged by commercial production animation houses, whose insatiable appetite for the latest and greatest visual effect is both enormous and endless. Pacific Data Images and Pixar are examples of such production facilities where, for example, the Michael Jackson music video *Black on White* and the short feature *Tin Toy* were produced. These commercial facility houses are trendsetters who popularize animation techniques.

Another key reason involves the modeling of the human face in three dimensions, which is difficult to do manually. Improvements in scanner technology, such as the Cyberware optical laser scanner [Cyb90], and the availability to buy predigitized data sets from companies such as View-point [Vie93] reduce this painful and labor-intensive bottleneck.

A third — and perhaps the most intriguing — influence is the the advent of believable social agents. The construction of believable agents breaks the traditional mold of facial animation; agents have to operate in real time, bringing along a new set of constraints. While the basic algorithms used to animate a real-time character are concurrent with production animation, nontraditional tools have to be developed to deal with issues such as lip synchronization and behavior interaction.

Two-dimensional facial character animation has been well defined over the years by traditional animation studios such as Disney Studios, Hanna-Barbera, and Warner Brothers. However, three-dimensional computer-generated facial character animation has not been well defined at all. Therefore this book is focused principally on realistic three-dimensional faces.

As a further aid to help the reader, code samples are available from the sites listed in the Appendices.

1.3.   A Brief Historical Sketch of Facial Animation

This section is a brief synopsis of key events that have helped shape the field, rather than a chronological account of facial animation. Most events in facial animation have been published in one form or another. The most popular have been the proceedings and course notes of the ACM SIGGRAPH Conference, followed by other related computer graphics journals and conferences proceedings.[1]

Historically, the first computer-generated images of faces were generated by Parke as part of Ivan Sutherland's computer graphics course at the University of Utah in the early 1970s. Parke [Par72] began with a very crude polygonal representation of the head, which resulted in a flip-pack animation of the face opening and closing its eyes and mouth. While at the university, Henri Gouraud was also completing his dissertation work on his then new, smooth polygon shading algorithm; to demonstrate the effectiveness of the technique he applied it to a digitized model of his wife's face. Parke used these innovative shading techniques to produce several segments of fairly realistic facial animation. He did this by collecting facial expression polygon data from real faces using photogrammetric techniques and simply interpolating between expressions to create animation. By 1974, motivated by the desire to quickly produce facial animation, Parke [Par74] completed the first parameterized facial model.

---

[1]The reader is encouraged to refer to the Bibliography for a more complete listing.

In 1971, Chernoff [Che71] first published his work using computer-generated two-dimensional face drawings to represent a k-dimensional space. By
using a simple graphical representation of the face, an elaborate encoding
scheme was derived. Also in 1973, Gillenson [Gil74] at Ohio State University reported his work on an interactive system to assemble and edit
two-dimensional line-drawn facial images with the goal of creating a computerized photoidenti-kit system.

From 1974 through 1978, three-dimensional facial animation development
was essentially dormant. However, during this period the development
of two-dimensional computer-assisted animation systems continued at the
New York Institute of Technology, Cornell University, and later at Hanna-
Barbera. These systems supported two-dimensional cartoon animation including facial animation.

In 1980, Platt [Pla80] at the University of Pennsylvania published his mas-
ters thesis on a physically based muscle-controlled facial expression model.
In 1982, Brennan [Bre82] at MIT reported work on techniques for computer-
produced two-dimensional facial caricatures. Also at MIT in 1982, Weil
[Wei82] reported on work using a video disk-based system to interactively
select and composite facial features. Later at MIT, based on this work, Bur-
son developed computer-based techniques for aging facial images, especially
images of children.

In the mid eighties developments in facial animation took off once more.
An animation short film, *Tony de Peltrie*, produced by Bergeron and Lachapelle [BL85] in 1985, was a landmark for facial animation. This was the
first computer-animated short where three-dimensional facial expression and
speech were a fundamental part of telling the story.

In 1987, Waters [Wat87] reported a new muscle model approach to facial
expression animation. This approach allowed a variety of facial expressions
to be created by controlling the underlying musculature of the face. In 1988,
Magnenat-Thalmann and colleagues [MTPT88] also described an abstract
muscle action model. In 1987 Lewis [LP87] and in 1988 Hill [PWWH86]
reported techniques for automatically synchronizing speech and facial animation.

Another ground breaking animation short was *Tin Toy*, which received
an Academy Award. Produced by Pixar, *Tin Toy* was an example of the
capabilities of computer facial animation. In particular a muscle model was
used to articulate the facial geometry of the baby into a variety of expressions [Par90].

The development of optical range scanners, such as the Cyberware optical
laser scanner [Cyb90], provides a new wealth of data for facial animation. In
1990, Williams [Wil90b] reported the use of registered facial image texture
maps as a means for 3D facial expression animation.

The new wave of enhanced image processing and scanning technology promises to usher in a new style of facial animation. In 1993, Lee, Terzopoulos, and Waters [LTW93] described techniques to map individuals into a canonical representation of the face that has known physically based motion attributes.

Another growth area is in medicine, where there is a focus on surgical planning procedures. In 1988, Deng [Den88] (and later Pieper [Pie91] in 1991) used a finite-element model of skin tissue to simulate skin incisions and wound closure.

Most recently there has been a surge of interest in facial analysis from the computer vision community. This interest is twofold: first, to provide the ability to track the human face, and second, to develop the ability to detect facial expression and thereby derive emotional states. There has been some early success in both areas. Two popular techniques are emerging: model-based [YCH89, BI94] and optical flow-based [BY95, EP94] techniques.

1.4. Application Areas

By far the largest motivator, developer, and consumer of three-dimensional facial character animation is the animation industry itself. Character animation in all forms of advertising and film production takes place on a need-by-need basis. Rarely do common components get reused in the next project; computer character animation is perhaps the most labor-intensive activity in animation production.

While the computer animation industry continues to shape how computers are used in animation, other emerging areas that influence animation are briefly mentioned below.

1.4.1. Games Industry

The games industry is dictated by the real-time performance characteristics of CPUs and graphics processors, which is in contrast to the expensive high-end graphics machines typically used in production animation. Examples of facial animation can be found in many educational software packages, such as Bright Star Technologies [Inc93], which animates a couple of talking two-dimensional cartoon characters call Bananas and Jack.

As CPU performance and graphics card capabilities continue to improve, so does the potential for more real-time three-dimensional graphics. As a result, we will undoubtedly see an increasing number of developments in character animation in the near future.

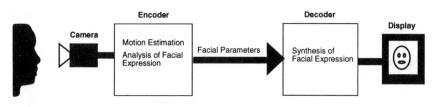

Figure 1.1.
A one-way video teleconferencing protocol.

1.4.2. Medicine

Computing in medicine is a large and diverse field. In the context of facial animation, two particular aspects are of interest: craniofacial surgical planning and facial tissue surgical simulation. In both cases the objective is to execute preoperative surgical simulation before the patient goes under the knife.

Craniofacial surgical planning involves the rearrangement of the facial bones due to trauma or growth defects [VMW83]. Because this involves the rigid structures of bone tissue, the procedure essentially becomes a complex three-dimensional cut-and-paste operation. Computer models are typically generated from computer tomography scans of the head and the bone surfaces generated from iso-surface algorithms such as the *Marching Cubes* [LC87].

For facial tissue simulation the objective is somewhat different. Here the objective is to emulate the response of skin and muscle after they have been cut and tissue has been removed or rearranged [Lar86]. Understanding and simulating skin tissue dynamics is the subject of Chapter 8.

1.4.3. Teleconferencing

The ability to transmit and receive facial images is at the heart of video teleconferencing. Despite the rapid growth of communication bandwidths, there still remains a need for compression algorithms. One active research area is in model-based coding schemes and in particular, algorithms applied to facial images [CHT90].

The process is illustrated in Figure 1.1. Each frame from a video camera is analyzed on the encoder end of the link, with the assumption that the principal object in it is a human face. Computer vision algorithms are then used to extract and parameterize properties, such as the shape and orientation of the head and face.

These few parameters are transmitted to the decoder, where a three-dimensional model of the human head is synthesized. As the head moves from frame to frame, new parameters are transmitted to the receiver and subsequently synthesized. This procedure is in contrast to existing video teleconferencing compression techniques that deal exclusively with image data.

1.4.4. Social Agents and Avatars

A rapidly emerging area for facial animation is in novel user interfaces that have characters or agents. The principle behind such agents, or avatars, is an ability to interact directly with the user. This ability can be as simple as a reactive behavior to some simple action such as searching for a file, or as complex as an embodiment or characterization of a personal assistant capable of navigating the Internet under voice commands and responding audibly and visually with a resulting find. Current popular themes are butlers or quirky characters that display their activity state through facial expressions.

Ultimately, these agents will understand limited spoken requests, speak to the user, behave in real time, and respond with uncanny realism. These new interfaces often are referred to as *social user interfaces* and are designed in an effort to supplement graphical user interfaces. For example, a character will appear to assist when you start a new application, but if you hesitate or ask for help, the agent will reappear to provide you with further guidance. In many instances these characters will be seen as active collaborators with personalities of their own.

At first sight, building this type of interface appears to be straightforward: construct a character, build a set of behavior rules, and switch the character on. Unfortunately it is not that simple. It is difficult enough to understand and model human-to-human behavior, let alone human-to-computer behavior. So by endowing a computer interface with some human characteristics, we turn on all our human responses. Most significantly we expect the interface to behave like a human, rather than a computer. Bearing this in mind, a useful social interface, such as a computer-generated humanoid with a face, has yet to be seen. However, many academic and industrial labs are actively developing prototypes.

1.5. Relationship to Conventional Animation

Undoubtedly Disney Studios has had the most dramatic impact on animation over the years. Most of the hard lessons it learned are directly applicable to computer animation, especially character animation. It also could be argued that there are no differences between traditional animation techniques and those applied in computer animation, suggesting that computers are merely more powerful tools at the disposal of animators. Essentially this is true. We therefore have a great deal to learn from traditional animation.

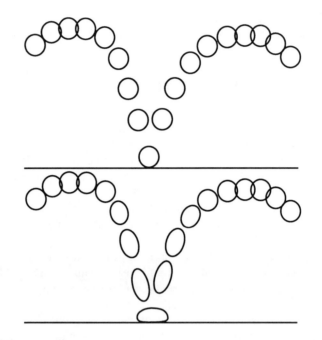

Figure 1.2.
In the motion of a ball bouncing, the ball can appear to have more
weight if the drawings are closer together at the top of the arc. In the
bottom illustration, a flattened ball on impact and elongation in
acceleration and deceleration are the beginnings of squash and stretch.

1.5.1. Disney's Twelve Principles of Animation

Frank Thomas and Ollie Johnston [TJ81] outlined twelve principles of animation, which applied to the way Disney Studios produces animation. These
"rules" are universally accepted as the cornerstone of any animation production and can be applied directly to the way computer character animation
is produced [Las87]. What follows are brief descriptions of those principles
that can also be applied to facial animation.

Squash and Stretch

Squash and stretch is perhaps the most important aspect of how a character
moves. A rule of thumb is that no matter how "squashy" or "stretchy"
something becomes, its volume remains relatively the same. Objects, such
as a bouncing ball, will compress when they hit an immovable object, such
as the floor, but they soon come back to their original shape (see Figure 1.2).

If a character or object is in motion, it will undergo certain changes within its overall shape. For example, a cat character falling through space stretches in the direction of the fall and squashes, or "splats," when it reaches the ground. The scaling may seem extreme when viewed in a single frame, but in motion it is remarkable how much the squashing and stretching can be exaggerated while still retaining a natural look. This elasticity can be used to imply weight, mass, or other physical qualities. For example, the shape of an iron balloon would not be affected by a drop to the ground, whereas a balloon full of water undergoes dramatic shape changes both as it is dropped and when it impacts the ground.

Anticipation

Anticipation is the act of hinting to the audience what is about to happen. This hint can be a broad physical gesture, or it can be as simple as a facial expression. The key idea is not to allow any motion to come unexpectedly, unless that is the desired effect. For example, before a character zooms off, it gathers itself up, draws back in the opposite direction, and then moves off in the other direction.

These anticipatory moves do not necessarily imply why something is being done, but rather they clarify what is being done. Once a movement has been implied through anticipation, animating a vastly different move can be used to introduce an element of surprise. For example, a car coiling up, ready to shoot forward but then zooming backward could be considered a sight gag.

Staging

Staging is the actual location of the camera and characters within the scene. Staging is very important and should be done carefully. Principles of cinema theory come into play in the way that shots are staged. In general there should be a distinct reason for the way that each shot in the film is staged. The staging should match the information that is required for that particular shot. The staging should be simple and clear, and it should enhance the action. A common mistake in the design of computer-generated films is to make the staging too dynamic simply because the computer has the capability to do so. As a consequence the scenes become confusing, or else distract from the action that is taking place.

One could easily write an entire paper on the meaning and importance of camera angles, lighting, and other film effects. Researching conventional film literature will enhance an animator's understanding of these theoretical film principles and is highly recommended. However, the most basic advice for good staging is that the most important information required from a scene should be clear and uncluttered by unusual or poor staging.

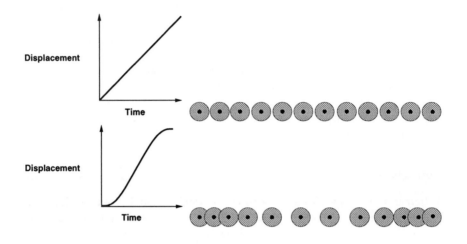

Figure 1.3.
The top profile illustrates a linear time displacement, while the bottom
profile shows how the ease-in and ease-out can give the impression of
acceleration and deceleration.

Follow-Through and Overlapping Action

If all the parts of a character stop or change motion at the same time, the
effect is one of extreme rigidity. To impart a sense of fluidity, animators delay
the movement of appendages. For example, consider a piece of animation
in which a character falls on the ground. Letting the arms lag one or two
frames behind the body impact imparts continuity and fluidity to the entire
motion. This effect is called *follow-through.*

Overlapping action also is important when moving the camera through an
environment or when zooming a logo through space. Early computer animation typically comprised of a move, a pause, a rotation, a pause, another
move, another pause, and so on. This process quickly becomes tedious. A
solution is to start the rotation before the move finishes, overlapping the
action instead of pausing. Follow-through is a common form of overlapping
action. Rather than abruptly stopping an action after it has been completed,
the additional motion eases out along the same path of action. For example,
a tennis swing is much more effective if the swing continues after the ball
has been hit.

Ease-In and Ease-Out

Newton's laws of motion state that no object with mass can start in motion abruptly without acceleration. Even a bullet shot from a gun has a short period of acceleration. Except under the most unusual of circumstances does the motion of an object have an instantaneous start or stop. *Ease-in* and *ease-out* are the acceleration and deceleration of an object in motion respectively. Eases may be applied to any motion track, including rotation, scaling, change of color, and translation. How an object eases helps to define the weight and structure of the object.

An ease is used at the beginning or end of a move to soften the transition from an active state to a static state. Many animation systems offer a choice of eases, the most common being a cosine ease (see Figure 1.3(b)). The linear motion, as in Figure 1.3(a), is continuous; all motion proceeds in a steady, predictable manner. However, linear motion does not lend itself to interesting animation, and thus it is the least desirable. Nonlinear eases are more widely used; their motion is fluid and more enjoyable. Being able to arbitrarily define eases for every action is the best alternative. Often a curve editor is used to interactively edit ease functions and, in combination with spline functions, to allow for an infinite number of possible eases. There are accepted algorithms defining the mathematical specifications of all the myriad eases, but actually seeing the curve dip down to its rest position is sometimes as useful as seeing the animation in preview. The ability to interactively adjust the curve that determines the rate of animation or transition between positions in a key frame is crucial.

Arcs

Most motion is nonlinear; that is, an object usually follows some curved path. Rather than linearly interpolating from one key frame to the next, passing a curve through the keys gives a more dynamic look to the animation. If animation has been completely interpolated using splines, however, the motion may be too uniform in velocity — in short, it will have no punch.

Any "oomph" lost by splining can be regained by editing curves by hand. Again, a function editor that gives an interactive graphic representation is ideal for defining motion curves. Most systems have some automatic interpolation functions available to the animator. One problem with cubic interpolating splines is that although they keep slope continuity from key frame to key frame, they also tend to overshoot when confronted with sudden changes in velocity. Since animators intend key frames to represent extremes in motion, these overshoots can have disastrous results. Feet go through the floor; fingers go through hands. Not overshooting cubic interpolating splines is necessary in a production animation environment to allow smooth motion without jumping in and out of a curve editor.

Secondary Motion

Secondary motion is the motion of objects or body parts which depend on primary motion. An example of secondary motion would be the motion of clothing over the surface of a moving figure. In general, secondary motion is caused by the motion of a primary object. In *Balloon Guy* [Wed87], the motions of the string, the dog's ears, and the person's head, are all secondary motions caused by the general motion of the characters themselves.

Exaggeration

Exaggeration involves making the motion more dramatic than one would observe in the real world. If a scene is animated with little or no exaggeration, the motion will be dull and listless. Animators use exaggeration to sell the action or the movement of a character.

The exact amount of exaggeration that is required is difficult to judge, but an interesting observation can be made. The version of the animation always looks more exaggerated than the final rendered frame. Exaggeration of motion is not always the way to go, but often exaggeration of motion characteristics is needed to create interesting motion. Exaggeration does not have to impart a cartoon feel to be effective. After the motion has been blocked out, it's up to the animator to decide which movements must be exaggerated in order to enhance the animation. Live action footage can be used for reference. The live action may be used to rough out the major movements, which are then subtly exaggerated to showcase aspects of the motion.

Appeal

The characters should *appeal* to the audience in some way. This is not to say that all the characters need to be cute, but rather that there should be some elements about the characters that make them interesting to watch.

1.6.   Facial Expression Analysis

Exactly how facial muscle actions interact to express emotional states concerned some noted scientists. One of the first published investigations of facial expression was by John Bulwer [Bul48, Bul49] in the late 1640s. He suggested that one could not only lip-read but also infer emotional state from the actions of muscles. Subsequently, in the later part of the nineteenth century, Charles Bell, Duchenne de Boulogne, and Charles Darwin all applied themselves to a more rigorous investigation of facial expression.

Table 1.1.
Completely independent expressive muscles.

Current name	Name used by Duchenne
m. frontalis	muscle of attention
superior part of *m. orbicularis oculi*	muscle of reflection
m. corrugator supercilli	muscle of pain
m. procerus	muscle of aggression

1.6.1. The Significance of Charles Darwin's Investigations

Ten years after the publication of Charles Darwin's [Dar72] seminal book *The Origin of Species*, he published *The Expression of the Emotions in Man and Animals*. Although this book never received the recognition as did his first, it remains an important departure for modern research in behavioral biology. Darwin was the first to demonstrate the universality of expressions and their continuity in man and animals. Over the next hundred years or so, scientists have classified and refined many of the theories postulated by Darwin at that time.

1.6.2. The Electrophysical Experiments of Duchenne

The most remarkable investigation of facial expression of its time was by Duchenne [Duc62]. It is remarkable because he documented his scientific research with the then new medium of photography. He investigated facial articulation by stimulating facial muscles with moist electrodes that delivered direct "galvanic" current to key motor points on the surface of face. Isolated muscle contractions could then be elicited by the careful positioning of the electrodes. Consequently, Duchenne could manipulate and record the activity of facial muscle at will and classify muscles, or small groups of muscles, that could be considered expressive. Armed with this relatively crude tool, Duchenne documented and classified muscles that were expressive, inexpressive, or discordantly expressive. He then published the results in *De la physionomie humaine ou analyse electro-physiologique de l'expression des passions applicable à la practique des arts plastiques*[Duc62].[2]

All researchers in this field, from Darwin to those of the present day, acknowledge the debt to Duchenne for his remarkable study of facial expression. While there may well be discrepancies between his classification and more recent research, he essentially defined the field. Tables 1.1 – Table 1.5, are directly from his classification.

---

[2]This book was first published in French and has been subsequently translated into English by R. Cuthbertson in 1990 [Duc90].

Table 1.2.
Incompletely expressive muscles and muscles that are expressive in a
complementary way.

Current name	Name used by Duchenne
m. zygomaticus major	muscle of joy
m. zygomaticus minor	muscle of moderate crying or weeping
m. levator labii superioris	muscle of crying

Table 1.3.
Completely independent expressive muscles.

Current name	Name used by Duchenne
m. levator labii superioris alaeque nasi	muscle of crying with hot tears
transverse part of m. nasalis	muscle of lust
m. buccinator	muscle of irony
m. depressor anguli oris	muscle of sadness, of disgust
m. mentalis	muscle of distain or doubt
m. platysma	muscle of fear, fright, and torture, and complimentary to wrath
m. depressor labii inferioris	muscle complementary to irony and aggressive feelings
alar part of m. nasalis	muscle complementary to violent feelings
m. maseter	muscle complementary to wrath and fury
palpebral part of m. orbicularis oculi	muscle of contempt and complementary to crying
inferior part of m. orbicularis oculi	muscle of benevolence and complementary to overt joy
outer fibers of m. orbicularis oris	muscle comlementary to doubt and distain
inner fibers of m. orbicularis oris	muscle complementary to aggressive or wicked passions
upward gaze	movement complementary to recollection
upward and lateral gaze	movement complementary to ecstasy and to sensual desire
downward and lateral gaze	movement complementary to defiance or fear
downward gaze	movement complementary to sadness and humility

Table 1.4.
Synoptic table: Expressions produced by the isolated contraction of muscles that are completely expressive.

Primordial expressions	Muscles that produce them
Attention	m. frontalis
Reflection	supererior part of m. orbicularis oculi, moderately contracted
Meditation	same muscle, but strongly contracted
Intentness of mind	same muscle, but very strongly contracted
Pain	m. corrugator supercilli
Aggression or Menace	m. procerus

Table 1.5.
Synoptic table: Expressions produced by the combined contraction of muscles that are incompletely expressive with those that are expressive in a complementary way.

Primordial expressions	Muscles that produce them
Weeping with hot tears	m. levator labii superioris alaeque nasi plus the palpebral part of m. orbicularis oculi
Moderate weeping	m. zygomaticus minor plus the palpebral part of m. orbicularis oculi
Joy	m. zygomatic major
Laughter	same muscles plus palpebral part of m. orbicularis oculi
False laughter	m. zygomaticus major alone
Irony, ironic laughter	m. buccinator plus m. depressor labii inferioris
Sadness or Despondency	m. depressor anguli oris plus flaring of the nostrils and downward gaze
Distain or Disgust	m. depressor anguli oris plus palpebral part of m. orbicularis oculi

Table 1.5 (cont.)
Synoptic table: Expressions produced by the combined contraction of muscles that
are incompletely expressive with those that are expressive in a complementary way.

Primordial expressions	Muscles that produce them
Doubt	m. mentalis plus the outer fibers of m. orbicularis oris (either the inferior portion or the two portions at the same time) plus m. levator labii superioris alaeque nasi
Contempt or Scorn	palpebral part of m. orbicularis oculi plus m. depressor labii inferioris plus m. transversus plus m. levator labii superioris alaeque nasi
Surprise	m. frontalis plus muscles lowering the mandible, but to a moderate degree
Astonishment	same combinations of muscles and lowering of the mandible, but a stronger contraction
Stupefaction	same combinations, maximally contracted
Admiration, agreeable surprise	the muscles of astonishment associated with those of joy
Fright	m. frontalis plus m. platysma
Terror	m. frontalis plus m. platysma and lowering of the mandible, maximally contracted
Terror, with pain or torture	m. corrugator supercilli plus m. platysma and muscles lowering the mandible
Anger	superior part of m. orbicularis oculi plus m. masseter plus m. buccinator plus m. depressor labii inferioris plus m. platysma
Carried away by ferocious anger	m. procerus plus m. platysma and muscles lowering the mandible, maximally contracted
Sad reflection	superior part of m. orbicularis oculi plus m. depressor anguli oris
Agreeable reflection	superior part of m. orbicularis oculi plus m. zygomatic major

Table 1.5 (cont.)
Synoptic table: Expressions produced by the combined contraction of muscles that
are incompletely expressive with those that are expressive in a complementary way.

Primordial expressions	Muscles that produce them
Ferocious joy	m. procerus plus m. zygomatic major plus m. depressor labii inferioris
Lasciviousness	m. transversus plus m. zygomaticus major
Sensual delirium	gaze directed above and laterally, with spasm of the palpebral part of m. orbicularis oculi, the superior portion of which covers part of the iris
Ecstasy	same muscles as sensual delirium, but without m. transverus
Great pain, with fear and affliction	m. corrugator supercilli plus m. zygomaticus minor
Pain with despondancy or despair	m. corrugator supercilli plus m. depressor anguli oris

1.6.3.   The Facial Action Coding System

While Duchenne pioneered the analytical study of human facial expression,
it wasn't until the 1970s that a more rigorous and precise study of the human
facial expression was undertaken.

The Facial Action Coding System (FACS), developed by Paul Ekman and
Wallace Friesen [EF78] in 1977, was particularly relevant to facial animation because it broke down facial action into small units called *action units*
(AUs). Each AU represented an individual muscle action, or an action of
a small group of muscles, into a single recognizable facial posture. In total they classified 66 AUs that in combination could generate defined and
gradable facial expressions. Chapter 4 describes the FACS in detail and Table 4.4 describes the Action Units by name, number, and anatomical basis.
Table 4.5 lists 11 additional AUs, several of which do not involve any of the
facial muscle actions. As a result FACS has been used extensively in facial
animation over the past decade to help animators interpret and construct
realistic facial expressions.

2

Anatomy of the Face, Head, and Neck

The form and function of the human body has been studied in great detail by artists over the centuries. In particular the Renaissance artists began the rigorous tradition of figure drawing so that they could produce realistic and detailed interpretations of the human form. For example, Leonardo da Vinci [Cla92] would often attend and perform cadaver dissections to understand human anatomy. His detailed comprehension of anatomy can clearly be seen in his remarkable drawings of the human body. The value of detailed anatomical understanding is reflected thoughout fifteenth-century art, and today it remains a foundation of art instruction [Hal65, Hog81].

One of the objectives in creating three-dimensional computer-generated faces is to design faces that not only appear realistic in static imagery but also move in animated sequences. Consequently, we can learn a great deal from anatomy in the same way that did the artists who studied the human form to produce realistic interpretations and renditions of the face.

While the artist's perspective is important in computer facial synthesis, twentieth-century medical anatomical reference books provide the most significant insight into human anatomy. The most widely used medical reference manual is *Gray's Anatomy* [WWDB89], which provides precise and detailed anatomical descriptions. Another particularly insightful reference manual is *Sobotta Atlas of Anatomy* [FS83]. This manual is graphically illustrated in color with drawings and photographs. Dissection manuals, such as Cunningham's *Manual of Practical Anatomy, Vol. 3: Head, Neck, and*

19

Brain, offer a different perspective by describing how the face can be taken apart piece by piece [Rom67]. Additional medical references include Fried's *Anatomy of the Head, Neck, Face, and Jaw* [Fri76] and Warfel's *The Head, Neck and Trunk* [Waf73].

One of the most frustrating aspects of medical reference manuals is the overwhelming quantity of information that is difficult to follow and digest. This chapter attempts to simplify the terminology and describes the anatomical features of the face that are useful for computer synthesis. Essentially the description breaks down into two parts: the facial skeleton and the facial muscles.

In Section 2.2., the individual bones of the skull that make up the skeletal framework of the face are described. This section is followed by Section 2.3. that describes the muscles of facial expression with their attachments and primary actions. Section 2.3.2. describes the muscles of mastication, followed by a description of the tempromandibular joint. The muscles of the tongue are described in Section 2.5., followed by a brief description of the muscles of the scalp, ear, and neck. The skin and its mechanical properties are described in Section 2.7.. Finally, a description of the eyes and eyeballs are given. The reader is encouraged to refer to anatomical references for more complete and comprehensive descriptions.

2.1. Nomenclature

Human anatomy has its own distinctive terminology based on the assumption that the person is standing erect, arms at the sides, the face and palms directed forward.[1] This posture is known as the *anatomic position* (see Figure 2.1). The location of body parts are described in relation to this pose and three imaginary planes:

- **Median plane.** This vertical plane cuts through the center of the body, dividing the body into equal right and left halves. A structure located closer to the medial plane than another is said to be *medial* to the other. A structure lying farther away from the medial plane than another is said to be *lateral* to the other.

- **Coronal plane.** This vertical plane divides the body into front and back halves. The coronal plane is at a right angle to the medial plane. The term *anterior* refers to the front of the body; *posterior* refers to the back of the body. A feature is described as anterior (or posterior) to

---

[1]While this section is rather dry, the reader is encouraged to spend the time to read, digest, and remember these fundamental terms, as all medical references use this type of nomenclature.

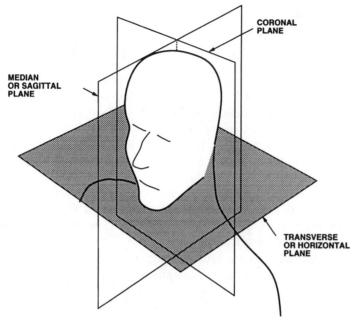

Figure 2.1.
Terminology commonly used in descriptive anatomy.

another feature when it is closer to the anterior (or posterior) surface
of the body.

- **Transverse horizontal planes.** These planes are at right angles to
  both the median and coronal planes.

Superior and *inferior* refer to relative positions with respect to the upper
and lower ends of the body. For example the lips are superior to the chin
but inferior to the eyes. *Superficial* and *deep* refer to the relative distance
of structures from the outermost surface of the body. The brain is deep
relative to the skull. The lips are superficial to the teeth. *Proximal* and *distal*
describe the relative distances from the roots of the limbs or other organs.
For example the ankle is distal to the knee but is proximal to the toes. The
tip of the tongue is distal to the root of the tongue. *Ipsilateral* refers to the
same side of the body, while *contralateral* refers to the opposite side of the
body. The left eye is contralateral with the right eye and ipsilateral with the
left ear.

2.2. The Skull

The skull is essentially a protective casing for the brain and provides a foundation for the face (see Figures 2.2 and 2.3). The bones of the skull can be divided into two major parts: the cranium, which lodges and protects the brain, and the skeleton of the face, of which the mandible is the only freely jointed structure. The cranium can be further subdivided into the calvaria and the cranial base. The cranial base is the bottom half of the brain case, and the calvaria is the top half. It should be noted that these are arbitrary divisions and that several bones contribute to both the cranial base and the calvaria, as well as the facial skeleton.

The facial skeleton is positioned below and anterior to the cranial base. The upper third of the facial skeleton consists of the orbits and nasal bones, the middle third consists of the nasal cavities and maxillae, and the lower third consists of the mandibular region.

For the most part it is the facial skeleton that is of particular interest in 3D facial modeling as it provides the framework onto which the muscles and skin are placed.

2.2.1. Bones of the Calvaria

Frontal Bone.   The frontal bone is a shallow, irregular cap forming the forehead. Posteriorly, it connects with the parietal bones. In the lower back, it joins the wings of the sphenoid bone on each side. Inferiorly, it connects with the ethmoid bone and lacrimal bones. Anteriorly, it connects with the zygomatic, maxillae, and nasal bones.

The curved, smooth area of the frontal bone is known as the *squama*. Anteriorly, two deep curved depressions form the roof of the orbit. Laterally, two projections, the right and left *zygomatic processes*, form the lateral wall of the orbit with the zygoma. The *supraorbital ridges* are curved elevations connecting the midportion of the frontal bone with its zygomatic process.

Occipital Bone.   The occipital bone forms the most posterior part of the skull and also contributes to the cranial base. It articulates with the atlas by way of the *occipital condyles* flanking the opening for the spinal cord. The various rough markings and eminences on the bone are related to the formation and attachments of various muscles, tendons, and ligaments.

Parietal Bones.   The parietal bones are a pair of quadrangular cup-shaped bones that form most of the cranial roof and sides. Inferiorly, they meet the temporal bone and the right and left great wings of the sphenoid bone. Anteriorly, they join the frontal bone.

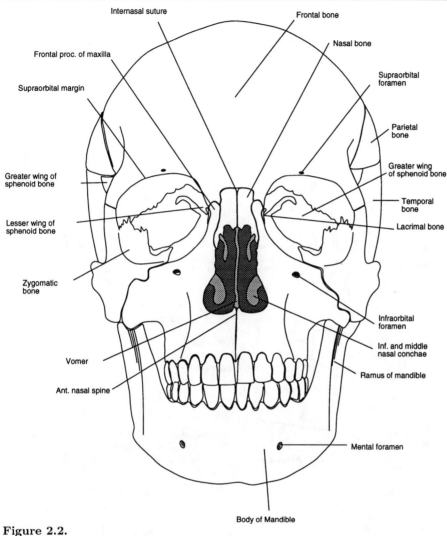

Figure 2.2.
The frontal view of the skull.

The outer surface of the parietal bone is smooth and convex. A curving eminence, known as the *inferior temporal line*, divides the lower third from the upper two-thirds. This eminence serves as the upper limit of the origin of the temporalis muscle.

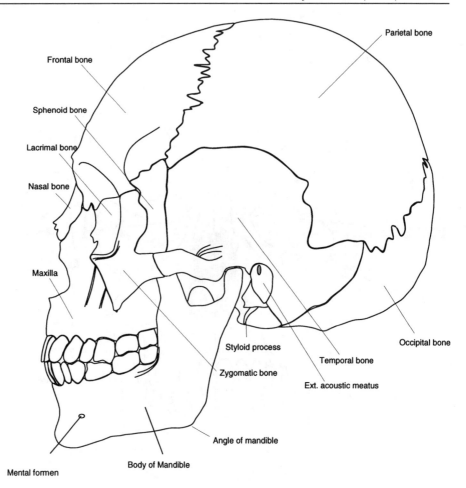

Figure 2.3.
The lateral view of the skull.

2.2.2. Bones of the Cranial Base

Temporal Bone. The temporal bone has a large flat portion known as the squama and forms part of the lateral wall of the skull. A depression on the inferior surface known as the *glenoid fossa* provides an articulate region for the mandible. Just superior to this fossa is a fingerlike projection, the *zygomatic process*, which joins with the zygoma anteriorly to form the *zygomatic arch*.

Immediately posterior to the root of the zygomatic process is a large opening. This opening is the entrance to the middle ear and is known as the *external auditory meatus*. Posterior to the meatus is a rounded, rough prominence, the mastoid process. Inferior and medial to the *external auditory meatus* is a pointed, bony projection, the *styloid process*, which serves as the attachment of several muscles and ligaments.

Sphenoid Bone. The sphenoid bone is a midline bone that is "wedged" between the frontal, temporal, and occipital bones. Anteriorly, it articulates with the maxillae and palatine bones. Superiorly, it joins the parietal bone, and anterosuperiorly, it meets the ethmoid bone and frontal bones.

The sphenoid bone has a central body, paired greater and lesser wings spreading laterally from it, and two pterygoid processes, descending from junctions of the body and the greater wings.

2.2.3. Bones of the Facial Skeleton

The facial skeleton is composed of the sphenoid bone, the ethmoid bone, the palatine bone, the maxillae, the inferior nasal concha, the sygomatic bones, the nasal bones, the lacrimal bone, the mandible, the hyoid bone, and the vomer.[2]

Ethmoid Bone. The unpaired ethmoid bone fits into the midportion of the anterior medial area of the frontal bone. It contains a midline perpendicular plate that crosses a horizontal cribriform plate. This cribriform plate is perforated to allow passage of the olfactory nerves between the brain case and the nose. Hanging off the outer lateral edge of the cribriform plate are the superior and middle nasal conchae, bilaterally. These each have multiple septa passing laterally to another more lateral paper-thin plate of vertical bone, the *lamina orbitalis* (*lamina papyracea*). Between the lamina orbitalis and the conchae, separated by these septa, are the *ethmoid air cells*. The lamina aids in the formation of the medial orbital wall.

Palatine Bone. The palatine bone is an extremely irregularly shaped bone that acts as a link between the maxillae and the sphenoid bone. It consists of two main parts, a horizontal plate and a vertical plate. The horizontal plate forms the posterior of the hard palate. This area is where the palatine bone articulates with the horizontal or palatine process of the maxilla. The horizontal plate of the palatine bone also articulates with the

---

[2]Each of these bones has a complex shape. To help the reader we have illustrated the significant bones useful for facial modeling. We have also ordered them in most proximal to least, since the deeper bone structures have less influence on the overall face shape.

horizontal plate of the palatine bone of the opposite side to complete the posterior hard palate.

The vertical plate reaches up behind the maxilla to contribute a small lip to the posterior orbital floor. On the posterior aspect of the vertical plate is the area of articulation for the lateral pterygoid plate of the sphenoid bone.

Maxillae. Except for the mandible, the maxillae are the largest of the facial bones; they are in the lower part into which the upper teeth are located. Each maxilla consists of a large, roughly pyramidal hollow body and four prominent processes.

The *frontal process*, arising from the anteromedial corner of the body, reaches to and connects with the frontal bone and forms the medial orbital rim. Posteriorly, this process articulates with the lacrimal bone, which joins the ethmoid bone, the three of which form the medial orbital wall with portion of the frontal bone. The medial rim of the frontal process fuses with the nasal bone. The *zygomatic process* arises from the anterolateral corner of the maxillary body. In conjunction with the zygomatic bone it forms the infraorbital rim and the greatest portion of the orbital floor. The horizontal *palatine process* arises from the lower edge of the medial surface of the body. It joins the process of the other maxilla to form the major part of the hard palate. Extending downward from the body of the maxillae is the rounded, elongated *alveolar process*, which serves to house the teeth. The posterior aspect of this process is known as the *maxillary tuberosity*. This area is somewhat rough and contains several foramina for the superior alveolar nerves and vessels.

The orbital surface is concave, with a sharp medial edge that joins the lacrimal bone anteriorly and the laminal orbitals of the ethmoid bone posteriorly. Laterally, the orbital surface articulates with the zygomatic bone and the frontal bone. It is separated from the sphenoid bone by the inferior orbital fissure.

The anterior lateral surface aids the zygomatic bone in the formation of the cheek. Its boundary posteriorly is the bony crest which begins at the tip of the zygomatic process and courses in a concave arc inferiorly to end at the alveolar process. Just inferior and medial to the infraorbital foramen is a smooth depression on the surface of the maxilla. This depression is the canine fossa.

Along the midline between the two palatine processes on the nasal surface is a sharp elevation, the *nasal crest*, which serves as the attachment for the nasal septum.

Inferior Nasal Concha. The inferior nasal concha is a small oval bone. It lies within the nasal cavity near the floor and articulates to the lateral wall of the nasal cavity formed by the maxilla.

Zygomatic Bones. Each zygoma forms the prominence of the check. It is composed of a diamond-shaped body with four processes. The frontal process, which forms part of the lateral orbital wall, attaches to the frontal bone. The temporal process joins the zygomatic arch with the temporal bone. The maxillary process, together with the zygomatic process of the maxilla, forms the infraorbital rim and part of the orbital floor. The fourth process joins the maxilla at the lateral wall of the maxillary sinus in an eminence, the jugal ridge, just above the molar region. The articulation of the zygoma with the great wing of the sphenoid occurs on the posterior aspect of the frontal process as it turns to help form part of the posterolateral orbital wall.

Nasal Bones. The nasal bones are paired and lie in the midline just above the nasal fossae. They fit between the frontal processes of the maxillae and articulate superiorly with the frontal bone. They are somewhat quadrilateral in shape, the outer surface is convex, and the inner surface is concave.

Lacrimal Bone. The lacrimal bone is an irregular thin plate of bone. It lies in the anteromedial aspect of the orbit and articulates with the lamina orbitalis of the ethmoid bone posteriorly, the maxilla inferiorly and anteriorly, and the frontal bone superiorly.

Mandible. The mandible is a strong, horseshoe-shaped bone that is the largest and heaviest bone of the facial skeleton (see Figure 2.4). The horizontal portion is known as the body and the right and left vertical sections are known as the *rami*.

The rami each have two terminal processes: one, called the *condyle*, is blunt and somewhat rounded; the other, serving as the insertion of the temporalis muscle, is the *coronoid process*. The deep curved notch between the two processes is the *sigmoid notch*. The condyle has a smooth rounded head that is attached to the ramus by a thinner elongated neck. The posterior border of the ramus meets the inferior border of the body at the mandibular angle. The right and left bodies meet at the chin point, the *symphysis*, on which is a variably elevated area, the *mental protuberance*.

On the lateral surface of the body, one sees the mental foramen lying just below the roots of the premolars. On the superior aspect of the body lies the alveolar process, which houses the mandibular teeth. The external oblique line begins just posterior to the mental foramen, passes posteriorly and superiorly to become the anterior border of the vertical ramus, and finally ends at the coronoid tip.

Medially, in the area of the symphysis, the bony mental (genial) tubercles or genial spines can be seen. Just posterior and lateral to these features is an oblique ridge of bone extending posteriorly and superiorly to end at the

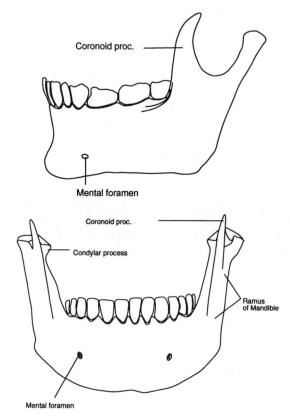

Figure 2.4.
The mandible and teeth.

crest of the alveolar ridge near the third molar. This area is the mylohyoid linear ridge. The depression on the medial aspect of the posterior portion of the body, just below the mylohyoid line, is the submandibular fossa. Above the line and more anterior, another depression, the *sublingual fossa*, is seen.

Almost exactly in the center of the medial surface of the vertical mandibular ramus, the inferior alveolar canal begins with a wide opening, the *mandibular foramen*. On its anterior surface is a bony process, the *lingula*. The inferior alveolar canal lies within the bone and follows the curvature of the mandible from the inferior alveolar foramen in the ramus to the mental foramen in the body. Here it begins a short canal to the mental foramen and then continues on in the bone to the symphysis region as the incisive canal.

Behind the last molar, on the crest of the alveolar process, is a small roughened retromandibular triangle.

Hyoid Bone. This bone contributes to the skeleton of the head and neck and acts as an important functional structure. The hyoid bone is suspended in the neck and lies superior and anterior to the thyroid cartilage (Adam's apple). It serves as the attachment for many muscles that lie in the anterior portion of the neck and as a point of fixation for the accessory muscles of mastication.

Vomer. The vomer is thin and flat, forming the posteroinferior portion of the nasal septum. It is situated in the midsagittal plane of the nasal fossa. It articulates inferiorly with the palatine and maxillary bones. The posterior portion of the anterior superior border meets the perpendicular plate of the ethmoid bone. The anterior portion connects with the cartilaginous septum of the nose.

2.2.4.   The Vertebral Column

The skeletal portion of the neck is known as the *cervical vertebral column*. There are seven cervical vertebrae. The first cervical vertebra is the *atlas* which serves as the connection of the vertebral column with the skull. The occipital bone of the skull articulates with the atlas. The body of the second cervical vertebra, the *axis*, is fused with that of the atlas. The five remaining cervical vertebrae are joined by movable joints. The neck is flexible at any one of these cervical joints. Fibrocartilaginous pads, the *intervertebral disks*, are spaced between adjacent surfaces of the vertebrae. These pads act as cushions between the articular surfaces.

2.3.   Muscles of the Face, Head, and Neck

In the general sense muscles are the organs of motion. By their contractions, they move the various parts of the body. The energy of their contraction is made mechanically effective by means of tendons, aponeuroses, and fascia, which secure the ends of the muscles and control the direction of their pull. Muscles usually are suspended between two moving parts, such as between two bones, bone and skin, two different areas of skin, or two organs.

Actively, muscles contract. Their relaxation is passive and comes about through lack of stimulation. A muscle usually is supplied by one or more nerves that carry the stimulating impulse and thereby cause it to contract. Muscles can also be stimulated directly or by any electrical activity emanating from any source. For example, in 1862, Duchenne de Boulogne applied electrical probes to the human face to solicit facial expressions by the activation of particular muscles or groups of muscles [Duc62]. He documented his research with 73 photographs of facial expressions, a rare and seminal example of photographs being used for physiological investigation (see Chapter 1

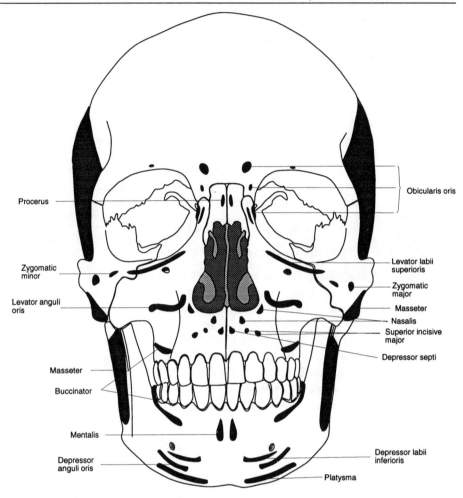

Figure 2.5.
The frontal view of facial muscle attachments.

for more details). Usually the stimulation for muscular contraction originates in the nerve supply to that muscle. Lack of stimulation to the muscle results in relaxation.

When a muscle is suspended between two parts, one of which is fixed and the other movable, the attachment of the muscle on the fixed part is known as the *origin*. The attachment of the muscle to the movable part is referred to as the *insertion*.

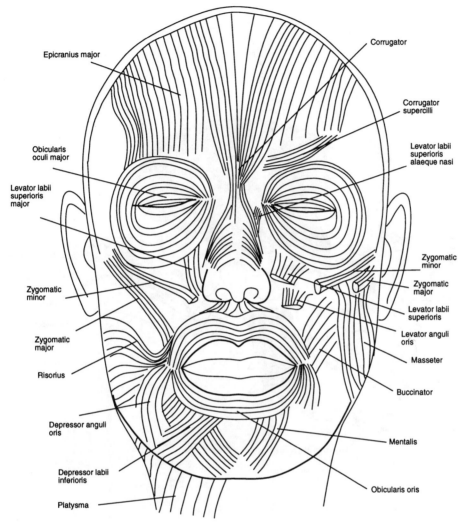

Figure 2.6.
The frontal view of facial muscles.

2.3.1. The Muscles of Facial Expression

The muscles of the face are commonly known as the muscles of facial expression. Some facial muscles also perform other important functions, such as moving the cheeks and lips during mastication and speech, or constriction (closing) and dilation (opening) of the eyelids. The muscles of facial expression are superficial, and all attach to a layer of subcutaneous fat and skin at

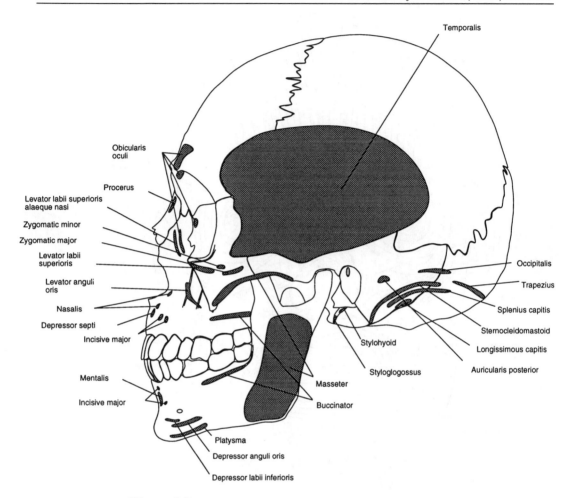

Figure 2.7.
The lateral view of facial muscle attachments.

their insertion. Some of the muscles attach to skin at both the origin and the insertion such as the obicularis oris. When the muscles are relaxed, the fatty tissues fill the hollows and smooth the angular transitions so as to allow the general shape of the skull to be seen. The illustrations in Figures 2.6 and 2.8 illustrate the superficial muscles of the face, while Figure 2.9 shows some of the deeper muscles. Finally, Figures 2.5 and 2.7 illustrate the location of facial muscle attachments.

The muscles of facial expression work synergistically and not independently. The group functions as a well-organized and coordinated team, each

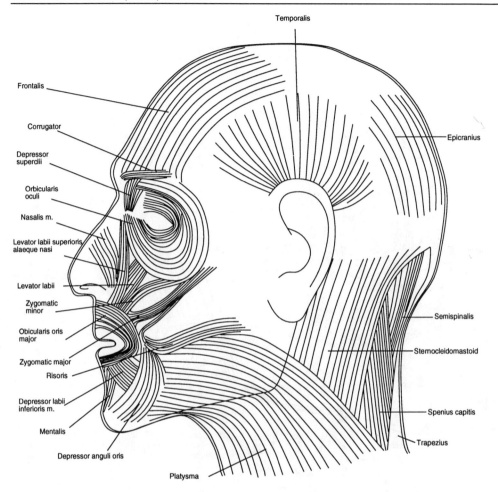

Figure 2.8.
The lateral view of superficial facial muscles.

member having specified functions, one of which is primary. These muscles interweave with one another. It is difficult to separate the boundaries between the various muscles. The terminal ends of these muscles are interlaced with each other.

In more general terms, the muscles of the facial expression can be grouped according to the orientation of the individual muscle fibers and can be divided into the upper and lower face. Three types of muscle can be discerned as the primary motion muscles: *linear/parallel* muscles, which pull in an angular direction, such as the zygomatic major and the corrugator supercilii;

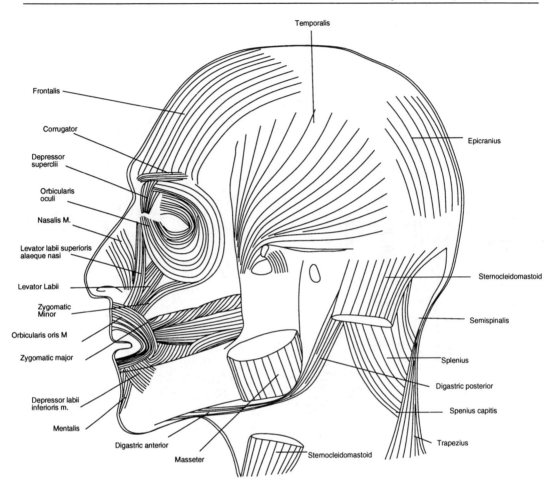

Figure 2.9.
The lateral view of deep facial muscles.

elliptical/circular sphincter-type muscles, which squeeze, such as the obicularis oris; *sheet* muscles, which behave as a series of linear muscles spread over an area, such as the frontalis. The following is a list of the facial muscles with description first, followed by each muscle's primary actions.

Circumorbital Muscles of the Eye

Orbicularis Oculi.   This muscle encircles the eye in concentric fibers that act as a sphincter to close the eye. It originates at the inner canthus of the eye from the frontal process of the maxilla and the lacrimal bone. The more superior fibers end in the skin in the lateral region of the eye.

Action. This muscle plays an important role in the protection of the eye. It firmly closes the eyelids to avoid dust and bright sunlight and to prevent contact of objects against the eye itself. The orbital part can act independently, drawing the skin of the forehead and cheek to the medial angle of the orbit. This activity causes wrinkles radiating from the outer margins of the eye. The palpebral part of the muscle exerts a much finer control over the individual eyelids. This fine control of the eyelids plays an important role in nonverbal communication. The lacrimal part dilates the lacrimal sac.

Corrugator Supercilii. This small paired pyramidal muscle is located at the medial end of each brow. Attached to bone at the medial end of the superciliary arch, it ascends laterally, interlacing and blending with the orbicularis oculi.

Action. This muscle exerts traction on the skin above the midpart of the supraorbital margin. It draws the brows medially and down, producing (with the orbicularis oculi) vertical wrinkles on the forehead.

Levator Palpebrae Superioris. This muscle arises within the orbit above the optic foramen and advances and spreads out to end in the upper eyelid.

Action. This muscle, when it contracts, lifts the upper lid.

Muscles of the Nose

These muscles are quite rudimentary; however, they do act to dilate and constrict the nasal openings.

Procerus. The procerus muscle originates from the nasal bone and passes superiorly to end in the skin of the brow and forehead.

Action. This muscle depresses the medial end of the eyebrow, producing transverse wrinkles over the nasal bridge and root. The action of this muscle aids in reducing the glare of bright sunlight.

Nasalis. The nasalis arises from the alveolar eminence over the lateral incisor and swings around the nose to insert on the superior surface of the bridge, at the tip of the nose and alar cartilages. The depressor septi and the dilator naris also are members of this group of muscles.

Action. The transverse part of this muscle compresses the nasal aperture at the junction of the vestibule and nasal cavity.

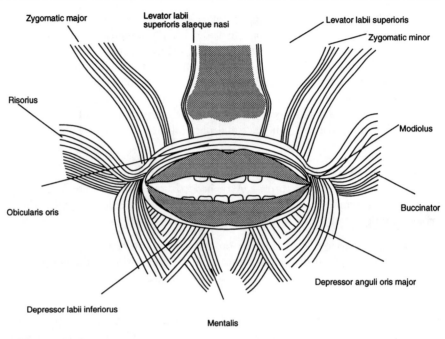

Figure 2.10.
The principle muscles around the mouth.

Depressor Septi.   This muscle is attached to the maxilla above the central incisor and ascends to the mobile part of the nasal septum.

Action. This muscle assists the alar part of the nasalis in widening the nasal aperture.

Levator Labii Superioris Alaeque Nasi.   This muscle is attached to the upper part of the frontal process of the maxilla; it then descends inferolaterally, dividing into a medial slip attached to the greater alar cartilage and the skin over it and a lateral slip prolonged inferolaterally across the vental aspect of levator labii superioris, and attaches successively to the dermal floor of the upper part of the nasolabial furrow and ridge.

Action. This muscle raises and inverts the upper lip and deepens the nasolabial furrow's superior part; the medial slip dilates the nostril.

Muscles of the Mouth

The numerous muscles of the mouth are important muscles of facial expression (see Figure 2.10). The principal muscles are the orbicularis oris, the buccinator, the levator labii superioris alacque nasi, the levator labii superioris, the zygomaticus major and minor, the levator anguli oris, the anguli oris, the depressor labii inferioris, the risorius, and the mentalis. One group opens the lips, and one group closes the lips. The muscles closing the lips are the orbicularis oris and the incisive muscles. The muscles opening the lips are known as the radial muscles, which are divided into the radial muscles of the upper and lower lips, superficial and deep.

Orbicularis Oris. This muscle consists of numerous strata of muscular fibers surrounding the orifice of the mouth. It consists in part of fibers derived from the other facial muscles that converge on the mouth. It is the buccinator that forms the deep layer of the orbicularis oris. Some of the fibers decussate at the corners of the mouth passing over the top of the lip and the underside of the lip. In addition, the levator anguli oris crosses at the corner of the lips and runs around the bottom lip. Likewise the depressor anguli oris crosses the corner of the mouth and runs around the top lip. Regarding the other muscles, the levator labii superioris, the zygomaticus major, and the depressor labii inferioris intermingle with the muscle fibers just described.

Action. The action of the orbicularis oris produces an almost endless control of the lips. The variety of lip shapes are used in speech and nonverbal communication. It is also important in chewing where it can hold food against the teeth. It also can narrow the lips and force them against the teeth, purse the lips, or protrude the lips.

Buccinator. The buccinator muscle is thin, wide, and flat, forming the major portion of the substance of the cheeks. Its arises both from the maxilla and the mandible opposite the first molar and from the pterygomandibular raphe. The fibers run forwards to blend with those of the orbicularis oris. The medial fibers decussate at the posterolateral to the angle of the mouth, so that the lower fibers run to the upper lip and the upper ones run to the lower lip. The interlacing of the deep buccinator muscles and some of the superficial muscles of the orbicularis oris forms the *modiolus*.

Action. The buccinators compress the cheeks against the teeth, thereby preventing the accumulation of food in the cheek.

Levator Labii Superioris Alaeque Nasi. This muscle originates from the frontal process of the maxilla and inserts into the skin of the wing of the nose and into the orbicularis oris, near the philtrum.

Action. This muscle raises the upper lip, deepening the nasolabial furrows and slightly dilating the nostrils.

Levator Labii Superiors. This muscle has a wide attachment to the bone of the orbit, zygomatic, and maxilla. It is embedded at the other end into the top lip between the levator anguli oris and the levator labii superioris alaeque nasi.

Action. This muscle raises the upper lip, deepening the nasolabial furrows like the levator labii superioris alaeque nasi.

Zygomaticus Major. This muscle arises from the malar surface of the zygomatic bone and is inserted into the corner of the mouth. The zygomatic major arises on the front surface of the zygomatic bone and merges with the muscles at the corner of the mouth.

Action. This muscle elevates the modiolus and buccal angle, as in laughing.

Zygomaticus Minor. The origin of the zygomaticus minor, the weakest of the three heads of the quadratus labii superioris, is the body of the zygoma in front of the origin of the zygomaticus major. It inserts in the skin of the upper lip, lateral to the midline.

Action. This muscle elevates the upper lip, exposing the maxillary teeth, and deepens the nasolabial furrow.

Levator Anguli Oris. This muscle is slightly deeper than the overlaying zygomatic muscles. It arises from the canine fossa and is inserted into the corner of the mouth, intermingling with the zygomaticus, depressors, and orbicularis oris.

Action. This muscle raises the modiolus and buccal angle, displaying the teeth and deepening the nasolabial furrows.

Depressor Anguli Oris and Depressor Labii Inferioris. These muscles arise from the mandible, and the fibers converge to the corners of the mouth.

Action. Both these muscles depress the corner of the lips downward and laterally.

Risorius. This muscle is one of those located at the corner of the mouth. It originates from the fascia of, and just below the anterior border of, the masseter muscle. It passes anteriorly in a horizontal line to insert under the skin and mucous membrane of the upper lip near the corner of the mouth.

Action. This muscle pulls the angle of the mouth laterally and is often referred to as the "smiling muscle."

Mentalis. This muscle originates in a circular area above the mental tuberosity. It passes in a lateral direction toward the skin. Some of the medial fibers converge and cross those of the contralateral mentalis muscle. The insertion is in the skin of the chin.

Action. This muscle's action is to elevate the skin of the chin aiding its protrusion/eversion, as in drinking.

Levator Anguli Oris. The levator anguli oris, also referred to as the caninus, is the only muscle in the deep layer of muscles that open the lips. It originates from the canine fossa, passes inferiorly and laterally, and inserts in the tendonous node of intertwining muscles at the corner of the mouth.

Action. The function of the caninus is to elevate the angle of the mouth.

Depressor Anguli Oris. This muscle arises from the area near the insertion of the platysma and inserts into the tendonous node at the angle of the mouth.

Action. This muscle depresses the modiolus and buccal angle laterally in opening the mouth and the expression of sadness.

Depressor Labii Inferioris. This muscle originates near the origin of the triangular muscle. It passes upward to insert in the skin of the lower lip.

Action. This muscle pulls the lower lip down and laterally in mastication.

2.3.2. The Muscles of Mandible Motion and Mastication

The movement of the mandible is complex involving the coordinated action of the muscles attached to it (see Figure 2.11). These muscles, like all muscles, work in groups with each other and with other muscles to perform a smooth, balanced, coordinated series of movements of the mandible. Four basic movements of the mandible are:

- *protraction* — pulling the mandible forward so that the head articulates indirectly with the articular tubercle of the temporal bone,

- *retraction* — pulling the mandible backward so that the head moves into the mandibular fossa,

- *elevation* — closing the mouth, and

- *depression* — opening the mouth.

These actions are described in more detail in Section 2.4.

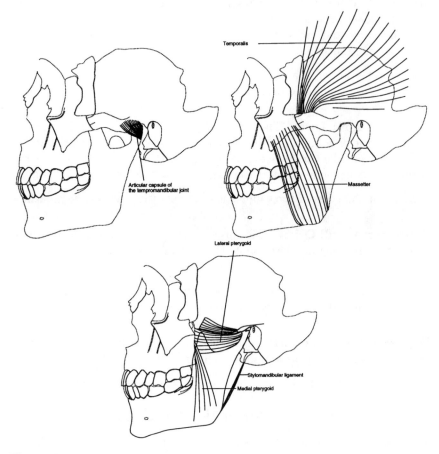

Figure 2.11.
The principal muscles influencing the temporomandibular joint.

Muscles which Elevate the Mandible

The muscles responsible for elevating the mandible are the masseter, the medial pterygoid, and the temporalis.

Masseter. The most superficial of the muscles of mastication is the masseter muscle (see Figure 2.11). It is a broad, thick, rectangular plate, which originates on the zygomatic arch and zygoma and passes inferiorly and posteriorly to insert on the lateral surface of the mandibular ramus at the angular region. The more superficial fibers of this muscle arise from the lower border of the zygoma. The more deeply situated fibers arise from the entire length of the zygomatic arch. The superficial fibers originate no farther posteriorly than the zygomaticotemporal suture.

Action. The action of this thick, powerful muscle is to elevate the lower jaw. The superficial fibers exert power at a right angle to the occlusal plane, whereas the deep fibers, along with their elevating action, exert a secondary retracting component, particularly when the mandible is in a protruded position. This balanced combination of elevation and retraction (retrusion) is important during the closing movement of the mandible.

Medial Pterygoid. The internal medial pterygoid muscle is the deep counterpart of the masseter muscle, but it is weaker (see Figure 2.11). It originates primarily in the pterygoid fossa and the medical surface of the lateral pterygoid plate. Some fibers arise from the palatine bone and maxillary tuberosity.

Action. This muscle acts as an elevator of the mandible so as to close the mouth. Because of the direction of the muscle fibers, it also pulls the mandible forward. When the medial and lateral pterygoid muscles on one side contract together, the chin swings to the opposite side. Such movements are important in chewing.

Temporalis. The temporalis is a broad, fan-shaped muscle that arises in the temporal fossa, a wide field on the lateral surface of the skull (see Figure 2.11). The fibers of the temporalis converge toward the space between the zygomatic arch and the skull. The apex of the coronoid process is located here. The anterior fibers are quite vertical, and the posterior fibers become increasingly oblique. The insertion occupies the coronoid process and extends inferiorly along the anterior border of the vertical ramus and external oblique ridge.

Two tendons of insertion are to be considered here. The outer or superficial tendon is attached to the anterior border of the coronoid and mandibular ramus. The deep tendon juts medially and inserts into the region of the lower third molar. The retromolar triangle is free from insertion of the temporal muscle.

Action. The fibers are somewhat longer and therefore the temporal muscle is less powerful than the masseter, but it provides for rapid movement of the mandible. The posterior fibers have a retracting component to their action, but the temporalis is still considered primarily as an elevator of the mandible.

Muscles that Retract the Mandible

The muscles responsible for retracting the mandible are the temporalis (described in Section 2.3.2), the digastric, and the geniohyoid.

Digastric. The digastricus is made up to two fusiform, fleshy parts, known as bellies, attached to one another, end to end. The posterior belly originates at the mastoid notch and passes anteriorly and inferiorly to the hyoid bone, where its anterior portion ends in a tendon. This tendon slides through a connective tissue pulley, which is attached to the greater horn of the hyoid bone. The anterior belly arises on this intermediate tendon and passes superiorly and anteriorly to insert on the medial surface of the symphysis of the mandible, near the inferior border, in a depression known as the digastric fossa.

The nerve supply to the posterior belly is via a branch of the seventh cranial nerve. The anterior belly is innervated by the mylohyoid branch of the third division of the fifth cranial nerve.

Action. With the mandible fixed, the digastric raises the hyoid bone and, with it, the larynx — an important action in swallowing. In addition, when the mandible is raised, the digastric assists in the retraction of the mandible, and if the hyoid is fixed, it can also depress the mandible.

Geniohyoid Muscle. The geniohyoid muscle arises from the anterior end of the mylohyoid line, near the genial tubercles, and passes posteriorly and inferiorly to the upper half of the body of the hyoid bone. It is supplied by the first and second cervical nerves.

Action. The geniohyoid muscle princiaplly assists the mylohyoid muscle in elevating the tongue. This muscle also elevates and fixes the hyoid bone and depresses the mandible.

Muscles that Protract the Mandible

The muscles repsonsible for protracting the mandible are the lateral pterygoid, the medial pterygoid (described in Section 2.3.2), and the masseter (described in Section 2.3.2).

Lateral Pterygoid. The lateral pterygoid muscle has two heads from which it arises. The inferior head, which is the largest, originates from the lateral surface of the lateral pterygoid plate. The infratemporal surface of the great wing of the sphenoid bone serves as the origin of the superior head. The muscle then passes posteriorly to insert on the anterior surface of the condylar neck.

Some fibers insert on the anterior surface of the temporomandibular joint capsule. The nerve and blood supply are from the same source as the other muscles of mastication.

Action. The lateral pterygoid muscle acts to open the jaw. It causes the mandible to shift to the opposite side when it contracts without the aid of its contralateral mate.

Muscles that Depress the Mandible

The muscles responsible for depressing the mandible are the digastric (described above), the geniohyoid (described above), the mylohyoid, and the platysma.

Mylohyoid. The mylohyoid muscle forms the floor of the mouth. The right and left muscles pass inferiorly and medially and unite with one another in the midline on a tendonous band, known as the raphe.

The origin is the mylohyoid line on the mandible. The posterior fibers insert on the body of the hyoid bone, but most of the fibers of this broad, flat muscle insert on the mylohyoid raphe. The posterior border is free. The mylohyoid muscle is inferior to the bandlike geniohyoid muscle and superior to the digastric muscle. It is innervated by mylohyoid branches of the third division of the trigeminal nerve.

Action. The primary function of this muscle is to elevate the tongue. When the fibers contract, the curvature is flatter; thus the floor of the mouth is elevated, and with it, the tongue. Only the posterior fibers of the mylohyoid muscle, running from the mandible to the hyoid bone, influence the position of the hyoid bone or the mandible.

Platysma. This thin, wide, flat muscle plate that covers most of the anterior and lateral portion of the neck is called the platysma (see Figure 2.8). It lies just below the skin. At its upper border, the platysma attaches to the lower border of the mandible and contiguous skin. It interlaces with the depressor anguli oris. The platysma arises from the fibrous connective tissue under the skin of the clavicle (collarbone) and shoulder. The fibers ascend anteriorly in an oblique course to their insertions.

Action. The action of the platysma is to raise the skin of the neck, as if to relieve the pressure of a tight collar. Also, the platysma draws the outer part of the lower lip down and depresses the mandible. This action is commonly seen in the expression of horror.

2.4.   The Temporomandibular Joint

The temporomandibular joint is the articulation between the mandible and the cranium (see Figure 2.12). It is one of the few joints in the body which contains a complete intra-articular disk, thereby dividing the joint space into upper and lower compartments. This feature facilitates the combined gliding and hinging movements around a transverse axis which passes between the two lingulae. Both articulating complexes of this joint house teeth. The shapes and positions of these teeth influence the function of the temporomandibular joint.

A fibrous capsule encloses the joint. Superiorly, it encircles the glenoid fossa. Below, it attaches to the circumference of the neck of the condyle just beneath the head of the condyle. The inner surface of the capsule is lined by a lubricating synovial membrane.

Inside the capsule is an articular disk. This is an oval plate of fibrous tissue shaped like a peaked cap and completely divides the joint. Its upper surface is sagittally concavoconvex to fit the articular tubercle and fossa, while its inferior concave surface is adapted to the mandibular head.

Three ligaments are associated with the tempromandibular joint: the lateral, the sphenomandibular, and the stylomandibular. Neither the stylomandibular ligament nor the sphenomandibular ligament has any influence upon the movement of the lower jaw.

Lateral Ligament.   This muscle has a broad attachment to the lower border and tubercle of the zygomatic bone. From here the fibers pass downward and backward, blending with the joint capsule to attach to the lateral and posterior parts of the mandible.

Sphenomandibular Ligament.   The sphenomandibular ligament is a bond of fibrous tissue arising from the spine of the sphenoid bone and attaching at the lingula of the mandibular foramen. It is located on the medial aspect.

Stylomandibular Ligament.   The stylomandibular ligament is another fibrous band. It extends from the styloid process to the mandibular angle. Only the temporomandibular ligament limits the joint.

2.4.1.   Movements of the Temporomandibular Joint

The movements of the temporomandibular joint can be described as depression, elevation, protraction, retraction, and lateral movement. All of these movements are used to some extent in chewing. The disk slides on the articular tubercle, and the condyle rotates on the disk when the jaw is opened and closed (see Figure 2.13). In protruding the mandible, both disks

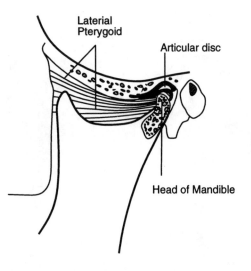

Lateral
Pterygoid

Articular disc

Head of Mandible

Figure 2.12.
The temporomandibular joint.

glide forward; rotation of the condyles is prevented by contraction of the elevating muscles of the mandible. When the mandible moves into lateral positions, one disk glides forward while the other remains stable in position. In chewing, first there is lateral movement; then the mandible is returned to position by the closing muscles. Opening is accomplished by contraction of the external pterygoid, digastric, mylohyoideus, and geniohyoideus muscles. Elevation is produced by the masseter, temporalis, and internal pterygoid muscles. The mandible is protruded by simultaneous action of both external pterygoids and the closing muscles. It is retracted by the posterior portion of the temporalis muscle. Lateral movement is accomplished by contractions of the pterygoid muscles. When the left pterygoid muscles are contracted, the left condyle glides forward, the right condyle stays in position, and the mandible shifts to the right.

2.5. Muscles of the Tongue

The tongue is a powerful muscular organ with a fantastic ability to alter its shape, configuration, and position (see Figure 2.14). The tongue is covered by mucous membrane. Other than its covering, the tongue is composed entirely of muscles, nerves, and blood vessels.

The muscles of the tongue are divided into two groups, the intrinsic and the extrinsic muscles. The intrinsic muscles lie within the tongue itself. The

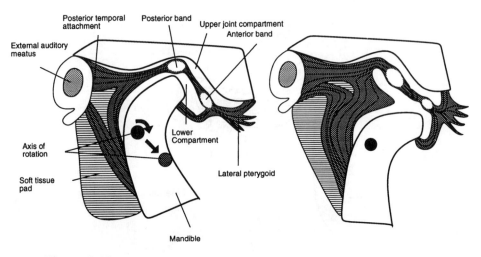

Figure 2.13.
Sagittal section of the two extreme positions during temporomandibular joint articulation. Notice that the axis of rotation glides forward and downward.

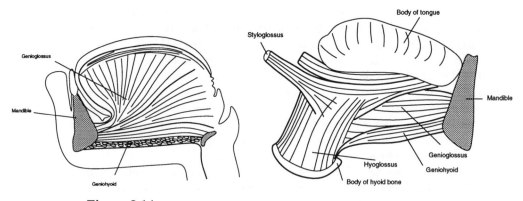

Figure 2.14.
The intrinsic and extrinsic muscles of the tongue.

extrinsic muscles originate outside the tongue and attach on and interlace with the intrinsic muscles.

The intrinsic and extrinsic muscles are also divided into pairs. The tongue is divided into two halves by a median fibrous septum, which extends throughout its length and is fixed below and behind to the hyoid bone.

Intrinsic Muscles of the Tongue

The varying shapes that the tongue can assume are quite complex but can be easily predicted once one considers what happens when the various intrinsic muscles contract. The intrinsic muscles of the tongue can be subdivided into longitudinal, transverse, and vertical.

Superior Longitudinal Muscles. The superior longitudinal fibers lie directly under the dorsal mucosa. They arise from the posterior submucous fibrous tissue and run forward and obliquely to insert on the edges of the tongue.

Inferior Longitudinal Muscle. The inferior longitudinal muscle, a narrow band of fibers, is situated on the undersurface of the tongue and extends from the root of the tongue to its tip.

Transverse Fibers. The transverse fibers originate on the median septum and pass laterally to the lateral borders of the tongue.

Vertical Fibers. The vertical fibers are found in the forepart of the tongue and extend from the upper surface to the lower surface.

Extrinsic Muscles of the Tongue

Genioglossus. This muscle is a flat, triangular muscle which originates at the superior genial tubercles of the mandible. It fans out and inserts into the tongue and hyoid bone. The inferior fibers are inserted on the body of the hyoid bone; the rest insert along the entire undersurface of the tongue from the root to the tip. The posterior fibers protrude the tongue, and the anterior fibers retract the tongue.

Hyoglossus. The hyoglossus acts to depress the tongue and draw its sides down. It originates from the hyoid bone and passes vertically behind the mylohyoid muscle to insert in the lateral portion of the tongue and mingle with other fibers.

Styloglossus. The styloglossus draws the tongue upward and backward. The origin of the styloglossus muscle is the styloid process. It passes down and forward and enters the tongue in two parts: one, longitudinal, blends with the inferior longitudinal muscle, and the other overlaps and intermingles with the hyoglossus.

2.6.   The Muscles of the Scalp, Ear, and Neck

This section describes the muscles of the scalp, the vestigial muscles of the ear, and only the large superficial muscles of the neck.

2.6.1.   Muscles of the Scalp

The four muscles of the scalp are the paired occipital and frontal muscles. They are related to one another by a common tendon known as the *galea aponeurotica*. The two frontalis muscles, the two occipital muscles, and the galea aponeurotica, as a unit, are known as the epicranial muscle. The frontalis is attached to the root of the nose and skin of the eyebrow. The occipitalis originates at the supreme nuchal line from the mastoid process to the midline.

Action. The frontalis acts to lift the eyebrow and furrow the skin of the forehead.

2.6.2.   Muscles of the Outer Ear

The auricularis anterior, superior, and posterior are the muscles of the outer ear. These muscles serve little or no function.

Action. Only a few people can activate the muscles of the outer ear voluntarily. Occasionally these muscles contract involuntarily when other muscles of facial expression are activated.

2.6.3.   Superficial Muscles of the Neck

The superficial muscles of the neck are the trapezius, platysma (described above), and the sternocleidomastoid.

Trapezius.   The trapezius is a large, flat triangular muscle covering the back part of the neck and the upper trunk (see Figure 2.15). It arises from the external occipital protuberance, the ligamentum nuchae, the spinous processes of the seventh cervical vertebra, and from the spines of all the thorasic vertebrae. The ligamentum nuchae is a fibrous band, extending from the occipital protuberance to the spinous process of the seventh cervical vertebra. The fibers of the trapezius converge as they pass laterally to their insertions on the shoulder girdle.

Action. When both the right and left trapezius muscles contract together, they pull the head backward; the trapezius also acts to rotate the scapula.

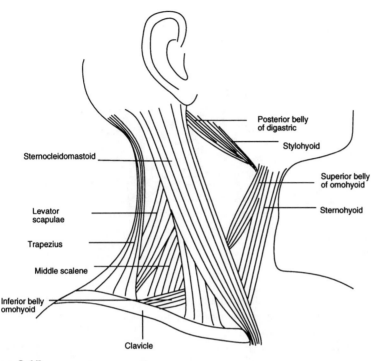

Figure 2.15.
Superficial muscles of the neck.

Sternocleidomastoid. This muscle ascends superiorly and posteriorly across the side of the neck from its two origins. One origin is the upper-most part of the sternum, and the other origin is the medial third of the clavicle. The two parts blend into one thick muscle that inserts into the mastoid process of the temporal bone and the lateral half of the superior nuchal line of the occipital bone.

Action. When this muscle contracts, the neck is bent laterally and the head is drawn toward the shoulders, as the head rotates. The chin is thus pointed upward and toward the opposite side. When the right and left sides contract together, the neck is flexed as the head is drawn forward.

2.7. Skin

The skin covers the entire external surface of the human form and is a highly specialized interface between the body and its surroundings. It has a multi-component microstructure, the basis of which are five intertwined networks

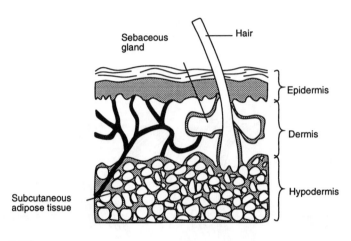

Figure 2.16.
Skin layers.

of collagen, nerve fibers, small blood vessels, and lymphatics, covered by
a layer of epithelium and transfixed at intervals by hairs and the ducts of
sweat glands (see Figure 2.16).

Facial tissue varies in thickness over the face; around the eyes it is thin,
whereas around the lips it is thick. Also, skin texture varies with thickness,
giving more of a pinkish color where thin, and a yellowish color where it is
thick. Many factors influence the appearance of skin tissue; thickness, age,
and disease are the primary effectors. Between males and females there is a
difference in underlying fatty tissue, there being less in men than in women.
Skin thickness is less in women than in men, giving a luster to the skin
surface of women. Facial wrinkles are caused in part caused by the loss of
fatty tissue as the person grows older, and the loss of elasticity in the skin
from aging causes further furrowing and wrinkling.

Human skin has a layered structure consisting of the epidermis, a superficial layer of dead cells, and the dermis, fatty tissue. The epidermis and the
dermis, at a finer resolution, have layers within themselves.

The mechanical properties of facial tissue are described in more detail
in Chapter 7, *Skin and Muscle-Based Facial Animation*, where a computer
model of facial tissue is developed.

2.7.1. The Epidermial Tissue

The epidermis is the outermost layer of skin and is composed mainly of
keratin. In this tissue there is a continuous replacement of cells, with a
mitotic layer at the base replacing lost layers at the surface.

2.7.2. The Dermal Tissue

The dermis consists of irregular, moderately dense, soft connective tissue. Its matrix consists of an interwoven collagenous network, with varying content of elastin fibers, proteoglycans, fibronectin and other matrix components, blood vessels, lymphatic vessels, and nerves.

2.7.3. The Subcutaneous Tissues

Underneath the dermis lies the superficial fascia, which consists of adipose tissue distributed in a network of connective fibres. This connective tissue is mostly collagen arranged in a lattice with fat cells. The intercelluar amorphous matrix is referred to as the *ground substance*. Beneath the superficial fascia, lies the deep fascia which coats the bones. This layer is formed mainly of aponeuroses, which are flat or ribbon-like tendons.

2.7.4. Skin Lines

The layered structure of skin is nonhomogeneous and nonisotropic [KGEB75, Lar86]. These features were elaborated in 1861 by Langer who made observations on many cadavers. His investigations were based on an earlier observation by Dupuytren (1834) that a circular puncture on the skin left an elliptical wound (see Figure 2.17). Langer hypothesized that skin is constantly in a state of tension due to the rhomboidal arrangement of the dermal fibers. Consequently, if the fibers were disturbed, the tension in the long axis of the rhomboid dominated, deforming the wound shape. The significance of this investigation was that surgical incisions should be made parallel to the lines of tension to minimize postoperative scarring. More recently Kraissl [WWDB89] in 1951 described lines of tension that were usually orthogonal to the line of action of subcutaneous muscle fibers. In some cases these lines would run at right angles to Langer lines. However, it is worth noting that Kraissl lines, for the most part, describe fundamental crease lines on the face.

2.8. The Eyes

The eyes are in reality a separate lobe of the brain springing from the distal extremity of the optic nerve. Situated in the skeletal orbits for protection, the eyes are the end organ of the sense of vision. The positioning of the eyes in the orbits provide rigid support and sites for muscular attachment. The muscles permit the accurate positioning of the visual axis under neuromuscular control to assist in determining the spatial relationship between the two eyes for binocular vision.

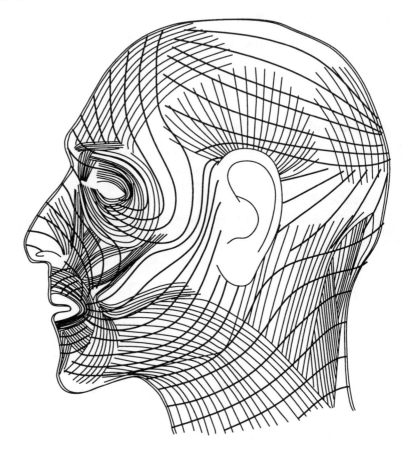

Figure 2.17.
Distribution of Langer's cleavage lines on the face.

When creating synthetic computer-generated facial images, careful attention should be paid to the details of the eyes. The eyes should converge and not stare into space, the pupil should be able to dilate, and the highlight reflection off the surface of the iris and cornea should be modeled with care. With these basic characteristics the computer model can maintain attention, thereby enhancing the realism of the face.

2.8.1.   The Eyeball

The eyeball consists of a series of concentric layers which enclose cavities filled with separate light-refracting media (see Figure 2.18). The eyeball is about 2.5 cm in diameter but is not perfectly spherical since the anterior cornea has a smaller radius of curvature than the rest of the globe.

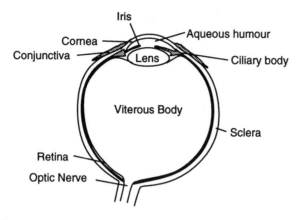

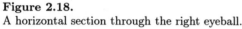

Figure 2.18.
A horizontal section through the right eyeball.

Sclera.   This area is the outermost layer of the eyeball and consists of a dense, collagenous coat; the posterior five-sixths is the white opaque sclera. The point where the optic nerve pierces the sclera is approximately 3 mm to the nasal side of the posterior pole and slightly inferior to the horizontal meridian.

Cornea.   The anterior sixth of the eyeball is known as the cornea. The cornea is a thin, bulging, transparent membrane set into the circular gap at the anterior pole of the sclera, with which it fuses at the sclero-corneal junction. The anterior surface of the cornea is covered with a layer of epithelium which is firmly bound to it, and is continuous with the conjunctiva at the margin of the cornea.

Iris.   The iris is an adjustable diaphragm around the central aperture of the pupil. The iris is the mechanism which automatically regulates the amount of light permitted to pass through the lens and is regulated by two sphincter muscles, one to dilate, the other to constrict. It lies anterior to the lens and is separated from the cornea by the anterior chamber. Its circumference is continuous with the ciliary body and is connected to the cornea by the pectinate ligament. The iris varies greatly in color and surrounds a central aperture, the pupil. The anterior surface shows faint radial striations.

   The accommodation of the lens to near and distant vision is accomplished by the action of smooth-muscle fibers of the ciliary body. These actions may be either automatic or voluntary, providing for unconscious or conscious accommodation.

Retina.   The retina is the innermost layer of the eyeball and is, in reality, an expansion of the optic nerve. It consists of ten layers of which the deepest is the layer of rods and cones. The entire space bounded by the retina, the ciliary body, and the posterior surface of the lens is occupied by the vitreous body, which is filled with a transparent, gelatinous substance.

3

Modeling Faces

3.1. Introduction

Developing a facial model involves determining geometric descriptions and animation capabilities that represent the faces of interest. It also involves the representation of additional attributes such as surface colors and textures. For our purposes, static models are not useful; the facial models must be constructed in ways that support animation.

The face has a very complex, flexible, three-dimensional surface. It has color and texture variation and usually contains creases and wrinkles. As shown in Chapter 2, the detailed anatomy of the head and face is a complex dynamic assembly of bones, cartilage, muscles, nerves, blood vessels, glands, fatty tissue, connective tissue, and skin. To date, no facial animation models which represent and simulate this complete, detailed anatomy have been reported. For some applications, such as medical visualization and surgical planning, complete detailed models are the ultimate goal. Fortunately, a number of useful applications, such as character animation, can be accomplished with facial models that approximate only some aspects of the complete facial anatomy.

3.1.1. Facial Mechanics

The modeled facial geometry and its animation potential are inseparably intertwined. The structure of the model determines its animation poten-

tial. The actions a model must perform determine how the model should
be constructed. Choices made early in the modeling process determine its
animation capabilities.

The mechanics of the face and head are extremely important when constructing these models. The jaw needs to work, the eyelids need to open and
close, the eyelids need to stretch over the eyeballs, and the cheeks need to
stretch. There are subtle points to consider as well. When the eyes look from
one side to the other, how much of the flesh surrounding the eyes moves?
When the mouth opens and closes, how much of the neck is influenced?
When the mouth opens, how much do the cheeks move and how far up the
cheeks is there an effect? How is the nose affected? Such details can be the
key to a character's age and personality.

The eyes and the mouth are the most expressive areas of the face. They
communicate the most information and elicit the greatest emotional responses. Care must be exercised with these regions so that the necessary
details and flexibility are included in the model.

3.1.2. Facial Diversity

Even though most faces have similar structure and the same feature set,
obviously there is considerable variation from one individual face to the next.
This subtle variation is exactly what makes individual faces recognizable.
One of the challenges of facial animation is to develop models that support
and allow these variations.

While most of the discussion in this book is centered on the representation of realistic faces, the spectrum of possible representation styles is wide.
Artists and illustrators have developed many approaches to depicting the
human face. These range from sketches and realistic renderings to cartoons
and abstract forms to surrealism — to name just a few. Almost any of these
artistic styles might be used as the basis for computer models of the face.

Caricatures

One popular form of facial representation is the caricature. Caricatures typically involve distorting or exaggerating the most recognizable features of a
specific face. This often is done in editorial cartoons of famous persons.
Brennan [Bre82] developed a computer-based automatic two-dimensional
caricature generator. By digitizing two-dimensional vector representations
of a number of faces and averaging them, a model or description of the
normal or average face was developed. Caricatures were then formed by
exaggerating the differences of individual faces from the computed normal
face. A similar approach could also be applied to three-dimensional faces.

Empathetic Characterizations

In animation we are usually concerned with telling a story, which means getting the audience involved with the characters. This involvement implies that we must develop our facial models so that the audience can establish an emotional response to the character. We want the audience to hate the villain, love the heroine, laugh with the comic, and feel sorry for the unfortunate victim. Developing such empathetic characters is a challenge.

3.2. Facial Geometry

The goal of the various animation techniques, which is discussed further in Chapter 4, is to control the modeled faces, over time, such that the rendered facial surfaces have the desired shapes, colors, and textures in each frame of the animated sequence. How do we geometrically represent faces in ways that allow both effective animation and efficient rendering?

3.2.1. Volume Representations

One approach to representing faces is to use one of the many volume representation techniques. These include constructive solid geometry (CSG), volume element (voxel) arrays, and aggregated volume elements such as octrees.

CSG is used successfully as the basis for a number of computer-aided mechanical design systems. For these systems the objects of interest are represented using Boolean set constructions of relatively simple regular mathematical shapes, such as planes, cylinders, and spheres. Unfortunately, realistic faces are not easily represented in this way. Therefore, CSG has not been a popular geometric basis for faces. However, one can imagine a particular style of three-dimensional cartoon faces that might be constructed using CSG techniques.

Volume element, or voxel, representation is a preferred way of describing anatomical structures in medical imaging. These representations may be assembled from two-dimensional data slices of three-dimensional structures. These two-dimensional slices may, for example, be obtained using computer tomography (CT) [BGP83] or magnetic resonance (MR) techniques [HL83]. There are numerous examples of this approach being used to create three-dimensional representations of the detailed interior structure of the human head [FZY84] [HVW85] [HDH83] [CDL+87]. Detailed voxel representations typically require huge amounts of memory.

There may be a future for voxel models in specific animation areas, such as surgical planning [BTTU84], where correct detailed understanding of interrelated interior structures is required. However, animation of such models is a problem. Animations based on simple rotations of the voxel data or moving slicing planes through the model are straightforward. However, the structural shape changes usually associated with facial animation are complex for voxel models. Possible animation approaches include interpolation between voxel data sets and the use of freeform deformations similar to those discussed in Section 3.10.5.

Direct voxel models are not currently used for facial animation. However, techniques such as the *Marching Cubes* algorithm developed by Lorensen and Cline [LC87] can be used to extract surface geometry models of the anatomical structures from the voxel data. Animation may then be done using the extracted surface models.

The extracted surfaces usually are constructed to follow specific structure boundaries in the voxel data. The structure boundaries are associated with transitions between regions of specific constant densities within the voxel data.

3.2.2. Surface Representations

Surface primitives and structures are the current preferred geometric basis for facial models. The surface structures used must allow surface shapes and shape changes as needed for the various facial conformations and expressions. Possible surface description techniques include implicit surfaces, parametric surfaces, and polygonal surfaces. Parametric surfaces include bivariate Bézier, Catmull-Rom, Beta-spline, B-spline, hierarchical B-spline, and NURB surfaces. Polygonal surfaces include regular polygonal meshes and arbitrary polygon networks.

Implicit Surfaces

One approach is to find an analytic surface or collection of surfaces to approximate the surfaces of the face. An implicit surface is defined by a function $F(x, y, z)$ that assigns a scalar value to each point in x, y, z space [Bli82]. The implicit surface defined by such a function is the set of points such that

$$F(x, y, z) = 0.$$

For example, a sphere of unit radius centered at $(0, .5, -.5)$ would be described by the implicit function

$$f(x, y, z) = x^2 + (y - .5)^2 + (z + .5)^2 - 1.$$

Any polynomial function $f(x, y, z)$ implicitly describes an algebraic surface. In particular, quadrics such as ellipsoids, cylinders, cones, and tori are implicit algebraic surfaces.

Given two implicit surface functions $f(x, y, z)$ and $g(x, y, z)$, additional implicit surface functions can be generated by *blending* the two given functions [Woo86]. Examples of blended implicit functions are Nishimura's *Metaballs* [NHK+85] and Wyvill's *Soft Objects* [WMW86].

Although implicit surfaces commonly are expressed analytically, Ricci [Ric73] pointed out that the defining functions could be any procedure that computes a scalar value for every point in space. Models constructed with such procedures are called *procedural implicit models*.

The blending and constraint properties of implicit surfaces allow creation of models that would be difficult to build with other techniques. However, interaction with implicit surface models is difficult [BW93]. Real-time display of surfaces is important for interactive design. With current techniques, implicit surfaces take more time to interactively manipulate and display than polygonal or parametric surfaces. In addition, methods that allow a high degree of user control over implicit surfaces have yet to be developed. As a result, implicit surfaces have yet to be used for facial animation.

Parametric Surfaces

Bivariate parametric functions are used widely to define three-dimensional surfaces. These surfaces are generated by three functions of two parametric variables, one function for each of the spatial dimensions. These functions typically are based on quadric or cubic polynomials.

The most popular of these surfaces, referred to as *tensor-product parametric surfaces*, are defined in terms of control values and *basis* functions. Examples of these include B-splines, Beta-splines, Bézier patches, and nonuniform rational B-spline surfaces (NURBS) [BBB87]. These surfaces can be expressed in the form

$$\mathbf{S}(u, v) = \sum_i \sum_j \mathbf{V}_{i,j} B_{i,k}(u) B_{j,m}(v)$$

where $\mathbf{S}(u, v)$ is the parametric surface, $\mathbf{V}_{i,j}$ are the control values, and $B_{i,k}(u), B_{j,m}$ are the basis functions of polynomial orders k and m, respectively. This formulation usually is recast into the matrix representation

$$\mathbf{S}(u, v) = [\mathbf{u}][\mathbf{B}_u][\mathbf{V}][\mathbf{B}_v]^T [\mathbf{v}]^T$$

where $[\mathbf{u}] = [1 \ u \ u^2 \cdots u^{k-1}]$ and $[\mathbf{v}] = [1 \ v \ v^2 \cdots v^{m-1}]$.

For each surface patch, the parameters u and v vary over the interval $[0.0, 1.0]$. The basis functions $\mathbf{B}_u$ and $\mathbf{B}_v$ are determined by the type and order of the surface. For uniform, bicubic B-splines, $k = m = 4$ and both $[\mathbf{B}]$ matrices are

$$\frac{1}{6}\begin{vmatrix} 1 & 4 & 1 & 0 \\ -3 & 0 & 3 & 0 \\ 3 & -6 & 3 & 0 \\ -1 & 3 & -3 & 1 \end{vmatrix}.$$

For bicubic surfaces the [**V**] matrix is a four-by-four array of control values. The relationship between these control points and the surface they define depends on the surface type. For B-splines these control values are in fact three-dimensional points which are near, but not typically on, the defined surface. For a Catmull-Rom surface [CR74] the surface will pass through its interior control points. For other surface types the control values may be points or other geometric entities, such as tangent vectors.

In most implementations the desired surface is defined and controlled using a large array of control values. Each four-by-four subarray of control values defines one portion or *patch* of the larger surface. These patches join together with specific surface continuity characteristics. The surface continuity is determined by the surface type. Bicubic B-spline surfaces, for example, have $\mathbf{C}^2$ continuity, which means that the surface has second-derivative continuity across the boundaries between the patches.

A few facial model implementations, such as Waite [Wai89] and Nahas et al. [NHS88], have used bicubic B-spline surface modeling techniques. These models produce faces with smooth curved surfaces that are defined using relatively few control points (typically a 16-by-12 array of control points). These models do have a few disadvantages:

- The density of control points used does not support the detailed surface definition and surface control needed around the eyes and mouth.

- Because of the array structure of the control points, adding detail requires adding complete rows or columns to the control points array.

- Creases in the face are difficult to implement since they require defeating the natural surface continuity properties.

Hierarchical B-Splines.   Forsey and Bartels [FB88] describe a way to increase local detail in B-spline surfaces without the need to add complete rows or columns of control points. By carefully controlling overlapping boundary conditions, it is possible to locally increase surface detail by overlaying a more detailed surface defined with additional control points only in the region of interest. These additional control points allow more detailed control of the surface. The additional detail is a refinement layered onto the original surface. The added detail is relative to the original underlying surface.

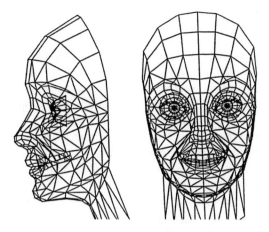

Figure 3.1.
An example polygon topology.

When the underlying surface is modified, the added detail follows accordingly. This approach is hierarchical and can be applied repeatedly, adding additional detail onto regions which already have enhanced detail.

Wang's *Langwidere* facial animation system [Wan93] was implemented using hierarchical B-spline surfaces. In this model, hierarchical refinement was used to add local surface detail, including the interior of the mouth and the eyes and eye sockets. Facial expression animation is controlled using simulated muscle functions to manipulate the hierarchical surface control points.

3.2.3. Polygonal Surfaces

Modern graphic workstations are adept at displaying polygonal surfaces and can update modest complexity facial models in near real time. Because of this efficiency, essentially all facial models are displayed using polygonal surfaces. Even the nonpolygonal surface techniques described above are approximated with polygon surfaces for display.

The vast majority of existing facial models are based on polygonal surface descriptions. These polygonal surfaces may be in the form of regular polygonal meshes or as arbitrary networks of connected polygons such as that shown in Figure 3.1.

3.2.4.   Developing a Polygonal Topology

In this context, *topology* refers to the way the polygons are connected to form the surface. The regular mesh topology organizes the polygon vertices into a rectangular array. These vertices are then connected with triangular or quadrilateral polygons to form the desired surface. Arbitrary polygonal networks are constructed by connecting vertices as needed to form the desired surface. Gouraud's [Gou71] original approach was to directly approximate the surface of a face with an arbitrary network of polygons. This network was constructed by sampling the surface at a number of points and connecting these points to form polygons. No attempt was made to impose a regular structure on the created polygons. The topology shown in Figure 3.1 is an example of an arbitrary polygonal network.

There are a number of things to keep in mind when approximating a face with polygons.

- The polygons must be laid out in a way that allows the face to flex and change shape naturally. If the polygons are not triangles, they should remain approximately planar as the face flexes.

- The polygons must approximate the face for each expression. The polygon topology may need iterative modification until it allows reasonable representation of the face in all of its possible expressions. The eyelids and lips require special attention to insure that they can open and close naturally.

- The density of surface-defining information should be distributed according to surface curvature. Areas of high surface curvature (the nose, the mouth, around the eyes, and the edge of the chin) need a high density of defining information, whereas areas of lower curvature (the forehead, cheeks, and neck) need less defining information. Higher density also is needed in those areas that require subtle surface control. These areas include the eye region and the mouth, which are the major expressive areas of the face.

- Use the smallest number of polygons consistent with good results. The goal is to have acceptable surface shape accuracy with a minimum number of polygons. A smaller number of polygons allows for faster image generation and minimization of the data acquisition problem.

- Polygon edges must coincide with the creases of the face (under the eyes, the side of the nose, the edge of the lips, and the corner of the mouth). Polygons should not span the creases.

- Special care is necessary if creases are to be visible in smooth shaded surfaces. Separate normals must be maintained for vertices along the crease that are in polygons on opposite sides of the crease. This action insures that there will be a shading discontinuity along the crease and that the crease will be visible.

- Polygon edges must coincide with color boundaries such as those associated with the lips and eyebrows. Polygons should not span color boundaries. If the model makes use of texture-mapped color information, these considerations may not be as important.

- Since the face is nearly symmetric, we may elect to model only one side of the face. The other side may be obtained by *mirroring* or reflecting about the plane of symmetry. This approach is not recommended when accurate models of specific faces are desired.

3.3. Face Features

A facial model is usually the sum of many parts and details. Much of the research on facial animation has focused on techniques for geometrically defining and manipulating the facial *mask*. A more complete approach is to integrate the facial mask, facial feature details, and hair into models of the complete head.

The Facial Mask. The facial mask corresponds to the visible external skin surface of the face and often includes the front part of the neck. Many face models have dealt only with this expressive facial mask, as shown in Figure 3.2(a). A face mask by itself is not very realistic. It is usually necessary to add facial features to be convincing. Complete faces include eyeballs, facial hair (eyebrows, eyelashes, beards, etc.), and the inside of the mouth, including the teeth, gums, and tongue. The details of the face are very important in achieving realistic results. Figure 3.2(b–d) shows the effect that details such as the eyes, eyebrows, eyelashes, teeth, and hair have on the realism of even a very simple face model.

Eyes. Detailed, dynamic eyes are very important to successful expression animation. Eye tracking motions and even pupil dilation changes add realism to the animation. Details of iris coloration and reflections from the eyeballs add life to the face. Each eyeball can be approximately modeled as a white sphere with color bands for the iris and pupil. Since only a small portion of the eyeball is actually visible, only the front part of the eyeball needs to be included in the model.

A better model would include a smaller superimposed reflecting transparent partial sphere as the cornea. An even better model might use texture

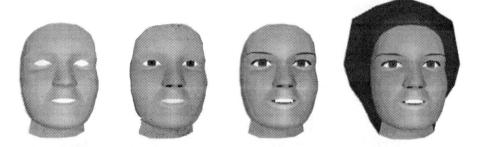

Figure 3.2.
The effect of facial features: (a) only the facial mask; (b–d) the effect of
additional feature details. (From [Par72].)

mapping for the color patterns of the iris and even the blood vessels visible
in the whites of the eyes. Sagar et al. [SBMH94] developed a very detailed
eye model for use in simulating eye surgery.

Lips.   The lips and surrounding tissues are extremely flexible and must be
modeled with sufficient curvature density and flexibility to take on the range
of possible mouth postures. The mouth and lips are instrumental in communicating emotional postures. The lips are also a major component of speech.
The lips help form the speech phonemes and their visual counterparts, called
visemes.

Teeth.   The teeth are at least partially visible during many expressions and
speech utterances. As a result, including teeth in the facial model is of some
importance. The teeth could be modeled in several ways. One of the simpler
approaches is that shown in Figure 3.2(c), where each tooth is represented
by a single forward-facing polygon. A more realistic — and more complex
— approach would be to model the detailed shape of each tooth. A third
approach would be to texture-map teeth images on a simple connected set
of polygons used to approximate the dental arch.

Other interior structures of the mouth may be visible in some facial postures. These include the gums, the tongue, and the other interior surfaces of
the mouth. Including these features increases the fidelity of the facial model.

Tongue.   The tongue is visible in many facial postures and is important
in distinguishing a number of speech postures. If the tongue is visible, is
it between the teeth or touching the roof of the mouth? For several of the

speech postures, tongue shape and position are the main characteristics that determine which visime is being represented. Including even a simple tongue can significantly increase the range of expressions and the ability of the facial model to support speech animation.

Ears. Ears are very individual and are important in capturing and representing *likeness*. They are also difficult to model. Real ears have complex surfaces which require a large number of polygons or complex bicubic surfaces with many control points. In some face models, simple approximations to the real ear shapes have been used effectively. In other face models the ears are simply not included, sometimes because they are covered with a hat or hair.

Asymmetries. There is strong temptation to model the face with exact left/right symmetry. This simplifies both the surface definition and the control aspects of face models. However, faces are not truly symmetric. Asymmetries occur in both conformation and expressions. Structural and expression asymmetries are important characteristics of both realistic and character faces. Much facial personality is the result of these asymmetries.

Hair. Hair, including eyebrows, eyelashes, and beards, is important for realistic facial models. Hair can be an important aspect of a character's personality. Just as in real life, hair and hairstyle can be a significant component in recognizing specific individual characters. Ideally, the hair should behave dynamically in response to head and air current motions.

Hair has been and continues to be a challenge for the modeler. Polygon or bicubic surfaces are not very good representations for hair, even when texture mapping techniques are used. Several recent implementations have modeled hair as collections of individual hair strands. Chapter 10 discusses techniques for modeling and animating hair.

3.3.1. Complete Heads

The face should be viewed as an integrated part of a complete head and, in turn, as a part of the complete character. A complete head model includes the face, ears, hair, the back of the head, and the neck. The ability to specify the shape of the head, the conformation of the ears, hair and hairstyle is important in representing faces of specific people or characters.

Integrating the face, head, and neck into the rest of the body is an important aspect of three-dimensional character animation. The head is connected with the rest of the body through the complex muscle and bone structures of the neck and upper trunk. The dynamics of head and neck motions are discussed in Peterson and Richmond [WR88].

3.4.   Sources of Facial Surface Data

Regardless of the geometric primitives used, a basic modeling goal is to create descriptions that faithfully represent the desired face or faces. Specifying the three-dimensional surface of a face or any other complex object is a significant challenge.

Four general approaches are used for determining surface shape for face models:

- three-dimensional surface measuring techniques,

- interactive surface sculpting,

- assembling faces from components, and

- creating new faces by modifying existing faces.

Most of the face models discussed in this book rely on measured three-dimensional surface data. Surface measurement can be accomplished using digitizers, photogrammetric techniques, or laser scanning techniques.

3.4.1.   Capturing Likeness

To capture likeness we need to obtain shape and shape change information from real faces. The ability to capture the subtleties of a particular face depends on the density of measured points and the corresponding number of surface polygons or patches. It depends also on the accuracy and resolution of the measuring system.

3.4.2.   The Time Element

Since faces are dynamic and change over time, it is necessary to *freeze* the desired facial postures. For real faces this outcome involves holding the face in a desired posture for the duration of the measurement process. Photographic techniques automatically freeze the desired posture at a specific time instant. Physical facial sculptures are another way to freeze facial postures.

3.4.3.   Contour Reconstruction

Three-dimensional surfaces can be constructed using digitized two-dimensional contour information from multiple stacked data slices. Surfaces are formed by creating a *skin* of polygons which connect the contours. Algorithms exist for automatically creating these polygon skins [FKU77]. Information from the contours also might be used as control points for parametric surfaces that approximate or interpolate the contour data.

3.4.4. Three-Dimensional Digitizers

Three-dimensional digitizers are special hardware devices that rely on mechanical, electromagnetic, or acoustic measurements to locate positions in space. The electromagnetically based Polhemus 3Space digitizer [Pol87] is probably the most widely used device for this purpose.

These digitizers require physically positioning a three-dimensional probe or locator at each surface point to be measured. The digitizing process requires considerable time if a large number of points are to measured.

The surface points measured may be the vertices of a polygon network or the control points for a parametric surface. Since real faces tend to move and change shape over time, digitizers work best with sculptures or physical models that do not change shape during the measuring process.

3.4.5. Photogrammetric Techniques

This method captures facial surface shapes and expressions photographically. The basic idea is to take multiple simultaneous photographs of the face, each from a different point of view. If certain constraints are observed when taking the photographs, the desired three-dimensional surface data points can be computed based on measured data from these multiple two-dimensional views [Par74] [Sut74]. Since this process *freezes* the facial surface at a given instant of time, it can be used for direct measurement of real faces as well as face sculptures.

3.4.6. Laser Scanning Systems

Laser-based surface scanning devices, such as those developed by Cyberware [Cyb90], can be used to measure faces. These devices typically produce a very large regular mesh of data values in a cylindrical coordinate system. They can digitize real faces as well as physical models and facial sculptures. Facial poses must be held constant during the short time needed to complete the scanning process. Newer versions of these scanning systems can simultaneously capture surface color information in addition to surface shape data.

Postprocessing of the scanned cylindrical data mesh is often required to extract the surface data needed for a particular face model. This postprocessing may include data thinning, spatial filtering, surface interpolation, and transformations from cylindrical to Cartesian coordinate systems.

3.4.7. Standard Form

It is often desireable to put the three-dimensional data into a standard form so that all measured faces will have certain common properties. We may, for example, want the symmetry plane of the face to be coincident with the plane defined by the x and z axes, with the x axis pointed toward the front of the face, and the z axis pointing up. We probably want the origin of the face coordinate system to be located near the center of the head. We also may want the data scaled so that the size of the head is within a specific range.

3.5.   Digitizer-Based Modeling

Three-dimensional digitizers involve moving a sensor or locating device to each surface point to be measured. The digitized points may be polygonal vertices or control points for parametric surfaces. These devices require that the positions be measured sequentially. This sequential requirement implies that the total surface digitizing time will depend on the number of points to be measured.

There are several types of three-dimensional digitizers, each based on a different physical measurement technique. They include digitizers based on mechanical, acoustic, or electromagnetic mechanisms.

Mechanical Digitizers.   Mechanical digitizers rely on positioning a mechanical measuring stylus at the surface points to be measured. The stylus may be attached to a mechanical arm linkage or to an orthogonal set of mechanical tracks. Potentiometers or shaft encoders embedded in the mechanism are used to convert the mechanical position of the stylus into electrical signals. These signals are in turn transformed into coordinate values. The mechanical structure of these devices may prevent them from reaching all points on the surface of some objects.

Acoustic Digitizers.   Acoustic digitizers rely on the time of flight of sound pulses to multiple sound sensors. Triangulation based on these propagation times allows spatial locations to be computed. The sound source is usually located at the measuring stylus. At least three sound sensors are located in the measuring environment to receive the sound pulses. Objects in the environment can occlude or distort the sound transmission paths, resulting in measurement errors.

Electromagnetic Digitizers.   Electromagnetic digitizers, such as the Polhemus 3Space digitizer [Pol87], work by generating orthogonal electromagnetic fields. Sensors attached to the stylus provide signals that can be converted to stylus location *and* orientation. These digitizers do not work well with objects that contain materials, such as metals, that can block or distort the electromagnetic fields.

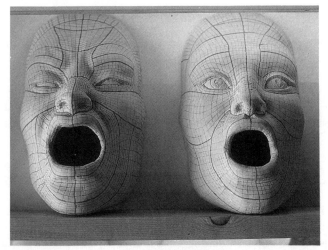

Figure 3.3.
Facial model sculptures. (Courtesy Jeff Kleiser.)

Digitizer Accuracy. The resolution and accuracy of these devices are limited by characteristics of the physical properties being measured and by accuracy of the sensors. The limitations may be in the form of accumulated mechanical tolerances, distortion of sound waveforms, or the strength and distortion of electromagnetic fields. The Polhemus digitizer, for example, has an accuracy of about .02 inches within a spherical working volume of diameter two feet. To achieve good positional accuracy, the digitized objects should fit within this working volume.

3.5.1. Digitizing Polygonal Surfaces

Kleiser [Kle89a] describes the use of a Polhemus digitizer to create polygonal facial models. In this instance, a number of plaster facial sculptures were created for the various facial expressions and speech postures of a specific character. Figure 3.3 shows two of these sculptures.

The same predetermined polygon topology was used to mark each of the face sculptures. Each vertex in the topology is identified. This identification may be in the form of row and column numbers for regular polygonal meshes, or as vertex numbers for arbitrary polygonal networks. For arbitrary networks, the facial topology is recorded by noting how the numbered vertices are connected to form the surface polygons.

The digitizer is used to sequentially measure the vertex positions for each sculpture. The measurements usually are taken in a predetermined order, such as in row or column order or vertex number order. These measurements could be taken in arbitrary order, but doing so requires specifying the vertex order as the digitizing takes place.

3.5.2. Digitizing Parametric Surfaces

Reeves [Ree90] describes an example of digitizing physical models to define parametric surface face models. In this case the face model was for Billy, the baby character in the film *Tin Toy* [Pix88].

The data for Billy's skin was a set of three-dimensional points along with information that specified how these points were ordered to define the surface. The surface was determined by fitting a smooth parametric surface through the data points.

The Digitization Process

A plastic doll head was used to test and debug the digitizing process. The actual Billy prototypes were sculpted in modeling clay. Using clay allowed small changes to the model when necessary. Identifying lines or marks were pressed into the clay surface where desired. The modeling clay allowed these marks to be easily changed when necessary. However, the soft clay also allowed the digitizing stylus to sink into the surface, which made digitizing fine detail difficult and could add error to the resulting data.

Billy's head and body were digitized using a Polhemus 3Space digitizer [Pol87]. Only one side of Billy's head was digitized. The other side was generated by reflecting the points about the center of the head.

The actual digitizing process was quite simple: position the digitizer stylus at a point on the clay model, hit a foot pedal to record the position, move the stylus to the next position, hit the pedal, etc.

Entering the connectivity information occurred concurrently. Connectivity was represented as ordered point sets that define each small surface element. This defining information was entered interactively by requesting a new element and then pointing at the points forming that set, one by one. This procedure is very similar to defining the vertices of a polygon. If polygons are defined by four-point sets organized in rows, a whole row of elements can be automatically specified by identifying the first and last points of the current row and of the previous row.

Surface Fitting

Reeves reports that the initial approach was to fit the data points with triangular Bézier patches. Triangles make it easy to tile a surface that makes transitions from high detail to low detail. Four-sided, five-sided, and n-sided patches can be handled easily since they can be subdivided into three-sided patches.

Unfortunately the surfaces produced were not smooth. While the triangular Bézier patch interpolates its corner vertices as well as its corner normals

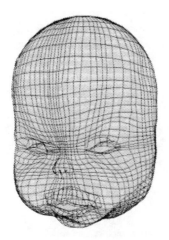

Figure 3.4.
Surface structure for the Billy model. (Adapted from [Ree90].)

and is $\mathbf{C}^1$-continuous across adjoining patches, there is no control over what happens interior to the patch. Under some conditions severe surface undulations can occur. The next approach tried was to use bicubic Catmull-Rom [CR74] patches, which are well suited for interpolating data points. Given 16 data points arranged in a four-by-four array, the defined surface patch passes through the four central data points and defines a smooth $\mathbf{C}^1$ boundary, with adjacent patches defined using shared points.

As discussed in Section 3.2.2, four-sided bivariate surfaces such as Catmull-Rom patches are hard to refine. To add detail to the surface, you have to add entire rows or columns of data points. Adding detail in one region also adds it in other regions where it is not needed. The need for relatively fine detail around Billy's mouth and eyes caused unneeded data points across the bottom of the cheeks, at the top of the neck, and around the ears. As a result, Billy's head, shown in Figure 3.4, was defined by about 2700 points forming about 2600 patches. These data took days to digitize. The hierarchical B-spline representation discussed in Section 3.2.2 is one approach to minimizing the number of data points needed for a given surface

Even using the Catmull-Rom surface, the modeled head was still too wrinkly. Fortunately, applying the concept of *geometric continuity* developed by DeRose and Barsky [DB88] to the Catmull-Rom surfaces finally achieved acceptable results. Geometric continuity introduces an additional shape parameter, called *beta*$_1$, for each curve segment. Reeves used a heuristic developed by DeRose and Barsky to automatically determine *beta*$_1$ values that smoothed the surface and removed most of its irregularities.

Figure 3.5.
Finished frame of Billy from *Tin Toy*. (Copyright 1988 Pixar.)

According to Reeves, Billy still had a *north pole* problem where patches came together at the top of his head, and Billy still had some bad surface undulations in the lower cheeks. Figure 3.5 shows Billy in a finished frame from *Tin Toy* which illustrates the result of this modeling effort.

3.6.   Photogrammetric Measurement

In this section we describe two photographically based approaches to measuring surface position data. The first is computationally simple but has limitations and inherent accuracy problems. The second is more robust but is also more computationally complex.

For both approaches it is necessary to locate and measure the same surface points in at least two different photographs of the surface. For smooth surfaces such as the face, it is difficult to identify corresponding points in multiple photographs unless the surfaces are somehow marked. One way to do this is to draw or paint a set of points or polygon vertices on the surface prior to taking the photographs.

3.6.1.   A Simple Photogrammetric Method

For the simple method we need only one pair of simultaneous photographs for each expression posture. Each pair consists of orthogonal views of the face: one taken from directly in front, and the other taken directly from one

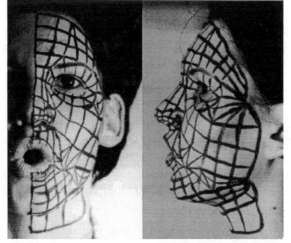

Figure 3.6.
Example image pair for the simple photogrammetric method.
(From [Par72]).

side. Once we have a face that has been marked with the desired points, we can capture a number of different poses, expressions, or phoneme utterances simply by taking a simultaneous orthogonal pair of photographs for each pose. Figure 3.6 shows an example pair of photographs.

We establish a three-dimensional coordinate system with a coordinate origin near the center of the head. This coordinate system might be chosen such that two of the coordinate axes lie in the symmetry plane of the face. The three-dimensional position of each surface point is measured directly from the photograph pairs. We get two of the three dimensions from one photo, and two more from the other photo. Of course, it is necessary to maintain correspondence between the points in each image.

One of the dimensions, usually the vertical dimension, appears in both images. It is necessary to scale measurements from one photo to match those from the other photo. This scaling usually is based on measurements in the dimension common to both photos.

The measurement can be done manually based on coordinate axes lines drawn directly on the images. A ruler or measurement grid is used to determine the coordinates of each point visible in each view. It is possible and highly desirable to semi-automate this measurement process by using a two-dimensional digitizer such as a data tablet.

This simple method has significant shortcomings. The photographs are not true orthographic projections but are in fact perspective projections. Therefore, the images are somewhat distorted. This distortion can be minimized by using long-focal-length lenses.

Some points on the face may not be visible in both views: for example, the inside corner of the eye and the underside of the chin. An estimate must be made for at least one of the coordinates of these occluded points. Clearly, a better method is desired.

3.6.2.   A Better Photogrammetric Method

The main objections to the simple method are the perspective distortion and the fact that some of the points may be occluded in one or both of the orthogonal views. The better method, described below, eliminates the perspective distortion and minimizes the occlusion problem. It also can be semi-automated using a two-dimensional digitizer.

Theory

A camera may be viewed simply as a device for projecting a three-dimensional space onto a two-dimensional space. This mapping can be described mathematically using homogeneous coordinates and the proper transformation matrix followed by a homogeneous division. If the projection transformation matrices are known, then by using two (or more) photographs of an object, it is possible to compute the three-dimensional position of points visible in at least two photos.

Let $P = [x, y, z, 1]$ be a point whose three-dimensional coordinates are to be found. Let $T1$ be the four-by-three transformation matrix which is used to map the point P into the two-dimensional space of the first photograph. Let $T2$ be the corresponding transformation for the second photograph.

$$[P][T1] = [P_1'] \qquad for\ photograph\ 1$$

$$[P][T2] = [P_2'] \qquad for\ photograph\ 2 \qquad (3.1)$$

or

$$\left|\ x \quad y \quad z \quad 1\ \right| \begin{vmatrix} T1_{11} & T1_{12} & T1_{13} \\ T1_{21} & T1_{22} & T1_{23} \\ T1_{31} & T1_{32} & T1_{33} \\ T1_{41} & T1_{42} & T1_{43} \end{vmatrix} = \left|\ x_1' \quad y_1' \quad h_1\ \right| \qquad (3.2)$$

and

$$\left|\ x \quad y \quad z \quad 1\ \right| \begin{vmatrix} T2_{11} & T2_{12} & T2_{13} \\ T2_{21} & T2_{22} & T2_{23} \\ T2_{31} & T2_{32} & T2_{33} \\ T2_{41} & T2_{42} & T2_{43} \end{vmatrix} = \left|\ x_2' \quad y_2' \quad h_2\ \right|. \qquad (3.3)$$

The coordinates of the point measured in the two-dimensional spaces of the photographs are:

$$x_{m_1} = \frac{x_1'}{h_1}$$

$$y_{m_1} = \frac{y_1'}{h_1}$$

$$x_{m_2} = \frac{x_2'}{h_2}$$

$$y_{m_2} = \frac{y_2'}{h_2}. \tag{3.4}$$

Therefore,

$$x_1' = x_{m_1} * h_1$$
$$y_1' = y_{m_1} * h_1$$

$$x_2' = x_{m_2} * h_2$$
$$y_2' = y_{m_2} * h_2. \tag{3.5}$$

Carrying out the matrix multiplications in (3.2) and (3.3) gives

$$x_1' = x * T1_{11} + y * T1_{21} + z * T1_{31} + T1_{41}$$
$$y_1' = x * T1_{12} + y * T1_{22} + z * T1_{32} + T1_{42}$$
$$h_1 = x * T1_{13} + y * T1_{23} + z * T1_{33} + T1_{43}$$

$$x_2' = x * T2_{11} + y * T2_{21} + z * T2_{31} + T2_{41}$$
$$y_2' = x * T2_{12} + y * T2_{22} + z * T2_{32} + T2_{42}$$
$$h_2 = x * T2_{13} + y * T2_{23} + z * T2_{33} + T2_{43}. \tag{3.6}$$

Substituting these equations into (3.5), collecting terms for x, y, z, and rewriting in matrix form gives

$$\begin{vmatrix} T1_{11} - x_{m_1}T1_{13} & T1_{21} - x_{m_1}T1_{23} & T1_{31} - x_{m_1}T1_{33} \\ T1_{12} - y_{m_1}T1_{13} & T1_{22} - y_{m_1}T1_{23} & T1_{32} - y_{m_1}T1_{33} \\ T2_{11} - x_{m_2}T2_{13} & T2_{21} - x_{m_2}T2_{23} & T2_{31} - x_{m_2}T2_{33} \\ T2_{12} - y_{m_2}T2_{13} & T2_{22} - y_{m_2}T2_{23} & T2_{32} - y_{m_2}T2_{33} \end{vmatrix} \begin{vmatrix} x \\ y \\ z \end{vmatrix} = \begin{vmatrix} x_{m_1}T1_{43} - T1_{41} \\ y_{m_1}T1_{43} - T1_{42} \\ x_{m_2}T2_{43} - T2_{41} \\ y_{m_2}T2_{43} - T2_{42} \end{vmatrix}$$

or

$$[A][X] = [B]. \tag{3.7}$$

The above is an overdetermined system of four equations in the three unknowns x, y, and z. In general, if we have n views with n T matrices, we will have $2n$ equations in the three unknowns. Multiplying both sides of (3.7) by $[A]^T$ gives

$$[A]^T[A][X] = [A]^T[B]. \tag{3.8}$$

This result is a system of three equations that can be solved using standard numerical methods such as Gaussian elimination with partial pivoting [CK80], to give a least-mean-square solution for the three unknowns x, y, and z.

The previous discussion assumes that we know the two transformation matrices, $T1$ and $T2$. To solve for these matrices, we note that each of the T matrices contains 12 element values. If we have six *reference points*, whose three-dimensional coordinates are known — visible in each photograph — then we can use the relationships shown in (3.1), (3.5), and (3.6) to construct a system of 12 equations with the 12 unknowns corresponding to the elements of the T matrix. In this case the known values are the three-dimensional x, y, and z values and the measured two-dimensional x_m and y_m values of the six reference points.

Since we are dealing with a homogeneous system, the matrix T will include an arbitrary scale factor; we are free to set one of the unknown $T_{i,j}$ values to any nonzero value. If we set $T_{43} = 1$, then the system described above becomes one with 12 equations of only 11 unknowns. We can solve this overdetermined system in the same way that we did for (3.7).

Since we get two equations for every reference point, we really need only $5\frac{1}{2}$ reference points to construct the required 11 equations in the 11 unknown T matrix values. On the other hand, if we happen to have more than six reference points, we certainly can include them in the construction of the overdetermined system of equations.

Implementation

For this method orthogonal views are not required. We are free to place the two cameras so that each sees as many points of the face as possible. In fact, this method can be extended to more than two cameras. Thus the occlusion problem may be minimized. However, as the camera positions approach each other, the accuracy of the method suffers. The cameras should not be placed close to each other.

This method can be extended by the use of strategically placed mirrors in the photographed scene. Mirrors, in effect, allow multiple views to be

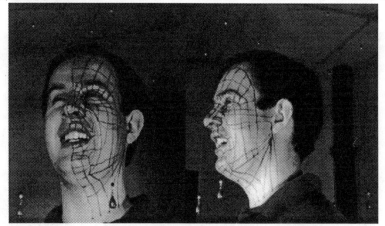

Figure 3.7.
Example photograph pair for the better photogrammetric method.
(From [Par74].)

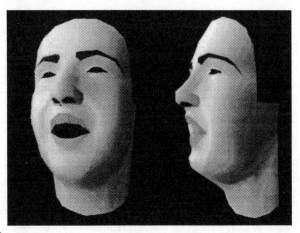

Figure 3.8.
Results from the better photogrammetric method. (From [Par74].)

captured within a single photograph. Mirrors can also be used to minimize
point occlusions.

One requirement is that we must know the T transformation matrix for
each photograph, which generally means including within each photograph
at least six reference points whose three-dimensional positions are known.

Figure 3.7 shows an example pair of photographs for this method. The
suspended beads act as the reference points. Figure 3.8 shows two views of
the resulting measured facial surface.

Figure 3.9.
Scanned surface range data. (From [WT91].)

If the camera position, the three-dimensional face coordinate system, and the two-dimensional photograph coordinate system are all held constant for a series of facial pose photographs, we need to solve for the T matrices only once for the entire series.

3.7.   Modeling Based on Laser Scans

Laser-based scanners, such as those produced by Cyberware [Cyb90], measure an object by moving a scanning apparatus in a circular path around the object. This action produces a large regular mesh of measured surface values in a cylindrical coordinate system. This mesh typically consists of 512 vertical scan columns, each with 256 or even 512 measured surface points. Each mesh entry is an integer range or radius value, indexed by azimuth angle and height.

Figure 3.9 shows a shaded three-dimensional terrain surface based on the range data from such a cylindrical scan. The height of the surface at each point is based on the measured range values, while the horizontal dimension corresponds to azimuth angle. These cylindrical coordinate data usually are transformed into Cartesian coordinates for use in facial models.

The scanner may simultaneously measure surface color, producing an image of the surface such as that shown in Figure 3.10. This color data set has the same resolution as the range data mesh and is registered point for point with the range data.

Figure 3.10.
Scanned surface color data. (From [WT91].)

3.7.1. Missing Data

One of the problems with laser-based range data is missing points. For various reasons the reflected laser beam may be obscured or dispersed so that the sensors see no range or color data for some surface points. Missing points commonly occur on the underside of the chin, in the nostril area, in the pupils of the eyes, and in areas with hair.

To make smooth shading and texture mapping possible, it is necessary to *fill in* the missing range and color data. At least two different approaches have been described for filling in this data.

Lee et al.[LTW95] used a relaxation membrane interpolation method described in [Ter88] to fill in the missing data. Relaxation interpolation creates successively better approximations for the missing data by iteratively using nearest neighbor values. This procedure is analogous to stretching an elastic membrane over the gaps in the surface. This approach also is used to fill in missing color values.

Williams [Wil90b] points out that processing digitized range surface data is very similar to image processing. Williams suggests restoring surface continuity as follows:

- The range data mesh is converted to a floating point array with the missing values set to 0.0.

- A second *matte* array is created and set to 1.0 where valid range data exist, and to 0.0 where gaps exist.

- In the regions around 0.0 matte values, a small blurring filter kernel is applied to both the matte data and the surface data.

- Where the blurred matte value increases above a threshold value, the surface sample is replaced by the blurred surface value divided by the blurred matte value.

- This filtering is recursively applied until no matte values are below the threshold.

The missing data points are replaced by smooth neighborhood estimates that gradually grow together. This same approach also can be used to fill in missing color values. This technique reportedly works well for the small regions of missing data. It is not expected to work well for missing data regions larger than the filter kernel used.

The scheme may be implemented so that the replacement regions slowly grow outward, smoothing valid data at the missing data boundaries. The matte threshold, region growth, and blur kernel can be varied for different results.

3.7.2. Surface Smoothing

The surface data from laser scanners tends to be noisy. It is often desirable to apply some data smoothing, to suppress noise that could result in spurious surface detail. Williams [Wil90b] suggests smoothing the data using a *Turky* or hysteresis blur filter. A smooth estimate of the surface at a point is computed using a three-by-three blur kernel with unity gain and center sample coefficient of 0.0. If the computed estimate differs from the center sample by greater than a threshold amount, the center sample is replaced by the estimate. Williams reports that this filtering process smoothed out a number of spurious surface details.

Filtering the Normals

Surface normals are extremely sensitive to surface perturbations. Williams [Wil90b] suggests that the usual methods of computing surface normals for polygon meshes are too local for the noisy, closely spaced data we get from laser scans. It is reasonable to smooth such local normal estimates, or to use normals of a surface somewhat smoother than the one actually displayed. In this way, satisfactory normal-based shading can be achieved without smoothing away surface features.

3.7.3. Polar Artifacts

The scanner works in a cylindrical coordinate system, but the head is roughly spherical. This difference results in a number of data problems near the top of the head. The scanned data samples become increasingly sparse near the top of the head, and the surface is poorly resolved in this region. Because of the scanning geometry, data near the top of the head are less accurate and more prone to error.

When filtering is applied to the cylindrical range data mesh, artifacts may occur near the poles, where sampling errors are greatest. Because sample spacing is far from uniform near the poles, filtering is very anisotropic in these regions.

One common way to work around these north pole-related problems is to ignore the scanned data near the pole and substitute a separately created *scalp mesh* which does not suffer from these problems.

3.7.4. Scanned Data Versus Desired Topologies

The scanner produces a huge amount of data with constant spatial resolution. These data are inefficient in terms of capturing the surface shape. There are usually more data than are needed in some areas, and perhaps fewer data than are really needed in others. In most cases we will want to reduce the data set to a more manageable size.

The data can be automatically *thinned* based on surface curvature. This reduction is done by throwing away data points in areas of lower surface curvature or in areas where the surface curvature is below a given threshold value. This process will generally replace the regular data mesh with an arbitrarily connected polygon network.

Another approach is to lowpass filter the range data, eliminating higher spatial frequency information, and then to resample the filtered data using a data mesh with fewer points.

The data points of the scans are not tied to specific facial features and can shift from one scan to the next. It is very difficult to reconcile data obtained in one scanning pass with data obtained in another scanning pass. We usually want to use a specific facial surface topology. The scanned data are not correlated to any specific facial topology.

Interactively Fitting a Topology

To be useful, the data need to be matched to the desired facial topology. One approach is to interactively associate each vertex of a polygon topology with the appropriate corresponding point in the scanned data mesh. For example, we want the polygons forming the lips to be fitted to the scanned data points for the lips.

This procedure might be done by loosely overlaying the desired vertex topology on the scanned data and then scaling and sliding the entire polygon set around to achieve an approximate match with the data. Each vertex would then be individually adjusted to align with its corresponding data point.

This interactive vertex matching could be done using the range data, or else it could be done using the surface color data. It could even be done using both data sets simultaneously. Remember there is an exact one-to-one correspondence between the range data mesh and the surface color mesh. To help identify facial features, we might apply an edge-enhancing image filter to the color data or a Laplacian filter to the range data [LTW93].

The Laplacian filter could be implemented using finite differences of the range data. The Laplacian $l_{i,j}$ at each data point is

$$l_{i,j} = l_{ij}^x + l_{ij}^y$$

where

$$l_{ij}^x = P(r_{i-1,j} - 2r_{i,j} + r_{i+1,j})$$
$$l_{ij}^y = P(r_{i,j-1} - 2r_{i,j} + r_{i,j+1}).$$

l^x and l^y are the positive second derivatives of range in the x and y directions, respectively. $P(x) = x$ if x is greater than zero and is zero otherwise. These equations assume that the discrete step size is one.

Face Topology Adaptation

Lee et al.[LTW93] [LTW95] propose fitting an adaptive canonical facial polygon network to scanned data using largely automatic techniques. The canonical network used is designed to provide an efficient surface triangulation with many small triangles in areas of high curvature or high surface articulation and with fewer larger triangles in other areas.

This topology is fit to the scanned data using the multistep procedure outlined below.

- Locate the highest range data point within the central region of the face. Globally translate the canonical face network so that the tip of the nose corresponds to this highest point.

- Locate the chin as the point below the nose with the largest positive range Laplacian.

- Locate the mouth as the point between the nose and the chin with the highest positive Laplacian.

- Rescale all vertex positions below the nose based on these located points.

- Locate the chin *contour* as those vertices lying between the latitude of the nose and the latitude of the chin. Rescale all vertices below the chin contour.

- Locate the ears as those points near the sides of the head and near the latitude of the nose with Laplacian values greater than a threshold value.

- Rescale all vertices horizontally to match the ear locations.

- Locate the eyes as those points with the greatest Laplacian values in the estimated eyes region.

- Rescale all vertices above the nose to match the located eyes.

In the original canonical face network, each vertex pair is connected by a modeled spring. These springs provide forces which are designed to keep the vertices optimally distributed across the surface. Once the network is rescaled as described above, these spring forces are activated. The spring forces adaptively adjust the new network, attempting to minimize network distortions based on the vertex spacing in the original canonical network. The located feature points identified in the steps above are treated as immobile boundary conditions for the adaptation process.

In some cases it may be necessary to interactively adjust some vertex positions after the adaptation step. This adjustment is particularly appropriate for points defining important facial features.

Note that the automated process described above assumes that the facial expression in the scanned data matches the facial expression of the canonical network. Lee et al.[LTW93] discuss extensions to this approach that may be used when the expressions do not match.

Adaptive Meshes

Creating a rectangular mesh model for the entire head from the scanned data is straightforward. A relatively low-density mesh is in effect overlaid on the scanned data by simply using every tenth data point in azimuth and elevation to form the polygon mesh. However, this mesh completely ignores the distribution of head and facial features. We really want to concentrate polygons in areas with articulated features such as the eyes and mouth and in areas of high surface curvature. Terzopoulos and Waters [TW91] describe an approach using *active* meshes to adapt the polygon mesh to the head and facial features. Active meshes adapt to features of interest, increasing vertex and polygon density in those areas. Active meshes include the notion of springs which connect each node to its eight nearest neighbors. As a node is moved, these springs create forces which influence its neighboring points.

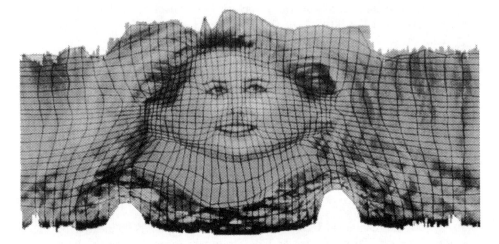

Figure 3.11.
An adapted mesh overlaid on its surface color data. (From [WT91].)

These points in turn influence their neighbor, and so on. When a point is moved, a new equilibrium configuration for the entire mesh is computed by iteratively simulating the node and spring dynamics.

In adaptive meshes, the mesh nodes or vertices automatically distribute themselves over the data. Each node acts as an *observer* of the data near its location and modifies its spring coefficients based on what it observes. These spring value changes require computing a new equilibrium configuration for the mesh. From these new positions, the nodes again consider the data near their locations and adjust their spring coefficients accordingly. This process is repeated until the equilibrium configuration becomes stable. Figure 3.11 shows an adapted mesh overlaid on the scanned color data.

If the node observations and spring value adjustments are appropriately related to the facial features of interest, the stable adapted mesh will be optimal for representing these features. The observations are typically based on range gradients and feature edge information extracted from the color data. The spring values are adjusted so that the nodes migrate toward features of interest. (See [TW91] or [WT91] for details.)

3.8.   Sculpting Facial Models

As an alternative to measuring facial surfaces, models may be created using operations analogous to those used by sculptors. These methods include assembling sculptures from various component parts and iteratively modifying sculpted surface shapes.

Interactive surface editors allow the face modeler to create and modify surfaces by interactively manipulating vertex positions or surface control points. Stereo display techniques can be a useful part of such systems. These techniques allow true three-dimensional perception of the surface shapes as those shapes are created or modified. Stereo display techniques present slightly different views of the surface to each eye. These views correspond to what each eye would see if the surface were a real three-dimensional object. Each eye sees only its view through the use of various optical techniques such as color filters, polarizing filters, or electro-optical shutters.

3.8.1. Assembling Faces from Simple Shapes

Not all facial models need to be complex, nor do they have to accurately resemble human faces. Sometimes a simple stylized character is better than a complex realistic one. It may be easier to stylize or caricature using simple facial models than with complex models.

Simple facial features can make the face easier to model, easier to animate, and even easier to render. The ways in which simple faces animate are not necessarily determined by the rules of real faces. However, like realistic models, these simple models must be capable of effectively expressing human emotions.

Simple face models can be assembled from basic shapes and can make use of simple control mechanisms. A wonderful example of a character created by assembling simple shapes is Tinny, from the film *Tin Toy* [Pix88], shown in Figure 3.12.

Simple Facial Shapes

The component shapes can be quite varied and may include basic geometric shapes such as spheres, cylinders, and cones. Other simple shapes might be constructed from simple parametric surface meshes.

Reeves [Ree90] describes what he calls the *bound* shape. This shape's outside perimeter is defined by eight points that lie on the surface of a defining sphere and by a central point whose position is the centroid of the eight perimeter points but offset from the sphere by a given amount. Four bicubic patches are fit to these data to form the bound's surface.

Each defining bound point is defined by its spherical latitude and longitude. The bound also uses four tangent parameters that control how the surface of the bound lifts off the defining sphere. Constructive solid geometry (CSG) operations may be used with bounds to form facial features. The mouth could be a bound that is sunk into the head using the *difference* operator. This operator subtracts the mouth cavity formed by the bound from the head sphere.

Figure 3.12.
Tinny from *Tin Toy*. (Copyright 1988 Pixar.)

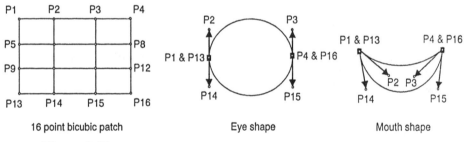

16 point bicubic patch   Eye shape   Mouth shape

Figure 3.13.
The patchedge structure. (Adapted from [Ree90].)

The character's eyes might be constructed using overlaying partial spheres or overlaying bounds. The white of the eye might be a bulge on the head defined by a bound. The iris, pupil, and eyelid could also be bounds, but ones which lie just above the surface of the eye.

Reeves also described a simpler shape called a *patchedge* [Ree90] that can be used to form eyes, mouths, and other facial features. A patchedge is a single bicubic patch defined by the 16 points arranged in a four-by-four array as shown in Figure 3.13(a). Patchedge features are animated by controlling the edge control points.

The four left edge points $P1, P5, P9$, and $P13$ are constrained to be the same point, and the four right edge points $P4, P8, P12$, and $P16$ are constrained to be another single point. The interior patch points are derived as weighted sums of the edge points. By controlling the tangents formed by the two top edge midpoints $P2$ and $P3$ and the two bottom edge midpoints $P14$ and $P15$, many different shapes can be formed, as shown in Figure 3.13 (b–c). With patchedges, the eye pupils might just be small disks, displaced a small distance above the surface of the iris. Eyelids might be independently animated patchedges, positioned above the eyes, that could close over the eyes or open to reveal them.

Language-Based Modeling

Reeves [Ree90] also points out that the assembly and manipulation of model components can be specified through the use of a modeling language. With this approach, the model is actually a program in a special language. Graphic primitives (such as spheres, cones, bounds, patches, and polygons) and operators (such as translate, rotate, and scale) are functions built into the language. The model program is executed to determine the positions and orientations of the graphical objects in the model.

Variables in such a language could include normal variables, which take on assigned values until new values are assigned, and *articulated* variables, which have values associated with keyframes. These articulated values are interpolated between the keyframes using various functions. For an animated model, the program is executed once for each frame time. Changing the model variable values for each frame creates the desired sequence of model postures.

As an example, the model might be a spherical head with simple features. The head could nod back and forth and twist from side to side based on the articulated variables $head_{nod}$ and $head_{twist}$. The nose, a small sphere positioned on the head, could be moved around on the surface of the head using additional articulated variables. The two eyes could be positioned anywhere on the head with appropriate articulation variables. The pupils of the eyes, which float just above the surface of the eyeballs, could be articulated with variables that control where the eyes are looking.

3.8.2. Successive Refinement

Elson [Els90] describes a successive refinement approach to surface sculpting using interactive modeling tools and techniques based on manipulating winged-edge polyhedral structures and the spatial displacement of the polyhedra vertices. These surface sculpting operations include tools for cutting surfaces into smaller pieces, forming extrusions, and pulling points to locally deform the surface.

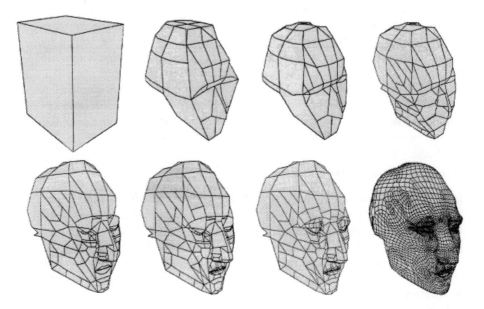

Figure 3.14.
Sculpting a head from a cube. (Adapted from [Els90].)

Winged-Edge Models. The common points-polygon surface representation is very compact, but simply moving one vertex interactively means searching through all of the polygons to find the ones that contain that point. The more polygons in the surface, the harder this search is to do. The winged-edge form allows construction of single surface models that can be easily modified [Bau72]. All the needed topology information is kept locally in edge data structures. Every edge knows the identity of its neighboring faces, end points, and the other edges that meet it at its end points. Therefore, making local topological changes is very straightforward. Surface editing is fast and independent of the size of the model.

For example, the head might begin as a cube. Cutting operations could be used to rough out the overall shape of the head. Extrusions and local surface deformations could be used to add features and feature detail. Finally, a *beveling* tool could be used to obtain the finished facial surface.

The beveling operation introduces new polygons into the structure by replacing existing edges or vertices with new polygons. This operation can be used iteratively, obtaining higher polygon density and smoother surface curvature on each iteration. Figure 3.14 shows the use of these operations to sculpt a detailed head model from a cube.

3.8.3.   Shapes Based on Intensity Painting

Williams [Wil90a] describes the use of methods normally associated with digital paint systems to interactively create three-dimensional surfaces. The key idea here is to interpret a painted two-dimensional image as a three-dimensional surface where intensity at each pixel is used as the z depth of the surface at that point. In effect, the intensities of the two-dimensional painting are interpreted as a surface relief map. Williams refers to this approach as *3D Paint*.

The two-dimensional painted images are usually grayscale images. Each grayscale value corresponds to a surface depth value. These images can be created and modified using standard painting tools such as freeform line drawing, area filling, and filter brushes. Colormap modification techniques also may be used to affect the final grayscale image values. These images could be initially based on scanned images, such as photographs, and then interactively manipulated to achieve the desired results. A key aspect of Williams' approach is to provide an interactive three-dimensional view of the painted surface in addition to the standard two-dimensional view of the intensity image. Williams made use of a special purpose real-time analog device which displayed the painted image as a stack of intensity profiles, with one profile for each scan line. This display gave real-time feedback, enabling the artist to immediately see the result of her painting actions. On many current graphics workstations this interactive three-dimensional view could be created in a second screen window using graphics primitives such as vectors or polygons to represent the painted intensity surface.

Figure 3.15 shows a regular polygon mesh face created using depth information based on image intensity. The density of polygon vertices shown is much less than the density of image intensity values. The polygon mesh was obtained by subsampling the dense image array. The painted intensity image typically has a resolution of at least a few hundred pixels on a side.

This approach is limited to single-valued surfaces. It is not possible, for example, to create a single surface to model the entire head using this technique. This limitation may be overcome by painting one surface for the front of the head and another surface for the back of the head. Stitching these two surfaces together forms the complete head.

3.9.   Conformation Guidelines

The following facial shape and conformation guidelines based on work by Kunz [Kun89], Halton [Hal65], and Hogarth [Hog81] are useful in the design of face models. These guidelines are generalizations. Considerable variations occur from one individual to the next.

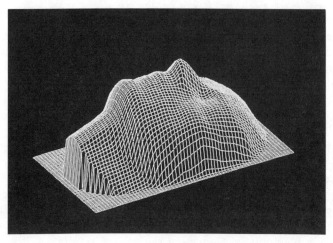

Figure 3.15.
Example intensity-painted three-dimensional face surface.

Overall Shape and Proportion.

- The skull and jaw fit into an egglike shape.

- From the side, the major axis of this egg shape is tilted, with the chin fitting into the narrow bottom. The shape widens at the top to fit the back of the skull.

- The eyes are located halfway between the top of the head and the bottom of the chin.

- The eyes are set back from the front of the face, nested into the eye sockets. The eyes are protected by the front part of the forehead, the cheekbones, and the inner side of the nose.

- The eyes are about one eye's width apart.

- The bottom of the nose is halfway between the eyebrows and the chin.

- The mouth is located one-third of the way from the bottom of the nose to the bottom of the chin.

- The tops of the ears are approximately even with the eyebrows and the bottoms of the ears are about even with the bottom of the nose.

- The ears are located just behind the midline between the front and back of the skull.

- Lines between the outer corners of the eyes and the tip of the nose form a right angle.

The Eyes and Eyelids.

- The eyeball is essentially a sphere. The upper eyelid slides up and down over the eyeball sphere. The lower lid moves very little. The upper eyelid is thicker than the lower.

- The highest point of the upper eyelid is shifted toward the nose. The lowest point of the lower eyelid is shifted away from the nose. The lower lid joins the upper lid at nearly a right angle at the outer corner.

- The eyelids are separated by a pink membrane at the inner corner. At the outer corner, the eyelids come directly together and the upper lid hangs slightly over the lower one.

- The upper eyelid follows the form of the eyeball much more closely than does the lower lid. The edges of both lids are thickened and have a square cross section. When they close, the two flat surfaces meet. The eyelashes project from the front edges of these flat surfaces. The upper lashes are generally longer and thicker than the lower lashes.

- The lower eyelid is seldom lower than halfway between the eyebrow and the top of the wing of the nose.

The Nose.

- The nose is a long wedge-shaped form attached to the forehead with a smaller wedge-shaped form. The nose is thinnest where these two wedges meet and becomes wider toward its bottom.

- Between the eyes, the nose has a concave profile curve between the brow and the narrowest part of the nose. The sides of the nose are steepest here.

- The bottom of the nose is formed by five pieces of cartilage; two form the nostrils, a third separates them, and the remaining two form the tip of the nose. This cartilage allows the lower part of the nose to flex and take on slightly different shapes for various facial expressions.

- The tip of the nose usually slants upward, whereas the nostrils slant down.

- Viewed from below, the nostrils slant towards each other at the tip of the nose.

The Mouth and Lips.

- The mouth is the most flexible of the facial features. The upper lip is longer and thinner than the lower lip.

- The upper lip extends out over the lower lip. The upper lip is flatter and more angular. The bottom lip is fuller and rounder. Under the bottom lip there is often a slight indentation.

- The upper lip has three sections; the lower lip has two sections. The center upper lip is directly under the nose; the highest points are close to the center. The lowest points of the lower lip are farther to the sides.

- The shapes of the mouth and lips are influenced by the teeth and the curved shape of the dental arch. A smile or laugh shows the upper teeth clearly. As the corners of the mouth are pulled back, they form a small depression where they meet the cheeks.

The Ears.

- Ears are unique to each person and should be modeled with the same care as the rest of the features. The ear has a fleshy lobe at the bottom but is structured with cartilage elsewhere. The curves and whorls in the center of the ear account for most of the individual differences.

- The ear is somewhat saucer-shaped at its perimeter. The central portion is shaped more like a bowl.

- The ears tend to run parallel to the plane of the side of the head. The outer rim of the ear is curved to catch sound waves.

- From the side, the ear usually slants at the same angle as the nose.

Male Versus Female.

- Dimensions of male and female heads are essentially the same. However, the angle of the jaw is much less pronounced in women. The distance across the jaw at the throat and the distances from cheekbone to cheekbone and from zygoma to zygoma are less for women. The cheekbones are less prominent and farther behind the chin, and the chin is more pointed in women.

- The head of a man is squared, and its parts project more definitely. The forehead is higher; the zygoma, cheek, and chin bones are more prominent; and the angle of the jaw is squarer and more pronounced. The front of the face at the mouth is flatter.

- In men, the lower third of the face frequently appears longer than the center third of the face.

- In women, the distance from the corner of the eye to the front of the ear is the same as the distance from the corner of the eye to the corner of the mouth. For men, the ear is a little farther back.

- In men, the width across the wings of the nose is equal to or greater than the width of the eye. In women, it is slightly less.

- The mouth is larger in men than women. The indentation under the lower lip is more noticeable in men.

- The height of the brows above the eyes varies considerably. It is mainly in women that the space between eye and brow is of any extent. In men, it is often hidden by the overhanging brow.

- The nose is narrower and the nostrils are more pinched-looking for women. The nostrils often have a dilated appearance in men.

Children.

- The overall proportions of the face and the ratio of the face to the rest of the head change dramatically from birth to maturity (at about 15 years of age). At birth, the face takes up a relatively small part of the head; the ratio of facial mass to cranial mass is about 1 to 3.5. The change in this ratio is most rapid in the early years of childhood. By the age of one, the ratio has become 1 to 3; by the age of four, the ratio has become 1 to 2.5. At maturity, the face makes up a much larger portion of the head; the ratio of facial mass to cranial mass is reduced to about 1 to 2.

- Rounded cheeks and smoothness between the brows suggests youth.

- The width across the wings of the nose is even less in children than in women.

- Noses in children are shorter and softer in appearance than in adults. The mouth is also smaller in children.

3.10. New Faces from Existing Faces

Several approaches have been proposed for creating new faces based on existing faces. These processes include interpolating between existing faces, applying deformations to existing faces, and transforming a canonical face into the faces of specific individuals.

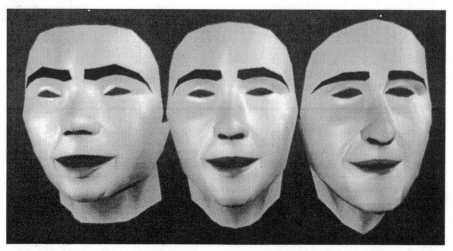

Figure 3.16.
Facial interpolation. The center face is an interpolated blend of the left
and right faces.

3.10.1. Interpolation for Modeling

Interpolation may be used to specify new faces or face components from
previously defined faces. The notion of interpolation is quite simple. In the
one-dimensional case, we are given two values and asked to determine an
intermediate value. The desired intermediate value is specified by a fractional
coefficient α.

$$value = \alpha(value_1) + (1.0 - \alpha)(value_2) \qquad 0.0 < \alpha < 1.0$$

This basic concept is easily expanded into more than one dimension by
simply applying this procedure in each dimension. The idea generalizes
to polygonal surfaces by applying the scheme to each vertex defining the
surface. Each vertex will have two three-dimensional positions associated
with it. Intermediate forms of the surface are achieved by interpolating each
vertex between its extreme positions.

Fixed Topology

In the simplest case, the polygonal facial topology must be the same for each
face being interpolated. The number of vertices defining the surface and their
interconnections must be identical for all faces. If the facial topology is fixed,
creating a new face involves just interpolating the vertex positions. Figure
3.16 illustrates the interpolated blending of one face with another.

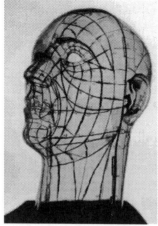

Figure 3.17.
Flexible facial topology storage device.

For this approach to work, a *single* sufficiently flexible topology must be developed that allows representation of a wide range of individual faces. Using such a topology, Parke [Par74] used the photogrammetric technique described in Section 3.6.2 to collect data for ten different faces. The topology used was first applied to the plastic head model shown in Figure 3.17. This marked plastic head model served as a storage device for the topology. It was used as a guide each time the topology was applied to a real face, which assured that the topology would be identical from face to face.

The data from these ten faces were used to create an animated film showing interpolated transitions from face to face. This film demonstrated that, at least for the faces used, a single topology could allow representation of different faces and would support reasonable interpolated transitions between the faces.

The general interpolation approach can be extended to parametric surfaces. The interpolation would be applied to the control points. Again in the simplest case, the faces being interpolated would have the same surface construction: the same type of surface, the same number of patches, and the same number of control points.

Variable Topology

How do we interpolate between faces if the faces do not have the same topology. The obvious method is to simply add or delete polygons and vertices from one or more of the faces until they have the same topology. However, algorithms to do this for arbitrary polygon networks are not obvious.

Another approach [MTMdT89] is to convert the arbitrary topology of each face into an m-by-n rectangular grid topology. Then interpolate between these grids. Note that in this approach the grid for one face is not required to be the same size as the grid for the next face.

If the grids are not the same size, a corresponding point in the smaller array is determined for each point in the larger array. The implication is that some points in the smaller grid will correspond to more than one point in the larger grid.

Conversion of the arbitrary polygon network into the desired regular grid is done by *resampling* the polygon surface in a specific way. Each of the n columns in the constructed grid surface corresponds to a face *profile* curve created by the intersection of a *slicing* plane with the original polygon network. The m points in each profile column are determined by resampling its profile curve. The number of points, m, in each column is determined by the length of the maximum length profile curve.

3.10.2. Transforming Canonical Faces

Essentially all human faces have the same structure and are similar in shape. This fact allows the construction of a *canonical* face model. Kurihara and Arai [KA91] describe a technique for creating specific faces from a single canonical model. Modeling specific faces consists of transforming the canonical facial model into the desired individual facial model.

The Transformation Method

The canonical facial model shown in Figure 3.18(a) is defined with about 3000 polygons which were obtained by digitizing a mannequin with a laser scanner. The transformation of this model is defined by a displacement vector for each polygon vertex. Rather than specifying the explicit displacement of each vertex, control points C_j are selected from the vertices. The desired transformations are expressed by displacing these control points. The displacements of the remaining vertices are determined by interpolation of the control-point displacements.

The displacement at each control point is expressed as a three-dimensional vector V_j which describes the spatial difference between the desired transformed position D_j of the control point and its position C_j in the canonical face. The interpolation of these displacement vectors is simplified by projecting the facial surface points into a two-dimensional cylindrical parameter space. A point $P(x, y, z)$ is mapped into $P_s(\theta, H)$ where

$$P_s(\theta, H) = (tan^{-1}(z/x), y).$$

The two-dimensional θ, H parameter space is triangulated by the control points using Delaunay triangulation [Sib78] as shown in Figure 3.19(a). The

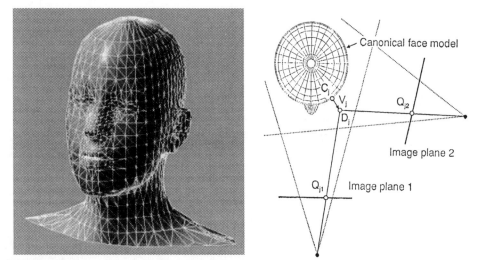

Figure 3.18.
(a) The canonical model. (Courtesy T. Kurihara.) (b) Determining the
destination points. (Adapted from [KA91].)

displacement vector for a given point is based on interpolating the vectors
of its three surrounding control points as shown in Figure 3.19(b).

A total of 58 control points are used for transforming the canonical face.
These control points are vertices that are important in specifying the overall
shape of the face and the shape and location of facial features such as the
eyebrows, the corners of the eyes, and the mouth. Eighteen of these points
are manipulated interactively to control facial expression.

The remaining 40 points are used to determine the shape of the face and
the shape and placement of the facial features. These points are computed
based on photographic measurements as described in the following section.

Photographic Transformation Control

While the control points used to create new faces might be interactively
manipulated, the creation of a specific facial model can be based on photographs.

The three-dimensional destination points D_j for the C_j control points
may be determined from their measured two-dimensional Q_{jk} positions in at
least two photographic views of the specific face as shown in Figure 3.18(b).
(The k subscript indicates which photograph.) There are no restrictions on
camera position and orientation, as long as all the destination points D_j
are seen in each view. The D_j positions are determined using the same
photogrammetric techniques discussed in Section 3.6.2.

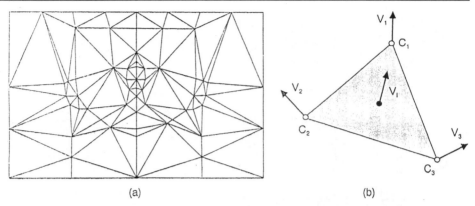

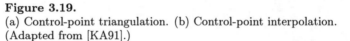

(a)   (b)

Figure 3.19.
(a) Control-point triangulation. (b) Control-point interpolation.
(Adapted from [KA91].)

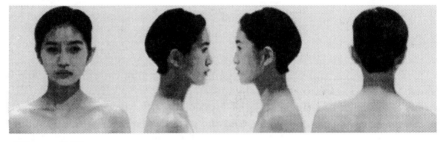

Figure 3.20.
Texture source photographs. (Courtesy T. Kurihara.)

Texture

The canonical model approach discussed in this section depends heavily on texture mapping to supply facial feature details. The texture map is constructed from four photographs of the individual face and head. These photographs are the front, right, left, and back views of the head as shown in Figure 3.20.

A complete cylindrical texture map, similar to those obtained with a laser scanner (see Section 3.7), is constructed by compositing the information from the four photographs. Each photograph is mapped onto its specific transformed face model and is then projected into cylindrical texture coordinates.

Figure 3.21.
Composited texture map. (Courtesy T. Kurihara.)

The composited texture, shown in Figure 3.21, is the weighted average of all the projected textures. The weighting function used is based on the *positional certainty* at each surface point. This positional certainty, in turn, is based on the inner product of the surface normal vector and the viewing vector at each point. The weighting function is zero where the positional uncertainty is below a certain threshold value.

3.10.3.   Growth Transformations

Todd et al [TLSP80] proposed that the shape change of the human head as it grows from infancy to adulthood can be modeled using a relatively simple geometric transformation. The reported work deals only with two-dimensional head profiles. Experimentally the best growth transformation, referred to as the *revised cardioidal strain transformation*, was specified as

$$R' = R(1 + k(1 - cos\theta))$$

$$\theta' = \theta$$

in polar coordinates. In Cartesian coordinates, R and θ are defined as

$$R = \sqrt{x^2 + z^2}$$

$$\theta = tan^{-1}x/z$$

where z is toward the top of the head and x is toward the front of the face. The origin is at the center of the head, and θ is zero at the top of the head. k is a coefficient related to age. k is zero for the infant profile and is increased to generate successively older profiles. Figure 3.22(a) shows the effect of this transformation.

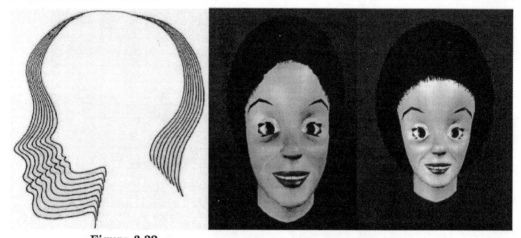

Figure 3.22.
Growth transformation. (a) Effect of the two-dimensional transformation. (Adapted from TLSP80.); (b) Effect of the three-
dimensional transformation: a mature face and a younger face.

Todd later indicated [Tod80] that the two-dimensional growth transformation could be extended into three-dimensional spherical coordinates as

$$R' = R(1 + k(1 - cos\theta))$$

$$\theta' = \theta$$

$$\phi' = \phi$$

where R is the radius, θ is the elevation angle, and ϕ is the azimuth angle.
Figure 3.22(b) shows the effect of a three-dimensional growth transformation.

3.10.4. Local Deformations

Local deformations are another way to obtain new faces from existing faces.
A local deformation is a transformation applied to only a portion of an object rather than to the entire object. Applying a local deformation requires
selecting the region of the object to be transformed and specifying the transformation to be used.

Magnenat-Thalmann et al.[MTMdT89] describe five ways of selecting the
deformation region of a polygonal model and four transformation methods.
The five selection schemes proposed are as follows:

- selecting specific vertex numbers,
- selecting vertices within a bounding box,

- selecting vertices within a cylindrical slice,

- selecting vertices with a specific color value, and

- selecting vertices that satisfy set operations between regions specified using one or more of the four previous methods.

The four proposed transformation methods are as follows:

- Percentage to a vertex — each selected vertex is moved toward a reference point a percentage of the distance between the vertex and the reference point.

- Guided translation — a translation vector is computed between a point A and a point B, and a specified percentage of this translation vector is applied to all selected vertices.

- Scaling to a plane — a scaling is applied to each selected vertex; the magnitude of the scaling is proportional to the distance between each vertex and a specified plane.

- Variable translation — a variation factor is used to control transformation within a selected region. If the variation factor is zero, then all selected vertices will be transformed in the same way. If the variation factor is 1.0, then a vertex at the center of the region will be fully effected while vertices at the edge of the region will not be effected at all. The vertices are modified according to a generalized *decay function* [AWW89] based on position relative to the center of the region.

DiPaola [DiP91] introduced local deformation based on ellipsoidal volumes and warping functions. In this approach ellipsoidal volumes are used to select the vertices to be transformed. The transformations used are warping or twisting functions of the form $\mathbf{f}(\mathbf{p} - \mathbf{o})$, where $(\mathbf{p} - \mathbf{o})$ is the direction vector from the origin $\mathbf{o}$ of the warping function to the vertex position $\mathbf{p}$. The warping functions used decay smoothly to zero so that they have only local influence.

Each vertex is displaced by the sum of all defined warping functions that have an effect at its location. In DiPaola's system up to 12 warping volumes and functions could be used. Each warping volume could be interactively positioned and scaled.

DiPaola used these warping volume deformations to create character changes such as the large asymmetric cranium and huge chin shown in Figure 3.23. These deformations could also be used to create small subtle changes such as muscle bulges, brow furrows, and double chins.

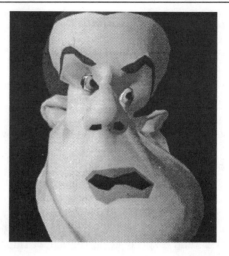

Figure 3.23.
New face created by applying ellipsoidal warping to an existing face.
(Courtesy Steve DiPaola.)

3.10.5.   Freeform Deformations

Another approach to modifying existing three-dimensional facial models is
the freeform deformation (FFD) technique, developed by Sederberg and
Parry [SP86]. Freeform deformation can be described through the use of
a physical analogy. Think of a flexible three-dimensional model immersed
in a block of clear, flexible plastic. This block of plastic can be bent or
twisted into various shapes. As the plastic block is reshaped, so is the model
embedded in it.

The block of plastic in our analogy corresponds to a parametric solid
defined by a three-dimensional cubic lattice of control points. As the control
points are manipulated, the parametric solid is deformed. As the parametric
solid is deformed, so is the embedded model. The basis for the parametric
solid is typically a trivariate tensor product Bernstein polynomial.

Freeform deformation is remarkably versatile. It can be applied to various
geometric primitives, including polygonal, quadric, parametric, and implicit
surfaces and solid models. Freeform deformation can be applied either locally to only a portion of a model or globally to all of a model. Freeform
deformations may be applied hierarchically, with each application modifying the results obtained by previous deformations. Adjoining deformations
can be constrained to maintain continuity across their common boundary.
Constraints also can be used to control how much the volume of a deformed
object changes.

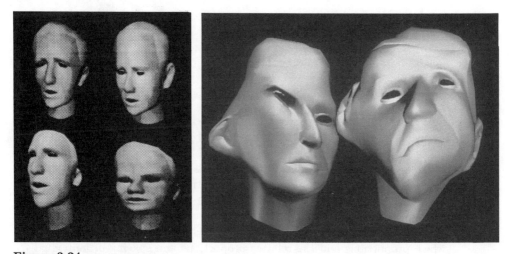

Figure 3.24.
Faces created using stochastic noise deformations: (a) mild
deformations, (b) strong deformations (also shown in Plate I).
(Courtesy John Lewis.)

The control points for the freeform deformation described above are arranged in a regular three-dimensional cubic lattice. Coquillart [Coq90] describes extensions that allow alternative control-point structures such as cylindrical lattices. These extensions allow additional flexibility in the kinds of shape deformations possible.

3.10.6. Stochastic Noise Deformations

Lewis [Lew89] suggests the use of vector-valued solid noise functions to create new models from existing models. The resulting stochastic deformations can be used to create individual *natural* objects based on prototype models.

For faces this method requires perturbing existing face models to get additional models that are random variations of the originals. Three independent scalar solid noise functions are used as the components of a vector field. This field is used to alter or deform the shape of the original face model. For polygonal models, each vertex position is perturbed based on the solid noise vector field.

The solid noise approach could also be applied to parametric surfaces and to volume models. For a parametric surface each control point would be perturbed.

The characteristics of the solid noise functions may be varied to produce a range of effects. The noise may be adjusted to create variations that correspond to those normally seen from one individual face to the next. The noise could also be adjusted to produce effects associated with caricatures or even completely surrealistic faces. Figure 3.24(a) shows deformations that correspond to normal individual variations; Figure 3.24(b) shows faces with deformations more like those associated with caricatures.

3.10.7.   Parameterized Conformation Models

Another approach, related to the approaches described previously in this section, is the use of parameterized facial models. In fact, parameterized models could be implemented using many of the techniques discussed above. The basic idea for a parameterized model is to create a desired face or facial expression based on some number of controlling parameter values. If the model supports *conformational* parameters, it can be used to generate a range of individual faces.

The conformation parameters might include control of overall head and face proportions and the relative proportions and spacing of individual facial features. The range of possible individual faces generated by the model depends on the number and type of control parameters and the permissible value range for each parameter. Chapter 6 presents a more detailed discussion of parameterized models.

4

Facial Animation

4.1. Fundamental Animation Techniques

There are at least five fundamental approaches to facial animation. These approaches are interpolation, performance-driven, direct parameterization, pseudomuscle-based, and muscle-based animation [Par91b].

The goal of the various animation techniques is to manipulate the surfaces of the face over time so that the faces have the desired expressions in each frame of the animated sequences. This process involves directly or indirectly manipulating the surface polygon vertices or the surface control-point positions over time.

Interpolation is perhaps the most widely used of the techniques. In its simplest form it corresponds to the *key-framing* approach found in conventional animation. The idea behind key-frame or *key-pose* animation is that the desired facial expression is specified for a certain point in time and then again for another point in time some number of frames later. A computer algorithm then generates the frames in between these key frames. Several films such as *Sextone for President* [Kle88] and *Don't Touch Me* [Kle89b] contain convincing facial animation achieved by digitizing the face in each of several different expressions and then interpolating between these expressions. Key-pose animation requires complete specification of the model geometry for each key facial expression. This specificity makes it a very labor-intensive approach.

Performance-based animation involves measuring real human actions to drive synthetic characters. Data from interactive input devices such as Waldos [deG89], data gloves, instrumented body suits, and laser- or video-based motion-tracking systems are used to drive the animation.

In the direct parameterized model approach [Par74], sets of parameters are used to define facial conformation and to control facial expressions. The direct parameterized models use local region interpolations, geometric transformations, and mapping techniques to manipulate the features of the face.

With pseudomuscle-based facial animation, muscle actions are simulated using geometric deformation operators. Facial tissue dynamics are not simulated. These techniques include abstract muscle action [MTPT88] and freeform deformation [SP86].

In the muscle-based approach, Platt and Badler [PB81] used a mass-and-spring model to simulate facial muscles. Waters [Wat87] developed a face model that includes two types of muscles: linear muscles that pull and sphincter muscles that squeeze. Like Platt and Badler, he used a mass-and-spring model for the skin and muscles. However, Waters' muscles have directional (vector) properties.

Terzopoulos and Waters [TW90] applied physical modeling techniques to the control of facial expressions. Facial muscle actions are modeled by simulating the physical properties of facial tissue, including the muscles.

4.2.   Control Parameterizations

A unifying theme proposed in this chapter is that, from the animator's point of view, facial animation may be viewed as the manipulation of a set of control parameters. It is argued that all currently used or anticipated facial animation schemes may be viewed as *parameterizations*. The animation control schemes may then be viewed as control parameterizations. Animation becomes the process of specifying and controlling parameter set values as functions of time.

The development of facial animation may be viewed as two *independent* activities: the development of control parameterizations and associated user interfaces, and the development of techniques to implement facial animation based on these parameterizations.

For any animation model, control interfaces or *control handles* for the animator are very important. The goal is to provide a wide range of natural and intuitive expression control.

From the animator's point of view, the interesting questions are:

1. What are the parameters?

2. Are the parameters adequate and appropriate?

3. How are the parameters actually manipulated?

The animator usually is not interested in the implementation algorithms or details, but rather in the animation functionality provided. The animation system may be viewed as a *black box* with, hopefully, a useful, predictable interface that allows the animator to produce the desired results. The animator really does not care how the black box works, only that it does work and does provide appropriate functionality.

From the implementer's point of view, the interesting questions are:

1. What parameters should be provided?

2. What user interface to these parameters should be provided?

3. What algorithms and techniques should be used to actually implement the system?

Most recent work has concentrated on specific techniques for implementing facial animation. Relatively little work has been done on establishing control functionality and animator interface guidelines. Questions concerning *useful, optimal,* and *complete* control parameterizations remain mostly unanswered. The functionality provided by each implementation has been influenced primarily by the characteristics of the particular implementation techniques rather than by any attempt to fulfill a well-understood set of functionality and interface goals.

There are two major control parameter categories. The more often addressed category concerns control of facial expressions. The other category concerns control of individual facial shape or conformation. Conformation control is used to select or specify a particular individual face from the universe of possible faces and is discussed in Chapter 3. Expression control is concerned with changes of facial expression and is the primary topic of this chapter. In the ideal case these two categories are *orthogonal*: conformation independent of expression and expression independent of conformation.

As we shall see, the development of *complete* low-level parameterizations enables the development of higher levels of control abstraction.

4.3. Interpolation

Interpolation is one way to manipulate flexible surfaces such as those used in facial models. Interpolation is probably the most widely used technique for facial animation. As shown in Chapter 3, the notion of interpolation is quite simple. In the one-dimensional case, we are given two values and asked to determine an intermediate value where the desired intermediate value is specified by a fractional interpolation coefficient α.

$$value = \alpha(value_1) + (1.0 - \alpha)(value_2) \quad 0.0 < \alpha < 1.0 \quad (4.1)$$

This basic concept is easily expanded to more than one dimension by applying this simple procedure in each dimension. The idea generalizes to polygonal surfaces by applying the scheme to each vertex defining the surface. Each vertex will have two three-dimensional positions associated with it. Intermediate forms of the surface are achieved by interpolating each vertex between its two extreme positions.

4.3.1. Key Expression Interpolation

Among the earliest and still most widely used schemes for implementing and controlling facial animation is the use of key expression poses and interpolation. Parke [Par72] first demonstrated the use of this approach to produce viable facial animation. The basic idea and the control parameterization for interpolations are very simple and also very limited.

The idea is to collect, by some means, geometric data describing the face in at least two different expression poses. Then a single control parameter, the interpolation coefficient, is used as a function of time to change the face from one expression into the other. A basic assumption underlying the interpolation of facial surfaces is that a single facial topology can be used for each surface. If the surface topology is fixed, manipulating the surface shape involves only manipulating the vertex positions.

To change the face from one expression to another is a matter of moving each surface control point a small distance in successive frames. The position of each point is determined by interpolating between the extreme positions.

As discussed in Chapter 3, it is known that a single topology allows representation of a wide range of individual faces. Can a single topology also be mapped onto a wide range of facial expressions? Will the transitions between these expressions be reasonable?

To answer these questions Parke [Par74] collected data for a number of real facial expressions. The topology used is the one shown in Figure 3.17. This simple topology uses about 300 polygons defined by about 400 vertices.

Using this data, an animation was created showing that a single topology would allow both representation of many expressions and reasonable interpolated transitions between the expressions. Figure 4.1 illustrates an interpolated transition between two expressions. The middle image is an interpolation between the two key poses.

Bilinear Expression Interpolation

Expression interpolation can be extended in several ways. More than two expression poses may be used. For cxample, if four expressions are available, then two interpolation parameters may be used to generate an expression

Figure 4.1.
Interpolation between expressions. [From Par74.] (Also see Plate II.)

which is a *bilinear* blend of the four key poses (see Plate III). If eight expressions are available, then *three* interpolation parameters may be used to generate a *trilinear* expression blend.

n-*Dimensional Expression Interpolation*

Four interpolation parameters and 16 key expressions allow blending in a four-dimensional interpolation space. Interpolation in higher dimensional expression spaces is possible but probably not useful to the animator since interpolation in these higher dimensional expression spaces is not very intuitive.

Pairwise Expression Interpolation

Another way of exploiting multiple expression poses is to allow pairwise selection of the poses from a library of expressions and to use a single interpolation parameter to blend between the selected poses. This method requires specifying three control values: the starting pose, the final pose, and the interpolation value.

Again, if many expression poses are available, they could be selected four at a time and used as the basis for bilinear expression blending. They could even be selected eight at a time as the basis for trilinear expression interpolation. The possible variations on these interpolation schemes seems quite open-ended; however, the usefulness of these approaches is not established.

Facial Region Interpolation

Another useful extension to expression interpolation is to divide the face into
a number of *independent* regions. Separate interpolation values may then be
applied to each region. This approach extends the control parameter space in
an intuitive way. An example of this approach, presented by Kleiser [Kle89a],
is to divide the face into an upper region and a lower region. The upper
region is used primarily for emotional expression, while the lower region is
used primarily for speech expression. This division allows some *orthogonality*
between emotion and speech control. Special care must be exercised in
manipulating the surface along the boundaries between the regions.

Nonlinear Interpolation

Since the face is governed by physical laws, its motions are not linear but
tend to accelerate and decelerate. The *linear* aspect of linear interpolation
refers to the fact that the interpolated value is computed using a linear
function of the two endpoints. There is, however, no restriction on the way
we manipulate the α interpolation coefficient as a function of animation
frame time. The α value may be a nonlinear function of time. Parke [Par72]
found that functions based on cosines of fractional time intervals were useful
acceleration and deceleration approximations.

In addition, the vast collection of parametric curve, surface, and volume
specification techniques such as B-splines, beta-splines [BBB87], and so on
might be used as the basis for generating nonlinear expression blends. The
key-pose vertices would provide the geometric basis for the control points
required by these techniques.

Limitations of Interpolation

The interpolation schemes outlined above have limitations. First, the range
of expression control is directly related to the number and disparity of expression poses available. An expression that falls outside the *bounds* of the
key-pose set is unattainable — except perhaps by extrapolation, an inherently risky approach. Also, each key pose requires an explicit geometric data
collection or data generation effort. For a large set of poses, this is a daunt-
ing task. If different individuals, as well as various expression poses, are to
be included, then the number of key poses needed may be very large. In all
but the simplest cases, providing intuitive, orthogonal control parameters to
the animator is difficult.

4.4. Performance-Based Animation

Performance-based animation involves using information derived by measuring real human actions to drive synthetic characters. Performance-based animation often uses interactive input devices such as Waldos [deG89], data gloves, instrumented body suits, and laser- or video-based motion-tracking systems.

Two performance-based approaches are discussed here: expression mapping and model-based persona transmission. Additional approaches to performance animation are discussed in Chapter 9.

4.4.1. Expression Mapping

The expressive facial animation developed by Bergeron, Lachapelle, and Langlois [BL85] for their 1985 animation *Tony de Peltrie* can be viewed as an early form of performance animation.

The first step in the process was to digitize 20 different expression and phoneme poses directly from a real person. This step was done using photographic digitizing techniques.

A correspondence was made between the neutral expression (E_0) of the real face and the neutral face of the character to be animated. Because the number of points defining the character face was larger than the number of points defining the real face, a one-to-n point correspondence was used. For each point of the real face, a correspondence to several points in the character face was defined. However, each point in the character's face had only one corresponding point in the real face.

Once this correspondence was defined, character expressions were computed using a function that mapped real face expressions to the character. This function was based on the differences between real face expressions. The difference between the neutral expression and the target expression $(E_T - E_0)$ of the real face was added to the neutral character expression. The difference for each point in the real face is added to its corresponding point group in the character. In this way the exaggerated features of the animated character are driven from the real face expressions by expression mapping. An amplification factor was used to increase or decrease the magnitude of the added differences.

A library of standard key expressions was computed by applying expression mapping independently to five areas of the face: the left and right eyebrows, the left and right eyelids, and the rest of the face, including the mouth. A three-dimensional curved interpolation algorithm [KB84] was then used to generate intermediate expressions between key character expressions. The key expressions used were from the standard library or were created as needed by combining standard expressions or by exaggerating existing expressions.

4.4.2. Model-Based Persona Transmission

Parke [Par82] suggested that a convincing synthetic representation of a person's face could be used to create a synthetic videophone if sufficiently powerful analysis techniques were developed capable of matching the motions of a synthetic image to those of an actual person. Such a system could operate over very low data rate channels, even over the standard telephone network [WSW90][Wel91]. This concept was introduced in Chapter 1 and is described in more detail here.

The image analysis and image synthesis aspects of this scheme are equally important. The image analysis needs to automatically extract all of the relevant parameters from the source image in real time. This analysis includes tracking head movements and identifying facial features and feature shapes. This extracted information is then transmitted to the remote image synthesis system to produce the corresponding synthetic facial images.

Success depends on generating convincing real-time synthetic faces. Real-time implementations of any of the animation techniques described in this chapter could be used to synthesize the necessary facial expressions.

Image Analysis. To match the synthesized image to the posture and expression of the real face, the boundaries of the head and shoulders, as well as the positions and shapes of the internal facial features, must be determined.

One analysis approach is an algorithm developed by Nagao for locating the eyes and mouth in a facial image [Nag72]. A large cross-shaped image mask is convolved with the facial image, which has the effect of low-pass filtering the image and applying a Laplacian or second-derivative operator. The output image is thresholded to produce a binary image. Thresholding isolates negative peaks in image luminance and effectively produces a line sketch of the face. The line elements in the image are referred to as *luminance valleys* [PR85].

The algorithm then scans this image from top to bottom, searching for the two vertically oriented luminance valleys corresponding to the sides of the head. The area between these sides is searched for the symmetrically located eyes. The positions of the eyes determine the orientation axis of the face. The algorithm then searches for luminance valleys corresponding the bottom of the nose, the lips, and the chin.

Snake-based algorithms also have been used for locating the boundaries of the head and shoulders [WW90]. A snake is an energy-minimizing spline guided by external constraint forces and influenced by image content so that it is pulled towards features such as lines and edges. Snakes can also be useful for estimating local feature motion. For example, lip tracking is shown in [KWT88]. In addition, feature motion vectors can be extracted using hierarchical block matching [Bie88].

An additional source of information about mouth shape comes directly from speech. The speech track may be analyzed to determine which sequence of mouth shapes should be displayed [MAH89].

4.5. Facial Expressions

For the animation approaches described in the previous sections, we did not need much understanding of the underlying structure and expression capabilities of the face. To continue our study we need to look more carefully at the expressive character of the face and to understand in more detail the expressive structure of the face.

4.5.1. The Universal Expressions

Research in facial expression has concluded that there are six *universal* categories of facial expressions that are recognized across cultures [Ekm89]. These categories are sadness, anger, joy, fear, disgust, and surprise, as shown in Figure 4.2. Within each of these categories there may be a wide range of expression *intensity* and some variation in expression details.

Faigin [Fai90] presents an excellent discussion, from an artist's point of view, of these expressions and their variations. Faigin describes each expression category and its variations in terms of the appearance of three facial regions and their associated facial wrinkles. The three expressive regions are the eyebrows, the eyes, and the mouth.

Sadness

In simple sadness the inner portions of the eyebrows are bent upward. The skin and soft tissue below the eyebrow are piled up above the upper eyelid. The eyes are slightly closed because of downward pressure from the tissue above the eyelid and because of upward motion of the lower eyelid. In simple sadness the mouth is relaxed. Sadness is illustrated in Figure 4.2(a).

The wrinkles associated with sadness include horizontal folds across the brow, trace vertical lines between the eyebrows, oblique folds above the upper eyelid, and a smile-shaped fold under the lower lip.

Sadness has many intensities and variations, including, open-mouthed crying, closed-mouth crying, suppressed sadness, nearly crying, and miserable. These variations may include completely lowered eyebrows, tightly shut eyes, a square-shaped open mouth, a bulge on the chin, and a very pronounced nasolabial fold.

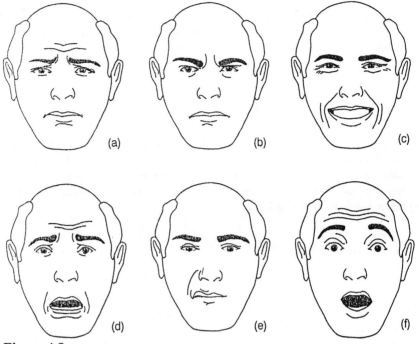

Figure 4.2.
The universal expressions: (a) sadness, (b) anger, (c) joy, (d) fear,
(e) disgust, and (f) surprise.

Anger

In simple anger the inner corners of the eyebrows are pulled downward and
together. The lower edge of the eyebrow is at the same level as the upper
eyelid. The eye is wide open, but pressure from the lowered brow prevents
the white of the eye from showing above the iris. The mouth is closed with
the upper lip slightly compressed or squared off. Anger is illustrated in
Figure 4.2(b).

The wrinkles for anger include horizontal folds above the upper eyelids
and vertical lines between the eyebrows.

Variations of anger include shouting rage, rage, and sternness. These
variations may include tightly compressed lips with a chin bulge or an open
mouth with a sneering upper lip and a straight lower lip, showing both the
upper and lower teeth.

Joy

In simple joy the eyebrows are relaxed. The upper eyelid is lowered slightly and the lower eyelid is straight being pushed up by the upper cheek. The mouth is wide with the corners pulled back toward the ears. If the mouth is closed, the lips are thin and pressed tight against the underlying bone. If the mouth is open, the upper lip is straight, showing the upper teeth; the lower lip is straight in the middle and angled near the corners. Joy is illustrated in Figure 4.2(c).

For joy the wrinkles are "crow's feet" at the corners of the eyes, a smile-shaped fold under the lower eyelid, dimples, and a deep nasolabial fold from nose to chin.

Variations on joy include uproarious laughter, laughter, open-mouthed smiling, smiling, stifled smile, melancholy smile, eager smile, ingratiating smile, sly smile, debauched smile, closed-eye smile, false smile, and false laughter. False smiles and false laughter are indicated by diminished crow's feet at the corners of the eyes and by only slight or absent folds under the lower eyelids.

Fear

Fear can range from worry to terror. In fear the eyebrows are raised and pulled together. The inner portions of the eyebrows are bent upward. The eyes are alert. The mouth may be slightly dropped open and stretched sideways. Fear is illustrated in Figure 4.2(d).

The wrinkles associated with fear include horizontal brow folds, vertical lines between the eyebrows, dimples above the eyebrows, and oblique folds above the upper eyelids.

In worry the lips are squeezed tightly together, and the lip margins disappear. There is a bulging below the lower lip and over the chin. In terror the eyes and mouth are wide open. The upper lip is relaxed while the lower lip is stretched wide and tight exposing the lower teeth. The nasolabial fold becomes straight and shallow. Bracket-shaped folds appear to the sides of the lower lip.

Disgust

Disgust ranges from disdain to physical repulsion. In disgust the eyebrows are relaxed. The eyelids are relaxed or slightly closed. The upper lip is raised into a sneer, often asymmetrical. The lower lip is relaxed. The nasolabial fold is deepest alongside the nose. Disgust is illustrated in Figure 4.2(e).

In disdain the eyelids may be partly closed with the eyes looking down. For physical repulsion the eyebrows are lowered, especially at the inner corners. The eyes may be mostly shut in a squint. The upper lip is raised in an intense sneer which may show the upper teeth. The lower lip is slightly pushed up. There are vertical lines between the brows, crow's feet and lower eyelid creases, wrinkles from the inner corner of the eye across the bridge of the nose, and a chin bulge.

Surprise

In surprise the eyebrows are raised straight up as high as possible. The upper eyelids are open as wide as possible with the lower eyelids relaxed. The mouth is dropped open without muscle tension to form an oval shape. In surprise, horizontal folds are formed across the brow. Surprise is shown in Figure 4.2(f).

4.5.2. Expressions of Physical States

There are many expressions that are not directly related to emotion. Faigin describes additional expressions associated with physical states such as pain and sleepiness. Faigin asserts that many of these expressions are also universally recognized. Faigin's list includes pain, exertion, drowsiness, yawning, sleeping, singing, shouting, passion, intensity, attention, perplexity, shock, and the facial shrug.

4.6.   Expression Coding Systems

Several systems or languages have been developed to describe facial expression. One of the earliest is the Mimic language, discussed in the following section. Another, and probably the most widely used in facial animation, is the Facial Action Coding System, which is also discussed below.

4.6.1. The Mimic Language

The *Mimic Language* developed by Hjortsjo [Hjo70] is one of the earliest attempts to investigate and systematize the muscular activities that create the diverse facial expressions. Hjortsjo's motivation was to develop a language for describing facial expression. According to Hjortsjo, mimicry includes the play of facial features, gestures, and postures.

In the underlying structure proposed by Hjortsjo, as shown in Figure 4.3, facial expressions are the direct result of both the static structural aspects of the face and the dynamic aspects of the face. In turn, the dynamic aspects are determined by both the mental condition and the emotional state of the individual. The static aspects also are presumed to be somewhat influenced by the individual's mental condition acting through the endocrine system.

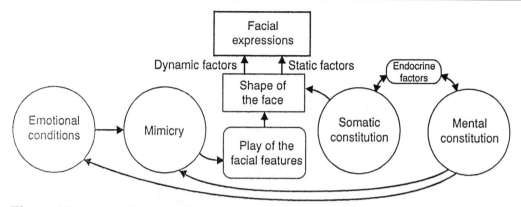

Figure 4.3.
Relationship between facial expression, physical structure, mental
condition, mimicry, and emotional state. (Adapted from [Hjo70].)

The purely static aspects of facial expression are determined by the facial
bones and the formation of the soft tissues of the face. The dynamic, living
facial expressions are produced by the play of the features — the changes of
form and appearance of the soft facial parts — created by the mimic muscles.

Using one of Hjortsjo's analogies, the soft parts of the face form the *in-
strument* that varies from person to person, while the mimic muscles play
the expression *melodies*. If the same expressions are played frequently, they
leave visible traces in the form of mimic wrinkles.

The Mimic Muscles of the Face

The mimic muscles are arranged primarily around the facial orifices: the
eye sockets, the nasal cavity, the mouth, and the auditory canals. Some of
these muscles are in the form of circular muscle fibers that contract to close
these openings. Other muscle fibers radiate from the orifice surroundings
toward the openings. Contractions of these fibers open or pull the orifice in
various directions. The mimic muscles never have both the origin and the
attachment to bone; the origin and the attachment are both to soft tissue,
or else the attachment is to soft tissue and the origin is to bone. When the
muscle contracts, the attachment moves toward the origin.

The vast majority of the mimic muscles are associated with the mouth
and eyes. In humans the muscles associated with the ears have little if
any expressive capability, and the ability to constrict and expand the nasal
opening is very limited.

The mimic muscles are innervated by the seventh cranial nerve, the *nervus
facialis*. This nerve begins with two small collections of nerve cells located
in the brain stem, the *facialis nuclei*. The nuclei are influenced by nerves

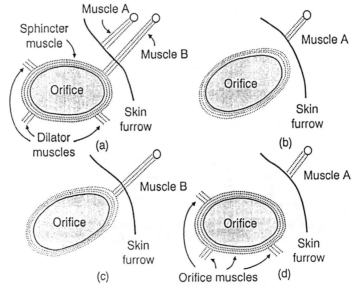

Figure 4.4.
Schematic representation of mimic muscle actions: (a) initial state, (b)
effect of furrow muscle, (c) effect of dilator muscle, and (d) effect of
furrow muscle and orifice muscles. (Adapted from [Hjo70].)

from the brain cortex and by nerves from the emotional centers of the brain.
The cortex nerves correspond to conscious control of facial expression, while
the nerves from the emotional centers correspond to unconscious, automatic
facial expressions.

A few of the mimic muscles lack direct relation to any orifice. They attach
superficially in the skin, often at the location of a skin furrow such as the
nasolabial furrow. When contracted, the skin is pulled toward the muscle
origin, possibly deepening or displacing a skin furrow. The soft tissue between the origin and attachment of the muscle also are affected. This tissue
is pressed together and may result in displacements, bulges, folds, and furrows. Small depressions or *dimples* can also appear where muscles attach to
the skin. Such soft tissue displacements play an important role in expression.

The effects of typical mimic muscle actions are illustrated in Figure 4.4.
Figure 4.4(a) shows an orifice and a skin furrow. The orifice is surrounded
by a sphincter muscle and a few dilator muscles. The muscle A runs from
its origin toward the orifice but does not reach it. It is instead attached to
the skin at the furrow. Muscle B runs parallel to muscle A but passes under
the furrow and attaches to the orifice. Muscle B is a true orifice dilator. In
Figure 4.4, muscle origins are indicated by small circles.

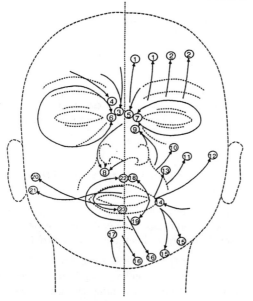

Figure 4.5.
Schematic of the mimic muscles. (Adapted from [Hjo70].)

In Figure 4.4(b), only muscle A is acting, which results in the middle part of the skin furrow being pulled toward the muscle origin. This action directly changes the shape of the furrow. The shape of the orifice is indirectly changed by the pull of stretched tissue between the orifice and the furrow. In Figure 4.4(c), only muscle B is acting, pulling the orifice toward the muscle origin. In this case, the middle part of the furrow is indirectly displaced by the compressed soft tissue. In Figure 4.4(d), muscle A is acting and displacing the skin furrow. However in this case, the orifice is not affected because the orifice muscles have been activated holding the orifice in place.

Figure 4.5 shows a schematic view of the mimic muscles. The small circles indicate the muscle origins, and the numbers in the circles correspond to the muscle numbers in the following annotated list. Hjortsjo refers to the actions of these muscles as the *letters* of the Mimic Language. See Chapter 2 for a more detailed discussion of these muscles and their actions.

1. The medial part of the frontalis muscle (*pars medialis frontalis*) raises the inner portion of the eyebrows.

2. The lateral part of the frontalis muscle (*pars lateralis frontalis*) raises the outer portion of the eyebrows.

3. The glabella depressor (*procerus* or *depressor glabelle*) depresses the inner portion of the eyebrows and brings the eyebrows together.

4. The eyebrow wrinkler (*corrugator supercilli*) depresses the middle portion of the eyebrows.

5. The eyebrow depressor (*depressor supercilli*) depresses the inner portion of the eyebrows.

6. The orbital part of the sphincter eye muscle (*pars orbitalis orbicularis oculi*) squeezes the eyes closed. It can depress the eyebrows and raise the upper part of the cheeks. It also creates folds and furrows around the eyes.

7. The eyelid part of the sphincter eye muscle (*pars palpebralis orbcularis oculi*) closes the upper eyelid.

8. The nasal muscle (*nasalis*) reduces the width of the nostrils and deepens the nasal wing furrow.

9. The upper lip and the nasal wing levator (*levator labii superioris alaeque nasi*) pulls up the nasal wings. They raise and deepen the nasolabial furrows and the infraorbital furrow. They may raise the outer part of the upper lip.

10. The upper lip levator (*levator labii superioris*) pulls the outer part of the upper lip up and out. It pulls the upper and middle portions of the nasolabial furrow up and out and pushes the inner cheek up toward the eye.

11. The lesser zygomatic muscle (*zygomatic minor*) pulls the lower part of the nasolabial furrow up and out. It also pulls the corners of the mouth up and out widening the mouth.

12. The greater zygomatic muscle (*zygomatic major*) pulls the corners of the mouth outward and upward. The lower part of the nasolabial furrow is deepened while being pulled out and up.

13. The levator of the corner of the mouth (*levator anguli oris or caninus*) pulls the corners of the mouth up and raises the nasolabial furrow. It may slightly open the mouth showing the upper teeth.

14. The smiling mouth (*risorius*) produces a small depression or dimple in the cheeks where it is attached.

15. The depressor of the corner of the mouth (*depressor anguli oris or triangularis*) pulls the corner of the mouth down. The depressor deepens the lower portion of the nasolabial furrow and pulls it downward.

16. The lower lip depressor (*depressor labii inferioris*) pulls the lower lip down and somewhat outward, slightly opening the mouth.

17. The chin muscle (*mentalis*) raises the soft parts of the chin, pressing the lower lip upwards. It emphasizes the chin-lip furrow.

18. The incisive muscles of the upper lip (*incisivi labii superioris*) pull the corners of the mouth inward, making the mouth more narrow and rounded. They smoothe the lower portion of the nasolabial furrow.

19. The incisive muscles of the lower lip (*incisivi labii inferioris*) pull the corners of the mouth inward, making the mouth more narrow and rounded. They smoothe the lower portion of the nasolabial furrow.

20. The lower cheek muscle (*buccinator*) pulls the corners of the mouth outward and slightly up. This muscle deepens the lower part of the nasolabial furrow and pulls it outward and stretches the skin over the chin.

21. The upper cheek muscle (*buccinator*) pulls the corners of the mouth outward and slightly up. This muscle deepens the lower part of the nasolabial furrow and pulls it outward.

22. The lip part of the mouth sphincter muscle (*obicularis oris*) constricts the mouth opening. If the red parts of the lips are relaxed, they are pushed out into a funnel shape.

23. The margin part of the mouth sphincter muscle (*obicularis oris*) constricts the mouth opening. It tightens the red parts of the lips, depresses the upper lip, and raises the lower lip. It can also roll the lips in over the teeth.

Table 4.1 presents a summary view of the regions of the face and the facial details affected by the mimic muscles. A * indicates an effect, and an o indicates a small effect.

Mimic Co-Movements

The concept of mimicry includes additional expressive movements in the form of gestures and postures that are characteristic manifestations of emotional states. Hjortsjo refers to these movements as the mimic *co-movements*, which include movements of the jaw, the neck, the shoulders, the arms, and the hands. In addition, the eyeballs may be rotated, directing gaze, and pupil dilation may change in response to changes in light or changes in emotional state. None of the co-movement muscles is innervated by the nervus facialis.

When the jaw is relaxed, the lower teeth are not pressed against the upper teeth, leaving a small gap called the *freeway space*. The position the relaxed jaws have in relation to each other is called the *rest position*. From this position the lower jaw can be raised, clenching the teeth. The lower jaw can also be lowered. The lower jaw can also be displaced forward and laterally side to side.

The neck allows the head position to bend and turn relative to the rest of the body. These motions include forward bending, backward bending, lateral tilting, and lateral turning to the right or left. Forward and backward bending can be combined with lateral turning. Lateral tilting may be combined with lateral turning.

Mimic Facial Expressions

The *words* of the Mimic Language correspond to the facial expressions. These words or expressions are formed by combining the *letters* of the language — the actions of the mimic muscles and the mimic co-movements.

Table 4.1.
Mimic muscle effects.

Regions	Eyebrow	Glabella Region	Eyelid	Infraorbital Triangle	Nasolabial Furrow	Nasal Region	Mouth Opening	Chin
Details	Forehead	Root of Nose	Palpebral Fissure	Infraorbital Furrow			Lips	
Muscles								
1,2	*	*	*	o		o		
1	*	*	*					
2	*		*					
3	*	*	o					
4	*	*	*					
5	*	*	o					
6	*	o	*	*	o		o	
7			*					
8						*		
9		o			*	*	o	
10					*	*	*	
11			*		*	*	*	
12			*	*	*	*	*	
13					*		*	
14				*				
15					*		*	
16					*		*	*
17							*	*
18,19					*		*	
20,21				*	*	*	*	*
22					*		*	
23					o	o	*	*

Hjortsjo describes the facial expressions corresponding to 24 emotions. These expressions are arranged in eight groups as shown in Table 4.2. Table 4.3 summarizes how these expressions are created using the mimic muscles and a few of the mimic co-movements. A * indicates that the muscle or co-movement contributes to the expression. An o indicates that the muscle or co-movement makes a small contribution.

4.6.2. Facial Action Coding System

A widely used scheme for describing facial expressions was developed by Ekman and his colleagues [EF78]. Although not intended for use in computer animation, this descriptive scheme has been widely used as the basis for expression control in a number of facial animation models. This system describes the most basic facial muscle actions and their effect on facial expression.

Table 4.2.
The mimic expressions.

Group	Number	Emotion
	1	Precise, resolute, firm, severe
A	2	Stern, angry
	3	Furious, incensed
	4	Mild, smiling, friendly
B	5	Happy
	6	Hearty laughter
	7	Ingratiating smile
C	8	Cunning, crafty, slyly smiling
	9	Self-satisfied smile
	10	Sad, worried, grieved
D	11	Mournful, almost in tears
	12	Physically hurt, tormented
	13	Suspicious
E	14	Observing, inquiring, examining
	15	Perplexed
	16	Surprised
F	17	Frightened
	18	Panic stricken, anguished
	19	Superior, scornful, ironic
G	20	Contemptuous, condescending
	21	Arrogant, self-satisfied
	22	Disgusted
H	23	Nauseated
	24	Bitter, woeful, disappointed

The Facial Action Coding System (FACS) describes the set of all possible basic *action units* (AUs) performable by the human face. Example action units are the inner brow raiser, the outer brow raiser, and the lid tightener. Each action unit is a minimal action that cannot be divided into smaller actions. According to Ekman, "FACS allows the description of all facial behavior we have observed, and every facial action we have attempted."

The primary goal of the Facial Action Coding System was to develop a comprehensive system which could reliably describe all possible visually distinguishable facial *movements*. Emphasis in the previous sentence is on visual, comprehensive, and movements. FACS deals only with what is clearly visible in the face, ignoring any invisible changes or any changes too subtle for reliable distinction. It only deals with movement and not with any other visible phenomena. FACS is concerned only with the description of facial motions, *not* in inferring what the motions mean.

Table 4.3.
The mimic muscle basis of the mimic expressions.

Expression	1	2	3	4	5	6	7	8	9	10	11	12	13	14	15	16	17	18	19	20	21	22	23	24
Muscles																								
1						o	*			o	*	*			*	*	*	*	*	*	*	*		*
2	o	*	*			o	*			o					*	*	*	*			*	*		*
3	*	*	*									*	*	*								*		
4									*	*							*	*						
5	*	*	*									*	*	*								*		
6					o		*	*	*	o		*									*	*		
7				*		*	*	*	*	o	o	*	*					*	*	*	*	*	*	*
8																						*	*	
9						*						*						o	o			*	*	o
10																		*	*	*		*		
11				*	*	*	*	*	*								o							*
12					*	*	*	*	*															
13				*	*	*	*	*	*															
14					*	*	*		*															
15		*	*						*	*			o					*	*	*				*
16	o	*	*				*															*		
17	o	*	*						*	*			*		*			*	*		*			*
18,19												*		o		*	*					*		
20,21	o	o	*		o	o	*		o		*		*											
22												*				*		*				*	o	
23	*	*	*				*	o	*			*		*							*			
Positions																								
head forward	o	o	o	o			*	*		*	*		*	*	o	o						*	*	
head back					o			o				*				*	*			o	*			
head tilted				o		*	*	*				*	*	*	*	o					o			o
head turned				o		*	*		*	*		*	*	*	o	o						*		o
teeth clenched	*	*	*						o			*		o				o				*	o	o
jaw dropped					o	*										*	*	*						
looking aside						*	*																	
looking down				o						*	*											*		

The use of FACS in facial animation goes beyond what was originally intended. FACS was intended only as a way to *score* or describe facial movements. In a number of facial animation systems, FACS is used as a way to control facial movement by specifying the muscle actions needed to achieve desired expression changes.

FACS was derived by analysis of the anatomical basis for facial movements. Since every facial movement is the result of some muscular action, the FACS system was developed by determining how each muscle of the face acts to change visible appearance. It includes all muscle actions that can be independently controlled.

The first step in developing FACS was to determine those muscles which can be voluntarily *fired* independently and to determine how each of these muscles changes facial appearance.

The next step was to determine if all the separate muscle actions could be accurately distinguished by appearance alone. There are instances where it is very difficult to differentiate among a set of muscles based on appearance only. In those cases, only one action unit was defined which might be the result of two or three different muscles. There is not a complete one-to-one correspondence between action units and separate muscles. Also, more than one action unit may be associated with a single muscle, as in the case of the frontalis muscle which raises the brow. Two different action units, corresponding to the inner brow and the outer brow are associated with this one muscle. Table 4.4 lists the name, number, and anatomical basis for each action unit.

Table 4.5 lists 11 additional AUs, several of which do not involve any of the facial muscles. FACS also includes descriptors which can be used to measure head and eye position.

FACS is limited to those muscles that can be controlled voluntarily. Any facial muscle not under voluntary control is not included in the FACS approach. The tarsalis muscle seems to be the only involuntary muscle of the face, and its effect on appearance is essentially the same as that produced by the levator palpebrae muscles.

FACS seems complete for reliably distinguishing actions of the brows, forehead, and eyelids. FACS does not include all of the visible, reliably distinguishable actions of the lower part of the face. The hinged jaw and the flexible lips allow an almost infinite number of actions, which is particularly true for actions associated with speech.

There are a total of 46 action units. Theoretically it is possible for as many as 20 to combine in a single facial movement. A facial movement also may involve only one action unit. Not all action units can be combined since some involve opposite actions. Also, some of the actions can conceal the presence of others.

Example Action Units

AU 10 — Upper-Lip Raiser. The muscles for this action run from roughly the center of the cheeks to the area of the nasolabial furrow. The skin above the upper lip is pulled upward and toward the cheeks, pulling the upper lip up. The center of the lip is drawn straight up. The outer parts of the upper lip also are drawn up, but not as high as the center portion. This action causes an angular bend in the shape of the upper lip. It also raises the cheeks and may cause wrinkling in the infraorbital furrows under the eyes. It deepens the nasolabial furrow and raises the upper part of the

Table 4.4.
Single facial action units.

AU	FACS Name	Muscular Basis
1	Inner Brow Raiser	Frontalis, Pars Medialis
2	Outer Brow Raiser	Frontalis, Pars Lateralis
4	Brow Raiser	Depressor Glabellae, Depressor Supercilli, Corrugator
5	Upper-Lid Raiser	Lavator Palpebrae Superioris
6	Cheek Raiser	Orbicularis Oculi, Pars Orbitalis
7	Lid Tightener	Orbicularis Oculi, Pars Palebralis
8	Lips Together	Orbicularis Oris
9	Nose Wrinkler	Levator Labii Superioris, Alaeque Nasi
10	Upper-Lip Raiser	Levator Labii Superioris, Caput Infraorbitalis
11	Nasolabial Furrow Deepener	Zygomatic Minor
12	Lip Corner Puller	Zygomatic Major
13	Cheek Puffer	Caninus
14	Dimpler	Buccinnator
15	Lip Corner Depressor	Triangularis
16	Lower-Lip Depressor	Depressor Labii
17	Chin Raiser	Mentalis
18	Lip Puckerer	Incisivii Labii Superioris, Incisivii Labii Inferiouis
20	Lip Stretcher	Risorius
22	Lip Funneler	Orbicularis Oris
23	Lip Tightener	Orbicularis Oris
24	Lip Pressor	Orbicularis Oris
25	Parting of Lips	Depressor Labii, or relaxation of Mentalis or Orbicularis Oris
26	Jaw Drop	Masetter; relaxed Temporal and Internal Pterygoid
27	Mouth Stretch	Pterygoids; Digastric
28	Lip Suck	Orbicularis Oris
38	Nostril Dilator	Nasalis, Pars Alaris
39	Nostril Compressor	Nasalis, Pars Transversa and Depressor Septi Nasi
41	Lid Droop	Relaxation of Levator Palpebrae Superioris
42	Eyelid Slit	Orbicularis Oculi
43	Eyes Closed	Relaxation of Levator Palpebrae Superioris
44	Squint	Orbicularis Oculi, Pars Palpebralis
45	Blink	Relax Levator Palpebrae and then contract Orbicularis Oculi, Pars Palpebralis
46	Wink	Orbicularis Oculi

Table 4.5.
Additional facial action units.

AU	FACS Name
19	Tongue Out
21	Neck Tightener
29	Jaw Thrust
30	Jaw Sideways
31	Jaw Clencher
32	Lip Bite
33	Cheek Blow
34	Cheek Puff
35	Cheek Suck
36	Tongue Bulge
37	Lip Wipe

furrow, producing a bend in the furrow shape. It widens and raises the nostril wings. If the action is strong, the lips will part.

AU 15 — Lip Corner Depressor. The muscles driving this action unit run from the sides of the chin upward, attaching at points near the corner of the lips. This action pulls the corners of the lips down. It changes the shape of the lips so that they angle down at the corners and are somewhat stretched horizontally. Pouching, bagging, or skin wrinkling may occur below the lip corners. The chin boss may flatten or bulge. This action may produce a medial depression under the lower lip. The nasolabial furrow will deepen and may appear pulled down or lengthened.

AU 17 — Chin Raiser. The muscle for this action runs from below the lower lip and attaches far down the chin. In this action, the skin of the chin is pushed up, pushing up the lower lip. The skin on the chin may wrench, and a medial depression may form under the lower lip. As the center of the lower lip is pushed up, the shape of the mouth changes to a *frown* shape. If strong, this action may cause the lower lip to protrude.

4.7. Direct Parameterized Models

Motivated by the difficulties associated with the key-pose animation, Parke [Par74] [Par82] developed *direct parameterized* models. The desire was to create an encapsulated model which would generate a wide range of faces and facial expressions based on a fairly small set of input control parameters. The goal was to allow both facial expression and facial conformation to be controlled by the parameter set values.

The ideal would be a model that allowed any possible faces with any possible expressions to be specified by selecting the appropriate parameter value set. The models created to date are certainly less than this ideal, but they do allow a wide range of expressions for a fairly wide range of facial conformations. Example faces generated using this approach are shown in Plate VI.

The challenge is to determine a *good* set of control parameters and to implement a model that uses these parameters to generate the desired range of faces and expressions. For the parametric models which have been developed, the parameter sets are fairly primitive and low level. The implementation approach has been to apply operations such as rotation, scaling, position offsets, and interpolation in combination to local regions of the face.

These models were developed with little theoretical basis and without careful attention to facial anatomy. They were experimentally derived to represent the visible surface features of the face based on observation and a general reference to the underlying structures. The control parameters provided include:

- *Expression* — eyelid opening, eyebrow arch, eyebrow separation, jaw rotation, mouth width, mouth expression, upper-lip position, mouth corner position, and eye gaze.

- *Conformation* — jaw width, forehead shape, nose length and width, cheek shape, chin shape, neck shape, eye size and separation, face region proportions, and overall face proportions.

About ten expression parameters allow the animator to specify and control a wide range of facial expressions. About 20 parameters are used to control a limited range of facial conformation. A detailed discussion of direct parameterized models is included in Chapter 6.

4.8. Pseudomuscle-Based Animation

The complex interaction between facial tissue, muscles, and bones and between the muscles themselves results in what are commonly called "facial expressions." It is evident that these interactions produce an enormous number of motion combinations. The idea, for the pseudomuscle approaches, is not to exactly simulate the detailed facial anatomy but rather to develop models with only a few control parameters that emulate the basic face muscle actions.

4.8.1.   Abstract Muscle Actions

Magnenat-Thalmann et al. [MTPT88] developed a pseudomuscle-based model
in which the parameters control *abstract muscle action (AMA)* procedures.
This approach is based on empirical models and not on physical simulation.

The AMA procedures are similar to but not the same as the FACS action
units. However, the FACS action units were used as the guide for constructing the muscle procedures. The action of each of these procedures is
typically more complex than the action of a single parameter in the direct
parameterized approach discussed above. The AMA procedures work on
specific regions of the face. Each AMA procedure approximates the action
of a single muscle or a group of closely related muscles.

For example, the vertical jaw action is responsible for opening the mouth.
It is composed of several motions: lowering the corners of the mouth, lowering the lower lip and parts of the upper lip, and rounding the overall lip
shape.

A partial list showing the most important of the 30 AMA procedures is
given below. These AMA procedures are *not* independent, so the ordering
of the actions is important.

Close Upper Lip	Close Lower Lip
Right Eyelid	Left Eyelid
Right Zygomatic	Left Zygomatic
Move Right Eyebrow	Move Left Eyebrow
Left Lip Raiser	Right Lip Raiser
Move Right Eye Horizontal	Move Left Eye Horizontal
Move Right Eye Vertical	Move Left Eye Vertical
Right Risorius	Left Risorius
Mouth Beak	
Vertical Jaw	
Compressed Lip	

This model allows facial control by manipulating the parameter values for
the *low-level* AMA procedures and also by manipulating composite parameters at a higher *expressions* level. *Expressions* are formed by controlling the
AMA procedures in groups. Two classes of expression level controls were
developed, *emotions* and *phonemes*.

4.8.2.   Freeform Deformations

Freeform deformation (FFD) is a technique for deforming solid geometric
models [SP86]. It can be used to control shape change for surface primitives
of any type or degree such as planes, quadrics, parametric surface patches, or
implicitly defined surfaces. As discussed in Section 3.10, FFDs correspond

to shape deformations of imaginary parallelepipeds surrounding the surface or object of interest. The appropriate analogy is the deformation of a clear, flexible plastic in which embedded flexible objects also are deformed. FFD involves a mapping from one three-dimensional space to another using a trivariate tensor product Bernstein polynomial. Deformations are specified by moving the lattice of control points from their initial positions.

Chadwick et al. [CHP89] describe a technique to simplify the task of specifying and controlling muscle actions based on deforming skin surfaces using freeform deformations. Freeform deformations provide a powerful basis for implementing pseudomuscle facial action procedures.

Rational Freeform Deformations

Rational freeform deformations (RFFDs) are an extension to basic FFDs which use rational basis functions in the formulation of the deformation. The rational basis functions incorporate weights for each control point in the parallelepiped control lattice.

Rational FFD's weights provide additional degrees of freedom when manipulating the deformations. When the weights at each control point are unity, the RFFDs are equivalent to the basic FFDs.

4.8.3. Facial Animation using RFFDs

Kalra et al. [KMMTT92] describe interactive techniques for simulating facial muscle actions using rational freeform deformations. Each particular muscle action is controlled by the displacement of the lattice control points for an RFFD defined in a facial region of interest.

To simulate the facial muscle actions, surface regions corresponding to anatomical regions of the desired muscle actions are defined. A parallelepiped control volume is defined around each muscle region. The muscle deformations corresponding to stretching, squashing, expanding, and compressing the surface region of interest are simulated by interactively displacing the lattice control points and by changing the weights assigned to each control point.

Interpolation is used to determine the deformation of points lying within the boundary areas between adjoining pseudomuscle regions.

Displacing a control point is analogous actuating a muscle. The resulting deformations can closely match the natural muscle actions. However, specifying the displacement of the control point is simpler than simulating the muscle.

4.9.   Muscle-Based Facial Animation

The detailed anatomy of the head and face is a complex assembly of bones, cartilage, muscles, nerves, blood vessels, glands, fatty tissue, connective tissue, skin, and hair, as discussed in Chapter 2. To date, no facial animation models based on this complete detailed anatomy have been reported. However, several models have been developed that are based on simplified models of facial bone structure, muscles, connective tissue, and skin. These models provide the ability to manipulate facial expression based primarily on simulating the characteristics of the facial muscles and facial tissue. A detailed look at the properties of human skin is presented by Pieper [Pie89].

Platt and Badler [PB81] developed an early dynamic face model in which the polygonal vertices of the face surface (the skin) were elastically interconnected with modeled springs. These vertices also were connected to the underlying bone structure of the model using simulated muscles. These "muscles" had elastic properties and could generate contraction forces. The face expressions were manipulated by applying muscle forces to the elastically connected skin mesh. The muscle actions used were patterned after the Facial Action Coding System action units.

Waters [Wat87] developed a dynamic face model that includes two types of muscles: linear muscles that pull and sphincter muscles that squeeze. Like Platt and Badler, he used a mass-and-spring model for the skin and muscles. However, Waters' muscles have directional (vector) properties that are independent of the underlying bone structure. These vectors make the modeled muscles independent of specific face topology. Each muscle has a zone of influence. The influence of a particular muscle is diminished as a function of radial distance from the muscle attachment point. The muscle control parameters of this model also are based on the FACS.

Extensions to the Waters model have been reported [TW90]. The same FACS-based control parameterization is retained, but the facial tissues are now modeled using a three-layer deformable lattice structure. These three layers correspond to the skin, the subcutaneous fatty tissue layer, and the muscles. The bottom surface of the muscle layer is attached to the underlying bone. A detailed discussion of muscle-based facial models is included in Chapter 7.

4.10.   Language-Based Animation

Language-based approaches to facial animation are used in the form of animation sequencers, animation scripting languages, and true animation programming languages.

4.10.1. Animation Sequencers

An animation sequencer is a program the takes as input a list of parameter or action descriptors and outputs a time-ordered list of animation control values. One set of values is generated for each frame of the animation. Sequencers allow fairly easy manual specification of many concurrent parameter or motion changes.

For each frame of a sequence, the sequencer scans its list of control action descriptors, checking the current frame number against the frame range of each descriptor. If the current frame is within the range of a descriptor, the sequencer computes the correct control values to output for the descriptor for this frame. The control value computations usually are based on interpolation or spline curve-fitting techniques.

Parke [Par74] used a control parameter sequencer to control the animations produced with his early parameterized model. In this case each parameter descriptor consisted of the parameter name, the beginning frame, the ending frame, the initial parameter, the ending parameter value, and the interpolation method to be used between the beginning and ending frames of this descriptor. Time gaps could be left in the specifications for a given parameter. The sequencer simply output the last computed value for that parameter for frames between input specifications.

Magnenat-Thalmann et al. [MTPT88] used a similar multitrack-based sequencer. Each of the independent *tracks* is a chronological sequence of key values for a given parameter. Each key value consists of a track ID, a frame value, and an intensity value. The track ID corresponds to the AMA parameter, and the intensity value is similar to the parameter value in Parke's sequencer. An interpolation scheme was used to compute AMA intensity values between the key values.

This system was extended to include an *expression* track in addition to the 30 AMA parameter tracks. Expression key values include an expression identifier. This identifier specified which predefined AMA-based expression group to use during a given time span. With this extension it is easy to define, for example, eye and eyebrow movements in an expression corresponding to a phoneme. This approach was used for the film *Rendez-vous à Montreal* [MTT87].

These early animation sequencers were not interactive. The parameter descriptors came from files created using text editors. However, the sequencer concept can be made interactive by applying interactive curve-fitting techniques to the various control value tracks.

4.10.2. Animation Languages

The language approach to animation can be very powerful. Reeves [Ree90], for example, describes an animation programming language developed at

Pixar. A face animation model could actually be a program in this special programming language. To animate the face, the time-dependent animation program is executed for the sequence of desired frame times. Many of the simple characters in Pixar films were modeled and animated using this language.

Graphical primitives such as spheres, cones, patches, and polygons and operators such as translate and rotate are defined as built-in functions in the language.

Variables in the language come in two forms: variables that take assigned values (and retain them until new values are assigned) and *articulated* animation variables. Articulated variables are never assigned. They take values that are based on key-frame values. The key-frame values are interpolated over time using various kinds of splines.

For example, a very simple facial model could be a head that is a sphere with its base sitting at the origin. This head could nod back and forth and twist from side to side with $head_{nod}$ and $head_{twist}$ articulated variables. The nose could be a small sphere that lies on the surface of the head. The nose could move around on the surface of the head with $nose_{ud}$ and $nose_{lr}$ articulated variables. Two eyes could be positioned anywhere on the head with appropriate articulation variables. In addition, each eye might have a pupil that is positioned to float just above the surface of the eye.

4.11. Interactive Animation Tools

The animator's task is to specify all of the control parameters that make the face come to life. A rich, interactive environment that supports the animator in this activity is highly desired. Interactive tools are the most productive and the most often used tools. Interactive animation tools consist primarily of interactive motion control tools, motion preview tools, and, to a limited extent, interactive surface sculpting tools.

4.11.1. Interactive Motion Control

For facial animation, the main desire is for interactive tools to specify and manipulate control parameters. Such tools usually include the capability to preview the specified animation in a real-time playback mode. One example is a system developed by Hanrahan and Sturman [HS85], which allows the animator to establish functional relationships between interactive input devices and control parameters.

For example, the animator might define a functional link between an input dial value and two facial control parameters. The dial value, RSMILE, might affect the right corner of the mouth by pulling it up and back as the dial value increases. The same RSMILE value also might affect the areas immediately surrounding the corner of the mouth, but using functional relationships that decrease the effect based on distance from the mouth.

At the same time another input value, say from the mouse, might be functionally linked to the raising of the eyebrows. This system provides great flexibility in defining the functional links between the input values and the generated control values. Such a system provides a great degree of precision and freedom in setting up the control values and control value sequences.

4.11.2. Interactive Surface Sculpting

One of the major limitations of interpolation-based animation is the requirement to capture or create all facial expression poses needed for a given animation. Interactive surface sculpting techniques can be used to reduce the effort involved in creating the required pose.

Paouri et al. [PMTT91] and Leblanc et al. [LKMT91] describe methods for interactively sculpting facial surfaces. These methods make use of a six-degree-of-freedom interactive input device called a Spaceball. The Spaceball is used in conjunction with a common 2D mouse. With the Spaceball in one hand and the mouse in the other, two-fisted three-dimensional interaction is achieved. The user can interactively view the object from different angles while performing various operations.

Sculpting the surface is accomplished by interactively selecting points, polygons, or regions and then applying various manipulation functions. Selected points in a defined region can be anchored. Anchored points will not move when sculpting operations are applied to the region.

4.12. Abstraction-Layered Facial Animation

Kalra et al. [KMMTT91] describe a facial animation system based on layered abstractions. A high-level language provides simple, general, extensible synchronization mechanisms. These mechanisms hide the time specifications.

Facial animation in this system is based on a multiple specification layers. Successively higher layers define entities in more abstract ways, starting with phonemes and working up through words, sentences, expressions, and emotions. The highest layer allows abstract manipulation of the animated entities, with assured synchronization of eye motion and emotions with the word flow of sentences.

4.12.1. The Abstraction Layers

The problem is decomposed into five layers. The highest layers are the most abstract and specify *what to do*; the low layers describe *how to do it*. Each level is an independent layer with its own inputs and outputs. The five defined layers are:

Layer 0: abstract muscles
Layer 1: minimal perceptible actions
Layer 2: phonemes and expressions
Layer 3: words and emotions
Layer 4: synchronization of emotions, speech, and eye motions

Layer 0: Abstract Muscles

This level corresponds to the most basic facial modeling and animation system. This implementation is based on the abstract muscle action procedures developed by Thalmann et al. [MTPT88] (see Section 4.8). At this basic level, the facial animation is based on a set of independent parameters that control specific abstract muscle emulations. Each abstract muscle has parameters such as the minimum value, the maximum value, and the current contraction value.

Layer 1: Minimal Perceptible Actions

Each minimal perceptible action (MPA) is a basic facial motion parameter. The range of each motion is normalized between 0 and 1 or between −1 and +1 (see Table 4.6). MPA specifications have the following general form.

$< MPA\ name >$ $< framenumber >$ $< intensity >$

Each MPA has a corresponding set of visible facial features such as movement of the eyebrows, the jaw, the mouth or other motions that occur as a result of contracting muscles associated with the region. MPAs also include nonfacial muscle actions such as nods and turns of the head and movement of the eyes.

Layer 2: Facial Snapshots

Snapshots correspond to specific phonemes or expressions. A snapshot is made up of one or more MPAs. The basic MPAs are combined to form the higher level expressions such as anger, fear, and surprise.

One can create natural expression snapshots as well as some unnatural and idiosyncratic snapshots. The intensity of an expression is directly determined by the intensity of its MPAs. A strong or feeble expression can be created by appropriately changing the intensities of the contained MPAs.

Table 4.6.
Minimum perceptible actions.

MPA Name	Value Range
Raise_eyebrow	-1 to 1
Squeeze_eyebrow	0 to 1
Move_horizontal_eye	-1 to 1
Move_vertical_eye	-1 to 1
Close_upper_eyelids	-1 to 1
Close_lower_eyelids	-1 to 1
Stretch_nose	-1 to 1
Raise_nose	0 to 1
Raise_upper_lip	0 to 1
Puller_lower_lip	0 to 1
Puller_corner_lip	0 to 1
Lower_corner_lip	0 to 1
Stretch_corner_lip	0 to 1
Mouth_beak	0 to 1
Zygomatic_cheek	0 to 1
Puff_cheek	-1 to 1
Nod_head	-1 to 1
Turn_head	-1 to 1
Roll_head	-1 to 1

library of expressions. Newly designed expressions may be added to the
predefined expression database.

Expression editing is, by design, independent of the low-level realization
of muscles and their actions. With this independence, the low-level implementation of an expression could be as simple as rotation or scale of a region
or as complex as a 3D finite-element model of the region. It would be possible to use entirely different implementation models for each MPA without
effecting high-level control.

Once defined, a snapshot has the following form:

$$< framenumber > \quad < snapshot > \quad < intensity >$$

Several snapshots may be active at the same time. This synchronuos
activity allows specifying a phoneme and a smile for the same time interval.

Layer 2a: Phonemes. A phoneme snapshot defines the position of the
mouth and lips during a particular sound emission. A phoneme is defined
by a set of interacting minimal perceptible actions such as:

```
[snapshot    pp=>
    [action    raise_sup_lip      30%]
    [action    lower_inf_lip      20%]
    [action    open_law           15%]
]
```

Layer 2b: Expressions. An expression snapshot is a particular posture of the face. These postures are generated using minimal perceptible actions in the same way as phonemes. The basic expressions as well as variants may be specified as snapshots.

Layer 3: Sequences of Snapshots

Words and emotions are defined as sequences of snapshots.

Words. A word may be specified as a sequence of component phonemes. A dictionary is used to store the phonemes for each word.

One problem is determining the duration of each phoneme, relative to the average duration of the phoneme, based on its current context. Duration is influenced by the phonemes prior to and following the current phoneme. Several heuristic methods have been proposed by researchers of text-to-speech synthesis [AHK87]. This system is able to generate the correct sequence of phonemes for a given time interval by using specifications such as:

How are you (pause 200 ms) Juliet?

Additional commands may be used to control the intensity, duration, and emphasis of each word. Pauses may be added to control rhythm and intonation of the sentence.

Emotions Emotions are defined as time-dependent changes in facial expression. The time-dependent behaviors are specified using expression intensity envelopes. The intensity envelopes are defined using time-based functions [Ekm77]. Each envelope has four stages:

- ATTACK — transition between the absence of the expression and the maximum expression intensity

- DECAY — transition between maximum intensity and stabilized expression intensity

- SUSTAIN — duration of the active expression

- RELEASE — transition back to the quiescent state

For each emotion the sequence of expressions and the durations of the expression stages are specified.

Generic Emotions. Each specific emotion has an average overall duration. However, time variation is context sensitive. For example, a smile may have a five-second average duration, but it may last as long as 30 seconds in some situations. The duration of each emotion stage is not equally sensitive to the time expansion. Expanding the overall duration of the emotion envelope expands the ATTACK and RELEASE stages proportionally less than the SUSTAIN stage. A duration sensitivity factor is associated with each stage.

Duration distributions are used to specify each generic emotion. For example, a stage duration may be defined as 5 ± 1 seconds based on a uniform distributed law, or an intensity level may be defined as 0.7 ± 0.05 based on a Gauss distribution.

Once a generic emotion is introduced in the emotion dictionary, it is easy to produce an instance by specifying its overall duration and magnitude.

Layer 4: Synchronization Mechanisms

There is a need for synchronizing various facial actions: emotions, dialogue, and eye motion. In this layer, language formalisms are introduced for specifying the starting time, the ending time, and the duration-independent action.

4.12.2. High-Level Script Language

The high-level script scheduler is a formalism for specifying the synchronization and the dependence between the various actions. An action is invoked as part of a specific sequencing with a specific execution duration as follows:

```
while   < duration >  do   < action >
```

Action Durations

Action durations may be specified in several ways:

- no specification (use the default value): [**emotion SMILE**]

- relative duration (% of the default value): [**emotion SMILE while 80% happyduration**]

- absolute duration: [**emotion SMILE while 30 seconds**]

- relative to another action: [**emotion SMILE while [say How are you?]**]

Action Sequencing

Actions may be sequenced as follows:

- $[A][B][C]$ — Action C follows action B which follows action A.

- $[A][forkB][C]$ — Actions B and C both follow action A in parallel.

- $[A]\cdots[forkB]\cdots]$ — Action A continues while action B is started and runs in parallel with action A.

- $[A][endforkB][C]$ — When action A ends, wait for the end of action B before starting action C.

- $[A\cdots[endforkB]\cdots]$ — Action A continues after parallel action B ends.

Action Synchronization

This system provides several types of action synchronization. These types include actor synchronization, emotion synchronization, and sentence synchronization.

Actor Synchronization. The use of actor names allows the actions of several actors to be synchronized.

```
[actor JULIET while
[       [say  "What's the time?"]
[actor ROMEO while
      [say "It's midnight..."]
]
[say "Oh, it's late..."]
 ]
]
```

Emotion Synchronization. The following statements generate a sequence of facial emotions for an actor. The emotions are assumed to be in the emotion dictionary.

```
[emotion FEAR]
[emotion ANGER while
      [say "Aghh"]
]
```

Sentence Synchronization. Word flow may be synchronized with expressions to form expressive sentences. Each word is considered an independent action with a starting time and a duration. It is possible to execute an expression action between words.

```
[say "My name is Juliet"
     [emotion WINK]
     "and yours?"
]
```

Combined Example. Combining these capabilities might result in the following dialog specification.

```
[actor ROMEO while
    [
  [say  "My name is Romeo"]
  [emotion HAPPY]
  [say  "What is your name?"]
  [emotion  QUESTIONING]
 [actor JULIET while
       [say "My name is Juliet"]
       [emotion WINK]
 ]
  [say "Oh, it's late..."]
  [emotion SURPRISE]
 [actor JULIET while
       [say "What time is it?"]
       [emotion CONCERN]
 ]
  [say "It's midnight"]
  [emotion SADNESS]
    ]
]
```

4.13. The Billy Animation

This section discusses an animation example which illustrates a few of the concepts presented in this chapter. This example is based on Reeves' description [Ree90] of animating the Billy baby face in PIXAR's animation *Tin Toy* [Las87].

To animate Billy's face (see Figures 3.4 and 3.5), a muscle-based model similar to the model proposed by Waters [Wat87] was used. Muscles were embedded in the surface model of Billy's head. As each muscle contracted, it pulled on the data points around it and moved the skin surface. The amount of contraction for each muscle over time was animated using keyframing and splining tools.

Two kinds of muscles were implemented: the linear and elliptical sphincters. A linear muscle was defined by two points, a bone attachment point that always remained stationary and a skin attachment point that would contract isotonically when the muscle operated. Other parameters for each linear muscle defined its zone of influence. A conical zone of influence with a circular cosine dropoff function was defined for each muscle.

The sphincter muscles pulled skin toward or away from a central point rather than tugging in a direction. Sphincter muscles were used around the mouth to purse the lips and around the eyes. A single point defined the center of the muscle. Three additional points defined the three axes used in establishing an ellipsoidal zone of influence. A circular cosine dropoff function was used to blend between maximal displacement at the center of the region and zero displacement at the edge of the region.

A total of 43 linear muscles and four sphincter muscles were used in Billy's face. The placement of the muscles was based on the illustrations shown in the Facial Action Coding System manual [EF78].

The muscle model, which supported linear and radial displacement, was not appropriate for the jaw or the eyelids. The skin in these areas is constrained by contact with another object, the jaw bone or the eyeball. When the skin moves in these areas, it is pulled over the object and moves rotationally or in an arc instead of linearly. A third kind of muscle, called a rotational muscle, was developed for these regions. Its zone of influence was defined using a partial torus centered about a point. A second point was used to specify the orientation of the torus. A third point specified the axis about which the torus points rotated. When the rotational muscle was actuated, all data points originally lying within the partial torus were rotated around the axis as a group by the same amount.

A relaxation mechanism was implemented to smoothly disperse some of the rotation movement to neighboring points. This relaxation step was responsible for moving points on the upper lip, cheeks, and neck in reaction to the jaw opening or closing.

Higher levels of control, called *macro muscles*, were developed. A macro muscle controls several low-level muscles. The amount of muscle contraction was weighted for each low-level muscle within a macro muscle. Thirty-three macro muscles were developed for Billy, but, only 12 of them were used for most of the film. The macro muscles saved time by encapsulating commonly used actions. However, the animator retained complete control of the underlying low-level muscles when needed.

The Billy facial and body model lacked one important characteristic: the skin was flexible but didn't simulate real tissue. The skin did not droop due to gravity or wobble due to inertia. This quality made Billy seem as if he were made of flexible stretchy plastic rather than skin.

4.14. Creating Good Animation

As introduced in Chapter 1, Thomas and Johnston [TJ81] outlined the animation principles developed by Disney Studios. These principles may be applied directly to computer character animation as discussed by Lasseter [Las87]. The principles that make great conventional animation great are those that can make computer character animation great. These principles insure that the animation is effective and truly communicates.

These principles cross the boundaries of animation technique and focus on the areas of story, design, and execution. Animation that lacks any of these aspects will suffer. Animation, computer or conventional, that succeeds at all of these levels will be successful.

4.14.1. Does It Communicate?

Successful animation implies much more than just moving objects from point A to point B. The primary goal of animation is communication. The fundamental test of good animation is how well it communicates. It must communicate the intended message clearly, creatively, and logically. Effective animation elicits a response from the viewer. It informs, captivates, and entertains. In short, it communicates!

Story or Content

The story or content is of fundamental importance in the success of an animation. Content largely determines the enjoyment the audience receives from the animation. Even if the concept is visually abstract, you are still telling a story. The story must be strong enough to justify the incredible time and energy required to produce the animation. If the content is trivial, the animation is probably not worth doing.

Design

Design in animation is very important. Since every element in an animation must be planned, considerable emphasis should be placed on the production design. Animation is really a form of cinematography. All cinematic approaches, techniques, and philosophies come into play. Design includes the determination of composition, balance, and color as well as film structure in terms of sequences, scenes, cuts, and pacing. Dynamic camera angles and creative editing procedures are all part of the process.

Characters should be designed so that they can accomplish the actions that the story requires. The character design must be appropriate for the sophistication of the software and hardware available. Characters should be designed so that they look and behave as three-dimensional entities.

Execution

Execution is very important and should be done well. The story and the design should allow good execution. The story and design should not overpower the available techniques and resources. It is easy to have story and design concepts that are beyond the capabilities of current techniques.

4.14.2. Use of Conventional Animation Techniques

The animator is skilled in fooling the eye into seeing something that may or may not be there. Observing the motion of an object, seeing the essence of its movement, and then knowing the best way to represent it are the most basic skills of an animator.

Animation is the art of making the inanimate come to life. Computer animators, like conventional animators, strive to bring life to the screen by creating effective image sequences. The principles of conventional animation can be used to enhance the quality of computer-generated animation.

Computer animation may borrow many of the techniques of conventional animation. It also may borrow the thinking process as well. Useful conventional animation techniques include the use of storyboards, a structured approach to animation production, and the use of pencil tests.

The Storyboard

Creating a storyboard is one way to communicate the combination of motions, events, and unfolding information of our story in a time sequence. It is a series of images, often simply drawings, by which the designer communicates the story concepts through visual choreography.

The purpose of the storyboard is to understand what is happening overall in the story and in the scenes. What precedes this shot? What comes after this shot? How does this shot fit within the scene and within the story?

Designing or choreographing computer animation via storyboards can save many hours and many production dollars. Concepts and ideas can be sketched, discussed, and revised prior to initial data input and execution on the computer.

Ideally, what we are trying to accomplish with a storyboard is the construction of a schedule of events that will fit into specifically allocated time slots. These events, simple or sophisticated, must communicate the intended message clearly, creatively, and logically.

The Structured Animation Approach

The production of computer animation, like conventional animation, may be structured, each scene composed of multiple scene elements.

The animation can be created one element at a time, which allows flexibility in producing the animation. Elements can be added and existing elements can be enhanced to arrive at the final animation. Changes in one element do not require redoing the entire animation, just recombining the scene elements.

The structured approach can be applied to the production activities as well. The production effort may be decomposed into multiple interlocking activities. Each activity accomplishes a part of the overall animation process.

Pencil Tests

In conventional cell animation, quick pencil tests are used to evaluate animation sequences prior to creating the finished animation cells. The same basic idea can be applied to computer animation. A low-effort animation test may be done before investing in the final animation production.

As an example, animation can be created using low-resolution models rendered as low-resolution images. When the tested animation is finalized, the low-resolution model motions will be applied to high-resolution models, creating the high-resolution images of the final animation.

4.14.3. Hints for Animating Simple Facial Models

Reeves' [Ree90] provides several animation hints, based on conventional animation techniques, that can make simple facial models more interesting and more alive.

- Motions and poses should not be symmetric. For example, make one eye slightly larger than the other. Turn one corner of the mouth down more than the other. When blinking the eyes, blink one eye a frame or two before the other.

- If the character talks, do not strain to attain perfect lip sync. It is most important to capture the ebb and flow of the dialogue.

- Caricature may be done by *cheating* facial expressions. For example, swing the mouth around the head so that it is almost below where the ears would be if there were ears. This action allows the camera to see the expression on the mouth while also showing a profile of the head.

- Exaggeration is a form of cheating. For example, when a character is shocked, his eyes might change scale three times in four frames: from normal size, to 1/4 normal, to three times normal, and back to normal again. Cheats like these, while not anatomically correct — and hence sometimes quite difficult to do with complex facial models — are very powerful in establishing the character and showing emotion. This is the power of animation, computer-assisted or not, over live action. It can create alternate realities !

4.15. Control Parameterizations Revisited

A number of facial animation techniques have been reviewed. Each of these has an associated control parameterization. In most cases, the control paradigm for the implementation is intimately related to its underlying techniques. The control of facial animation may be viewed as control parameterization and control interface issues. The development of control parameterizations and the development of animation system implementations should be *decoupled*. Parameterization research should focus on developing high-quality interfaces and parameterizations, and implementation research should focus on developing optimum techniques for modeling faces and generating facial expressions based on these parameterizations.

4.15.1. Ideal Parameterizations

The ideal parameterization and interface is one that allows the animator to *easily* specify any individual face with any speech and expression sequence. This is in fact the definition for a *universal parameterization*, one that enables all possible individual faces and all possible expressions and expression transitions. No implemented facial parameterization to date is even close to being universal.

The FACS system seems the best current basis for low-level expression parameterization, but it is probably not ideal from the animator's viewpoint. None of the existing facial animation systems actually implements the complete set of FACS action units.

Input and guidance from animators is certainly needed in the development of good, useful parameterizations. The focus should be on developing powerful control parameters sets that are motivated by the needs of the facial animator, *not* based on the characteristics of a particular implementation scheme.

Developing a truly *universal* parameterization appears very difficult and may not be possible. However, developing useful, broadly applicable parameterizations seems quite feasible and very worthwhile. Such low-level parameterizations would support the development of higher level, more abstract levels of control, including behavior-driven and story-driven animation.

4.15.2. Quality of Control Parameterizations

Assuming that truly universal parameterizations are not possible, at least in the near term, what are the metrics for judging the quality of a control parameterization? Attributes such as control range, complexity, number of parameters, intuitiveness, naturalness, and powerful interfaces immediately come to mind. Certainly an important measure is the range of possible faces and expressions that can be specified. How much of the universe of faces and facial expressions is covered by the parameterization? Judgment of this aspect is somewhat application-dependent. For example, if the application requires animation of only one specific character, conformation control is not an issue.

Intuitive and natural parameters, the number of parameters, and parameter complexity are all directly related. The number of parameters provided and the overall complexity of the parameterization should just be sufficient. Unnecessary parameters or parameter complexity should be avoided. Ease of use will be strongly coupled to how natural and intuitive are the parameters and the interface to those parameters.

Subtlety and orthogonality also are measures of parameterization quality. Subtle variations in expression and conformation often are needed. The ability of a parameterization to support these subtle variations is highly desired. Mutual independence of the parameters is also an issue. The change in one parameter value should have minimal and predictable interaction with other parameters. Change in one parameter value should not require reworking the other parameter values. This feature is particularly true for the interactions between expression and conformation parameters and between speech and expression parameters.

Another measure of an effective parameterization is its capability to serve as the basis for higher levels of control abstraction. As in the case of speech animation, the construction of control parameters at the phoneme or at higher levels of abstraction built on top of the basic parameterization should be possible.

4.15.3. High-Level Control Abstraction

A major focus of future efforts should be on the development of powerful models with the effective low-level parameterizations discussed above. The availability of such models would greatly facilitate development of very capable character animation systems. The development of complete low-level parameterizations enables the development of higher levels of control abstractions. Several high-level control abstractions are outlined below.

Speech-Driven Level

Much facial animation is related to speech. One particularly useful higher-level control abstraction would be at the speech level. A second-level speech parameterization would be in terms of phonemes and perhaps emotions. The phoneme-level parameters would in turn control the low-level lip shape deformation parameters.

Animating the face directly from a speech soundtrack is an intriguing concept. It involves analyzing the speech to identify the various phonemes and pauses and their durations. At a higher level it involves analyzing the speech for emotional content as well. These concepts are discussed in more detail in Chapter 8.

Behavior-Driven Level

An area of considerable interest in the computer animation community is the development of animation techniques that operate at the behavior level. At this level, the animator/director expresses the desired actions in terms of high-level *behaviors* rather than in detailed low-level motions. Work in this area has concentrated on activities such as legged locomotion and grasping objects. The underlying detail-control parameters for these particular activities are well defined and well understood.

The ability of the animator to specify facial actions in terms of high-level behaviors is certainly desired. An example would be the ability to simply supply dialogue text along with emotional directions and have the face *act out* the scene.

Another example would be the ability to specify a character's *personality* and have the animation system ensure that the facial actions conform to the specified personality traits.

Work in this area is just beginning.

Story-Driven Level

Takashima et al. [TST87] outline the development of a story-driven animation system. This system is an example of animation control at a very high level of abstraction. It is limited to simple children's stories. However, it does demonstrate a useful framework of such systems. This framework is based on three major activities: story understanding, stage direction, and action generation. Story understanding and stage direction are largely knowledge-based AI activities. Behavior-driven animation systems as discussed above would be a part of the action generation activity. One can envision future story-driven systems that include synthetic facial *acting* rather than just facial animation.

5

Facial Image Synthesis

Once we have created a facial model and determined how we want it to move, the next step is to actually generate the sequence of facial images that form the desired animation. The generation of synthetic images has been the focus of intense research and development over the last 30 years. There is a vast body of literature on synthetic image generation and a wide range of synthesis techniques exist. It is not the intent of this chapter to provide in-depth discussion of image synthesis, but rather to introduce the major aspects of image synthesis, to provide pointers into the literature, and to highlight aspects that are particularly relevant to facial images.

5.1. Synthetic Images

At the lowest level, computer-created synthetic images are simply large two-dimensional rectangular arrays of image fragments called *pixels*. Each pixel of the array has the same size and shape. Each pixel has a *color value*. When one of these color value arrays is displayed on an appropriate device, such as a color monitor, we perceive an image. The task of image synthesis is to compute the correct color value for each pixel in the desired images.

The size of the pixel array and the range of color values for each pixel determine the maximum visual information an image can represent. Common sizes for images range from a few hundred to a few thousand pixels in each dimension. Color values range from a few bits to as many as 36 bits per pixel. Colors are typically represented as triples of 8 bit values; one 8 bit value for each of three primary color components.

5.1.1. The Image Synthesis Tasks

Image synthesis includes three major tasks:

- transforming the geometric model and model components into the viewing coordinate system,

- determining which surfaces are visible from the viewing position, and

- computing the color values for each image pixel based on the lighting conditions and the properties of the visible surfaces.

5.1.2. Coordinate Transformations

The various components making up the scene to be synthesized may be defined in a number of different coordinate systems. Coordinate system transformations are used to move objects from one coordinate system into another coordinate system. The transformations used include operations such as translation, rotation, and scaling [FvDFH90].

These transformations may be defined as sets of equations that operate on coordinate values defined in one system to create new coordinate values in another system. It is often convenient to express these operations using matrix notation. For example, the rotation of a three-dimensional point could be expressed as:

$$
\begin{vmatrix} X' \\ Y' \\ Z' \end{vmatrix} = \begin{vmatrix} R_{11} & R_{12} & R_{13} \\ R_{21} & R_{22} & R_{23} \\ R_{31} & R_{32} & R_{33} \end{vmatrix} \begin{vmatrix} X \\ Y \\ Z \end{vmatrix}
$$

where X', Y', Z' are the coordinates of the rotated point; $R_{11}, \ldots, R_{33}$ are the terms specifying the desired rotation; and X, Y, Z are the original point's coordinates. The rotation terms are based on sines and cosines of the rotation angles.

Note that the rotation of a point within a coordinate system is exactly the same as the opposite rotation of the coordinate system itself.

Homogeneous Coordinates

We typically make use of four-dimensional homogeneous coordinates and coordinate transformations when describing and manipulating geometric models. The three-dimensional point X, Y, Z becomes the point $X, Y, Z, 1$ in a four-dimensional homogeneous system.

Homogeneous coordinates and transformations provide several advantages. All coordinate transformations of interest can be easily expressed using four-by-four transformation matrices. These four-by-four transformation matrices can be multiplied together to express complex transformations. For example, the following matrix expression is used to specify a coordinate transformation involving translation, scaling, and rotation.

$$
\begin{vmatrix} X' \\ Y' \\ Z' \\ 1 \end{vmatrix} = \begin{vmatrix} R_{11} & R_{12} & R_{13} & 0 \\ R_{21} & R_{22} & R_{23} & 0 \\ R_{31} & R_{32} & R_{33} & 0 \\ 0 & 0 & 0 & 1 \end{vmatrix} \begin{vmatrix} S_1 & 0 & 0 & 0 \\ 0 & S_2 & 0 & 0 \\ 0 & 0 & S_3 & 0 \\ 0 & 0 & 0 & 1 \end{vmatrix} \begin{vmatrix} 1 & 0 & 0 & T_1 \\ 0 & 1 & 0 & T_2 \\ 0 & 0 & 1 & T_3 \\ 0 & 0 & 0 & 1 \end{vmatrix} \begin{vmatrix} X \\ Y \\ Z \\ 1 \end{vmatrix}
$$

The same transformation, after multiplying the matrices, may be expressed as

$$
\begin{vmatrix} X' \\ Y' \\ Z' \\ 1 \end{vmatrix} = \begin{vmatrix} R_{11}S_1 & R_{12}S_2 & R_{13}S_3 & R_{11}S_1T_1 + R_{12}S_2T_2 + R_{13}S_3T_3 \\ R_{21}S_1 & R_{22}S_2 & R_{23}S_3 & R_{21}S_1T_1 + R_{22}S_2T_2 + R_{23}S_3T_3 \\ R_{31}S_1 & R_{32}S_2 & R_{33}S_3 & R_{31}S_1T_1 + R_{32}S_2T_2 + R_{33}S_3T_3 \\ 0 & 0 & 0 & 1 \end{vmatrix} \begin{vmatrix} X \\ Y \\ Z \\ 1 \end{vmatrix}
$$

As we see, the result of concatenating several transformations may also be expressed as a four-by-four matrix. And, as we shall see below, the perspective transformation can also be expressed by a four-by-four matrix.

Modeling Transformations

Different parts of a geometric model often are defined in different coordinate systems. Coordinate transformations are then used to put the various pieces together to form the complete model. Modeling transformations include: scaling to change object size, rotation to change object orientation, and translation to change object location. The coordinate system of the complete model or the complete scene is called the *world* coordinate system.

For example, when modeling the face, each eye usually is defined in its own coordinate system. This separation allows the eye to be rotated independently of the head and then translated into its proper location within the head.

Note that the order of transformations is important. Rotating an object and then translating it usually has a very different result than translating the object and then rotating it.

Viewing Transformations

In addition to assembling the components of a three-dimensional scene, coordinate transformations are used to put the assembled scene into the desired viewing coordinate system. This process is sometimes referred to as the *look-at, look-from* problem. The viewing system usually is specified by establishing the viewing position and the viewing direction in the world coordinate system.

The world coordinate system is translated so that the look-from position becomes the viewing system origin. Then the coordinate axes are rotated so that the Z axis (the depth axis) is pointed toward the look-at position. Then additional transformations may be applied so that the X and Y axes of the viewing system correspond to the X and Y axes of the desired image or display screen. These additional transformations may include switching from a right-handed to a left-handed coordinate system and rotating around the Z axis so that the viewing system is oriented to give the desired image [FvDFH90].

Perspective

We often want our images to have perspective similar to that which we see in the real world. In perspective, objects appear smaller as they move away from us.

To achieve simple perspective, we again make use of homogeneous coordinates. We first transform the scene elements already in the viewing coordinate system by a perspective transformation. We then project the resulting homogeneous point positions into a three-dimensional screen space by dividing X', Y', and Z' by the homogeneous W coordinate as shown below.

$$\begin{vmatrix} X' \\ Y' \\ Z' \\ W \end{vmatrix} = \begin{vmatrix} 1 & 0 & 0 & 0 \\ 0 & 1 & 0 & 0 \\ 0 & 0 & 1 & 0 \\ 0 & 0 & 1/d & 0 \end{vmatrix} \begin{vmatrix} X \\ Y \\ Z \\ 1 \end{vmatrix}$$

$$X_s = X'/W$$

$$Y_s = Y'/W$$

$$Z_s = Z'/W$$

d is the distance from the viewing system origin to the image projection plane. X_s and Y_s are the projected image coordinates, and Z_s is a function of the distance from the viewer to the point.

Simple perspective is only one of many possible viewing projections [FvDFH90]. In general, viewing projections map a three- or four-dimensional space into a two-dimensional image space.

Perspective transformations more complex than the one shown above may be used. But the basic notion of a perspective transformation in homogeneous four-dimensional space, followed by a homogeneous division, (thus projecting the points back into a three-dimensional screen space), remains the same. A more useful perspective transformation is to substitute $tan(\alpha)$ for the $1/d$ term in the transformation shown above. The angle α is one-half the desired field of view [NS79].

5.2. Visible Surface Determination

Since our facial models are merely mathematical surfaces and not real objects, we must explicitly determine which surfaces are actually visible from a given viewpoint. The development of visible surface algorithms has been an area of active research since the early days of computer graphics. Many such algorithms have be developed [FvDFH90] [Joy88].

5.2.1. Visible Surface Algorithm Taxonomies

Several taxonomies have been proposed for classifying the many visible surface algorithms. The first of these was proposed by Sutherland et al. [SSS74]. This taxonomy classifies ten visible surface algorithms based largely on three criteria: whether the algorithm is for image space or object space, the sorting order used, and the sorting algorithms used.

Grant [Gra88] has proposed other taxonomies based on the type of sampling used, the type of geometric subdivision used, and the sorting order used. The sampling types include continuous sampling and point sampling. The geometric subdivision types include: object-based, space-based, scan plane, scan line, and screen area.

Image Space/Object Space

In object space algorithms, surface visibility is computed prior to being projected into screen space. The visibility computations are done at the precision used to represent the geometric primitives. Examples of object space algorithms include those proposed by Roberts [Rob63] and Appel [App67].

In image space algorithms, surface visibility is computed in the screen coordinate system after being projected from the world coordinate system. Visibility computations are done only for each pixel and only at the precision needed for a valid screen space solution. Most of the algorithms described below are image space algorithms.

Sorting Order and Algorithms

The sorting operations and the sorting order used is one way to classify the approaches to visible surface computation. The sorting operations used include bucket sorting and bubble sorting [Knu69]. Bucket sorting partitions a set of objects into a predetermined number of groups. Bucket sorting may be used to sort polygon edges into scan line groups based on the minimum Y value of each edge. Bubble sorting orders members of a set by iteratively exchanging neighboring elements until the elements of the set are in the desired order. Bubble sorting may be used to add a new element to an already sorted list simply by appending to the end of the list. The new element is then exchanged with its neighbors until it is positioned so the augmented list is completely sorted again.

Sorting orders used by visible surface algorithms include depth sort first, Y sort first, and its corollary, X sort first. In each of these approaches, usually additional sorting along the other dimensions is used to complete the visibility determination.

5.2.2. Use of Coherence

Visible surface algorithms often make use of various forms of scene and image coherence to minimize the amount of work needed to complete the visibility computations [FvDFH90]. For example, *object coherence* might be used to reduce the sorting effort. If one object is completely separated from another object in one or more dimensions then it is not necessary to compare all of the components of one object with all of the components of the other object.

Since properties usually vary smoothly across surfaces, *surface coherence* allows the use of incremental techniques to compute variation of these properties across the surface. *Edge coherence* means that a surface edge can only change visibility when it crosses another edge or when it penetrates another surface.

Scan line coherence means that the visible spans along one scan line are likely to be very similar to the visible spans in adjacent scan lines. *Area coherence* means that adjacent groups of pixels are often covered by the same visible surface. *Depth coherence* means that adjacent areas of a single surface typically have similar depth values, while adjacent areas of different surfaces typically have significantly different depth values.

Frame coherence means that the visible surfaces in one frame of an animation are usually very similar to the visible surfaces in adjacent frames.

5.2.3. Depth Sort Algorithms

Several algorithms make use of the depth first sorting order. These algorithms include the Painter's algorithms, the Newell algorithm, and the binary space partition (BSP) algorithm. The BSP algorithm uses a spatial partitioning scheme to determine depth. The Newell algorithm makes use of additional sorting to determine visibility. The Painter's algorithm use no sorting beyond the initial depth sort.

Painter's Algorithm

For the Painter's algorithm, the surfaces in the scene are sorted or ordered into a depth priority list. The surfaces are then rendered into the image buffer in reverse priority order. The lowest priority surface, or the surface farthest away, is rendered first. As the scene is rendered or *painted* from back to front, the correct visibility image is formed.

Schumacker et al. [SBGS69] describe a very early form of the Painter's algorithm implemented in real-time hardware using surface and object priorities to order the scene polygons into a priority list.

Newell Algorithm

The algorithm due to Newell, Newell, and Sancha [NNS72] first sorts all polygons based on the farthest Z depth coordinate of each polygon. If polygons overlap in X or Y and also in Z depth, one or more of the polygons is split so that a definite polygon ordering in Z can be achieved.

The depth ordered list of polygons is scan converted from back to front. The scan conversion used does not require an image buffer but rather makes use of an X sorted list of visible span segments for each image scan line. As each polygon is converted into scan line segments, the segments are added to the segment lists for the scan lines. The scan line segment lists are sorted in X. Where these segments overlap in X, the previously established depth ordering of the polygons is used to determine visibility.

BSP Trees

The binary space partitioning algorithm developed by Fuchs, Kedem, and Naylor [FKN80] [FAG83] creates a tree-structured spatial partitioning of the scene. Each node in the partitioning tree corresponds to a plane that divides the scene space into two half-spaces. Additional nodes in the subtrees correspond to additional planes that further partition the scene. The tree is extended until all surface primitives are uniquely partitioned. The leaf nodes of the tree correspond to the partitioned surface primitives. It may be necessary to subdivide surfaces to create a valid spatial partitioning.

The depth priority for the scene from a particular viewpoint is determined by traversing the partitioning tree. At each node, a test is made to determine on which side of the partitioning plane for that node the viewpoint is located. The result of this test determines which subtree at that node is traversed first. A complete traversal of the tree for a given viewpoint results in a visibility priority list for the scene. The traversal order for one viewpoint will likely be different than the order for another viewpoint. Different traversal orders create different visibility lists.

5.2.4. Scan Line Algorithms

Scan line algorithms typically first sort the scene polygons based on their Y values. Starting at the top of the image, polygons are added to an active polygon list based on the scan line Y value. Polygons are maintained on the active list as long as the current scan line intersects the polygon.

For each scan line a set of spans, from the active polygons, is ordered in X. Where these spans overlap, visibility is determined based on Z depth. A number of scan line algorithms have been developed, including those by Wylie et al. [WREE67], Romney et al. [RWE69], Watkins [Wat70], Bouknight [Bou70], and Bouknight and Kelley [BK70]. These algorithms differ primarily in the ways they sort the polygons in Y, the ways they X order the scan line spans, and the ways they resolve depth where the spans overlap in X. There are also some differences in how image coherence is exploited.

Area Subdivision Algorithms

Rather than subdividing the scene based on image scan lines, Warnock [War69] recursively subdivides the scene into smaller and smaller areas. The algorithm starts by considering the entire scene. If the scene is "simple enough," it is rendered. If it is too complex to render directly, it is cut into four smaller regions by dividing it in half in both the X and Y dimensions. Each smaller region is then considered. If the region is simple enough it is rendered. If not, it is divided again into four smaller regions. This area subdivision is continued until each region is simple enough or until the size of the region reaches the size of the image pixels.

The "simple enough" criteria varies with implementation. "Simple enough" means that the visible complexity of the region can be directly rendered by the implementation. Typical examples include the cases where only the background is in the region, where only one polygon covers the region, where only one visible polygon covers the region, and so on.

Weiler and Atherton [WA77] propose an alternative area subdivision algorithm where the polygons in the scene are clipped by the edges of the other polygons in the scene. This alternative results in an irregular subdivision of the image. Within each clipped region, the algorithm determines which polygon fragment is visible and renders it.

5.2.5. Z-Buffer

The depth-buffer or Z-buffer algorithm is probably the simplest and by far
the most widely used visibility algorithm. Because of its simplicity it is easy
to implement in either software or fast dedicated hardware.

For each pixel in the image, a record is kept of the current distance from
the closest surface to the viewpoint. This collection of depth distances is
referred to as the Z-buffer [Cat74]. The color of the closest surface at each
pixel is also stored in an image buffer.

As each surface primitive is rendered, the Z depth value and the surface
color value are computed for each pixel within the primitive. If the newly
computed Z value at a pixel is closer to the viewer than the stored Z value,
the new Z value and the new color value for this pixel are stored in the buffers.
After all surface primitives are rendered, the image buffer will contain the
final rendered image.

Porter [Por83] proposed a scan line version of the Z-buffer algorithm. In
this approach the scene is sorted in Y order as in the scan line algorithms
described above, but the visibility on each scan line is computed using a one
line Z-buffer.

The Z-buffer is inherently a point sampling algorithm and suffers from
the aliasing problems outlined in Section 5.5. Carpenter [Car84] describes
an extended form of the Z-buffer called the A-buffer. The A-buffer keeps a
list of visible objects for each pixel. A 32-bit coverage mask is used to record
which part of the pixel is covered by each visible object. Complex coverage comparisons are implemented using Boolean operations. The A-buffer
provides better images with reduced aliasing at an increased computational
cost.

5.3. Surface Shading

The computed colors for the image pixels are determined by the surface
properties of the visible surfaces and the modeled lighting conditions.

5.3.1. Surface Properties

Surface properties include color, texture, reflectivity, and transparency.

Surface Color

Color is a modeled attribute associated with each surface. Color may be
uniform across a surface, or it may vary across the surface. For polygonal
surfaces, color may be assigned as a vertex attribute, allowing each vertex to

have a different color. Color values across the surface between these vertices are determined using color interpolation.

A particular color can be described by specifying its location in a three-dimensional color space. A number of different standard color spaces might be used. Probably the most common is the RGB color space, in which each color has a specific value in red, green, and blue. Other color spaces include the HSV (hue, saturation, and value) color space and the YIQ color space used in color television.

Colors that are difficult to specify in one color space may be easy to specify in another. For example, skin tones are much easier to specify in the HSV space than in the RGB space. Transformations exist that can convert colors defined in one space into the equivalent colors in another space [Smi78].

Texture Maps

Another way to specify colors that vary across a surface is to use a *texture map* [Cat74]. A texture map is simply a two-dimensional color pattern. This pattern can be synthetically generated or it can be from an image.

A *UV* coordinate system is introduced to associate the texture map with the modeled surface. The texture map is defined in the two-dimensional *UV* coordinate system. For polygonal surfaces, each vertex has an assigned *UV* texture coordinate. For points on the surface between vertices, the *UV* texture coordinates are interpolated.

Each *UV* coordinate pair corresponds to a specific location in the texture space. The color for each point on the surface is determined by finding the *UV* value for that point and then looking up the corresponding color value in the texture map.

Since the texture map is essentially a two-dimensional array of color values, it has values defined only for integer *UV* values. *UV* interpolation across textured surfaces can result in *UV* values that fall between these integer values. When this happens, bilinear interpolation may be used to compute the texture value. The fractional portions of the interpolated *UV* values are used as interpolation coefficients to find the required texture color from the four closest surrounding values in the texture map.

Williams [Wil83] introduced the *mipmap* concept of repeatedly prefiltering the texture map to obtain multiple representations of the texture data. Each filter repetition results in a texture map with less detail and lower spatial frequencies. Aliasing effects (see Section 5.5) can be minimized by selecting the appropriate texture representation level. Aliasing can be further reduced by using trilinear interpolation. Trilinear interpolation involves bilinear interpolation in each of two adjacent representation levels, followed by interpolation between the levels. The interpolation within each level is just as described above and is based on the fractional *UV* values. The two representation levels used and the interpolation coefficient between the levels are determined by the screen size of UV increments across the surface. As the surface becomes smaller on the screen, more heavily filtered versions of of the texture map are used.

Volume Textures. The concept of texture maps can be extended to three-dimensional volume textures [Per85] [Pea85] [Per89]. Here each location in space or each polygon vertex has a three-dimensional UVW texture coordinate. These coordinates specify locations in a three-dimensional texture array or are used as variables in a three-dimensional texture function.

The texture coordinates may be embedded in the space containing the model, or else the texture may be attached to the object. If the texture is embedded in the space, then the texture of the object will change as it moves through the space.

Bump Maps. As we will see, the surface normal is fundamental to reflection calculations, and the normal is also fundamental in shading calculations. Blinn [Bli78] proposed the use of surface normal *variation* as a way of specifying additional surface shading complexity. Variation in the surface normals can be used to create wrinkled or bumpy-looking surfaces. The underlying surface geometry is not changed, just the surface shading, which is based on the modified surface normals.

Bump maps are one way to specify the desired surface normal variations or perturbations. The bump map is defined in a UV space similar to that of a texture map. The bump map entries are accessed using the UV values associated with modeled surfaces. Interpolation techniques may be used for bump maps just as for texture maps.

Bump maps are vector valued arrays. Each UV coordinate in the map has a vector value. These vectors are used to modify the surface normal vectors.

Reflection Properties

Light reflection properties are associated with the modeled surfaces. These properties are usually specified in terms of diffuse reflection, specular reflection, and transparency.

Diffuse. Diffuse light reflection is actually a subsurface property. Light falling on the surface penetrates below the surface and is internally reflected multiple times and eventually emerges from the surface. Diffuse reflection can be modeled using Lambert's law, which states that the amount of diffuse light leaving the surface seen by the viewer depends only on the angle between the surface normal and the direction of the light source illuminating the surface:

$$I = I_s K_d cos\theta,$$

where I is the diffuse reflected light, I_s is the intensity of the light source, K_d is the diffuse reflection coefficient of the surface material, and θ is the incident angle of the light. The color of diffuse reflected light is primarily a property of the surface material.

Specular. Specular light reflection occurs at the surface of the material. It is the kind of reflection that we see from the surface of polished chrome. The specular reflection a viewer sees depends on her location relative to the light source and the orientation of the surface. Light incident on a specular surface will be reflected along a vector that is determined by the incident light vector and the surface normal vector. The reflection vector will be in the plane defined by the incident vector and the normal vector. The reflection vector is the incident vector mirrored about the normal vector.

The amount of specular reflection the viewer sees depends on the angle between the reflection vector and the vector from the surface to the viewer position. For a perfect reflector, the viewer's position must lie directly on the reflection vector to see the reflected light. For less-than-perfect reflectors, which include most specular surfaces, the viewer will see some reflected light even if not positioned directly on the reflection vector. As the angle between the viewing vector and the reflection vector increases, the amount of light seen decreases. This relationship can be expressed as

$$I = I_l K_s cos^p \gamma,$$

where I is the amount of reflected light, I_l is the intensity of the incident light, K_s is the specular coefficient of the surface, γ is the angle between the viewing vector and the reflection vector, and p is an exponent that determines how rapidly the light falls off as the viewer moves away from the reflection vector. The color of specular reflected light is primarily a property of the light source.

Reflection Maps. Blinn and Newell [BN76] extended the notion of specular reflection to include reflection maps. A reflection map is essentially a panoramic wrap around image representing the peripheral part of a modeled scene. Vectors from the viewer position toward the modeled surfaces are specularly reflected. The directions of these reflected vectors are used to access elements of the reflection map. The directions of the reflected vectors are usually specified in terms of azimuth and elevation angles. What the viewer sees reflected from the surface depends on where the reflection vector points in the reflection map. As with texture maps, interpolation of the map elements may be used to compute the values returned from the reflection map.

Transparency

Transparency is a measure of how much light is transmitted through a material. An ideal transparent material would let all light falling on one side pass through to the other side. Most transparent materials attenuate light transmission to some extent. The attenuation may be color or wavelength dependent. Opaque materials transmit no light.

Careful modeling of transparency also includes refraction of the light as it enters the material at one surface and as it leaves the material at another surface.

The Eye as an Example

The eyeballs are an example that illustrates the texture, reflection, and transparency concepts. Texture mapping is a very effective way to represent the complex color patterns in the iris of the eye. These patterns would be very difficult to model using just polygon geometry. Texture mapping could also be used to represent the detailed blood vessel patterns visible on the white of the eye.

Because the surface of the eye is wet, light reflected from the eye is predominately specular. However, diffuse reflection does contribute significantly. Diffuse reflection is the dominate factor in determining the colors of the iris.

A detailed model of the eye depends on transparency to model the lens of the eye. Light passes to and from the interior of the eye and to and from the iris through the lens. Specular reflection from this transparent curved surface creates the dominate highlights we expect to see on the eyes.

5.3.2. Lighting

Lighting in a synthetic scene is controlled by placing light sources in the modeled environment. These light sources include ambient light, directional lights, local lights, and spotlights.

Ambient Light. Ambient light is a nondirectional, nonlocational source of light. Ambient light is used to approximate the light in a scene due to reflections between the various surfaces. Ambient light intensity usually is specified for the entire scene. Each modeled surface will also have an ambient light reflection coefficient to determine how much ambient light it will reflect.

Directional Lights. Directional light sources are located at an infinite distance in a specific direction. Since these lights have only a direction and not a specific location, some lighting calculations are simplified for directional lights.

Local Lights. Local lights have a specific location in the scene. Lighting calculations are more complex for local lights since the relevant lighting vectors vary across surfaces and throughout the scene.

Spotlights. Spotlights are local lights but with constraints on the direction of the light. The light is bounded to be within a cone around a specified direction vector. The angular size of the bounding cone is a part of the spotlight specification.

Shadows

Shadows in synthetic images fall into two broad classes: those that occur simply because no light happens to illuminate some portion of an object, and those that are caused by one object blocking light that would otherwise fall onto the surface of another object.

The first kind of shadowing may occur even in very simple scenes containing just one object. Those surfaces that are on the side of the object away from all light sources will be in shadow.

Cast shadows are created when objects are positioned between light sources and other objects. For a given single light source, the cast shadow problem is essentially the same as the visible surface problem, but from the point of view of the light source. Surfaces that are not visible to the light source will be in a shadow cast from that light source.

5.3.3. Polygonal Shading Models

Several shading models have been developed to fill in the pixel color values for polygonal surfaces. These include flat shading, smooth or Gouraud shading, and Phong shading.

Flat Shading

For flat shading, one color value is computed for each polygon. This color value is based on a single surface normal vector for the entire polygon. Flat shading produces surface shading discontinuities at the boundaries between adjacent polygons. The shaded surface appears *faceted*.

Gouraud Shading

In Gouraud shading [Gou71] a color value is computed for each polygon vertex. Pixel values between the vertices are computed using linear interpolation. The color value at each vertex is based on a surface normal vector for that vertex. Usually the normal vector at a vertex is computed by summing the normal vectors for all polygons that share that vertex. Since shared vertices have a common normal vector, they will usually have a common vertex color. Gouraud shading eliminates first-order shading discontinuities between adjacent polygons, and the surface appears smooth.

Phong Shading

Phong Bui-Tuong [BT75] extends the Gouraud approach to interpolate the vertex surface normals across the polygons. The vertex normals are computed as in the Gouraud approach. However, a new normal vector is interpolated and renormalized for every pixel. This pixel normal vector is then used to compute the pixel color.

The Phong approach requires significantly more computation but produces better surface shading. Phong shading minimizes the higher order shading discontinuities between adjacent polygons. Phong shading allows effective specular highlights; Gouraud shading does not.

5.3.4. Ray Tracing

Ray tracing, first proposed by Kay [Kay79] and Whitted [Whi80], combines visible surface determination, lighting, shadows, and surface shading into a single algorithm. A simple ray-tracing algorithm applies a recursive procedure to each image pixel to find its color.

This procedure creates a directed line segment or ray from the viewer's eye through the center of the screen pixel. This line is tested to see if it intersects any surfaces in the modeled scene. If so, information about the first surface encountered is stored and new rays are created. One of the new rays is the surface reflection of the original ray. Another new ray is a refracted ray if the surface is transparent.

Each of these new rays is tested to see if it intersects any surfaces in the scene. Each time a ray intersects a surface, new rays are spawned. The rays are organized in a tree structure. When a ray fails to intersect any surface, a default color value is assigned to that node in the tree and no new rays are spawned. When a ray intersects a light source, the light characteristics are assigned to the node and no new rays are spawned.

When all spawned rays for a given pixel are completed, the ray tree is traversed from the leaf nodes back to the original pixel node. Node color values are computed as the tree is traversed. The final result is a single color value for the pixel. This color is based on what the original ray and its descendants encountered in the scene. Ray tracing is good at representing scenes that contain objects with shiny specular surfaces. It is not so good for objects with diffuse surfaces.

Ray tracing is a simple concept but requires significant computation. In the simplest implementations each ray must be tested against every surface to find possible intersections. When intersections are found, the new rays also must be exhaustively tested. Spheres are a favorite modeling primitive for ray tracing because intersection, reflection, and refraction calculations are fairly simple for spheres.

A number of optimizations have been proposed to increase the efficiency and reduce the cost of ray-tracing calculations [Gla84] [KK86] [Gla89].

Distributed Ray Tracing

The simple ray-tracing algorithm outlined above is inherently a point sampling algorithm and as such is subject to spatial aliasing artifacts (see Section 5.5). One approach to reducing aliasing is to trace several rays for each pixel and use a weighted sum of the results. For example, each pixel could be subdivided into four, nine, or 16 subpixels; each subpixel corresponds to one traced ray.

Cook, Porter, and Carpenter [CPC84] proposed a scheme in which a number of rays are traced for each pixel. Instead of spacing the rays based on a regular subpixel array, however, the rays are distributed randomly throughout the pixel. The number of rays traced may be adaptively adjusted. When the summed pixel color converges to a stable value, additional rays are not computed since they are probably not needed.

5.3.5. Radiosity

Rather than approximating the light due to reflections between objects in the scene with an ambient light term, Goral et al. [GTG84] and Nishita and Nakamae [NN85] proposed explicitly modeling these interactions using mathematics originally developed to model radiant heat flow. This *radiosity* approach models the steady-state light energy transfer between the light sources and the surfaces in the scene. Radiosity models diffuse reflection from the surfaces, not specular reflection.

The result of this complex calculation is independent of viewer position and remains constant for a given scene. If some aspect of the scene lighting or surface placement is changed, then the radiosity solution must be recalculated. However, since the calculation is iterative, the previous solution provides an excellent, economical starting point for determining a new solution.

5.4. The OpenGL Lighting Model

A typical polygonal lighting model is the one used in OpenGL [NDW93]. In this model a surface color is determined for each polygon vertex. The pixel colors between vertices are determined using Gouraud shading. The surface color at each vertex is the sum of three components: a surface material emission component, a global ambient light component, and the sum of contributions from all specified light sources. This complete sum is expressed as:

$$color_{vertex} = emission + ambient_{global} + \sum light_{sources}. \qquad (5.1)$$

Each of these components has contributions in three primary colors: red, green, and blue. The resulting color values are *clamped* or limited to be in the range [0,1.0]. This model does not include any cast shadow calculations and does not incorporate light reflected from objects onto other objects.

5.4.1. Emission Term

The emission term is the simplest. It models light coming from self-illuminating objects, i.e., objects that *glow*. It is a triplet of RGB light values associated with the object.

5.4.2. Global Ambient

The global ambient component is calculated by multiplying a global ambient light term by the ambient material property at the vertex:

$$ambient_{global} = ambient_{light} * ambient_{material}. \qquad (5.2)$$

This calculation is done for each of the RGB color contributions:

$$R_{ag} = R_{al} * R_{am}$$
$$G_{ag} = G_{al} * G_{am}$$
$$B_{ag} = B_{al} * B_{am}. \qquad (5.3)$$

5.4.3. Contributions from the Light Sources

The contributions of all light sources are summed together. For each light source, its contribution is computed using ambient, diffuse, and specular terms, an attenuation factor, and a possible spotlight effect as shown below:

$$light_n = attenuation_n * spotlight_n * (ambient_n + diffuse_n + specular_n). \qquad (5.4)$$

This computation is done for each of the RGB components.

The attenuation factor for a *local* light is based on the distance between the light source and the vertex and on three attenuation coefficients:

$$attenuation = 1/(K_c + K_l d + K_q d^2), \qquad (5.5)$$

where d is the distance, K_c is a constant attenuation coefficient, K_l is a linear attenuation coefficient, and K_q is a quadratic attenuation coefficient.

If the light source is *directional* rather than local, then the attenuation factor is set to 1.0. A directional light source is located at infinity in a particular direction.

If the light is not a spotlight then the spotlight term is set to 1.0. If the light is a spotlight, but the vertex is outside the illumination cone of the light, then the spotlight term is set to 0. If the light is a spotlight and the vertex is inside the cone of illumination, the spotlight term is calculated as follows:

$$spotlight = max(v \bullet t, 0)^{spot}, \qquad (5.6)$$

where $v \bullet t$ is the dot product of the two vectors, v is the unit vector that points from the spotlight to the vertex, and t is the unit vector in the direction the spotlight is pointing.

This dot product varies as the cosine of the angle between these two vectors. Objects directly in line with the spotlight get maximum illumination, while those off the spotlight axis get less illumination. The cone of illumination is determined by checking the dot product value against the cosine of the spotlight's cutoff angle. The *spot* exponent determines how fast the spotlight illumination falls off as an object moves away from the center line of the spotlight.

The vertex ambient term for each light is the product of the light source ambient light term with the ambient term of the surface material.

$$ambient = ambient_{light} * ambient_{material}. \qquad (5.7)$$

The diffuse contribution for each light is computed as follows:

$$diffuse = max(l \bullet n, 0) * diffuse_{light} * diffuse_{material}, \qquad (5.8)$$

where $l \bullet n$ is the dot product of the unit vector l, which points from the vertex to the light source, and the unit surface normal vector n, at the vertex. The $diffuse_{light}$ term is a property of each light, while the $diffuse_{material}$ term is a property of the surface material.

If $l \bullet n \leq 0.0$ for a light, then there is no specular component for the light. If there is a specular component for the light, it is computed as shown below:

$$specular = max(s \bullet n, 0)^{shininess} * specular_{light} * specular_{material}, \qquad (5.9)$$

where $s \bullet n$ is the dot product of the unit vector s and the unit surface normal vector n, at the vertex. The unit vector s is formed first by adding the vector from the vertex to the light source and the vector from the vertex to the viewpoint and then by normalizing the result. The $specular_{light}$ term is a property of each light, whereas the $specular_{material}$ term is a property of the surface material. Shininess is also a property of the surface material. It determines how shiny the surface is. Chrome has a high shininess value, and felt has a low shininess value.

5.5.   Aliasing

It is important to remember that the pixels of the image array are representations of small image areas and not simply point locations in the image. A fundamental flaw in most early image synthesis algorithms was that they simply point sampled the projected scene data when determining the color value for each pixel. This approach, while computationally attractive, does not take into account basic sampling theory and thus results in various objectionable image artifacts such as jagged *stairstep* edges and pixel scintillations in animations.

5.5.1.   Spatial Aliasing

Sampling theory tells us that for point sampling to faithfully represent the sampled signal, we must sample at a rate more than twice the highest frequency in the signal. If we fail to do so, the high-frequency components in the signal will not be correctly represented and will appear to be signal components of lower frequency. This misrepresentation is called *aliasing* [Cro76][FvDFH90].

For images the frequencies of interest are the image spatial frequencies. High spatial frequencies are associated with sharp edges and image detail. Blurry or fuzzy images have relatively low spatial frequencies.

Convolution

The correct way to determine the value for a pixel is to *convolve* the projected two-dimensional scene information with a sampling filter function that preserves the spatial frequencies that can be represented in the image and eliminates the spatial frequencies that cannot be represented [GW87][FvDFH90]. The filter functions are continuous two-dimensional weighting functions. *Convolution* involves a two-dimensional integration of the projected scene information multiplied by the filter function. This integration is done for each pixel in the image with the sampling filter aligned to that pixel.

There are many possible filter functions. Some have finite extent, and some have infinite extent. Some filters do a good job of rejecting unrepresentable frequencies, while others do not. An example of an infinite-extent filter is the function $sin(x)/x$ where x is the radial distance from the center of the

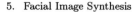
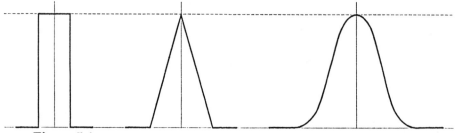

Figure 5.1.
Cross sections of several image filter functions: (a) the *box* filter, (b) the *triangle* or *tent* filter, and (c) the *Gaussian* filter.

current pixel. It is also the ideal filter function. One simple finite-extent filter is the *box* filter, which has the value 1.0 in the region corresponding to the area of the pixel and has a value of 0.0 everywhere else. The box filter gives much better results than simple point sampling, but it is far from an ideal filter. Better finite-extent filter functions include the *triangle* or *tent* filter, and the *Gaussian* filter as shown in cross section in Figure 5.1. These filters usually cover an area larger than the pixel.

The size and shape of the filter function have a dramatic effect on the spatial frequency characteristics of the produced image and on the perceived quality of the image. For example, a wide Gaussian filter will produce soft, fuzzy images with relatively low spatial frequencies.

Super Sampling

As you would expect, the convolution-based approach to image synthesis can be enormously expensive. As a result a number of computationally less expensive techniques have been developed which, while not theoretically correct, give good *approximate* results. These techniques include *super sampling* and *stochastic super sampling* [Coo86]. Both approaches approximate the convolution integration by summing a number of weighted point samples in and around the region of each computed pixel. In stochastic super sampling, the locations of the point samples are randomly selected; for super sampling, the point sample locations are on a fixed grid. The weightings used for the point samples may be uniform or may vary based on functions similar to the convolution filter functions.

Area Coverage Anti-Aliasing

Another approach is to determine the area coverage for all visible surface fragments within each pixel region. Catmull [Cat78] did this determination for polygons by clipping the scene polygons along polygon boundaries and along pixel boundaries. This action produces a set of polygon fragments for each pixel. Using essentially a box filter, the color for each pixel is computed by summing the color contributions of all visible polygon fragments within the pixel. The contribution of each fragment is formed by weighting its color with the area it covers in the pixel.

5.5.2. Temporal Aliasing

Image aliasing can also occur because of poor *temporal* sampling. Each image in an animation represents a finite time span, not just an instant of time. If the time duration of animation images is ignored, temporal aliasing will occur.

Motion blurring is the most obvious manifestation of temporal sampling. Temporal sampling is accomplished in film cameras because the shutter is open for a finite duration while exposing the film. A similar time-dependent sampling occurs in video cameras.

For synthetic images the correct solution involves a combined temporal and spatial convolution of the image information. This convolution involves a three-dimensional integration of the temporally changing projected scene information, multiplied by a three-dimensional filter function. The third dimension here is time. This solution requires truly heroic amounts of computation.

Temporal super sampling offers a computationally tractable approach. Multiple spatial samples are computed at multiple times within each animation frame. These samples, regularly distributed in both space and time, are summed to form the value for each image pixel. A weighting function, similar to the three-dimensional filter function of the convolution, may be applied to the samples when forming the pixel sums.

Temporal super sampling may be extended to stochastic temporal super sampling. In stochastic temporal super sampling, multiple samples distributed in both time and space are summed to determine each pixel value. These samples are randomly distributed in both time and space. A weighting function, similar to the three-dimensional filter function of the convolution, may be applied to these random samples when forming the pixel sums.

5.6. Generating Synthetic Human Skin Texture

For synthetic actors, detailed surface structure should be considered in rendering human skin. While surface texture information may be obtained from photographs or created with a computer paint system, it would be useful to directly generate synthetic human skin textures.

Early work in synthetic skin-like textures includes the work of Miller, Kaufman, and Nahas et al. Miller [Mil88] created reptile skins using bump map and color map techniques. Kaufman [Kau88] created reptile skin patterns using a high-level texture synthesis language. Nahas et al. [NHRD90] described a method for creating skin texture using texture data obtained from laser scans.

Ishii et al. [IYT93] developed a synthetic texture generation model specifically for human skin. This model has two components: a skin geometry model and a skin surface reflection model. The geometry model creates detailed three-dimensional skin structures consisting of small furrows and ridges. Surface reflection is based on a multilayer skin model. In this case, the surface reflection model is based on the optical features of real skin, which has a number of distinct layers. Light absorption and scattering occur within each skin layer. Light reflection and transmission occur at the boundaries between skin layers.

5.6.1. Skin Surface Geometry

The skin surface consists of four elements: ridges, furrows, hair follicle openings, and sweat gland openings. The furrows and ridges are the dominant geometric features that determine the appearance of the skin. The configuration of these features determines our overall impression of the skin surface. Skin furrows cross the skin surface like a net. Skin ridges lie within the domains produced by the furrows. Hair grows from the follicles which are located in the furrows. Sweat gland openings are located on the ridges.

In the model proposed by Ishii et al., the overall two-dimensional pattern of the skin is generated using a Voronoi division. Variation of furrow shapes is created using pseudofractal subdivision. For some skin surfaces, such as around the wrist, the configuration of furrow and ridge patterns is anisotropic.

The three-dimensional curved ridge surfaces are defined and controlled using Bézier curves. The hierarchical structure of ridge polygons is described recursively. The hierarchical three-dimensional ridge surfaces are the basis for bump-mapped skin surface images.

Pattern Generation

Voronoi division is used to divide the two-dimensional skin plane into mutually exclusive initial polygons representing the skin furrow pattern. For natural-looking furrow variations, pseudofractal subdivision is applied to the polygon edges.

Ridge pattern variations are created by changing both seed point positions in the Voronoi division and the subdivision deformation magnitude. Pattern anisotropy is created by expanding or contracting vertex positions in particular directions. Figure 5.2 shows results of the Voronoi division and the subdivision methods. Figure 5.3 shows the effect of changing the seed

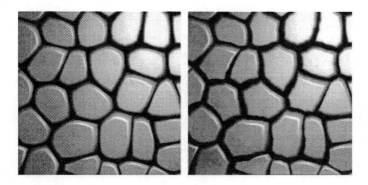

Figure 5.2.
Voronoi division and pseudofractal subdivision results.
(Courtesy T. Ishii.)

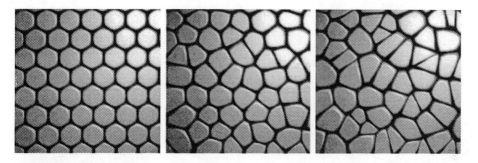

Figure 5.3.
Effect of seed point perturbation, increasing from left to right.
(Courtesy T. Ishii.)

points. Magnitude of perturbation increases from left to right. The fundamental configuration of seed points is a triangular lattice, and the placement perturbation is based on uniform random numbers.

Hierarchical Skin Structure

The skin ridges have a hierarchical structure that determines the skin surface pattern. Small polygons are formed inside the initial polygons, and these small polygons in turn have smaller ridges. This hierarchical structure is created by applying a Voronoi division to each polygon to generate smaller polygons. This polygon division is recursively executed until the desired hierarchical structure is generated. Ishii et al. indicate that three hierarchical levels are sufficient. Figure 5.4 shows the effect of the hierarchical levels.

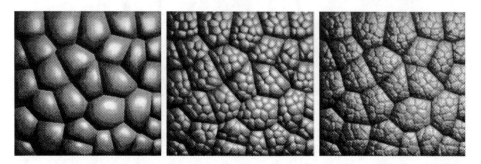

Figure 5.4.
Effect of hierarchical levels: (a) one level, (b) two levels, (c) three levels.
(Courtesy T. Ishii.)

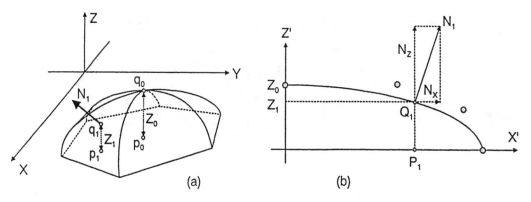

Figure 5.5.
(a) Ridge shape. (b) Ridge shape cross section.

Ridge Surface Shape Definition

The shape of each ridge component in the hierarchy is defined by its base
polygon.   Each ridge component has a curved three-dimensional surface
whose height increases from its sides to its center. See Figure 5.5.

Cubic Bézier curves are used to define these shapes. Assuming that the
base polygon is on the XY plane and the point $P_1(x_1, y_1, 0)$ is on the polygon,
we can determine both the height from P_1 to a point $Q_1(x_1, y_1, z_1)$ on the
component surface and the normal vector at Q_1 as follows. First, define a

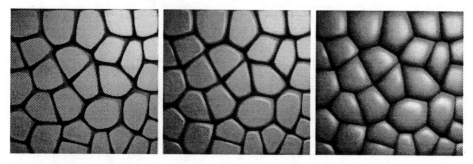

Figure 5.6.
Effect of Bézier curve slopes: (a) discontinuous surface derivatives,
(b) steep slope with continuous surface derivatives, (c) a mild slope.
(Courtesy T. Ishii.)

coordinate system for the ridge component by:

- defining the origin at the center point P_0 of the base polygon,

- defining the X' axis along the direction from point P_0 to point P_1, and

- defining the Z' axis in the direction perpendicular to the base polygon.

Second, specify the half cross-sectional shape of the ridge component with a cubic Bézier curve defined by four control points in the $X'Z'$ plane.

The height Z_1 from the base polygon to the ridge component surface and the normal vector S_1 on the surface can be derived from the defined Bézier curve as shown in Figure 5.5. Different surface shapes can be formed from the same base polygons by changing the control points defining the Bézier cross-sectional curves. The overall surface shape of the skin is formed by compositing the surface shapes of the hierarchy levels.

Figure 5.6 shows the effect of changing the Bézier curve control points, in turn controlling the ridge surface slopes.

5.6.2. Shading Calculation

The shade value of each point on the surface is computed by determining its normal vector. For each point, the base polygons in each hierarchical level are determined. (See Figure 5.7(a).) The parent-child relationship can be efficiently used to find these polygons. For each base polygon, the height and normal vectors at this point are determined using the scheme described above. The height and normal vectors at each level are composed to determine the height and the normal vector for the skin surface at this point. Figure 5.7(b) illustrates this process. The composite normal information forms the bump map used to shade the skin surface.

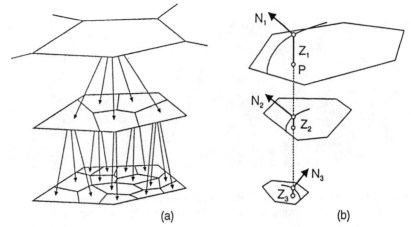

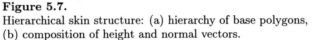

(a)   (b)

Figure 5.7.
Hierarchical skin structure: (a) hierarchy of base polygons,
(b) composition of height and normal vectors.

5.6.3. Texture Geometry Control Parameters

The geometry control parameters for the Ishii et al. model are the following.

- *Placement of the seed points.* Three types of placement are used: triangle lattice, square lattice, or random lattice. The placement may be perturbed using random values. Figure 5.3 shows the effect of changing the seed points.

- *Pseudofractal variation of the base polygon edges.* This variation is controlled by specifying the largest distance between the deformed edge and the original edge. The effect of pseudofractal edge variation is shown in Figure 5.2.

- *Anisotropic scaling.* For anisotropic ridge configurations, the base polygon vertices are transformed using asymmetric scale values. Figure 5.8 shows the effect of isotropic structure, vertical asymmetry, and horizontal asymmetry.

- *Number of hierarchy levels.* Figure 5.4 shows the effect of hierarchical levels.

- *Bézier curve control points.* For each hierarchical level, the control point parameters include the number of the curve segments and the placement of the four control points for each segment. Figure 5.6 shows the effect of changing the Bézier curve control points, in turn controlling the ridge surface slopes.

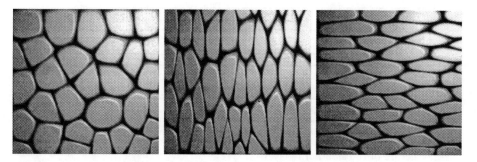

Figure 5.8.
Effect of anisotropic skin structure. (Courtesy T. Ishii.)

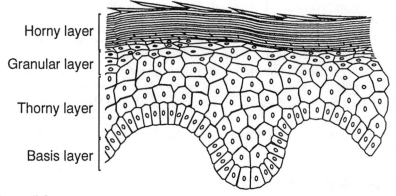

Figure 5.9.
Layers of the epidermis.

5.6.4. Skin Surface Reflection

Real skin surface consists of the epidermis, the dermis, and the subcutaneous regions. The epidermis, in turn, consists of the horny layer, the granular layer, the thorny layer, and the basis layer, as shown in Figure 5.9.

Skin cells are generated in the basis layer by cell division. These cells move upward and change into thorny cells, granular cells, and horny cells. When horny cells reach the top of skin surface, they are washed or worn off. This process is the *keratinization* process of epidermis cells.

Usually, the word *skin* is used to refer to the horny layer. The horny layer itself has a multilayer structure: the sebaceous layer, a number of horny cell layers, and a number of intercellular substance layers (see Figure 5.10). Horny cell layers and intercellular substance layers alternate. The optical characteristics of the skin depend on the number of horny cell layers, the thickness of each layer, and skin moisture content. The number of horny cell

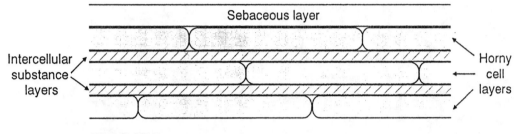

Figure 5.10.
Structure of the skin horny layer.

layers is usually about 14. Normal appearance of skin surface depends on normal keratinization and proper moisture in the horny layer.

The Ishii et al. reflection model is based on the optical properties of the horny layer. This model includes absorption and scattering within each horny layer, reflection and refraction at the boundaries between layers, and multiple reflections among the horny layers. This model also includes light reflection at the surface boundary between the air and the first horny layer. The *glossy* appearance of the skin surface is determined by specular reflection, whereas the *soft* appearance of the skin is determined by diffused reflection.

Multiple Light Reflections

It is assumed that the horny layers are essentially parallel (see Figure 5.10). Parallel light enters a layer from its upper boundary. Part of this light is absorbed or scattered within the layer. Light arriving at the lower boundary is divided into reflected light and transmitted light according to a boundary reflection factor.

Each layer has three modeled light components: parallel light reflected upward from the upper boundary, parallel light transmitted downward at the lower boundary, and the light scattered within the layer.

The scattered light is divided into upward energy and downward energy. These energies are reflected multiple times within a single layer as shown in Figure 5.11(a). Upward scattered light is divided into transmitted light and reflected light at the upper boundary based on an upward reflection factor. Downward scattered light is treated similarly. The reflected scattered light turns into new scattered light within the layer.

Four factors are defined for the combined multiple reflections within each layer. These are the reflection factor, the transmission factor, scattered light transmission up, and scattered light transmission down. These factors are applied iteratively from the first layer to the last layer, and from the last layer back to the first layer, as shown in Figure 5.11(b).

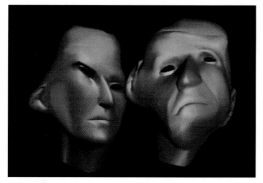

Plate I
Faces created using stochastic noise distortion. (Courtesy J. Lewis.)

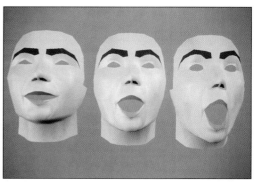

Plate II
Interpolation between facial expressions.

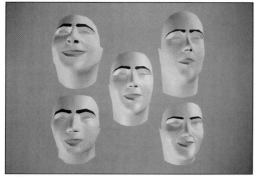

Plate III
Bilinear interpolation between faces.

Plate IV
Wind blown hair. (Courtesy K. Anjyo.)

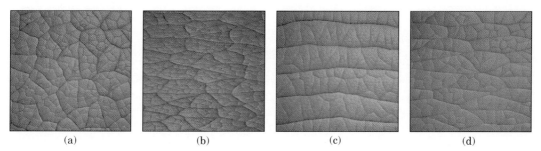

(a)   (b)   (c)   (d)

Plate V
Four synthetic skin surface textures. (Courtesy T. Ishii.)

(a) (b) (c) (d)

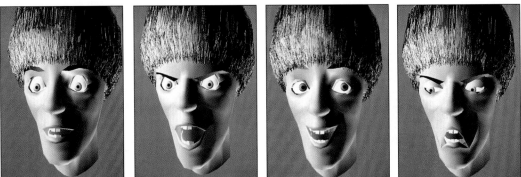

(e) (f) (g) (h)

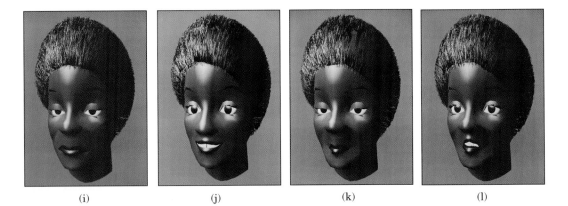

(i) (j) (k) (l)

Plate VI
A variety of facial expressions and conformations created using direct
parameterized models.

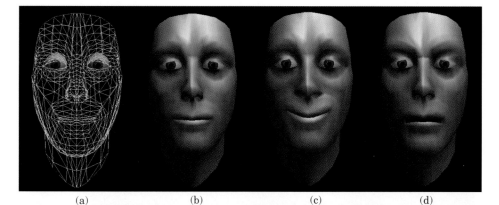

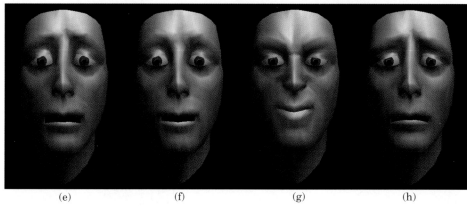

Plate VII
Images (a) and (b) illustrate the static geometry. Images (c)–(h) illustrate the six primary expressions created by the muscle model. (a) static wire frame, (b) static shaded, (c) happiness, (d) anger, (e) fear, (f) surprise, (g) disgust, (h) sadness.

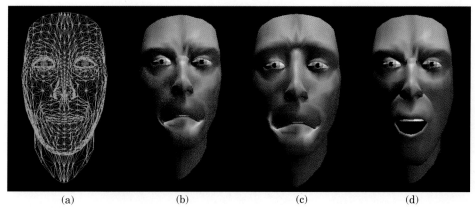

Plate VIII
Images (a)–(d) illustrate facial action created by the physical model. (a) Wireframe geometry, (b) anger, (c) worry, (d) jaw drop and brows furrowed.

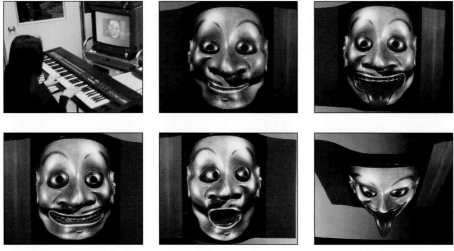

Plate IX
Example expressions of a real-time performance Kabuki mask developed at the Sony Research Laboratory.

Plate X
Four images from an animated sequence using Cyberware data and a physically-based model. These images are from an animation called *Bureaucrat II*.

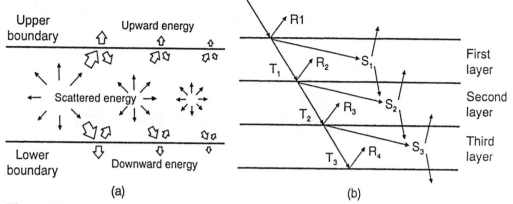
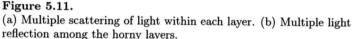

Figure 5.11.
(a) Multiple scattering of light within each layer. (b) Multiple light reflection among the horny layers.

The parameters that control the appearance of synthesized skin surface are:

- the total number of modeled layers, which affects both the glossy and soft appearance,

- the thickness and scattering coefficients, which affect soft skin appearance, and

- the refraction indices, which affect glossy skin appearance.

Refraction indices, absorption coefficients, and scattering coefficients change with horny layer moisture content.

5.6.5. Rendering Calculations

For the Ishii et al. model, skin rendering consists of two parts: calculating a table of light reflection energies and rendering the skin images. After assigning the number of layers and setting values for thickness, refraction index, absorption coefficient, and scattering coefficient for each layer, light reflection energies are calculated. The table of reflection energies is computed based on the incidence angle of light at the skin surface. This table enables quick image shading calculations.

For different skin colors, the reflection energies have different values. The reflection energies are calculated for wavelengths which represents the red, green, and blue color components. The diffusion factor value also varies with wavelength.

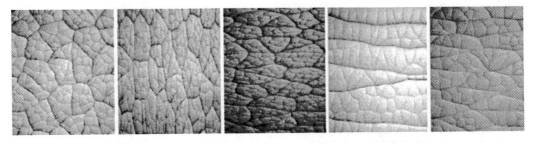

Figure 5.12.
Five skin surface textures synthesized with the Ishii et al. model.
(Courtesy T. Ishii.) (Also see Plate V.)

Figure 5.12 and Plate V show several synthetic skin textures created by combining the skin surface geometry model with the skin surface reflection model.

5.6.6. Vascular Skin Color Effects

Skin color is partially determined by the flow of blood to and through the skin. Changes in physical and emotional state can affect this blood flow [KMT94]. Increased blood flow is associated with physical exertion and emotions such as joy and anger. Decreased blood flow is associated with emotions such as shock and fear.

Increased blood flow causes the skin to appear flushed. Decreased blood flow causes the skin to become more pale. Skin temperature also is reflected in skin color. Hot skin, either from exertion or from being in a hot environment, is associated with increased blood flow and redder skin. Cold skin is associated with decreased blood flow and paler skin. Physical well-being is associated with *rosy* or *glowing* skin, whereas illness is associated with skin pallor.

Although changes in skin color generally apply to the entire face, some areas may be more affected than others [Pat95]. The cheeks, ears, neck, lips, and forehead may be more or less affected. For example, the blushing associated with embarrassment is usually more noticeable on the cheeks and ears.

5.7. Lighting the Face: Lessons from Portrait Photography

The task of the portrait photographer is to capture optimal facial images. This job is done by arranging the pose, selecting the camera placement, and controlling the lighting. Lighting the face is one of the most important aspects [Kod61]. There are important lessons to be learned for portrait lighting that can be directly applied to the creation of synthetic facial images.

There are two broad classes of portrait lighting: directional lighting and diffused lighting [FPC63]. Directional light includes bright sunlight and artificial light sources such as floodlights and spotlights. Directional lights create distinct highlights and shadows. With directional light, the relative positions of the face, the light sources, and the viewpoint are critical. If the face turns or if the position of the lights change, the lighting effect is changed. With directional lights, the interplay of light and shadow on the face can be used to achieve many effects. Lights can be used to emphasize form and texture or to flatten them out.

Light and shadow can be used to emphasize or de-emphasize facial features. Lighter areas in an image are perceived as coming forward, and darker areas are perceived as receding. Highlights on the forehead, nose, chin, and cheeks, along with shadows on the neck and sides of the face, can help create a three-dimensional appearance to the face.

Diffused light is relatively soft and even. It is truthful lighting. It reveals all facial features with equal emphasis. It includes light from a single large light source, light from multiple distributed light sources, light reflected from light-colored surfaces, daylight from a window or skylight, and the light of a gray overcast day. With diffused light, the relative positions of the face, the light sources, and the viewpoint are not critical. Diffused light does not allow the control of light effects that can be achieved with directional lights.

A basic principle of directional portrait lighting is that there should be one dominant light source, with all other light sources subordinate. The placement of this main or key light in relation to the face and to the camera is a primary consideration.

5.7.1. Single-Source Lighting

The simplest lighting situation is the use of a single directed light source. The lighting effect produced is critically dependent on the relative position of the light source, the viewpoint, and the position and orientation of the face. A number of lighting combinations and the resulting effects are described below.

Full Face — Viewpoint Directly in Front of the Face

For these poses the viewpoint or camera position lies on the symmetry plane of the face, directly in front of the face, looking at the full face.

Light on the Symmetry Plane of the Face.   The single light is located in front of the face, on the symmetry plane of the face, and shines in the

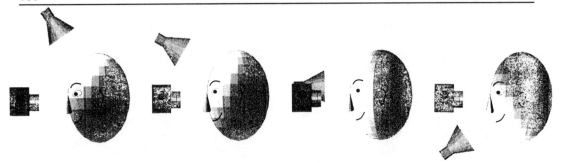

Figure 5.13.
Single-source symmetry plane, full face lighting (side views): (a) light
high above the viewpoint, (b) light above the viewpoint, (c) light at the
viewpoint, (d) light below the viewpoint.

direction of the face. The variations here are primarily in the height of the
light source relative to the face and the viewpoint position. These lighting
setups are shown in Figure 5.13.

- *Light high above the viewpoint.* The cheeks and forehead appear rounded. The eyes disappear into the shadows of the eye sockets. A shadow
  from the nose is cast down onto the mouth. The face has an overall
  gloomy, tragic look. The cast shadow of the head is not usually visible
  on the background.

- *Light above the viewpoint.* This lighting strongly shows the structures
  of the face. The height of the light should be adjusted so that a catchlight — a tiny reflection of the light source — is visible on each eye.
  These catchlights add *life* to the face. The nose shadow shouldn't quite
  touch the upper lip. Slight adjustments in the height of the light can
  significantly change the overall lighting effect.

- *Light at the viewpoint.* This placement produces lighting that is not
  very interesting. It flattens facial curvature and washes out facial textures and wrinkles. The head may cast a visible shadow on the background.

- *Light below the viewpoint.* The nose and other facial features cast
  shadows upward. The eyes catch a lot of light, and the face looks
  unusual. This lighting can lend an air of mystery and is often used in
  mystery and horror movies.

Light 45 Degrees to the Side, 45 Degrees Above. Here the light
source is moved 45 degrees to one side of the face and raised so that the
light is falling on the face at a 45-degree angle from above. This placement

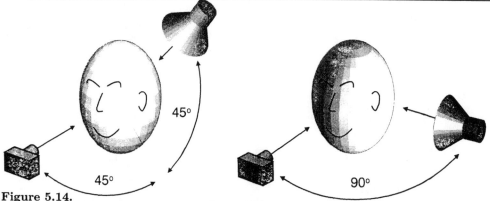

Figure 5.14.
Single-source full face side lighting: (a) light 45 degrees to the side and
45 degrees above the viewpoint; (b) light directly to the side of the face.

provides a flattering illumination of the face which emphasizes the cheekbones. With the light position properly adjusted, a triangle of light will fall
in the upper cheek opposite the light. There should be a reflection from the
light visible in both eyes. The result is the classic 45-degree portrait lighting,
which can also be used with the head turned partially to the left or right.
This setup is shown in Figure 5.14(a).

Light Directly to the Side of the Face (90 Degrees). Moving the
single light directly to the side of the face creates a very dramatic effect.
One side of the face is lighted while the other side is completely in shadow.
The light can be adjusted in height but is usually at the same height as the
face. This setup is shown in Figure 5.14(b).

Three-Quarter Pose

In this pose the face is turned slightly away from the viewpoint. The light
usually is located somewhat above the face. The height of the light is adjusted so that it creates a catchlight in both eyes as seen from the camera.
The exact height of the light also may be adjusted to flatter particular facial structures. For example, prominent cheeks can be de-emphasized by
lowering the light. A short nose appears longer when the light is raised.

There are three categories of lighting for this pose, each determined by
the side-to-side placement of the light. These lighting setups are shown in
Figure 5.15.

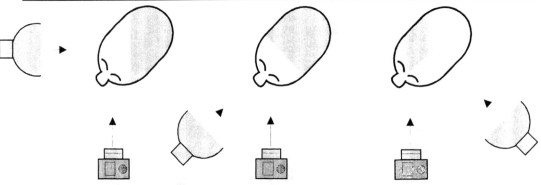

Figure 5.15.
Three-quarter pose lighting setups (top views): (a) short lighting,
(b) butterfly lighting, (c) broad lighting.

- *Short Lighting.* The light is located on the side of the face away from the camera, fully illuminating the side of the face away from the camera. This placement emphasizes facial contours and makes the face appear narrower.

- *Butterfly Lighting.* The light is placed directly in front of the face and casts a butterfly-shaped shadow under and in line with the nose. This placement is used most successfully with normal-width faces. It may highlight the ears, making them undesirably prominent.

- *Broad Lighting.* The light is on the side of the face toward the camera, fully illuminating the side of the face toward the camera. This placement de-emphasizes facial texture and makes narrow faces appear wider.

Facial Profiles

For facial profiles the camera is positioned directly to one side of the head. The single light may placed in various positions.

- Placing the light close to the viewpoint is often the most effective profile lighting.

- Placing the light so that it points directly at the front of the face flattens the curvature of the face but emphasizes the jaw line with a strong shadow.

- Moving the light farther from the camera produces a partial backlighting effect. Most of the head will be in shadow, but light does hit some areas of the face. The effect is dramatic, and the contour of the profile is strongly emphasized.

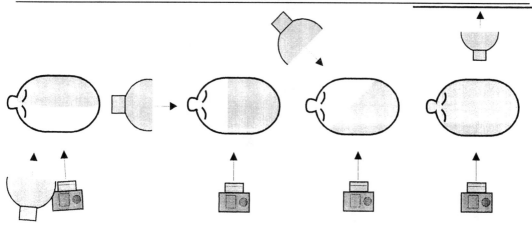

Figure 5.16.
Lighting for profiles (top views).

- A complete profile silhouette is obtained by moving the light completely behind the head and turning it to only illuminate the background. No light falls directly on the face.

These lighting setups are shown in Figure 5.16. In addition, the single-light setups previously described may be used with the viewpoint simply moved to the side of the head.

5.7.2.   Multiple-Source Lighting

Most portrait lighting setups use multiple lights. The main or key light corresponds to the single-source lighting discussed above. In addition to the main light, there may be one or more fill lights, a background light, one or more hair lights, and perhaps a back light. The basic multiple source lighting setup is shown in Figure 5.17.

- *The main or key light* generally is located higher than the face and about 45 degrees to one side of the face. It can be in either the *short* or *broad* light position, as discussed above. The main light can be a diffuse or direct light source depending on the desired effect. A diffuse main light will minimize facial texture.

The main light should be positioned so that:

  - the far cheek is illuminated with a triangular highlight,
  - the nose shadow extends downward toward the far corner of the mouth, and
  - prominent catchlights appear at about the 11 o'clock or one o'clock position on the eyes as seen from the camera position.

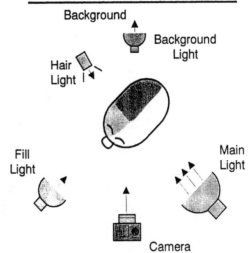

Figure 5.17.
The basic multiple-source lighting setup (top view).

- *The fill light* is placed on the side of the face opposite that of the main light. It usually is placed at about the same height as the viewpoint. Its exact side-to-side placement can be used to control facial highlights. If this light is positioned too far to the side, it may cause unwanted shadows from the cheeks across the mouth. Varying the intensity ratio between the main light and the fill light can be used to create various effects. This intensity ratio is usually about 3 to 1. The ratio can range from as low as 2 to 1 to as high as 6 to 1.

- *The background light* is used to illuminate the background, providing tone and color separation between the face and the background. It can also provide additional visual interest to the background. This light usually is placed behind the head midway between the head and the background. It is placed so that it is not visible from the viewpoint.

- *The hair light* adds detail and highlights to the hair. If the head has no hair, this light is not needed. It is placed high above and slightly behind the face. It can be placed directly overhead or to one side or the other. It should be placed so that it does not shine directly on the face causing distracting highlights. The intensity of this light is adjusted depending on the color and refection properties of the hair. Dark hair in general will require more light. Multiple hair lights may be used.

- *The back light* is used to partially outline the silhouette of the head or shoulder separating them from a dark background. It is usually a spotlight placed slightly above and behind the face. It is usually, but not always, on the same side of the face as the main light.

Wrap-Around Lighting

Sometimes two fill lights are used rather than just one. By positioning the second fill light about halfway between the main light and the normal single fill light, a pleasant wrap-around lighting effect is obtained. The height of the second fill light is usually midway between the height of the main light and the height of the first fill light. The middle fill light helps blend highlight and shadow areas. There is gradual transition from light to dark, which gives the face a more rounded appearance.

5.7.3. Use of Make-Up

Make-up is used to modify the properties of the skin or the facial hair. These modifications change skin or hair color or change skin reflection characteristics. The purpose of make-up is to emphasize or de-emphasize facial features. Features may be de-emphasized by making them darker or putting them in shadow. Features may be emphasized by making them lighter.

Make-up can be used to change the apparent contours of features such as the cheekbones. Make-up also can be used to change the color and shape of the eyebrows, the color of the eyelashes, and the shadows around the eyes. Lipstick can be used to change the shape, color, and reflection properties of the lips.

5.8. Animation Rendering and Perception

There is a strong correlation between the characteristics of the human visual system and the methods used to create animation. All film and video media rely on the ability of the human visual system to form a coherent view of dynamic scenes from a rapid sequence of essentially *still* images. The basic frame rates used for these image sequences are the result of compromises based on visual perception characteristics and economics. Human visual system characteristics determine the lower bound on these rates, while technical and economic realities set the upper bound. A frame rate that is too low to sustain the perception of smooth, flicker-free motion is not acceptable. It is also unacceptable for economic and perhaps technical reasons to choose a frame rate so high that it does not further enhance perceived image quality and motion.

Experience and experimentation has determined that 30-Hz-interlaced video is near the lower bound of acceptability. Video frame rates in excess of about 80 Hz contribute very little to perceived quality. For film, a rate of 24 frames per second, with projectors that show each image multiple times, is near the lower acceptability bound. Film systems based on frame rates up to 60 per second have seen limited use. Essentially all computer and conventional animation is produced for either the 30-Hz video (25-Hz in some countries) or the 24-Hz film standards.

Animators have long had at least an intuitive understanding of additional visual perception characteristics. For example, if the action is slow, a new image is not needed at every frame time. A frame may be held for 2, 3, 4, or even 6 frame times.

If the action is very fast, then intentionally blurring the moving portions of the animated images works well. In computer animation, correct temporal sampling blurs the moving parts of the images. These methods and other effective animation techniques [Mad69] work well, because they match human visual perception characteristics.

Research over the past two decades has demonstrated that human visual perception is supported by two major neurological systems which operate in parallel. These two perception channels are referred to as the *sustained* and the *transient* systems [KT73] [Tol75] [Len80]. The sustained system has poor temporal response but has good spatial resolution. It is specialized for pattern and detail detection. The transient system has poor spatial resolution but has good temporal response. It is specialized for motion detection.

The visual system seems designed to give highest priority to moving objects. Motion and scene changes impair the perception of detail, which is the result of a stimulus masking phenomenon. This masking occurs both backward and forward in time, because the activity of the sustained channel is pre-empted by the faster transient channel en route to the deeper visual processing areas of the brain [BG76]. An abrupt motion will mask detail perception for about 250 milliseconds.

Perception experiments [GGB85] also indicate that the visual system is relatively insensitive to high-spatial-frequency color information. It is much more sensitive to high-spatial-frequency luminance information.

Rendering for single still images and rendering for animation sequences are not necessarily optimized in the same ways. Rendering systems designed for animation can take advantage of the temporal characteristics of the visual perception system. Computational economies can be obtained by computing spatial detail only when and where it actually can be perceived in the animation [Par91a].

6

Direct Parameterized Face Models

As discussed in Chapter 4, there are many approaches to facial animation. For example, in key-pose animation the desired shape articulations are specified at two time points. An interpolation algorithm is then used to generate the necessary poses for the in-between frames. However, using this approach, each key pose must be completely specified. Developing the required three-dimensional key-pose descriptions is difficult at best. As the number of key poses needed becomes large, this approach quickly becomes impractical.

Motivated by the difficulties of key-pose interpolation, Parke [Par74] developed *parameterized* face models. Direct parameterized facial models originated as an extension to key-pose animation. The desire was to create an encapsulated model that could generate a wide range of faces and facial expressions based on a small set of input control parameters. Once an appropriate parameterized model is developed, a wide variety of animation can be produced with relatively little effort.

Parameterized models are powerful tools for facial image synthesis and animation, even as implemented in the relatively primitive models developed to date. The value of parameterized models to the animator is that she only needs to manipulate a limited amount of information — the parameters — to create a sequence of images. With the development of better, more complete facial parameter sets and the application of more sophisticated image synthesis techniques, parameterized models will allow even better facial animation.

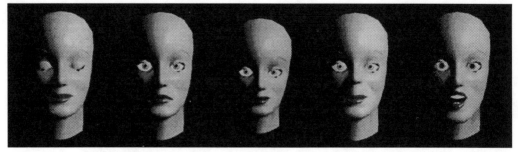

Figure 6.1.
Faces created using a parameterized model.

The ideal parameterized model would be one that allowed any possible face with any possible expression to be specified by merely selecting the appropriate parameter values. A parameterization that enables all possible individual faces and all possible expressions and expression transitions is referred to as a *complete* or *universal* parameterization.

The *ad hoc* direct parameterized face models created to date certainly fall far short of this ideal, but they do allow a wide range of expressions for a fairly wide range of individual facial conformations. Several faces generated using one parameterized model are shown in Figure 6.1. (Also see Plate VI.)

Direct parameterized models appear to have at least a short-term advantage over physically based simulation models in terms of simplicity, computation speed, varying facial conformation, and the ability to support exaggeration. Physically based models likely have a long-term advantage in applications requiring close fidelity to real facial motion and expression. Hybrid models relying on physical simulation for facial motion and expression control coupled with parameterized conformation and exaggeration control seem promising.

6.1. Parameterized Model Concepts

There are three basic ideas involved in the creation of parameterized graphic models. One is the fundamental concept of parameterization. Another is the development of appropriate descriptive parameter sets. The third is the development of parameterized models coupled with image synthesizers to create the desired images.

6.1.1. The Basic Parameterization Concept

Consider a class of objects for which individual members have identifiable differences. If the differences between member objects can be associated with a set of differentiation or specification criteria, then individual members of the class can be described or specified by these criteria values. These criteria are the *parameters*.

A *complete* set of specification criteria or parameters is one that allows every member of an object class to be specified by selecting an appropriate set of parameter values. If certain members of the class can be differentiated but not uniquely described by parameter values, the parameter set is not complete. In a complete set, every possible unique member of the class can be described by a unique n-tuple of parameter values. Some parameters might have values from finite discrete sets, while others might have values from bounded or unbounded continuous ranges.

A simple example of this notion is the class of objects called cubes. The description or specification for a particular cube consists of a set of parameter values such as the length of its edges, the color of each face, its weight, material, etc. If the set of parameters is complete, one can specify every possible cube by specifying the appropriate n-tuple of the parameter values. However, even for such simple objects, it may be difficult to develop truly complete parameterizations.

6.1.2.   The Synthesis Model

Given a parameterization scheme, the remaining task is to develop a synthesis model to produce images based on the parameter values. Figure 6.2 illustrates the major components of animator interaction with such a model. It has two major parts, the parameterized model and the image synthesis routines.

At the heart of the process is the set of algorithms, functions, and data that form the parameterized model. This model takes as input the parameter values specified by the animator. It produces as output a set of graphic description primitives such as vector or polygon descriptors. These graphics primitives are passed as input to the synthesis routines that actually create the images.

In an interactive environment, the animator can interactively adjust the parameter values to achieve the desired images or poses. Ideally, the model designer, the model implementor, and the animator interact closely in determining the actual parametric characteristics of the model.

Part of the model development process is determining the type of images to be produced. These types might be simple vector images generated using line segment descriptions. At the other end of the complexity spectrum, they might be images based on textured bicubic surfaces [Cat74] rendered using complex lighting models. A typical choice is to use polygonal surfaces rendered using fairly simple lighting and surface shading rules [Gou71].

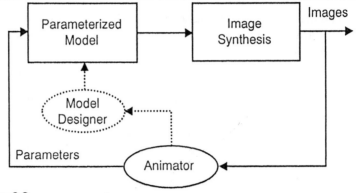

Figure 6.2.
Animator interaction with a parameterized model.

6.2. Facial Parameterization

Given this conceptual framework, developing the desired parameterized model consists of two distinct tasks:

- developing an appropriate set of parameters, and

- developing the parameterized model to implement this parameter set.

The first step is to determine the appropriate set of facial parameters. We would, of course, like to develop a complete parameter set for creating and specifying any possible face with any possible expression. However, the feasibility of developing such a complete parameterization is an open question.

If a complete parameterization is not practical or even possible, can useful parameterized models be developed? Are the parameters appropriate and efficient? Are they the correct parameters? Are they natural and intuitive to use? Do they meet immediate needs? Can the needed range of faces and expressions be generated using the chosen parameter set? Furthermore, can useful parameter sets be developed for which the number of parameters is relatively small?

No implemented facial parameterization to date is even close to being complete. The challenge is to determine a *good* set of control parameters and then to implement a model that uses these parameters to generate the desired range of faces. Several useful parameterizations, using only a few parameters, have been demonstrated [Par74] [Par82].

6.2.1.   Developing Facial Parameter Sets

How are facial parameter sets developed? One approach is to simply observe the surface properties of faces and to develop *ad hoc* parameters that allow specification of these observed characteristics.

A second approach involves studying the underlying facial structures or anatomy, and developing a set of parameters based on this anatomy (see Chapter 2). The models developed by Platt and Badler [PB81] and Waters [Wat87], for example, were developed based on simple models of the underlying structures that control facial expression.

A hybrid approach to developing a facial parameter set blends these two approaches. In the hybrid approach, parameters are based on structural understanding wherever possible and are supplemented as necessary by parameters based on observation. The direct models developed to date fall into this hybrid category.

Input and guidance from animators is certainly needed in the development of good, useful parameterizations. The focus should be on developing powerful control parameter sets that are motivated by the needs of the facial animator.

6.2.2.   Expression Versus Conformation

There are two broad categories of parameters; those that control the conformation, or shape, of an individual face, and those that control the face's expression, or emotional aspects. To some extent these two sets overlap, but conceptually they can be considered distinct. Control provided by the early parameterized models includes:

- *Expression parameters* — These parameters, including eyelid opening, eyebrow arch, eyebrow separation, jaw rotation, mouth width, mouth expression, upper-lip position, mouth corner position, and eye gaze, allow the animator to specify and control a range of facial expressions.

- *Conformation parameters* — These parameters, including jaw width, forehead shape, nose length and width, cheek shape, chin shape, neck shape, eye size and separation, face region proportions, and overall face proportions, are used to control a limited range of facial conformation.

The most general parameterized models are those that allow a wide range of both facial conformation and facial expression. However, models that allow variation only in conformation or only in expression are often useful. For example, the animation of a specific character may only require variation in facial expression. Such limited models often have the advantage of simplicity and efficiency.

Most facial models have focused only on expression control. The early work by Parke [Par74] and DiPaola's extensions [DiP89] [DiP91] also include conformation control as part of the parameterization.

6.2.3.   Expression Parameters

Of primary importance in expression are the eyes and the mouth [Mad69] [Fai90]. Therefore, most of the expression parameters relate to these areas. The *best* expression parameter set remains undetermined.

With only a few parameters it is possible to develop a model that allows interesting expression animation that can be matched to a spoken soundtrack [Par74]. Parameters that have been successfully used in past and current models are discussed below.

Expression parameters useful for the eyes include eyelid opening, pupil size or dilation, eyebrow shape and position, and the direction in which the eyes are looking. Useful expression parameters for the mouth include jaw rotation (which strongly influences mouth shape and opening), width of the mouth, mouth expression (smiling, frowning, etc.), position of the upper lip, and positions of the corners of the mouth.

Other useful expression parameters include the orientation of the face and head with respect to the neck and the rest of the body. The ability to orient the head, to turn and tilt it, was not included in early models and was obvious by its absence.

Facial Action Coding System

The muscle based *Facial Action Coding System* notation developed by Ekman and Friesen [EF78] is one possible foundation for expression parameterizations. The FACS system includes about 45 independent facial actions. These actions are based on the activity of facial muscles (see Chapter 4). The actions can occur separately or in combination to form expressions. The FACS system currently appears to be the most complete single basis for developing low-level expression models.

6.2.4.   Conformation Parameters

Changes in the conformation of faces, those aspects that vary from individual to individual and make each person unique, require a distinct set of parameters.

Conformation parameters control the relative size, shape, and positioning of the facial features. A few conformation parameters, such as the overall height to width aspect ratio of the face, apply globally to the face. The global parameters include a transformation, suggested by Todd et al. [TLSP80] that attempts to model facial growth (see Section 3.10.3). Other conformation parameters control skin and feature colors. Color control may include texture control in more elaborate models.

The variations in facial structure from one individual to another are less understood than the ways in which a given structure varies from one expression to another. Sources of conformation information include facial anatomy, physical anthropology, and those art disciplines concerned with realistic human form representation. Conformation principles from sculpture and portraiture may be useful. The notions of distortion and exaggeration from conventional character animation also play a role. The development of truly complete conformation parameter sets appears to be very difficult.

6.2.5. Quality and Scope of Direct Control Parameterizations

As discussed in Chapter 4, the *quality* of a parameter set refers to the appropriateness and efficiency of the parameters. *Scope* refers to the range of possible faces and expressions that can be generated using the chosen parameter set.

Assuming that truly universal parameterizations are not available, at least in the near term, what are the metrics for judging the quality of a control parameterization? Attributes such as range of control, complexity, parameter set size, intuitiveness, naturalness, and control interfaces immediately come to mind. Are they the correct parameters and are they natural and intuitive to use?

Certainly an important measure is the range of possible faces and expressions that can be specified. How much of the universe of faces and facial expressions is covered by the parameterization? Judgment of this aspect may be application dependent. If, for example, the application only requires animation of one specific character, then conformation control is not an issue.

Complexity, number of parameters, and intuitive and natural parameters are all directly related attributes. The number of parameters provided and the overall complexity of the parameterization should be just sufficient. Unnecessary parameters or parameter complexity should be avoided. Ease of use is strongly coupled to how natural and intuitive the parameters are and the interface to those parameters.

Subtlety and orthogonality are also measures of parameterization quality. Subtle variations in expression and conformation are often needed. The ability of a parameterization to support these subtle variations is highly desired. Mutual independence of the parameters is also an issue. The change in one parameter value should have minimal and predictable interaction with other parameters. Change in one parameter value should not require reworking the other parameter values. The above is particularly true for the interactions between expression and conformation parameters and between speech and expression parameters.

Another measure of an effective parameterization is its capability to serve as the basis for higher levels of control abstraction. In the case of speech animation, for example, the construction of control parameters at the phoneme or higher levels of abstraction built on top of the basic parameterization should be possible.

6.3. Implementation of a Direct Parameterized Model

Formal procedures for developing models that generate facial images based on a direct parameter set do not currently exist. The model [Par74] described in this section was developed with little theoretical basis and without careful attention to facial anatomy. It was experimentally derived to represent the visible surface features of the face based on observation and a general understanding of the underlying structures.

This model produces faces constructed of three-dimensional polygonal surfaces. The faces are manipulated through the use of parameters that control procedural shaping, interpolation, translation, rotation, and scaling of the various facial features.

This early parameterized facial model has many shortcomings by today's standards. However, it is a viable model and illustrates one approach to direct parameterized models. It has been widely distributed and is sufficiently robust to serve as the basis for subsequent use by other researchers. It has served as the basis for additional work in speech animation [LP87] [WHP88]. This model and its descendants have proved useful to psychologists interested in expression and communication, including the study of multimodal visual speech communications [CM90][CM93][CM94].

This model is both data and parameter driven. Data files define the polygon topology and the extreme vertex positions used for interpolation. The parameter values are entered interactively or, for animated sequences, from command files. The model generates polygon descriptors, which in turn drive polygon rendering routines. Models of this complexity can be animated in real time on current high-end graphics workstations.

6.3.1. Polygon Topology

For this model, image generation is based on polygonal surfaces. The facial mask is one polygonal surface, and each eyeball is another; the teeth are separate polygons. As shown in Figure 6.3(a), the polygon topology for the facial mask is an arbitrary network rather than a regular grid. The polygonal connections, or topology, of each surface remains constant, but the three-dimensional position of each vertex can vary according to the parameter values, eye orientation, and face orientation. As the vertex positions change, the polygonal surfaces flex and stretch, allowing the face to change shape.

This topology is the result of trial-and-error experience. It contains about 300 polygons defined by about 400 vertices. The polygons are sized and positioned to match the features of the face. There are many small polygons in areas of high curvature and fewer, larger polygons in the flatter regions.

Skin Creases

Skin creases are a way of adding detail to the facial model without adding polygons. The skin creases are specified in the input data and are not directly controlled by the parameters. Skin creases are generated by controlling the way vertex normals are calculated at the desired skin crease locations. Normals on one side of the crease are computed independently of the normals on the other side of the crease. These separate normals cause a shading discontinuity along the crease. The crease vertices are shown in Figure 6.3(a) as small circles.

Single Topology Assumption

A basic assumption underlying the parameterized face model is that a single facial topology can be used. If the facial topology remains fixed, manipulating the face only involves manipulating the vertex positions.

From earlier work [Par72] it was known that a fixed topology would allow a specific face to change expression. To determine if a single sufficiently flexible topology could reasonably model different faces, ten different faces were digitized using the technique described in Section 3.6. All ten data sets used the single polygonal topology shown in Figure 6.3(a).

This topology was first applied to a plastic model of the head. This model, shown in Figure 6.3(b), served as a storage device for the topology. The plastic model was used a guide each time the topology was applied to a real face, which assured that the topology would be identical from face to face.

Data from the ten faces were used to create an animation that showed transitions from face to face. This animation demonstrated that, at least for the faces used, a single topology would allow representation of many faces and reasonable transitions between faces. Figure 6.4 shows a transition between two of these faces.

6.3.2. Model Data

The parameterized model is based on data measured from the plastic head shown in Figure 6.3(b). Since this head is symmetric, only one side of the face was measured. Except for the eyes, one side of the face is a mirror image of the other side.

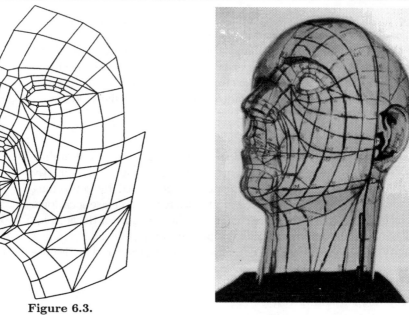

Figure 6.3.
(a) Data collection facial topology. (b) Plastic model topology storage device [Par74].

Figure 6.4.
Transition from one face into another [Par74].

Manipulation techniques were then developed to transform this static data into a dynamic, parametrically controlled facial model. These manipulation techniques included interpolation, translation, rotation, and scaling of the various facial features.

6.3.3. Interpolation Basis

Providing useful shape control is crucial to successful face models and facial animation. Polygonal surfaces allow explicit, direct control of all vertex positions. The polygonal approach also *requires* that each vertex position be explicitly specified. Recognition that interpolation is a good way to specify flexible polygonal surfaces was a key factor in the development of this early face model.

Interpolation generalizes to polygonal surface shapes by applying it to each vertex defining a surface. Each vertex has two or more three-dimensional positions associated with it. Intermediate forms of the surface are achieved by interpolating each vertex between its associated positions. For interpolation to work, the surface topology must be constant. That is, the number of vertices defining the surface and their interconnection must be identical in all forms of the surface.

6.3.4. Operations

For this model, operations, such as interpolation, are applied independently to local regions of the face rather than globally to the entire face. Figure 6.5 gives an overview of the model structure. The parameters affecting the various features are shown. An * indicates the use of interpolation to implement that parameter.

Five operation types are used to determine vertex positions from the parameter values. Although sometimes applied globally to the face, instances of these operations are in most cases applied independently to specific facial regions. These operations are usually order dependent.

- *Procedural* construction is used to model the eyes. The eyeball procedure accepts parameters for eyeball, iris, and pupil size and for the color of the iris, the eye position, and eyeball orientation. It then procedurally generates the polygon descriptors needed for the desired eyes.

- *Interpolation* is used for most regions of the face that change shape. These regions include the forehead, the cheekbones, the neck, and the mouth. Each of these areas is independently interpolated between defined extreme shapes and associated with a parameter value. For a given vertex in one of these regions, two extreme positions are defined. Parameter values control interpolation between the extreme positions.

- *Rotation* is used to open the mouth by rotating the lower portion of the face around a jaw pivot axis. The effect of this rotation is tapered from the lower jaw up to the middle of the cheeks.

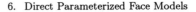

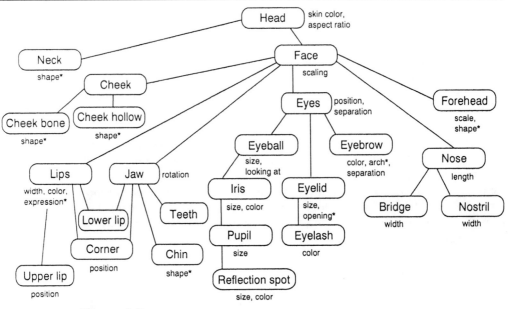

Figure 6.5.
Structure of the parameterized model [Par74].

- *Scaling* controls the relative size and placement of facial features. For example, the chin's prominence and the widths of the nose, jaw, and mouth are controlled by scaling. The scale factors are applied only to vertices within specified regions of the face.

- *Position Offsets* control the length of the nose, the corners of the mouth, and the raising of the upper lip. Position offsets move collections or regions of vertices as a group. The effect of some offset operations is tapered to blend into surrounding regions.

6.3.5. Eyes

The eyes are arguably the most important part of a facial model. Walt Disney once commented that the audience watches the eyes, and that is where time and money must be spent if the character is to be convincing.

The initial step in developing this model was the creation of realistic eyes. This development was done in two steps: first the eyeballs and then the eyelid mechanism.

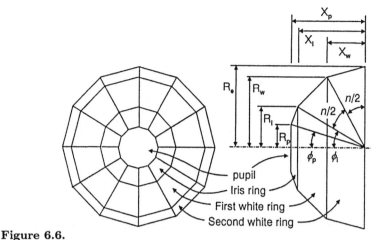

Figure 6.6.
Construction of the eyeball [Par74].

The Eyeball Model

The eyeballs are modeled as partial spheres. The eyeball sphere is created using concentric bands. The center band forms the pupil, while several surrounding bands are used to model the iris. The outer bands form the white of the eye. Several parameters are devoted to controlling the size and spacing of the pupil and iris bands as well as the iris colors.

The eyeballs are created by a procedure called for each eyeball instance. This procedure models the eyeball as a polygonal approximation to a hemisphere as shown in Figure 6.6. This hemisphere consisted of a 12-sided pupil polygon surrounded by three rings of 12 quadrilaterals each. The first of these rings forms the iris while the other two form the white of the eye. The decision to use 12 polygons per ring was a compromise between eyeball complexity and the desire for the pupil and iris to appear nearly circular.

The following relationships are used in the construction of the eyeballs.

$$\phi_i = sin^{-1}(R_i/R_e)$$

$$\phi_p = sin^{-1}(R_p/R_e)$$

$$n = \pi/2 - \phi_i$$

$$R_w = R_e sin(\phi_i + n/2)$$

$$X_w = R_e cos(\phi_i + n/2)$$

$$X_i = \sqrt{R_e^2 + R_i^2}$$

$$X_p = \sqrt{R_e^2 + R_p^2}$$

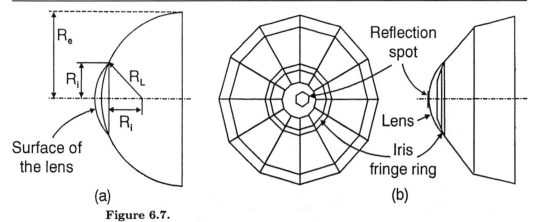

Figure 6.7.
(a) The eyeball lens. (b) The reflection spot and the iris fringe [Par74].

where R_e is the radius of the eyeball, R_i is the radius of the iris, and R_p is the radius of the pupil.

To achieve more realistic eyes, a reflection of the light source was included on each eye. Eye reflections are almost always visible over some portion of the pupil or iris. These visible reflections are due to the fact that the eyeball is not really spherical, but has a smaller partial sphere, the lens, superimposed on it as shown in Figure 6.7(a). R_L is the radius of the lens. The reflection spot is modeled as a six-sided polygon tangent to the surface of the eye lens and is free to move over the lens surface as shown in Figure 6.7(b). The exact positions of the reflection spots depend on the position and orientation of the eyes within the head, the location of the light source, and the location of the viewer relative to the head.

Further realism was obtained by adding an additional ring of polygons to each iris. This ring was used to add a color fringe around the iris as shown in Figure 6.7(b). Figure 6.8(a) shows a rendering of the eyeballs produced by the eyeball procedure.

6.3.6. The Eye Tracking Algorithm

Real eyes have the ability to look at or track objects in their environment. An eye tracking capability is included in this model. Like real eyes, the left and right eye track independently. The orientation angles of each eye depend on the position being looked at and the position of the eyes within the head.

The eyeballs generated by the procedure are centered at the origin of the eye coordinate system with the X axis passing through the center of the pupil. The desired orientation angles are those that will rotate each eyeball so that it will be looking in the desired direction when positioned in the face.

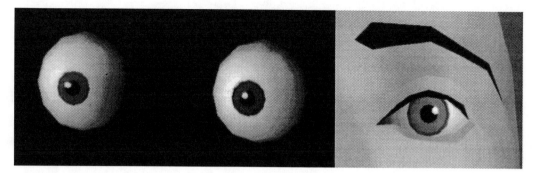

Figure 6.8.
(a) The eyeballs with iris fringes and reflection spots. (b) Eyeball
positioned within the face [Par74].

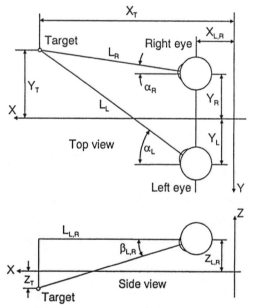

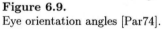

Figure 6.9.
Eye orientation angles [Par74].

Referring to Figure 6.9 we see that each eye has two orientation angles, α
and β. These angles are computed independently for each eye. The following
equations are used to determine these angles.

$$\alpha_R = arctan((Y_T - Y_R)/(X_T - X_R))$$
$$\alpha_L = arctan((Y_T - Y_L)/(X_T - X_L))$$

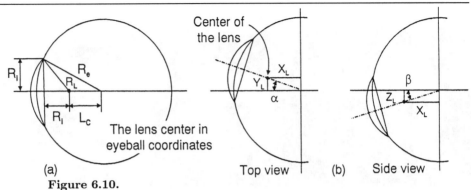

Figure 6.10.
(a) The lens center in eyeball coordinates. (b) The rotated lens center
[Par74].

$$\beta_R = arctan((Z_R - Z_T)/L_R)$$

$$\beta_L = arctan((Z_L - Z_T)/L_L)$$

where

$$L_R = \sqrt{((Y_T - Y_R)^2 + (X_T - X_R)^2)}$$

$$L_L = \sqrt{((Y_T - Y_L)^2 + (X_T - X_L)^2)}$$

6.3.7. The Eye Reflection Spot Algorithm

The first step in positioning the reflection spots is to determine the position
of the center of the lens sphere in the eyeball coordinate system. As shown
in Figure 6.10(a), we see that the center of the lens is displaced a distance
L_c along the X axis of the eyeball, where

$$L_c = \sqrt{(R_e^2 - R_i^2)} - R_i.$$

When the eyeball is rotated by the α and β angles computed above, the
center of the lens will be located at the position X_L, Y_L, Z_L in the eyeball
coordinate system as shown in Figure 6.10(b).

$$Z_L = L_c sin(-\beta)$$

$$Y_L = L_c cos(-\beta)sin(\alpha)$$

$$X_L = L_c cos(-\beta)cos(\alpha)$$

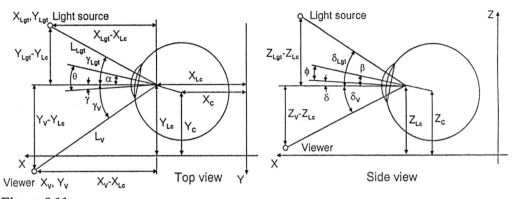

Figure 6.11.
Reflection spot orientation angles [Par74].

When the reflection spot polygon is generated by the eyeball procedure, it is centered on and perpendicular to the X axis of the eye. It is located a distance R_L from the center of the eye along the X axis. The angles θ and ϕ are used to rotate the reflection spot about the center of the eye lens into its proper orientation. See Figure 6.11.

$$\gamma_{Lgt} = arctan((y_{Lgt} - y_{Lc})/(x_{Lgt} - x_{Lc}))$$

$$\gamma_v = arctan((y_v - y_{Lc})/(x_v - x_{Lc}))$$

$$\gamma = (\gamma_{Lgt} + \gamma_v)/2$$

$$\theta = \gamma - \alpha$$

$$L_{Lgt} = \sqrt{((y_{Lgt} - y_{Lc})^2 + (x_{Lgt} - x_{Lc})^2)}$$

$$L_v = \sqrt{((y_v - y_{Lc})^2 + (x_v - x_{Lc})^2)}$$

$$\delta_{Lgt} = arctan((z_{Lc} - z_{Lgt})/L_{Lgt})$$

$$\delta_v = arctan((z_{Lc} - z_v)/L_v)$$

$$\delta = (\delta_{Lgt} + \delta_v)/2$$

$$\phi = \delta - \beta$$

In this coordinate system, angles are positive in the counterclockwise sense.

The generated reflection spot is rotated by θ and then by ϕ about the center of the eye. It is then displaced along the X axis of the eye by the distance L_c. Expressed in terms of transformation matrices this is:

$$\mid T_{spot} \mid = \mid T_\theta \parallel T_\phi \parallel T_{L_c} \mid .$$

Next the reflection spot and the rest of the eye are rotated about the center of the eye by α and then by β:

$$\mid T_{orient} \mid = \mid T_\alpha \parallel T_\beta \mid .$$

Finally the entire eye is displaced by x_c, y_c, z_c to assume its proper position in the face:

$$\mid T_{eye} \mid = \mid T_{orient} \parallel T_{face} \mid .$$

The reflection spot is transformed by T_{spot} and then by T_{eye}. The rest of the eye is transformed only by T_{eye}.

6.3.8.   Eyelids

The eyes are installed by generating eyeballs of the size needed and then positioning them in the head coordinate system. Initially the eyelids were fit over the eyeballs using a *spherical mapping* technique.

The eyelids are fit by computing the spherical coordinates (origin at the center of each eyeball) of the eyelid polygon vertices. The spherical radius coordinate of each eyelid vertex is then adjusted to be slightly larger than the radius of the eyeball. The vertex positions are then converted back into Cartesian coordinates for display.

This initial approach did not allow the eyelids to open and close — the eyelids remained in the position defined by the fit eyelid polygons. The ability to open and close the eyelids was implemented by combining a variation of the spherical mapping technique with linear interpolation.

Figure 6.12 shows the eyelid polygon structure used. The vertices enclosed by the dashed line are the ones involved in opening and closing the eyelid. These vertices are defined in only two dimensions, width and height. The third dimension is obtained by projecting the vertices back onto a sphere slightly larger than and centered on the eyeball.

The edges of the eyelids are modeled as a thin strip of polygons whose inner vertices are projected back onto a slightly smaller sphere.

Using two sets of two-dimensional data values, one for wide open eyes and one for closed eyes, intermediate eyelid openings can be interpolated. Projecting the interpolated two-dimensional vertices back onto the eyelid sphere produces the desired eyelid. The parameter controlling the eyelid opening is

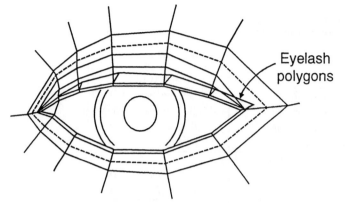

Figure 6.12.
Two-dimensional eyelid topology [Par74].

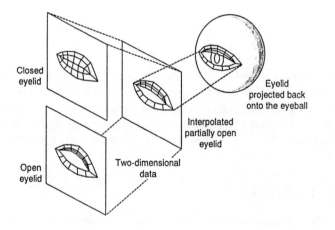
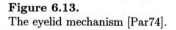

Figure 6.13.
The eyelid mechanism [Par74].

the one controlling the two-dimensional interpolation. This process is analogous to the real eyelid mechanism where two membranes are stretched across a spherical surface. This procedure is illustrated in Figure 6.13. The result of fitting the eyeballs into the face is shown in Figure 6.8(b).

Table 6.1.
Eye Region Parameters.

Parameter	Value Range
Eyebrow Arch	$0.0 \leq value \leq 1.0$
Eyebrow Separation	$-25.0 \leq value \leq 25.0$
Eyebrow Opening	$0.0 \leq value \leq 1.0$
Eyeball Size	$50.0 \leq value \leq 100.0$
(fraction of eyeball size)	
Iris Size	$0.0 \leq value \leq 1.0$
Reflection Spot Size	$0.0 \leq value \leq 1.0$
(fraction of iris size)	
Iris Fringe Size	$0.0 \leq value \leq 1.0$
Pupil Size	$0.0 \leq value \leq 1.0$
Iris Color	any valid color
Iris Fringe Color	any valid color
Reflection Spot Color	any valid color

Eyelashes

The eyelashes are modeled as a set of five polygons as shown in Figure 6.12. These polygons are included as part of the upper eyelid. Like the eyelid polygons, they are only defined in two dimensions. The inner vertices of the eyelashes are projected back onto the same sphere as the main eyelid vertices. However, the outer eyelash vertices are projected onto larger spherical surfaces.

6.3.9.   Eyebrows

The dynamic expression properties of the eyebrows are implemented using a combination of interpolation and translation. Two sets of shape data for the eyebrow vertices are specified. The eyebrows are varied from high to low arch by interpolating between these two data sets. An additional parameter uses translation to vary the separation of the eyebrows across the bridge of the nose.

6.3.10.   Eye Region Parameters

The following table lists the parameters that affect the eye region of the face model. Figure 6.14 shows the effect of varying only two of these parameters: eyelid opening and eyebrow arch.

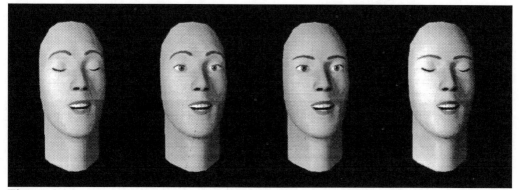

Figure 6.14.
Effect of eyebrow arch and eyelid opening parameters [Par74].

6.3.11. Mouth and Jaw

The mouth is opened by rotating the vertices of the lower part of the face about a jaw pivot axis. Jaw rotation is necessary for the mouth to assume its various speech and expression postures. This rotation is tapered. The vertices along the jaw are rotated by the full amount specified in the rotation parameter, but the rotation applied to those points above the jaw and below the mouth tapers so that the amount of rotation gradually diminishes for points higher in the face. While the lower lip rotates, the upper lip does not; therefore the mouth opens.

The vertices located between the dashed lines in Figure 6.15 are the vertices affected by jaw rotation. The jaw axis of rotation is parallel to the Y axis and passes through the indicated jaw pivot point. The lower lip, lower teeth, and the corner of the mouth rotate with the jaw. Positive jaw rotation has the effect of opening the mouth.

The center points of the lower lip are rotated with the jaw. Other points along the lower lip are rotated by amounts that taper toward the corners of the mouth. Vertices closer to the corners rotate by smaller amounts. The corners of the mouth rotate by one-third the jaw rotation. This scheme gives a natural oval-looking mouth.

Another parameter allows the upper lip to be raised and lowered. The effect of this translation is tapered from the center of the lip to the corners of the mouth. The center vertices receive the full effect, while the corner vertices are not affected.

The mouth can vary in shape by interpolating between two expression data sets. These data sets represent two expression extremes such as *smile* and *neutral.*

The model has several additional mouth manipulation parameters. A scaling factor is used to control the width of the mouth. A translation

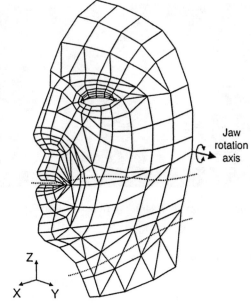

Figure 6.15.
Vertices affected by jaw rotation [Par74].

parameter allows the lips to move forward away from the teeth. Another parameter controls the thickness of the lips at the corner of the mouth. Three translation parameters allow the corners of the mouth to move in all three dimensions. A translation parameter is used to tuck the lower lip up under the front teeth — the position assumed by the mouth when forming the f and v sounds. The teeth are modeled as 32 four-sided polygons arranged along an approximation to the dental arch.

6.3.12. Mouth Region Parameters

The following table lists the parameters affecting the mouth region of the face model. Figure 6.16 show the effects obtained using three of these parameters: jaw rotation, upper-lip position, and mouth expression.

6.3.13. Conformation Parameters

A set of parameters is included in the model that allow the face to change in conformation. Conformation is used here to mean those features of the face that vary from one individual to another as opposed to features that change from expression to expression.

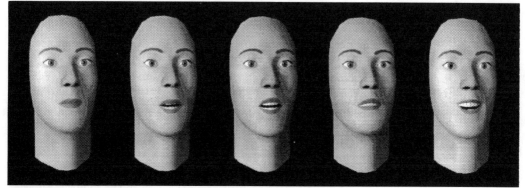

Figure 6.16.
Effect of jaw rotation, upper-lip position, and mouth expression [Par74].

Although the following parameterization is clearly not complete, it does allow a wide variety of facial conformations within the implied limits. These parameters are implemented by means of interpolation, scaling, or translation.

Parameters Implemented by Interpolation

The shape of the chin and neck are changed using interpolation. The forehead shape can be varied from sloping to bulging. The cheekbone can range from not noticeable to very pronounced. The hollow of the cheek can change from convex to concave.

Table 6.2.
Mouth Region Parameters.

Parameter	Value range
Jaw Rotation	$0.0 \leq value \leq 20.0$
Mouth Width	$0.5 \leq value \leq 1.5$
Mouth Expression	$0.0 \leq value \leq 1.0$
Upper-Lip Position	$0.0 \leq value \leq 20.0$
Forward Lip Offset	$0.0 \leq value \leq 30.0$
Mouth Corner Width	$0.0 \leq value \leq 25.0$
X Corner Displacement	$-25.0 \leq value \leq 25.0$
Y Corner Displacement	$-25.0 \leq value \leq 25.0$
Z Corner Displacement	$-25.0 \leq value \leq 25.0$
"f" Tuck	$-20.0 \leq value \leq 0.0$

Parameters Implemented by Scaling

Three parameters determine the overall *aspect ratio* of the face and head by scaling the entire head in each of the three dimensions.

Two parameters are used to control the width and height of the eyelids. Varying the values of these parameters controls the shape and size of the eyelids.

The nose is affected by two scaling parameters. One controls the width of the bridge of the nose. The other determines the width of the lower portion of the nose including the nostrils.

Three scale parameters are used to control the vertical proportions of the face. One parameter scales the region from the chin to the mouth. Another parameter scales the region from the chin to the eyes. The third parameter scales the region above the eyes.

Additional parameters scale the width of the cheeks and the width of the jaw. The effect of the jaw scaling is tapered. The maximum effect is applied to the lower forward point of the jaw. The scaling effect diminishes to zero at the upper rear of the jaw.

Parameters Implemented by Translation

It is possible to move the chin up and down as well as forward and back in relation to the rest of the face. The lower portion of the nose can be moved forward, backward, up, or down. The eyebrows also may be displaced up or down.

Table 6.3 lists the conformation parameters and their value ranges. Figure 6.17 illustrates the effect of several conformation parameters.

Additional Parameters

A number of additional parameters affect the face or its environment. These parameters include the position of the eyeballs within the head, where the modeled eyes are looking, where the light source is located, where the viewer is located and where she is looking. Other parameters control the field of view, the colors of facial features, and the shading model.

6.3.14. Parameter Ordering

Several regions of the face are affected by many parameters. The results of applying the parameter controlled operations are dependent on the order in which the operations are performed. The ordering depends on the specific implementation of a given parameterized model. This ordering is essentially arbitrary. In this particular model the parameter operations are applied in the order listed below.

Table 6.3.
Conformation Parameters.

Parameters	Value Range
Interpolation Forehead Cheekbone Cheek Hollow Chin Shape Neck Shape	$0.0 \leq value \leq 1.0$
Scaling Head X Scale Head Y Scale Head Z Scale Chin-to-Mouth Chin-to-Eye Eye-to-Forehead Eyelid X Scale Eyelid Z Scale Jaw Width Cheek Width Nose Bridge Width Nose Nostril Width	$0.5 \leq value \leq 1.5$
Translation Chin X Offset Chin Z Offset End-of-Nose X Offset End-of-Nose Z Offset Eyebrow Z Offset	$-50.0 \leq value \leq 50.0$

6.4. Animation Using the Parameterized Model

A parameterized model allows the animator to create facial images by simply specifying the appropriate parameter values. Animation is reduced to varying the parameter values over time. A sequence of images can be created by specifying the parameter values for each image in the desired animation sequence.

The difficult part of the task is to determine how the values must change over time to achieve a desired effect. The solution usually involves varying several parameter values simultaneously over any given time period.

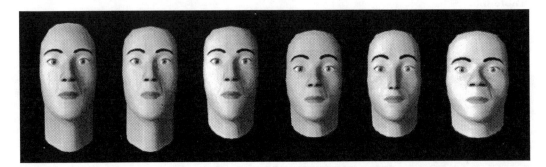

Figure 6.17.
The effect of several conformation parameters: (a) the initial face;
(b) changed forehead shape; (c) changed neck shape and jaw scale;
(d) changed chin-to-mouth scale, changed chin-to-eye scale, and
increased vertical scale; (e) end of the nose moved down, horizontal scale
decreased, and the cheekbones slightly more prominent; (f) increased
horizontal scale, raised and widened end of nose, narrowed bridge of
nose, lowered eyebrows, more prominent cheekbones, and more concave
cheek hollows [Par74].

6.4.1. Key Framing in Parameter Space

Key framing can be applied to the parameter values required to specify the
face poses rather than directly to the face poses. For each parameter, a
timed set of values is specified. At each frame of the animation sequence, a
function is evaluated for each parameter. This function is usually a simple
interpolation based on the time-tagged key parameter values.

A control program was developed to create the parameter commands required for each frame of an animation sequence. Inputs to this program
consist of a set of parameter specifications. Each specification consists of
the parameter ID, the frame range, the initial parameter value, the ending
parameter value, and the interpolation function to be used. The interpolation could be linear or could use an ease-in, ease-out, or both an ease-in and
ease-out function.

The control program stores each parameter specification and then searches
this data for each frame of the animation. If the current frame is within the
frame range of a specification, then the appropriate parameter command is
computed and output to the facial model. The parameter value is computed
based on the current frame, the frame range of the parameter specification,
the parameter value range, and the specified interpolation function.

Table 6.4.
Parameter Operation Ordering.

```
Scale the head
Interpolate the forehead shape
Fit the eyelid
Interpolate the cheekbone shape
Interpolate the cheek hollow shape
Interpolate the chin shape
Interpolate neck shape
Move the chin
Interpolate the mouth expression shape
Move the mouth forward
Scale the mouth width
Raise the upper lip
Tuck the lower lip
Chin-to-mouth scaling
Chin-to-eye scaling
Eye-to-forehead scaling
Rotate the jaw
Interpolate eyebrow shape
Move the eyebrows
Move the end of the nose
Scale the end of the nose
Scale the bridge of the nose
Move the corner of the mouth
Scale jaw width
Scale cheek width
```

6.4.2. Speech Animation

One of the goals for this model was to support speech animation. Speech animation is achieved by manipulating the facial parameters so that the facial expression and lip motions match a spoken soundtrack. Madsen [Mad69] indicates that the capabilities listed below are required for lip animation (see Chapter 8 for a detailed treatment of speech animation).

- Open lips for the open vowels — a, e, and i.

- Closed lips for the accent consonants — p, b, and m.

- An oval mouth for u, o, and w.

- Tucking the lower lip under the front teeth for f and v.

Table 6.5.

Lip Animation Parameters
Jaw Rotation
Upper Lip Position
Mouth Width

Expression Parameters
Mouth Expression
Eyebrow Arch
Eyebrow Separation
Eyelid Opening
Pupil Size
Eye Tracking

- The ability to move between these lip positions as required.

A number of the parameters described in the previous sections are used for speech animation. These parameters include jaw rotation, mouth width, lower-lip tuck, upper-lip raising, moving lips forward from the teeth, and manipulation of the corner of the mouth. Manipulation of the eyebrows, eyelids, and the mouth expression are used in conjunction with the speech parameters to convey emphasis and emotion.

Fewer than ten parameters are needed to do a reasonable job of speech animation. The parameters found most effective for facial expression and speech animation are listed below.

6.5. Parameterized Model Extensions

DiPaola, Pearce, and Cohen have each created extended direct parameterized models based on the original Parke model. These extensions are discussed in this section. Possible future extensions are also presented.

6.5.1. DiPaola Extensions

DiPaola created a second generation parameterized model [DiP89] [DiP91] based on the early model described above. This implementation is sometimes referred to as the Facial Animation System (FAS). It was designed to integrate with a production animation system.

This model was extended to include about 80 parameters for controlling the face, head, and facial hair. Like the earlier model, the operations controlled by the parameters include interpolation, translation, rotation, and scaling applied to particular subregions of the face or head. These operations usually taper their effect on vertices near the subregion boundaries. More of the parameters in this model control procedural operations than in the earlier model. The development of the parameter operations was based primarily on visual results.

Broader Range of Facial Types

One of the main attributes of this extended system is its ability to specify and animate a wider range of facial types. The original model implemented parameters that applied only to realistic human faces and to realistic facial movements. This extended system deals with faces outside the range of realistic human conformation. It includes conformation parameters that allow stylized humanoid faces, caricatures, and cartoon-like faces as well as realistic faces.

Parameters controlling localized deformation functions, such as those described in Section 3.10.4, are examples of the parameter controlled procedural operations used to extend the range of facial types.

Global and local squash and stretch parameters have been added to the model. The squash and stretch parameters, patterned after squash and stretch in conventional animation, preserve the volume of the face and head.

If an animator chose to scale the eyes to half the size of the head, the eye scale parameters would also have to influence neighboring regions, such as the forehead and the cheek regions. This capability is supported by this model. Broadening other parameters in this way adds additional flexibility. It also adds algorithmic complexity and longer computation times.

Since different facial types are just extreme variations in facial conformation parameters, different facial types can morph into each other by simply interpolating the conformation parameter values.

Asymmetry

Natural looking faces need to be asymmetrical. If the topology of the facial model is asymmetric the model will continue to be asymmetric even when symmetric expression parameters are applied to it. However, asymmetric expression parameters are also desired.

Most expression parameters for this model are implemented as dual parameters, with both left and right components. The left component affects the left side of the face while the right component affects the right side of the face. These components can also be used in a dual mode where both are changed as one symmetric parameter. This flexibility allows the animator a great deal of control.

Additional Expression Parameters

Puffed upper cheeks were added as a necessary companion to closed or
squinted eyes. Flared nostrils were added as a complement to many mouth
positions including the angry mouth expression. Neck rotations were added
to allow appropriate head gestures.

Eyes

The eyes are capable of being scaled in all directions, producing, among other
shapes, large elongated oval eyeballs. For this distortion to work, the neighboring facial areas must accommodate as required. The skin surrounding the
eyeballs must stretch appropriately, and the eyelids must close naturally, no
matter how the shape of the eyes is exaggerated. DiPaola's model is designed
so that most of these compensations occur automatically. Therefore specific
accommodation parameters are not needed and the eye-control parameters
need only include eyeball scales, eyelid positions, and eyeball rotations.

The eyeball is modeled as a high resolution sphere. The iris and pupil
are modeled with a second smaller sphere that intersects the larger eyeball
sphere. This added curvature closely approximates the curvature of the real
human eye. With this complex curvature, reflections are rendered over the
iris most of the time.

Texture mapping was used to define the iris and pupil area. This texture
was derived from a photograph of an actual eye. The texture used must have
any specular reflections removed by retouching or by mirroring one-half or
one-quarter of the scanned iris image.

Complete Heads

The early parameterized models included only the face and the front of the
neck. This extended model is more complete including the ears, the back of
the head, and facial hair.

Ears

Ears are very individual and important in representing individual likeness.
They are also difficult to model. Ears have complex shapes with higher
surface curvature than most other regions of the head. To model them well
requires a large number of polygons or complex bicubic surfaces with many
control points.

The amount of data needed to represent detailed ear curvature can be
large and may be out of proportion to the importance of the ears in the
overall model. Overly detailed ears may actually draw attention away from
the rest of the face.

The obvious solution of lowering the modeled detail of the ears can result in overly simplified, very unnatural ears. The compromise used in this model is to model the ears with a relatively low resolution polygonal surface. Skin creases corresponding to curvature boundaries are then used to emphasize ear surface curvature.

Facial Hair

Facial hair includes the eyebrows and a mustache or beard if present. The facial hair is modeled with *hair globs*. These hair globs are small irregularly shaped polygonal surfaces. The shapes of these surfaces are intended to mimic small tufts of hair. The hair globs are procedurally positioned and automatically aligned to the topology of the face. The hair flexes and moves with the face as it is animated.

Paths are defined on the face where the hair is to be located. These paths pass through points tied to the topology of the face. The type of hair glob and the number of globs for each path are specified. The hair globs are automatically positioned and aligned along the defined paths. Additional parameters are implemented to animate the hair regions independent of the face motions.

Eyebrows

Eyebrows are extremely expressive, capable of achieving a very wide range of positions. In the case of cartoons and caricatures, the variety of eyebrow shapes is almost limitless.

The eyebrows are created using hair globs. Several parameters are used to create the overall eyebrow shapes by controlling a number of facial points. A cubic spline is passed through these points defining a smooth eyebrow shape. Hair globs of the necessary size and orientation are positioned at intervals along this shape.

Matching Facial Animation with Body Animation

This facial model was combined with a full body model animated on a standard key-frame system. The body model was first animated with a dummy place holder head rather than the detailed facial model. To coordinate the facial animation with the completed body animation, the hierarchical head transformation information from the body animation was read into the facial animation system. This action made it possible to transform the face into the proper positions and orientations needed to match the body animation.

Neck

In addition to rotation parameters, the neck has parameters controlling its length and width. These parameters aid in attaching the face to an independent body model.

Facial-Expression Libraries

The use of facial-expression libraries is supported by this model, which allows reuse of previous expression descriptions and animation sequences.

The system is capable of saving and retrieving facial information to and from library entries. Library entries are simply parameter value sets that can be applied to the current face or animation sequence. A library entry may contain any or all of the facial parameters. The animator may select a library entry and edit it for a specific situation.

Library entries might contain conformation parameter values used to specify particular facial types or specific characters. The entries might also be used to specify particular expression poses such as angry, surprised, or happy. The entries could also be used to store parameter values for the various phoneme postures.

Interactive Control and Real-Time Playback

This facial model incorporates interactive control and real-time playback much like a *track-based* key-frame animation system. As with a key-frame animation system, the animator can create key poses, choose interpolation schemes, edit parameter value tracks, and preview animation in real time. The major difference for the facial system is that parameter values rather than hierarchical transformations are saved, interpolated, and applied to the model.

In addition to using entire key poses or individual parameter tracks, facial *region* tracks can be used. Region tracks are composed of parameter groups for specific facial regions.

With the region tracks, it is possible to animate the various facial regions separately. For example, an eye blinking sequence can be duplicated at various points of the animation without affecting other regions. The eye blinking instances could be scaled in time as necessary to fit the action.

6.5.2. Pearce Extensions

Pearce [PWWH86] reimplemented and extended the original model to directly support phoneme-based speech animation. The main extension was to provide phoneme-based control, which was done by mapping phoneme specifications into parameter value sets. This mapping also included time duration information. Transitions between sequential phonemes therefore included not only the parameter values for each phoneme but also information about how the parameter values changed over time during the transition.

These transitions are specified using nonlinear interpolation. The transition timing between phonemes is dependent on the specific phoneme sequence.

6.5.3. Cohen Extensions

To support work in *visible speech* [CM90] [CM93] Cohen implemented a number of extensions to the original parameterized model. These extensions included additional lip and tongue parameters, the use of image texture mapping, the use of skin transparency, and implementation on a high performance workstation.

Additional Lip and Tongue Parameters

To allow better speech articulation, four additional lip control parameters were added to the model. These are:

- Raise the lower lip.

- "Roll" the lower lip.

- Adjust lip thickness.

- Jaw thrust — translate the jaw forward or backward.

Two of the original lip parameters were modified to have more global effects. Raising the upper lip also raises some of the facial area above the lip. When the lips protrude, the cheeks are pulled inward.

Since the tongue is important for representing detailed speech articulation, a simplified tongue was added along with four tongue shape and position control parameters. This tongue was modeled as a polygonal mesh surface. The tongue control parameters are:

- Tongue length.

- Tongue width.

- Tongue thickness.

- Tongue angle.

Cohen briefly discusses the implementation of a more complex and detailed tongue model controlled by 13 parameters. However, manipulation of this complex tongue model was too slow for real-time speech representation.

Image Mapping

The implementation was extended to support the mapping of two-dimensional facial images onto the polygonal surface of the face. These images are typically obtained from video sequences. The images are scaled and centered to match the face model. In addition, the face shape conformation parameters are adjusted to conform to the shape of the facial images.

Once the image is scaled and centered and the face conformation is adjusted to achieve the best match between the image and face surface shape, the image is *attached* to the polygonal surface. The mapped image then moves with the parameter-controlled facial-surface articulations.

Skin Transparency

An additional parameter was used to control the transparency of the polygons representing the skin of the face. Transparency makes visible the speech articulations inside the mouth.

Interactive Parameter Control

Implementation on a high performance graphics workstation allows real-time animation and interactive control of the facial parameters. A menu of interactive *sliders*, one for each parameter, was added, allowing complete control of the facial postures.

6.5.4.   Future Extensions

Several possible future extensions to direct parameterized models are discussed below.

Use of Parametric Surfaces

A lesson learned from the early parameterized models is that the polygon data density for the facial surfaces was too sparse. Higher polygon density is needed to represent the subtle shape variations associated with subtle expression and conformation changes. The data density certainly needs to be increased in the major expressive areas of the face, the eyes, and the mouth.

The use of parametric surfaces, such as bicubic surfaces, presents an attractive alternative to the polygonal approach. With such representations, the facial control parameters would manipulate surface control points rather than the surfaces directly.

Texturing

Texture mapping is a very effective way to increase perceived image quality and detail. Texturing has been used occasionally in facial animations. Most often it has been used to animate mouth detail and to provide more detailed eyes. Williams [Wil90b] has described an approach to facial animation based almost entirely on texture mapping. Parameterized facial models could certainly benefit from well-integrated texture mapping techniques.

Animation Control

For any animation model, the question of control interfaces or control handles for the animator is very important. The integration of facial models into complete character animation systems and the development of better facial animation interfaces would be very useful extensions.

Better Parameterizations

The goal is to provide natural and intuitive parameters that allow a wide range of conformation and expression control and flexibility.

Better parameter sets are needed. This need is particularly true for the conformation parameters, but it is also true for the expression parameters.

One area of improvement might be the more effective use of parameter-controlled procedural construction and manipulation of facial features.

Another possibility would be to include automatic *secondary actions* in the model. This addition could possibly reduce the size and complexity of the parameter set for a given level of capability. The effect of each parameter would be extended to support any secondary actions associated with its main function.

Higher Level Direct Parameterizations

Parameters for the direct models have been specified at a fairly low level such as width of mouth, upper-lip position, etc. There is a need for parameterizations specified at higher levels of abstraction. Examples of these higher level parameters might be age, ethnic type, speech phonemes, etc. These new parameters would allow facial conformation and animation control at a much higher level.

The high-level parameterizations might be built on top of existing or future lower level parameterizations. They could be implemented using groups of operations similar to those used in the current low-level parameterized models.

At an even higher level would be parameterizations more like the *language* used by directors in guiding live actors. These parameters might include controlling overall expression, moods, and attitudes.

Nonhumanoid Faces

Facial models in general and parameterized models in particular have generally been limited to humanoid faces. However, conformation parameters might be extended to include nonhumanoid faces such as primates. They might be extended to include animal faces and even fanciful or alien creature faces.

7

Skin and Muscle-Based Facial Animation

The detailed anatomy of the head and face is a complex assembly of bones, cartilage, muscle, nerves, blood vessels, glands, fatty tissue, connective tissue, skin, and hair. To date no facial animation, based on this level of anatomical detail, has been developed. However, it is possible to reduce the complexity of the anatomy and mechanical properties to construct a simple animated model of the face. These models manipulate facial expression based on the physical characteristics of facial muscle and skin.

Recently, simulating skin tissue dynamics has received attention, particularly in surgical planning, where it is desirable to visualize the effects of surgery before the actual operation. Some of these techniques have been applied to facial animation to enhance the dynamic behavior of facial models, in particular skin tissue deformations, that produce subtle deformations such as furrowing. Therefore, this chapter focuses on some of the techniques that people have addressed to date.

7.1. The Mechanics of Facial Tissue

A description of facial tissue was described in Chapter 2, so this chapter focuses on the mechanics of facial tissue. Skin tissue deformation under

223

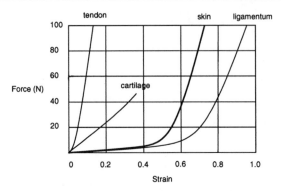

Figure 7.1.
Force-deformation relations for a selection of excised human tissues
tested in uniaxial tension.

applied loads has been the subject of a number of biomedical investigations [RVK78, KGEB75, Har77, Wri77, Lar86]. These investigations adopt
an engineering point of view, similar to that taken by researchers in material
science and continuum mechanics [Atk80]. What is evident from the experiments on living tissue is that there is a much greater complexity displayed
than that exhibited on structural materials for construction and manufac-
turing.

As a unit, soft tissue is *viscoelastic* in its responses to *stress*, the force of
load, and *strain*, the deformation or stretch. The result is that it has properties of both an elastic solid and a viscous liquid. The elastic nature of soft
tissue refers to its storage of energy and tendency to return to its rest shape
when the load is removed. The relationship between load and deformation
is nonlinear, even in the range of deformations commonly encountered in
living subjects. Figure 7.1 illustrates the relationship between stresses and
strains in soft tissue under typical uniaxial tension.

Tissue is viscous such that the internal forces generated due to a deformation is dependent not only on the amount of deformation but also on the rate
of deformation. The viscoelastic nature of soft tissue displays additionally
the following phenomena:

- **Hysteresis** refers to a change in the response of the material under
  cyclic loading and unloading as illustrated in Figure 7.2.

- **Stress relaxation** is the reduction in the force opposing a deformation
  held constant in time.

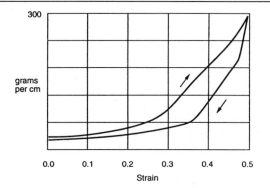

Figure 7.2.
Loading versus unloading force elongation curves of a skin patch. The
separation of the two curves illustrates a hysteresis effect.

- **Creep** is the increase in strain over time in a material under the influence of a constant load.

- **Preconditioning**, is when repeated applications of the same load result in different deformation responses.

The mechanical properties of skin are the result of the interaction of two
cellular bases: elastin and collagen. The behavior of elastin, which is a
major component of blood vessels, is very similar to an ideal rubber with an
essentially linear stress/strain response over a wide range of deformations.
Collagen, the material of tendons, has a much stronger stress response to
applied load and has a more limited range of deformation. The low stress
response to small strains may be due to the stretching of elastin, since the
collagen is arranged in a deformable lattice structure. The sudden increase
in stress may be due to the stretching of collagen once it is aligned with
the deformation. The pattern of the collagen lattice is not symmetric and
tends to form contour lines of fibers with common orientation. These lines
correspond to lines of anisotropic deformation of the skin called Langer's
lines [War73] as in Figure 2.17 in Chapter 2.

The fat cells and the ground substance, which are composed mostly of
water, account for the viscous properties of skin. They also account for the
behavior of the tissue under compression, where the collagen lattice on its
own would merely collapse. Instead, since the water in the fat and ground
substance is incompressible, they are forced outward perpendicular to the
line of compression. This phenomenon is called the *Poisson effect*. Extension
of the tissue also causes contraction along the plane, perpendicular to the
line of extension.

The composition of the soft tissue of the face changes with age [GuF65].
In the dermis of a newborn, there is a large proportion of collagen compared

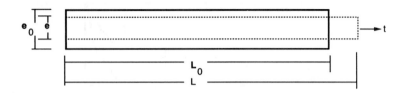

Figure 7.3.
A material of length L_0 elongated to a length L by a force t. The width
changes from e_0 to e.

to the amount of elastin, but this ratio inverts in old age so that elastin
is present in much higher concentrations than collagen. In addition, skin
becomes thinner with age due to the reduction of adipose tissue. Folds form
along lines of the skin adherence and muscle insertion causing characteristic
wrinkle lines.

7.1.1. Biological Solids

When considering a computer model of a biological solid, it is useful to
consider some basic engineering principles. In particular forces are defined
to be applied per unit area and can be related either to the original cross-
sectional area or to the deformed cross-sectional area. A force, or stress,
placed on a material acts in a specific direction and therefore is defined as a
stress vector.

When a material is deformed, the change in length is defined in terms of
strain. Take for example the material illustrated in Figure 7.3. This material
is deformed from an original length L_0 to an elongated state L. A variety of
ratios can then be used to represent this change in length $\lambda = \frac{L}{L_0}$ with the
corresponding strain measures.

- $e = \frac{L-L_0}{L_0}$, $E = \frac{L-L_0}{L}$

- $e = \frac{L^2-L_0^2}{2L^2}$ and $\xi = \frac{L^2-L_0^2}{2L_0^2}$

These strains are all roughly equal for very small deformations but become
different under larger deformations.

A deformable material often is defined as a Hookean elastic solid following
Hooke's law: $\sigma = Ee$, where σ is stress, E is a constant known as Young's
modulus, and e is strain. Hooke's law can be exactly applied to materials
with linear stress/strain relationships. When defining a three-dimensional
solid, multiple elastic constants are required. However, the equations can be
simplified for materials that are isotropic (equal stress produces equal displacement in any direction) rather than anisotropic materials characterized

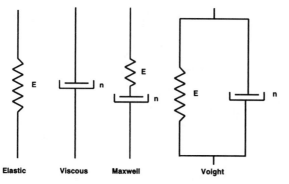

Figure 7.4.
Mechanical models for viscoelastic soft tissue.

by directional variations. When considering a two-dimensional isotropic material, further simplifications can be made. Only two elastic constants need be defined: E or Young's modulus, and v or *Poisson's* ratio, which is the ratio of the contraction of the surface in one direction when it elongates in the other.

Whereas elastic materials can be realized as Hookean solids, liquids can be realized as Newtonian fluids. Liquids traditionally are modeled according to the principles of hydrodynamics where a viscous liquid obeys Newton's law:

$$\sigma = \frac{\eta de}{dt} \tag{7.1}$$

where η is viscosity, e is strain, and t is time.

Many biological materials combine both elastic solid and viscous liquid behavior and subsequently called are viscoelastic. The properties of viscoelastic materials have already been described as hysteresis, stress relaxation, and creep. By using both Hooke and Newtonian laws, models of viscoelastic materials can be simulated. Essentially, these materials are a combination of a linear spring with a Young's modulus E and a dashpot with a viscosity η. As a result the spring creates a deformation proportional to the load, while the dashpot becomes a shock absorber producing a velocity proportional to the load. These two basic components can be combined in a variety of ways to simulate viscoelastic materials [TF88b]. Two simple combinations are the Maxwell and Voight, as illustrated in Figure 7.4, that have been used to describe the effects of muscle and tendons. For example, Hill's [GH24] muscle model, illustrated in Figure 7.5, was developed by the observation of isolated frog muscles.

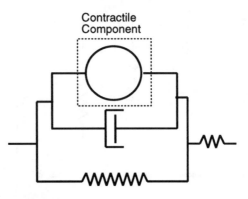

Figure 7.5.
Hill's muscle model consisting of a contractive component and a parallel
viscous unit coupled to additional elastic units.

7.2. The Mechanics of Muscles

Muscles are the principle motivators of facial expression such that when a
muscle contracts, it attempts to draw its attachments together. For facial
muscles this action usually involves drawing the skin towards the point of
skeletal subsurface attachment.

Muscle fibers come in many lengths, sometimes stretching the whole length
of the muscle, and are usually 10 to 100 microns in diameter. The muscle
fibers are composed of still smaller elements called myofibrils that run the
whole length of the fiber. Each myofibril is about 1 to 2 microns thick.
As a result, a single muscle fiber contains hundreds to several thousands of
myofibrils.

Along the longitudinal axis of each myofibril is a repeating pattern of
filaments called *sarcomeres*. The sarcomere is the actual functional unit of
contraction in the muscle. Sarcomeres are short — only about 1 to 2 microns
long — and contract developing tension along their longitudinal axis. It is
this shortening, in series, of many sarcomeres that creates the shortening of
a single muscle fiber; the subsequent overall shortening of a muscle is created
by the contraction of many fibers in parallel.

At the most fundamental level two contractive proteins, actin and myosin,
form the filaments within a sarcomere. In cross section they are packed
hexagonally with six thin myosin filaments surrounding each thick actin
filament. A theory of sliding filament muscle contraction was developed by
Huxley [HN54] in 1954 by the careful observation of isolated frog muscle.
Essentially, he observed that during muscle contraction, the actin filaments
were drawn into the A-bands, between the myosin rods (see Figure 7.6).

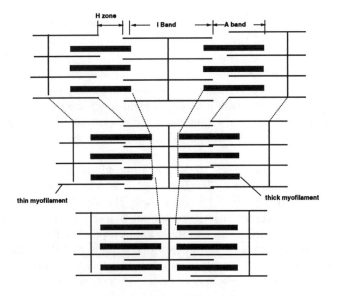

Figure 7.6.
A schematic diagram illustrating the changes (top to bottom) in myosin
and actin banding patterns observed by Huxley.

Effectively, muscles behave like tunable springs such that forces generated
by them are a function of length and level of neural activation [BCH82]. By
attributing spring-like and viscous qualities, a displacement becomes proportional to force and stiffness. This result is simply a restatement of Hooke
and Newtownian laws in a biological context.

7.3.   A Muscle Model Process

The anatomical and mechanical characteristics described so far illustrate
the complexity of the systems we are attempting to model. One approach
is to ignore many of the physical attributes and simply mimic the primary
biomechanical characteristics of facial tissue displacements by a geometric
distortion function. This procedure is by far the most computationally in-
expensive solution and produces reasonable results.

What follows is the description of the three primary muscles types: *linear,
sphincter,* and *sheet* [Wat87]. Linear muscle and sheet muscle are described
as linear muscle vectors, whereas the sphincter muscle is described as an
elliptical contraction.

7.3.1. Muscle Vectors

Muscle vectors, as the name suggests, follow the major direction and insertion of muscle fibers. Whereas real muscle consists of many individual fibers, the computer model assumes a single direction and attachment. With this simplifying assumption, an individual muscle can be described with direction and magnitude in both two and three dimensions; the direction is toward a point of attachment on the bone, and the magnitude of the displacement depends upon the muscle spring constant and the tension created by a muscular contraction.

In linear, or parallel, muscle the surrounding skin is contracted toward the static node of attachment on the bone, until, at a finite distance away, the force dissipates to zero. In sphincter muscle, the skin tissue is squeezed toward an imaginary center, like the tightening of a string bag. This squeezing can be described as occurring uniformly about a point of contraction. Sheet muscle is a broad flat area of muscle fiber strands and does not emanate from a point source. As a result it contracts to a localized node, rather than to a group of separated muscle fiber nodes. In fact, the muscle is a series of almost parallel fibers spread over an area.

The behavior of the linear, sphincter, and sheet muscles result from low-level muscle fiber contractions. Therefore, the requirement of the muscle model is to compute the displacement of surface nodes to new locations thereby emulating real skin deformation.

7.3.2. Linear Muscle

For the linear muscle it is necessary to compute how adjacent tissue, such as the node $\mathbf{p}$ in Figure 7.7(b), is affected by a muscle vector contraction. It is assumed that there is no displacement at the point of insertion in the bone and that maximum deflection occurs at the point of insertion into the skin. Consequently, a dissipation of the force is passed to the adjoining tissue, both across the sectors $\mathbf{A}$ and $\mathbf{B}$ in Figure 7.7(a).

To compute the displacement of an arbitrary node $\mathbf{p}$ in Figure 7.7(b), located on the mesh to a new displacement $\mathbf{p}'$ within the segment $v_1 p_r p_s$ towards v_1 along the vector p, v_1, the following expression is employed:

$$\mathbf{p}' = \mathbf{p} + akr \frac{\mathbf{pv_1}}{||\mathbf{pv_1}||}. \tag{7.2}$$

Here the new location $\mathbf{p}'$ is a function of an angular displacement parameter

$$a = \cos(a2), \tag{7.3}$$

where $a2$ is the angle between the vectors $(\mathbf{v_1}, \mathbf{v_2})$ and $(\mathbf{v_1}, \mathbf{p})$, D is $||\mathbf{v_1} - \mathbf{p}||$, r a radial displacement parameter

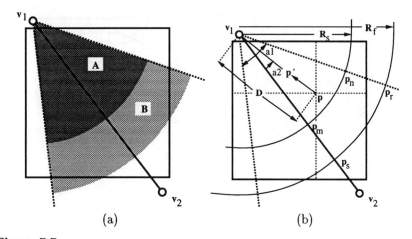

Figure 7.7.
The linear muscle zones of influence.

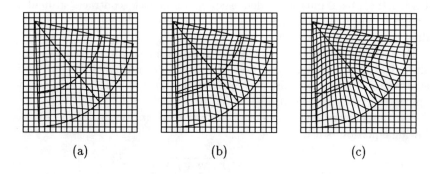

Figure 7.8.
A progressing sequence of muscle contraction with a linear cosine
activity. The mesh is a regular lattice of 20 x 20 units, and the
contraction factor is (a) 3, (b) 5, and (c) 10.

$$r = \begin{cases} \cos(\frac{1-D}{R_s}); & \text{for } \mathbf{p} \text{ inside sector } (\mathbf{v}_1\mathbf{p}_n\mathbf{p}_m\mathbf{p}_1) \\ \cos(\frac{D-R_s}{R_f-R_s}); & \text{for } \mathbf{p} \text{ inside sector } (\mathbf{p}_n\mathbf{p}_r\mathbf{p}_s\mathbf{p}_m), \end{cases} \qquad (7.4)$$

and k a fixed constant representing the elasticity of skin. By varying the
contraction factor of the muscle, the displacement of skin will appear to
move along the main axis of the muscle toward the root of the vector as
illustrated in Figure 7.8.

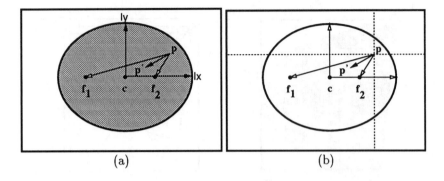

Figure 7.9.
Description of the sphincter muscle zones of influence.

7.3.3.   The Sphincter Muscle

Unlike the linear muscle model, a sphincter muscle contracts around an imaginary central point. As a result, the surface surrounding the mouth is drawn together like the tightening of material at the top of a string bag.

Essentially, the sphincter muscle is elliptical in appearance[1] and can be simplified to a parametric ellipsoid with a major and minor axis, lx representing the semimajor axis, and ly the semiminor axis about a imaginary epicenter c as illustrated in Figure 7.9.(a).

To compute the displacement of node **p** to **p**′ in Figure 7.9.(b), the following equation is used:

$$f = 1 - \frac{\sqrt{ly^2 p_x^2 + lx^2 p_y^2}}{l_x l_y}. \tag{7.5}$$

Figure 7.10 illustrates the contraction of a sphincter muscle influence with an increasing contraction.

7.3.4.   Sheet Muscle

Sheet muscle consists of strands of fibers which lie in flat bundles. An example of this type of muscle is the frontalis major, which lies on the forehead and is primarily involved with the raising of the eyebrows.

Whereas the linear muscle has a radial component, a sheet muscle neither emanates from a point source, nor contracts to a localized node. In fact, the muscle is a series of almost-parallel fibers spread over an area, as illustrated

---

[1]See Chapter 2 for more anatomical details. In particular refer to Figure 2.10.

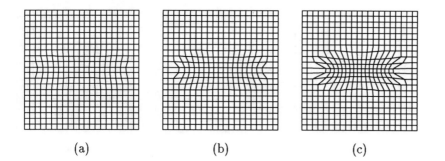

Figure 7.10.
A progressing sequence of sphincter muscle contraction with a linear
cosine activity. Mesh size is 20 x 20. Muscle contraction is (a) 0.5,
(b) 1.0, and (c) 2.5.

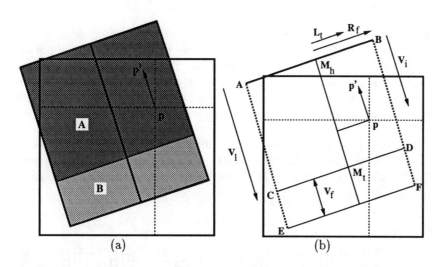

Figure 7.11.
The sheet muscle zones of influence.

in Figure 7.11(b). The computation of a node $\mathbf{p}$ can then be defined as

$$d = \begin{cases} \cos(1 - \frac{L_t}{R_f}); & \text{for } \mathbf{p} \text{ inside sector } ABDC \\ \cos(1 - \frac{L_t}{R_f} * (\frac{V_i}{V_t} + V_f)); & \text{for } \mathbf{p} \text{ inside sector } CDFE. \end{cases} \quad (7.6)$$

Figure 7.12 illustrates the contraction of a sheet muscle influence with an
increasing contraction.

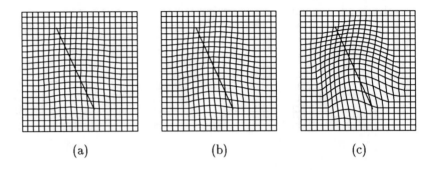

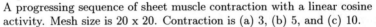

(a)   (b)   (c)

Figure 7.12.
A progressing sequence of sheet muscle contraction with a linear cosine
activity. Mesh size is 20 x 20. Contraction is (a) 3, (b) 5, and (c) 10.

7.3.5.   Varying the Elastic Properties

The linear, sphincter, and sheet muscles use a cosine function as a first-
order approximation to the elastic properties of skin. While this approach
produces adequate results, it is evident that the elasticity of skin varies with
age and from person to person [GuF65]. By replacing the cosine function
with a nonlinear interpolant, or power function, it is possible to vary the
elasticity of the mesh and thereby emulate the lower elasticity of the skin as
it ages.

A power function increases the falloff to zero at the boundaries of the
muscle vectors. Figure 7.13 illustrates the cosine function raised to a power
50. This technique allows a more flexible approach to the modeling of the
primary muscle vectors.

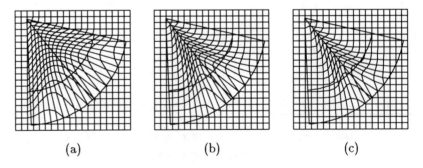

(a)   (b)   (c)

Figure 7.13.
The cosine muscle activity raised to powers (a) 0, (b) 20, and (c) 50.
Muscle contraction is 2.0, and mesh size is 20 x 20.

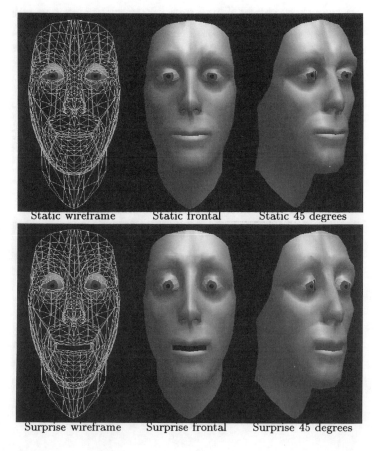

Static wireframe   Static frontal   Static 45 degrees

Surprise wireframe   Surprise frontal   Surprise 45 degrees

Figure 7.14.
Static and surprise facial expressions created from the muscle model
process.

7.4. Modeling the Primary Facial Expressions

Extensive research by psychologists of nonverbal communication has established a basic categorization of facial expressions that are considered to be
generic to the human race [Ekm73]. Ekman, Friesen, and Ellsworth [EFE72]
propose happiness, anger, fear, surprise, disgust/contempt, and sadness as
the six primary effect categories. Other expressions such as interest, calm
bitterness, pride, irony, insecurity, and skepticism can be displayed on the
face, but they have not been as firmly established as fear, surprise, disgust
and sadness.

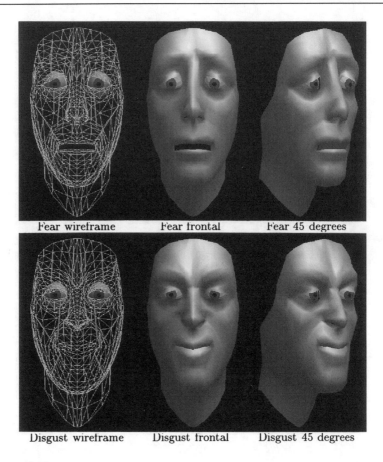

Figure 7.15.
Fear and disgust facial expressions created from the muscle model
process.

The Facial Action Coding System (FACS), developed by Ekman and
Friesen [EF78], psychologists of nonverbal communication, is a widely used
notation for the coding of facial articulation (for more details see Chapter 4).
FACS describes 66 muscle actions (some muscle blends) which in combination can give rise to thousands of possible facial expressions. These discrete
units can be used as fundamental building blocks or reference units for the
development of a parameterized facial muscle process.[2] What follows in the
next sections describes the synthesis of the six primary facial expressions:
surprise, fear, disgust, anger, sadness, and happiness.

---

[2]See Chapter 4, Table 4.4 for a complete listing of all the action units in the Facial
Action Coding System.

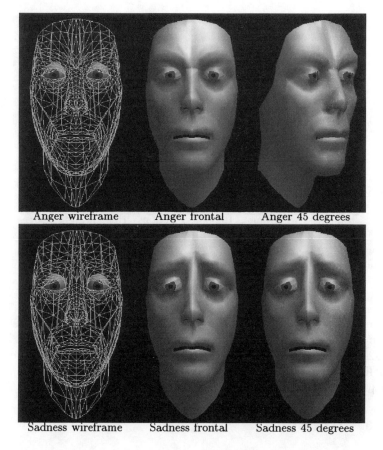

Anger wireframe   Anger frontal   Anger 45 degrees

Sadness wireframe   Sadness frontal   Sadness 45 degrees

Figure 7.16.
Anger and sadness facial expressions created from the muscle model
process.

7.4.1.   Surprise

Surprise is perhaps the briefest expression. In the upper face the brows are
curved and raised (AUl + AU2). There are no distinctive muscle actions in
the midsection of the face. The jaw drops, causing the lips and teeth to part.
The more extreme the surprise, the wider the jaw becomes (Figure 7.14 and
Plate VII(f)).

7.4.2.   Fear

Fear varies in intensity from apprehension to terror. In the upper face, the
brows appear raised and straightened (AUl + AU2 + AU4). The eyes are

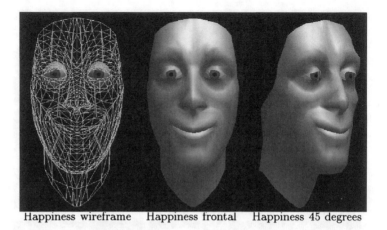

Happiness wireframe   Happiness frontal   Happiness 45 degrees

Figure 7.17.
Happiness facial expression created from the muscle model process.

tense during fear, with the upper lid raised and the lower lid tense. In the midsection of the face, the corners of the lips may be drawn backward (AU20), tightening the lips against the teeth. In the lower face the teeth usually are exposed by the downward pull of the lip (AU15 and/or AU16) (Figure 7.14 and Plate VII(e)).

7.4.3. Disgust

Disgust is an expression of aversion, such as the taste of something you want to spit out. In the upper face there could be a lowering of the brows (AU4); however, the primary cues to the expression are found in the midregion of the face around the nose and upper lip. Usually the upper lip is raised (AU9 and/or AU10), drawing up the flanges of the nose. The lower lip may be drawn downward or raised (AU17) (Figure 7.15 and Plate VII(g)).

7.4.4. Anger

In the emotional state of anger, a person is most likely to harm someone purposefully. The brows are drawn down and together (AU2 + AU4), while the eyes stare in a penetrating fashion with the eyelids wide (AU5). In the midregion of the face, the flanges of the nose can be drawn upward (AU10). In the lower face region there can be two distinctive types of motion: the lips closed hard against the teeth (AU24), or the lips parted to bare teeth (AU25) (Figure 7.15 and Plate VII(d)).

7.4.5. Happiness

Happiness is a positive emotion and can vary in intensity from mildly happy to joy or ecstasy. In the upper face the brows hardly change, while the eyelids are slightly compressed by the cheek, which is up (AU6). The most prominent action is the raising of the corners of the lips that widens the mouth into a broad grin (AU12). This action usually is combined with deepening nasolabial folds (AU11) (Figure 7.16 and Plate VII(c)).

7.4.6. Sadness

Sadness is endured stress, and unlike surprise it is often prolonged in duration. In sadness, the inner portion of the brows are drawn together and raised (AU1 + AU2 + AU4). The eyes usually are cast downward and the lower eyelids slightly raised. The mouth displays subtle motions that are akin to the expression of disgust, where the corners of the mouth are pulled downward (AU15) (Figure 7.15 and Plate VII(h)).

7.5. Parametric Surface Patches

The polygon is one of the basic primitives in every computer graphics system. In most cases a sequence of polygons is sufficient to approximate a curved surface. However, obtaining satisfactory smoothness, especially when considering the face, often requires large amounts of data. Furthermore, even with continuous Gouraud or Phong shading models, undesirable visual artifacts can arise, such as Mach banding [Gou71].

Chapter 3 described a variety of representations capable of producing continuous surfaces and thereby reducing such artifacts. A popular representation is the class of parametric surfaces such as B-splines, NURB surfaces, Catmull-Rom splines, Beta-splines, and hierarchical B-splines. These representations produce faces with smooth curved surfaces using relatively few control points.

While the parametric representation is attractive from a facial modeling point of view, it does complicate the manipulation of the surface for facial animation. The next three sections describe a variety of approaches to date taken to overcome the issues that arise in facial animation.

7.5.1. Bicubic B-spline Patches

The ideal layout for B-spline patches is a regular lattice of control points, which was employed by Waite [Wai89] to model and animate the face with a muscle model. The muscles were coordinated with the Facial Action Coding System to create a facial expression editor.

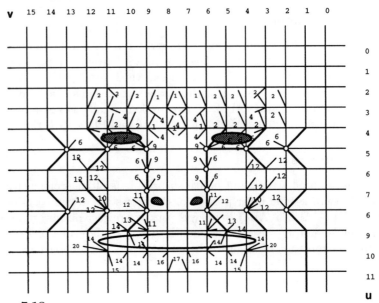

Figure 7.18.
A B-spline face patch. The u, v Facial Action Coding Unit mappings
for the left side of the face were as follows:
AU1 Left=(3,9)(3,8)(4,9)(4,8), AU2 Left=(3,11)(3,10)(4,11)(4,10),
AU4 Left=(2,11)(2,8)(3,10)(3,9)(4,9)(4,8)(3,11),
AU6 Left=(4,12)(4,11)(4,10)(4,9)(5,9)(5,11)(5,13)(6,9)(7,9),
AU9 Left=(5,9)(6,9)(7,9), AU10 Left=(8,10), AU11 Left=(8,9)(9,9),
AU12 Left=(9,11)(10,11)(8,9)(8,11)(8,13)(7,12)(7,11)(6,11)(6,12),
AU13 Left=(9,9), AU14 Left=(9,10)(9,9)(10,10)(10,9),
AU15 Left=(9,11)(10,11), AU16 Left=(10,9)(10,8),
AU17 Left=(10,8)(10,7)(11,8)(11,7), AU20 Left=(9,11)(10,11)

To achieve an animated face Waite determined the activation regions of the
face aligning muscles, or small groups of muscles, to the Facial Action Coding
System. The result was a 16 by 12 rectangular face patch as illustrated in
Figure 7.18. Within the face patch, five holes were trimmed out to represent
the eyes, nostrils, and mouth. Furrow lines, such as the nasiolabial and
infraorbital furrows, were created by doubling up control points, thereby
lowering the continuity at that location by one factor. Finally, the mappings
between the action units and the u, v space of the patch were defined.

Perhaps the biggest limitation of this approach is that the face doesn't
conform to a rectangular geometry configuration and has to be deformed
into a face shape.

7.5.2. Combining Bicubic and Catmull-Rom Splines with a Muscle Model

In the animation of *Tin Toy* [Ree90], the geometry of the baby's face was constructed from four-sided bicubic Catmull-Rom patches. [3] The complete geometry for the face consisted of some six thousand three-dimensional node vectors, far too many to control in an animation sequence.

The animation of the face was achieved by a muscle-based model similar to Waters' [Wat87], and two kinds of muscles were implemented: linear and elliptical sphincters. A linear muscle was defined by two vectors: a bony attachment and a skin attachment. The sphincter muscles were used around the mouth to purse the lips and around the eyes. In this case a single point defined the center of the muscle contraction and three other points defined the axes from which an ellipsoid zone of influence was created. In both cases a cosine function was used to blend between the maximal displacement at the center of the region of the ellipse and the edge of the linear muscle.

While having 50 muscle controls was a significant reduction in the total number of parameters in the face, further reduction was necessary for the animators. This reduction was achieved by creating macro muscles. A macro muscle is a single control, that when contracted causes several low-level muscles to contract. The amount of contraction is weighted by a scaling factor for each low-level muscle. For example, a contraction of 1 on the left brow macro muscle pulls 0.3 on the left1a, 0.5 on left1b, and 0.8 on left2a. A total of 33 macro muscles were defined, and approximately 12 were in use for most of the animation. While the macro muscles saved time by encapsulating commonly used actions, the animator retained complete flexibility because the underlying low-level muscles could be tweaked as well. Figure 3.4 illustrates the geometry and Figure 3.5 shows a rendered frame of the baby displaying an expression.

7.5.3. Hierarchical B-splines

A cubic B-spline patch is defined by 16 control points. While spline patches can define almost any arbitrary surface, only so much detail can be defined from the original 16 control points. To increase detail, more control points can be added in a hierarchy [FB88] to allow detail to be added only where desired (see Figure 7.19). This is achieved by overlays of more finely subdivided spline patches that conform to the surface to be refined. As a result, changes to a single control point affects the surface up to two control points distant. For example, a single central control point will affect a grid of five-by-five control vertices. By increasing the size of this grid, one line of control points on each side at each subdivision, the refined surface can

---

[3] Additional work done to improve smoothness contraints with shape parameters for each curve segment is derived from [DB88].

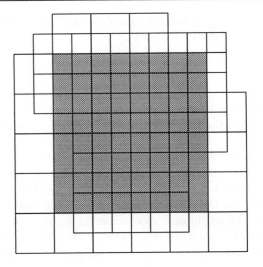

Figure 7.19.
An example of control point location after hierarchical subdivision.

guarantee to conform smoothly to the underlying control points at all times, creating a single continuous surface with continuity on both first and second derivatives.

7.5.4. Muscles and Splines

Having created a geometric representation of the face, the next task is to animate the face (see Figure 7.20).

7.5.5. Gradient-Based Muscles

One of the problems with the muscle model is that node displacements do not curve around the surface [Wan93], which is most noticeable in areas of high curvature. To overcome this limitation, it is possible to calculate the surface derivative in the direction defined by the muscle vector (see Figure 7.21). The point displacement is then scaled by the direction derivative as well as the relative strain rate along the projected vector to produce the final result.

7.6. Physical Models of Facial Tissue

The purely geometric nature of prior facial models ignore many of the complexities of the human facial tissue as described in Chapter 2. This is understandable when one considers the granularity and detail involved.

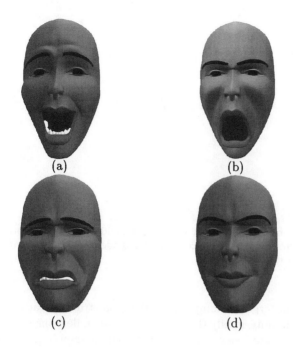

Figure 7.20.
Animated hierarchical B-spline model. (Courtesy of D. Forsey.)

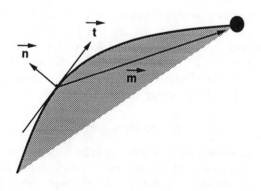

Figure 7.21.
Gradient-based displacement. Vector $\vec{n}$ is normal to the surface, $\vec{t}$ is the tangent vector, and $\vec{m}$ is the normal direction of displacement of the muscle model.

Figure 7.22.
A brow patch of a tension net model. The solid square represents the
bone attachment, the solid circle a muscle node, and the open circle the
skin node attachment.

One of the largest assumptions of the geometric approach is to consider the
skin as an infinitesimally thin surface with no underlying structure, on which
deformations are generated by geometrically manipulating the surface. Consequently, attempts to mimic many of the subtle facial tissue deformations,
such as wrinkles and furrows, are spurious.

7.6.1. A Tension Net

The simplest approach to skin tissue emulation is a collection of springs connected in a network, or tension net described in [Pla80]. In this model the
skin is represented as a warped plane of skin nodes, connecting their neighbors by arcs (Figure 7.22). The arcs have elastic material properties that
make them behave like Hookean springs where the extension is proportional
to the force divided by the spring constant k:

$$extension \propto force/k. \tag{7.7}$$

Forces are generated by synthetic muscles. In this model muscles are
collections of fibers connected at one end to skin and at the other to bone.
While real muscle consists of many individual fibers, for simplicity this model
considers only one or two macroscopic fibers per muscle (see Figure 7.22).
One arc, that is a macroscopic fiber, consists of two parts; the tail that
connects to bone, and the head connecting to a skin node. When a simple
muscle fiber contracts, a force is applied to a muscle node in the direction of
its tail (bone attachment). This force causes a displacement of the muscle

node. The force is then reflected along all arcs adjacent to this node; these reflected forces are then applied to their corresponding adjacent nodes. In this way, an applied force is propagated out from the initial node across the face.

The spring lattice approach to facial expression modeling has a distinct advantage over a purely geometric technique because the displacment of one node can influence all the other nodes in the surface. Consequently, muscle forces "blend" together, providing a unified approach to facial expression modeling. Furthermore, the inherent nature of springs helps maintain some geometric integrity allowing the surface to dimple and bulge, which is characteristic of facial tissue.

The tension net is a variation of a discrete deformable model which will be described in the following section.

7.6.2. A Deformable Lattice of Skin

Deformable models are physically models of nonrigid curves, surfaces, and solids [TF88a] and often the fundamental element is the spring connected to point mass nodes [Gre73]. Models with diverse topologies can be constructed by allowing springs to share nodes; the elements may be chained together to form deformable curves, or they may be assembled into more complex composite units, which are the building blocks of deformable surfaces and solids. What follows is a description of a basic discrete deformable model.

Nodes

In the most fundamental form a single node i can be described where $i = 1, \ldots, N$ has a point mass m_i and a three-space position $\mathbf{x}_i(t) = [x(t), y(t), z(t)]'$. The velocity of the node can be described by $\vec{v}_i = d\mathbf{x}_i/dt$, and its acceleration by $\vec{a}_i = d^2\mathbf{x}_i/dt^2$.

Springs

A single spring unit k, which connects two nodes x_i and x_{i+1}, has natural length l_k and stiffness c_k as illustrated in Figure 7.23. The actual length of the spring is $||\vec{r}_k||$, where $\vec{r}_k = \mathbf{x}_i - \mathbf{x}_{i+1}$ is the vector separation of the nodes. The deformation of the spring is $e_k = ||\vec{r}_k|| - l_k$, and the force the spring exerts on a node can be described as

$$\vec{s}_k = \frac{c_k e_k}{||\vec{r}_k||} \vec{r}_k. \tag{7.8}$$

The spring force is a nonlinear function of node positions because $||\vec{r}_k||$ involves roots of sums of squares.

Figure 7.23.
The fundamental building block, two nodes m_i, m_{i+1}, and a connecting
spring.

7.6.3. Integration

The discrete Lagrange equation of motion for the dynamic node/spring system is the system of coupled, second-order ordinary differential equations

$$m_i \frac{d^2 \vec{x}_i}{dt^2} + \gamma_i \frac{d\vec{x}_i}{dt} + \vec{g}_i = \vec{f}_i, \qquad i = 1, \ldots, N, \tag{7.9}$$

where

$$\vec{g}_i(t) = \sum_{j \in \mathcal{N}_i} \vec{s}_k \tag{7.10}$$

is the total force on node i due to springs connecting it to neighboring nodes
$j \in \mathcal{N}_i$, and where $\vec{f}_i$ is a net force acting on node i, which may include
application-dependent driving forces and forces due to boundary conditions
and constraints. The quantity γ_i is a velocity-dependent damping coefficient
for dissipating the kinetic energy of the deformable lattice through friction.

To simulate the dynamics of a deformable lattice, we provide initial posi-
tions $\vec{x}_i^0$ and velocities $\vec{v}_i^0$ for each node i for $i = 1, \ldots, N$ and numerically
integrate the equations of motion forward though time. At each time step
$\Delta t, 2\Delta t, \ldots, t, t + \Delta t, \ldots$, we must evaluate the forces, accelerations, velocities, and positions for each node. A simple and quick time-integration
procedure is the explicit Euler method [PFTV86].

7.6.4. Layered Tissue Models

Having described the basic mathematics of discrete deformable models, we
can construct a variety of geometric structures to represent soft objects, in
particular skin tissue. Figure 7.24 illustrates three basic geometric configurations for spring lattices.

For facial tissue an idealized discrete deformable skin lattice structure
is illustrated in Figure 7.25. Each line in the figure represents a biphasic
spring. The springs are arranged into layers of pentahedral and hexahedral
elements cross-strutted with springs to resist shearing and twisting stresses.

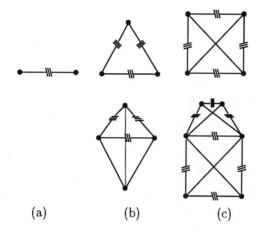

Figure 7.24.
The fundamental building blocks of deformable models. The top row
represents 2D configurations; the bottom row are 3D composite lattice
structures: (b) is a tetrahedal element, and (c) is a hexahedral element.

The springs in the three layers — representing cutaneous tissue, subcutaneous tissue, and the muscle layer — have different stiffness parameters in accordance with the nonhomogeneity of real facial tissue. The topmost surface of the lattice represents the epidermis (a rather stiff layer of keratin and collagen), and the spring stiffnesses are set to make it moderately resistant to deformation. The springs underneath the epidermis form pentahedral elements which represent the dermis. The springs in the second layer, which contains hexahedral elements, are highly deformable, reflecting the nature of subcutaneous fatty tissue. Nodes at the bottom of the second layer represent the fascia to which the muscle fibers that run through the hexahedral elements in the third layer are attached. Nodes on the bottom-most surface of the lattice are fixed onto the bone surface.

Translating this configuration into a facial topology is nontrivial. To automate the facial model assembly the procedure starts with the triangular facial mesh, whose nodes and springs represent the epidermis. First, it projects normal vectors from the center of gravity of each triangle into the face to establish subcutaneous nodes and forms tetrahedral dermal elements by connecting them to epidermal nodes using dermal springs. Second, it forms subcutaneous elements by attaching short weak springs from the subcutaneous nodes downward to muscle layer nodes. Third, it adds the muscle layer, whose lower nodes are constrained, anchoring them in "bone." Finally, it inserts the muscle fibers through the muscle layer from their emergence in "bone" to their attachments at muscle layer nodes. Figure 7.26(b)

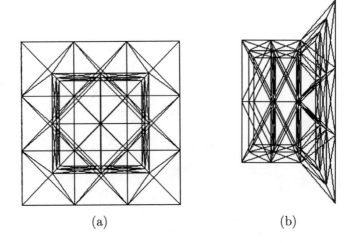

(a)   (b)

Figure 7.25.
Trilayer facial tissue model. (a) Top view. (b) Side view showing (right
to left) epidermal surface, dermal layer (pentahedral elements), and
subcutaneous and muscle layers (hexahedral elements).

and Plate VIII(a) illustrate a facial topology after the automatic assembly.
The synthetic tissue includes about 960 elements with approximately 6,500
springs in total. The physics-based face model then can be simulated and
rendered at interactive rates.

To incorporate both volume preservation and skull penetration forces, a
variation of the scheme described above was developed such that they could
be added to Equation 7.9 [LTW95]. In this model a volume preservation
force is computed for each element, represented as a discrete set of nodes.

$$\mathbf{q}_i^e = k_i(V^e - \tilde{V}^e)\mathbf{n}_i^e + k_2(\mathbf{p}_i^e - \tilde{\mathbf{p}}_i^e) \tag{7.11}$$

where V^e and $\tilde{V}^e$ are the rest and current volumes for the element e; $\vec{n}_i^e$
is the epidermal normal for the node i; $\bar{p}_i^e$ and $\tilde{\mathbf{p}}_i^e$ are the rest and current
nodal coordinates for i with respect the center of gravity of the element; and
k_1, k_2 are scaling force constants.

As previously mentioned in Section 7.5.5., it is important to maintain the
curvature aspects of the facial tissue as it slides over the underlying skull.
To model this effect there has to be an underlying geometry for the skull
which can be either estimated or computed as an offset to the surface geometry [LTW95]. Once again the additional force can be added to Equation 7.9.
The penalizing force can be computed as follows:

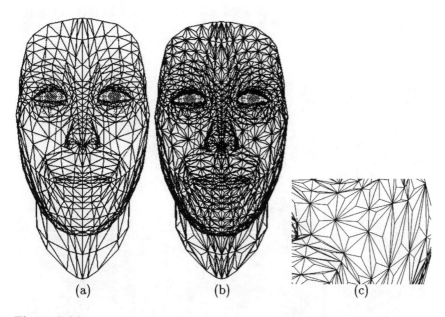

Figure 7.26.
An illustration of the skin layer construction. (a) shows the surface
polygon topology, (b) is the tetrahedral dermal elements, and (c) shows
a closeup of the cheek region of the face.

$$\mathbf{s_i} = \left\{ \begin{array}{ll} -(\mathbf{f}_i^n \cdot \mathbf{n}_i)\mathbf{n}_i & \text{when } \vec{f}_i^n \cdot \mathbf{n}_i < 0 \\ 0 & \text{otherwise} \end{array} \right. \tag{7.12}$$

where $\vec{f}_i^n$ is the net force on the facial node i, and $\vec{n}_i$ is the surface normal
at that node.

The result of using a physically based approach with range data collected
from a Cyberware scanner is illustrated in Plate X.

7.6.5. Muscles

Muscles that apply forces to the tissue lattice run through the second layer
of the synthetic tissue (Figure 7.30). Muscle fibers emerge from some nodes
fixed onto the bone at the bottom of the third layer and attach to mobile
nodes on the upper surface of the second fascia layer.

Let $\vec{m}_i^e$ denote the point where muscle i emerges from the "bone," with
$\vec{m}_i^a$ being its point of attachment in the tissue. These two points specify
a muscle vector $\vec{m}_i = \vec{m}_i^e - \vec{m}_i^a$. The displacement of node j in the fascia

Figure 7.27.
Four images from an animated sequence using a physically based model.
The individual was modeled using Cyberware range data.

layer from $\vec{x}_j$ to $\vec{x}_j'$ due to muscle contraction is a weighted sum of m muscle activities acting on node j:

$$\vec{x}_j' = \vec{x}_j + \sum_{i=1}^{m} c_i b_{ij} \vec{m}_i, \qquad (7.13)$$

where $0 \le c_i \le 1$ is a contraction factor and b_{ij} is a muscle blend function that specifies a radial zone of influence for the muscle fiber. Defining $\vec{r}_{ij} = \vec{m}_i^a - \vec{x}_j$,

$$b_{ij} = \begin{cases} \cos\left(\frac{\|\vec{r}_{ij}\|}{r_i}\frac{\pi}{2}\right); & \text{for } \| \vec{r}_{ij} \| \le r_i \\ 0; & \text{otherwise} \end{cases}, \qquad (7.14)$$

where r_i is the radius of influence of the cosine blend profile. Figure 7.29 illustrates a circular zone of muscle influence and with an associated displacement falloff profile.

Once all the muscle interactions have been computed, the positions $\vec{x}_j$ of nodes that are subject to muscle actions are displaced to their new positions $\vec{x}_j'$. As a result, the nodes in the fatty, dermal, and epidermal layers

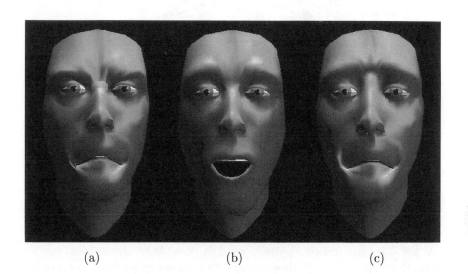

(a)   (b)   (c)

Figure 7.28.
Three examples of a physically based model under muscular control.

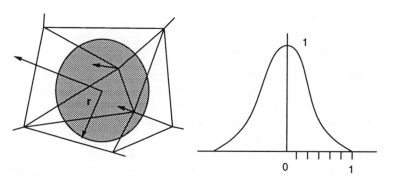

Figure 7.29.
The direction of muscle displacement of the lattice structure and the
nonlinear displacement function.

that are not directly influenced by muscle contractions are in an unstable
state, and unbalanced forces propagate through the lattice to establish a
new equilibrium position.

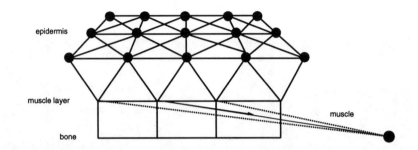

Figure 7.30.
A cross section of the trilayered tissue model. The muscle vector
influences only the nodes in the muscle layer.

7.6.6.   Examples

By orchestrating muscle contractions it is possible to create facial expressions that are superior to those created by a purely geometric deformations.
In particular, furrows on the brow can be pronounced by the contraction
of the corrigator muscle, which draws the brows together as illustrated in
Figure 7.28(a) and Plate VIII(b). The same is true for the furrows around
the mouth which occur naturally as the physical model contracts (see Figure 7.28(b), Plate VIII(b), and Plate VIII(c)).

7.6.7.   Finite-Element Skin Tissue Simulation

The finite-element method has a history in the application of structural analysis of materials and is used regularly in CAD/CAM as well as nonstructural
fields such as fluid mechanics, heat conduction, and biomedicine. A detailed
description of finite elements is beyond the scope of this book; the reader is
therefore referred to books on the subject such as [Bat82].

Essentially, the finite-element method is a technique to approximate the
solution of a continuous function with a series of trial shape functions.
The finite-element method (FEM), like the discrete simulation approach described so far, also divides the geometry into regions (elements) that, taken
together, approximate the behavior of material being simulated. The difference between the two methods lies in the way information is passed from
element to element as the material deforms. For FEM, the material properties of the elements are combined into a global stiffness matrix relating
loads on the material at the nodal points to the nodal point displacements.
This matrix then can be used directly to find the static solution. This is
in contrast to the discrete simulation method, where the nodal points are
iteratively displaced until the load contributions of all adjacent elements are
in equilibrium.

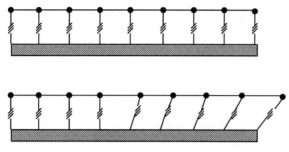

Figure 7.31.
Conceptualization of the finite-element model, where the skin is an elastic membrane divided by a series of nodes. The subcutaneous attachments are represented by springs attaching each node to an immobile surface.

7.6.8.   Skin Flap Design

One of the first skin tissue models of skin tissue deformation using FEMs was constructed by Larrabee [Lar86]. His approach attempted to model the effect of skin flap design for preoperative surgical simulation. His work was well motivated because models of wound closure, at that time, were based almost completely on plane geometry or paper models. Furthermore, these geometric approaches ignored the elastic properties of skin and skin attachment.

Figure 7.31 illustrates the idealized elastic membrane he created with nodes spaced at regular intervals. Attached to each node is a small spring representing the subcutaneous attachments. The stress and strain properties of the skin are related by the standard equations of classical elasticity, with the following variables: (1) E or Young's modulus, which represents the slope of the stress/strain curve; (2) v or Poisson's ratio, which is 0.5 for an incompressible material; and (3) k, the spring constant of the subcutaneous attachment, assuming a linear relationship between nodal displacement and force. The equations of the model were as follows:

- σ_{11} = stress along the side perpendicular to x_1 axis in the x_1 direction.

- σ_{12} = stress along the side perpendicular to x_1 axis in the x_2 direction.

- σ_{21} = stress along the side perpendicular to x_2 axis in the x_1 direction.

- σ_{22} = stress along the side perpendicular to x_2 axis in the x_2 direction.

Force equilibrium for a small element of area $dxdy$, as in Figure 7.32, leads to the equations:

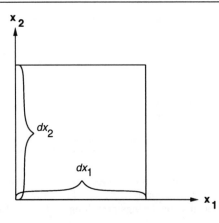

Figure 7.32.
Layout of a small square of skin dx_1, dx_2.

$$\frac{\partial_{11}}{\partial \mathbf{x}_1} + \frac{\partial_{21}}{\partial \mathbf{x}_2} - ku_1 = 0, \qquad (7.15)$$

$$\frac{\partial_{12}}{\partial \mathbf{x}_1} + \frac{\partial_{22}}{\partial \mathbf{x}_2} - ku_2 = 0, \qquad (7.16)$$

where u_1 and u_2 are the displacements of the element in the x_1 and x_2 directions, respectively, and ku_i is the force per unit area in the x_i direction.

The stresses are related to the displacements by

$$\sigma_{11} = \frac{E}{1-v^2}\frac{\partial u_1}{\partial \mathbf{x}_1} + \frac{vE}{1-v^2}\frac{\partial u_2}{\partial \mathbf{x}_2}, \qquad (7.17)$$

$$\sigma_{22} = \frac{vE}{1-v^2}\frac{\partial u_1}{\partial \mathbf{x}_1} + \frac{E}{1-v^2}\frac{\partial u_2}{\partial \mathbf{x}_2}, \qquad (7.18)$$

$$\sigma_{12} = \sigma_{21} = \frac{E}{2(1-v)}\left(\frac{\partial u_2}{\partial \mathbf{x}_1} + \frac{\partial u_1}{\partial \mathbf{x}_2}\right), \qquad (7.19)$$

where E is Young's modulus and v is Poisson's ratio. To solve these equations for u_1 and u_2, triangular finite elements were used.

7.6.9. Deng

Larrabee's approach was the first attempt to simulate the behavior of skin tissue. This method was soon followed by a more rigorous approach by Deng [Den88]. Her work attempted to simulate and analyze the closure of skin excisions on an idealized three-layer model of facial tissue. The computer simulation then minimizes *dog ears*, raised areas of skin that tend

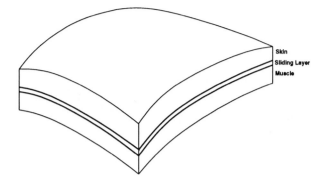
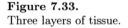

Figure 7.33.
Three layers of tissue.

to form at the end of a closed wound and closing of excisions traversing Langer's lines.

The model itself was constructed as a thick shell, as illustrated in Figure 7.33, consisting of three layers: a skin layer, a sliding layer, and a muscle layer. The model was then discretized into three layers of 16 node prism elements. Figure 7.34 illustrates a quarter of the model used in the skin excision simulations. The sliding layer was unique since it facilitated sliding of the skin over the muscles by making the layer incompressible with a low shear moduli. The skin tissue moduli were defined from a variety of different experimental sources which were plugged into ADINA (Automatic Dynamic Incremental Nonlinear Analysis), which performed the numerical computations.

7.6.10. Pieper

Pieper's work is a natural outgrowth of Deng's work by the application of FEMs to facial data collected from scanners. The problem that Pieper addressed was how to map scanned facial data into the continuum mesh that could then be given to a finite-element solver [Che92].

The solution was to use Cyberware data and CT (Computer Tomography) data presented in cylindrical coordinates. One advantage of using CT data is that both the extracted skull and skin surfaces are in perfect registration, as shown in Figure 7.35. The next task was to provide a mapping between the source data and normalized cylindrical coordinates. In cylindrical coordinates z represents the vertical axis, while θ is the angle from 0 to 360 degrees around the head. r provides the distance from the z axis to represent the skin surface at each point (θ, z) as illustrated in Figure 7.36.

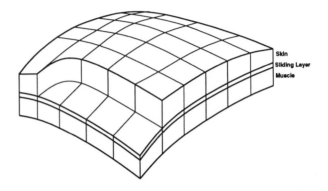

Figure 7.34.
Three layers of tissue discretized into 16 node prisms. This figure
illustrates a quarter of the total model. The cut-out on the top surface
represents a skin excision.

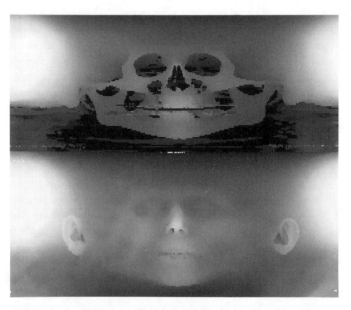

Figure 7.35.
An example of CT (computer tomography) data cast into cylindrical
coordinates [Wat92]. The top image was extracted at a specific iso-value
for bone surfaces, while the bottom was extracted at the skin surface.

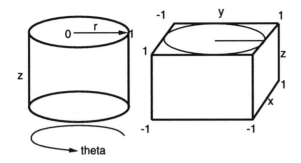

Figure 7.36.
The relationship between the source radial data and the normalized
cylindrical coordinate space.

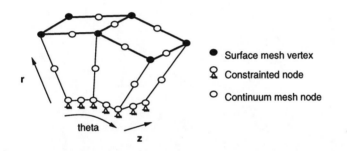

Figure 7.37.
An example of two elements from the continuum meshing process
discretized into 16 node cuboids.

The continuum meshing, necessary for the FEM computation, is created
from the skin to the bone surface geometries along the r axis. Triangles are
extruded into wedge elements, and quadrilatrials are extruded into cuboid
elements. Figure 7.37 illustrates a cross section of the nodes and elements
created by the continuum meshing. The FEM procedure employed by Pieper
involved a home-grown static displacement-based formulation of the finite-
element method to solve elasticity equilibrium equations. This was closely
based on procedures described in [Bat82]. The result was that he was able
to demonstrate simple facial surgical simulations, for example, Z-plasty, a
particular type of skin tissue excision and closure [GWJS86].

8

Speech Synchronized Animation

In traditional animation, synchronization between the drawn images and the speech track is usually achieved through the tedious process of reading the prerecorded speech track to find the frame times of significant speech events. Key frames with corresponding mouth positions and expressions are then drawn to match these key speech events. The mouth positions used are usually based on a canonical mapping of speech sounds into mouth positions [Bla49].

Reading the track traditionally involves transferring the soundtrack to magnetic film with sprocket holes. This film is then manually analyzed by passing it back and forth over a magnetic playback head to locate the frame locations of speech events. Today, this task would most likely be done by converting the soundtrack to digital form and then locating the speech event times using a computer-based sound editor.

For a more realistic correspondence, a live actor is filmed or videotaped while speaking. These recorded frames are then rotoscoped to obtain the correct mouth positions for each frame or for each key frame.

Parke [Par74] used both the speech track reading and the rotoscoping approaches in his early speech synchronized facial animation work. Animation was created based on manually reading the speech track to determine the corresponding timed sequence of speech-related parameters. Animation was also created using parameter sequences determined by rotoscoping images of the actor reading the speech track. These timed parameter sequences were used to drive a parameterized face model.

The techniques outlined above assume that the speech track is created first and the animation images are then created to match. This production ordering is usually preferred. However, sometimes the reverse is required where the speech track is created to match an existing animation sequence. And, as we shall see, computer-based speech animation allows a third possibility: speech and images created simultaneously.

8.1. Cartoon Lip Animation

According to Madsen [Mad69], simplicity is the secret to successful cartoon character lip animation. Attempts at extreme accuracy in lip motion for these characters usually appear forced and unnatural. For character animation the goal is not to imitate realistic lip motions but to create "a visual shorthand that passes unchallenged by the viewer." The effective simple approach is to use a visual pattern of vowel lip motions accented by the consonants. A visual pattern where open lips generally match the open vowels is usually sufficient. Madsen provides the following lip animation steps based on manually reading the speech track:

1. Determine the overall timing, the number of frames within and between each word.

2. Find the accented words containing the sounds b, m, and p. Within these words locate the frame times where the lips meet. These locations are the key frames that synchronize the lips with the consonants. Also locate the distinctive open vowels such as o and w.

3. Create the in-between frames with a simple visual pattern that approximates the rest of the spoken phrases.

Madsen also offers the following guidelines:

- Consonants are the accents of animated speech. Precision of the consonants gives credibility to the generalized patterns of the vowels. Perfect synchronization of each b, m, and p sharpens the animation.

- Letters like o and w require an oval mouth shape.

- The letters f and v require tucking the lower lip under the upper front teeth. This tuck tends to make the character look cute. Underanimate each f and v unless humor is desired.

- Pronunciations of a, c, d, e, g, h, i, j, k, l, n, q, r, s, t, x, y, and z are formed primarily by the tongue and do not require precise lip animation.

- When animating lip motions, the emotional qualities have to be created also. An angry "no" is different than a whispered "no."

8.2.   Speech Basics

Speech sound generation may be modeled as a broadband sound source passed through a filter [WI82]. The sound source is the vibrations of the vocal cords in the case of voiced sounds and air turbulence in the case of *whispered* sounds. Sounds where the vocal cords are open, relaxed, and not vibrating are termed *voiceless*. For example, the sounds t and d differ only in that the vocal cords vibrate during the d posture, but not during the t posture.

For voiced sounds the vocal cords in the larynx periodically collide producing a pitched buzzing sound that contains a spectrum of harmonic frequencies. The power in these harmonics falls off as the harmonic frequencies increase (see Figure 8.1(a)).

These sounds pass through the vocal tract which includes the throat, mouth, tongue, lips, and sometimes the nasal cavity. The energy in this noise is redistributed by the resonant properties of the vocal and nasal tracts. The vocal tract filters the sound, forming resonant energy peaks in the spectrum called *formants* (see Figure 8.1(b) and Figure 8.1(c)). While vocal tract filtering determines the particular phoneme produced, voice pitch, amplitude, and whether the sound is voiced or whispered are characteristics of the sound source. Mouth positions and the vowels formed are entirely independent of the sound source characteristics.

Each class of voice sounds is associated with a particular configuration of the vocal organs. These configurations are referred to as speech postures. If, for example, the jaw is rotated a certain amount and the lips are held in a particular position, with the tongue moved high or low, and back or forward, a specific vowel sound can be produced that is characterized by a particular energy distribution in the frequency domain. As the speaker articulates different sounds, these speech postures change. As the formant peaks move up and down the frequency scale, the voice sounds change.

The formant frequencies are changed by varying the position and shape of vocal tract constituents. The vowel sounds can be characterized by the frequencies of the first two formants. The formants change relatively slowly during vowels and change rapidly or disappear altogether during consonants and vowel-consonant transitions. This characteristic is especially true for consonants like b, d, g, p, t, and k which are commonly called the *plosives* or the stop consonants.

The nasal sounds such as m and n are articulated much like the plosive sounds. These sounds involve rapid shifts in formant frequencies and rapid

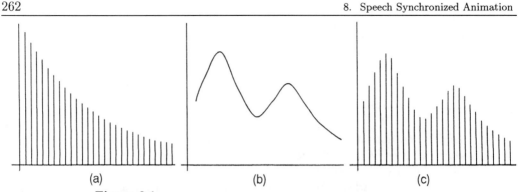

Figure 8.1.
Speech harmonic spectrum and the formants: (a) the vocal cord
generated harmonic spectrum, (b) the vocal tract spectrum filter,
(c) the resulting speech sound with resonant formant peaks.
(Adapted from [Lew91].)

changes in general spectral quality when the vocal tract is quickly connected
and disconnected to the nasal spaces by the velum, a valve in the back of
the mouth formed by the soft palate.

Various hiss-like noises are associated with many consonants. During or
just after the articulation of these consonants, air from the lungs is rushing
through a relatively narrow opening, in turbulent flow, generating the random hiss-like noises. Consonants are distinguished from vowels mainly by a
higher degree of constriction in the vocal tract. It is completely stopped in
the case of the stop consonants.

Whispered speech also involves turbulent airflow noise. But, because this
turbulence occurs in the initial part of the vocal tract, it is shaped by the
vocal tract resonances and has many of the qualities of ordinarily spoken
sounds.

8.2.1. Realistic Speech Postures

According to Walther [Wal82] lip reading is based on observing the visemes
associated with 45 English phonemes. Visemes are the visually distinguishable phoneme classes. Nitchie [Nit79] discusses lip reading based on 18 visually distinct speech postures involving the lips, teeth, and tongue. These are
summarized in Table 8.1 and illustrated in Figure 8.2. The visible differences
between similar speech postures may be quite subtle.

Table 8.1.
Speech postures.

Posture Name	Speech Sound	Posture Description
Narrow	long *e* as in "we"	Lips assume a narrow slit like opening, mouth corners slightly drawn back and parted
Lip to teeth	{em f and *v* sounds	Lower lip rises and touches upper teeth
Lips shut	*b*, *m*, and *p* sounds	Lips naturally shut
Puckered lips	long *oo* as in "moon"	Lips are puckered, showing only a small mouth opening
Small oval	short *oo* as in "good" *w* as in "we" *wh* as in "wharf"	Lips form a small oval, lips less puckered than in puckered posture
Widely open	*a* as in "farm"	Mouth open widely, tongue drawn back slightly
Elliptical	*u* as in "up" *u* as in "upon", *u* before *r* as in "fur"	Intermediate open position with elliptical shape
Elliptical puckered	*r* as in "free"	Elliptical shape but with mouth corners slightly puckered
Relaxed narrow	*i* as in "pit" long *e* as in "believe" *y* as in "youth"	Similar to narrow posture, but mouth corners are not drawn back and parted
Front tongue	*th* as in "thin" and "then"	Front of the tongue visible between the teeth
Tongue to gum	*t* as in "time" *d* as in "dime" *n* as in "nine"	Tongue touches the upper gum while while the lips are in the relaxed narrow posture
Tip to gum	*l* as in "leaf"	Only the tip of the tongue touches the upper gum while the lips are in the elliptical posture
Spherical triangle	*a* as in "all" *o* as in "form"	Lips are open in the shape of a spherical triangle
Tightened narrow	*s* as in "see" *z* as in "zebra"	Narrow mouth opening with the muscles at the corner of the mouth slightly tightened, teeth close together
Large oval	short *a* as in "mat"	Lips form large oval with corners slightly drawn up
Protrusion	*sh* as in "ship" *s* as in "measure" *ch* as in "chip" *j* as in "jam" *g* as in "gentle"	Mouth forms oval shape with the lips protruding forward
Medium oval	short *e* as in "let" *a* as in "care"	Similar to the elliptical posture but with the mouth corners further apart
Undefined open	*k* as in "keep" *g* as in "go" *nk* as in "rank" *ng* as in "rang"	Mouth open with shape similar to the closest associated vowel

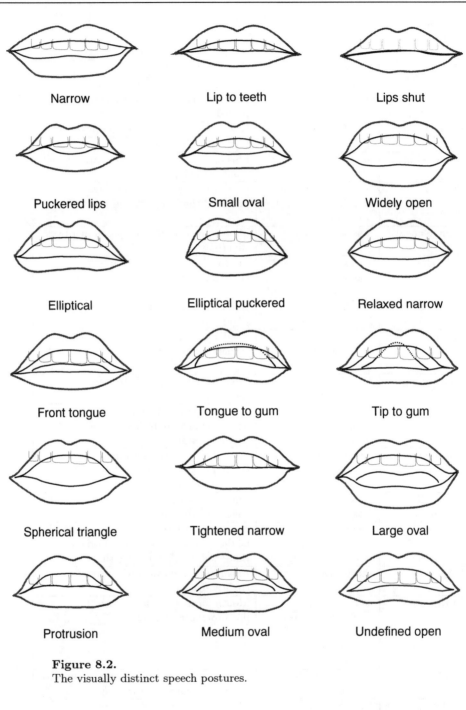

Figure 8.2.
The visually distinct speech postures.

8.2.2.   Coarticulation

Speech can be decomposed into a sequence of discrete units such as syllables and phonemes. However, in actual speech production there is overlap in the production of these sounds. The boundaries between these discrete speech units are blurred.

The vocal tract motions associated with producing one phonetic segment overlap the motions for producing surrounding phonetic segments. This overlap is referred to as coarticulation [KM77]. Coarticulation is the consequence of the physical dynamics of the vocal tract and the vocal tract postures required for various sounds. There are physical limits to how quickly the speech postures can change. Rapid sequences of speech sounds often require that the posture for one sound anticipate the posture for the next sound. Or, that the posture for the current sound is modified by the previous sound.

Coarticulation should be considered in speech animation so that incorrect mouth positions can be avoided. A simple approach to coarticulation is to look at the previous, the present, and the next phonemes to determine the current mouth position [Wat87]. This examination is not always sufficient, since the correct mouth position can depend on phonemes up to five positions before or after the current phoneme [KM77].

Forward coarticulation occurs when articulation of a speech segment depends on upcoming segments. The speech posture for one phonetic segment is anticipated in the formation of an earlier segment in the phonetic string. Backward coarticulation occurs when a speech segment depends on preceding segments. The speech posture for one segment is carried over to a later segment in the phonetic string.

Forward coarticulation can occur when a sequence of consonants is followed by a vowel. The lips can show the influence of the following vowel during the first consonant of the sequence. An example is the rounding of the lips at the beginning of the word "stew." The difference in articulation of the final consonant in a word depending on the preceding vowel is because of backward coarticulation.

Computing Coarticulation Effects

Pelachaud [Pel91] has proposed a three-step algorithm for determining the effects of coarticulation. This algorithm depends on the notion of clustering and ranking phoneme lip shapes based on how deformable they are. In this context, deformability refers to the extent that the lip shape for a phoneme cluster can be modified by surrounding phonemes. Ranking is from the least deformable, such as the f, v cluster, to the most deformable clusters, such as s and m. This deformability is also dependent on speech rate. A person talking slowly moves her lips much more than a person speaking rapidly.

The first step in this algorithm is to apply coarticulation rules to those highly deformable clusters that are context dependent. These forward and backward coarticulation rules consist of looking ahead to the next highly visible vowel and looking backward to the previous highly visible vowel. The lip shape for the current phoneme is adjusted to be consistent with the previous and next vowel shapes.

The next step is to consider the relaxation and contraction times of the mouth shape muscles [Bou73]. This step checks to see if each action has time to contract after the previous phoneme or to relax before the next phoneme. If the time between two consecutive phonemes is smaller than the contraction time of the muscles, the previous phoneme is influenced by the contraction of the current phoneme. Similarly, if the time between consecutive phonemes is smaller than the relaxation time, the current phoneme will influence the next one.

In the last step, geometric relationships between successive actions is taken into account. For example, closure of the lips is easier from a slightly parted position than from a puckered position. Also, the magnitude of speech actions are scaled depending on phoneme and context.

Dominance and Blending

In their study of synthetic bimodal visual speech communication, Cohen and Massaro [CM93] implemented a model for coarticulation based on Lofqvist's [Lof90] gestural theory of speech production. This model uses the concepts of dominance and blending functions.

In this model, each phoneme segment has an associated target set of facial control parameter values. Each phoneme segment also has a dominance function. Dominance is modeled using the following negative exponential function:

$$D_{sp} = \alpha_{sp} e^{-\theta_{sp}|\tau|^c}. \tag{8.1}$$

The dominance of a phoneme segment parameter, D_{sp}, falls off exponentially according to the time distance τ from the segment center raised to the power c modified by a rate parameter θ_{sp}. The coefficient α_{sp} gives the magnitude of the dominance function for this parameter for this segment s. Different coefficients are generally used for θ_{sp} prior to the segment center and after the segment center. τ is computed as follows:

$$\tau = t_{c_{sp}} + t_{o_{sp}} - t,$$

where $t_{c_{sp}}$ is the time center of the segment and $t_{o_{sp}}$ is a time offset for the dominance function peak.

$$t_{c_{sp}} = t_{start_s} + (duration_s/2).$$

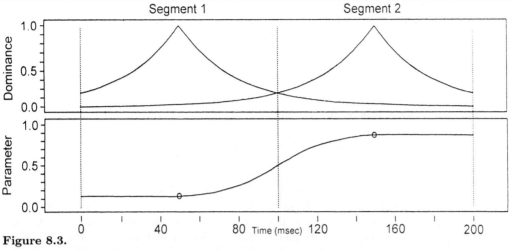

Figure 8.3.
Example dominance functions and a resulting blended control
parameter. (Adapted from [CM93].)

The actual parameter value used at a given animation frame time is determined by blending the dominance functions for that parameter using a
weighted average:

$$F_p(t) = \sum_{s=1}^{n}(D_{sp}(t)T_{sp})/\sum_{s=1}^{n}D_{sp}(t), \qquad (8.2)$$

where n is the number of phoneme segments in the utterance and the T_{sp}
are the segment target parameter values. Figure 8.3 illustrates this approach
for a simple two segment utterance. The characteristics of the dominance
functions and the blended results are controlled by the θ_{sp}, α_{sp}, and c values
used.

The dominance function blending approach automatically incorporates the
speech rate dependent aspects of coarticulation.

8.2.3. Intonation

Intonation is the melodic feature of an utterance. It is also the feature of
speech most noticeably absent in synthetic speech. Intonation is important
in conveying the emotions associated with a speaker's messages.

Intonation can be decomposed into three components: the type of utterance, such as interrogative or declarative; the attitude the speaker wants to
show to the listener, such as politeness or irony; and finally the involuntary
emotional aspects of the speaker's speech [SLS84]. The emotional component is differentiated by subjective pitch, perceived loudness, global pitch

contour, speech tempo, and pauses. Anger, for example, is characterized by a high pitch level, wide pitch range, and large pitch variations. Angry speech is loud on average but has wide loudness fluctuations. Articulation is precise and speech tempo is fast. Sadness, on the other hand, is characterized by low pitch level, narrow pitch range, and small pitch variations. Sad speech is soft, with small fluctuations in loudness. The tempo of sad speech is slow with a number of long pauses [Cah89] [LSS85] [WS81].

8.2.4. Bimodal Communication

There has been considerable research indicating that multiple information sources are useful in human recognition and understanding of spoken language [CM93] [CM94]. Being able to see a speaker's face seems to provide the listener with additional information valuable in understanding the speech. This concept is particularly true in noisy environments or other situations where the audio speech information is degraded. This research implies that both speech and accurate synchronized facial animation may be important components of human-computer interaction interfaces.

8.2.5. Speech as a Second-Level Parameterization

Any control parameterization for facial animation should support speech animation. Speech animation control is often a good example of *second-level* parameterized control. In these cases, speech animation is controlled by using a higher level parameterization built on top of a lower level basic parameterization.

The second-level parameterization used in speech animation is usually in terms of speech phonemes. The higher level control is specified in terms of phoneme transitions. The phoneme transitions are transformed into detailed lower level parameter transitions.

A fairly small number of visually distinct phonemes are needed to produce convincing animation. Since the same words may be spoken with different emotional overlays, the speech parameterization should be orthogonal to the emotional parameters.

The second-level phoneme parameterization approach has been used by Bergeron and Lachapell [BL85], Lewis and Parke [LP87], Hill et al. [HPW88], and Magnenat-Thalmann et al. [MTPT88] to produce successful speech animation.

8.3. Automated Synchronization

For automated synchronization, the visible speech postures, the positions of the lips and tongue, must be related in some identifiable way to the speech sounds. The source-filter speech model implies that lip and tongue positions are functions of the phonemes. Therefore analyses that result in the representation of speech as timed phoneme sequences are suitable for creating synchronized animation.

8.3.1. Performance Measures

The viability of an automated synchronization method depends on the nature and purpose of the facial representation. Realistic or semirealistic characters offer the greatest challenge, demanding more precise lip motions. They invite comparison with real people. The more fanciful the character, the more latitude we have in animating its speech and expressions.

Most people cannot read lips and cannot easily determine the sound corresponding to a given mouth position, but can identify good and bad synchronization. Accurate rhythm in mouth movement is fundamental for acceptable speech synchronization, while accuracy of mouth positioning becomes necessary in close-up views of the realistic faces. Performance measures for speech synchronization are not well defined. There are probably several useful levels of performance. These levels include the performance level useful for general character animation (described in Section 8.1), the performance level required for realistic animation, and the very high-quality standards necessary for lip-reading.

8.3.2. Taxonomy of Approaches

We would like computer-based systems that automatically synchronize facial animation with speech. Figure 8.4 shows a taxonomy of possible computer-based approaches. In this taxonomy, the primary differentiator is the initial form of the speech information. The speech may be available as text, prerecorded speech, both prerecorded speech and text, or as speech images.

Text-Driven

The idea here is to extract phoneme information from input text, then use a library of phoneme-based mouth shapes and durations to generate the synchronized facial animation. The text is also used to drive speech synthesis which creates synthetic speech synchronized to the face animation. Examples of this approach are discussed in Section 8.4.

Speech-Driven

The idea here is to analyze the prerecorded speech on a frame-by-frame basis to determine speech information. This information is used to create facial animation that matches the speech segment. The complete animation is

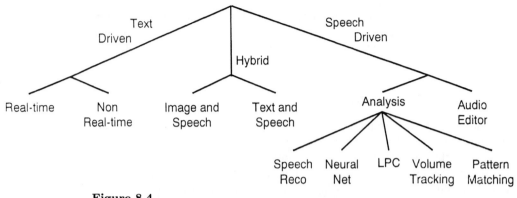

Figure 8.4.
Speech synchronization taxonomy.

formed by merging the prerecorded speech with the generated animation. Speech-driven examples are discussed in Section 8.5.

Hybrid — Text-and-Speech-Driven

Morishima and Harashima developed a hybrid approach [MH93] that depends on having both prerecorded speech and corresponding text information. A bottoms-up speech analysis is used to identify vowels and speech segmentation including pauses and speech component durations. Vowel recognition is done using pattern matching. Speech segmentation is based on speech waveform power changes and frame-to-frame changes in the speech spectrum. Top-down analysis of the text information is used to identify consonants.

The vowel and speech segmentation information is used to associate timing information with the phoneme information from the text input. The text and phoneme duration rules are used to determine consonants and the detailed timing used to drive the facial animation.

Hybrid — Image-and-Speech-Driven

Guiard-Marigny et al. [GMAB94] and LeGoff et al. [LGMCB94] describe an approach to speech synchronization which is essentially automated rotoscoping. The shape of the generated mouth is determined by analyzing lip postures in a sequence of video images. The shape of the generated lips is computed using five parameters measured from real lip images. The five parameters are the height and width of the interior opening of the lips plus three lip protrusion values as shown in Figure 8.5.

The generated lips are modeled using 320 polygons organized in four contour bands around the mouth. A set of continuous functions was devised

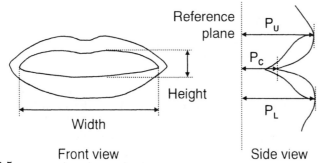

Figure 8.5.
Measured lip parameters. (Adapted from [LGMCB94].)

that fits the shape of the lips to the viseme shapes. These functions are controlled by coefficients, derived from the five measured parameters, which specify the equations that best fit the viseme lip contours.

The complete synthetic face is created by superimposing the lips on a parametrically controlled polygonal face model [Par74] [CM93] [CM94]. For this animation one additional parameter is measured from the video images to control the jaw rotation of the synthesized face. The created animation is used to support visual speech synthesis research where the generated facial animation is combined with the recorded speech.

8.4. Text-Driven Synchronized Speech

An appealing approach is to type in text and have both synthesized speech and synchronized facial animation created automatically. Synchronized synthetic visual speech is a general approach that lends itself to entirely automatic generation of speech animation. The major drawback is that qualities of current synthesized speech are far from those of natural speech. This approach is reported by Pearce et al. [PWWH86] and Hill et al. [HPW88]. Waters and Levergood [WL93] extended this approach to create the speech and animation simultaneously in real time.

The user inputs text that is automatically translated into the corresponding phonetic symbols. The system may also use other information such as models of spoken rhythm and intonation and a set of composition rules that provide appropriate modeling of the natural movement from one target to the next.

8.4.1. Speech Synthesis

A full treatment of speech analysis and synthesis is given in [WI82]. The first speech synthesizer that modeled the vocal tract was the Parametric Artificial Talker, invented in the 1950s. This device modeled the various sound energy sources (periodic or random), the spectral characteristics of noise bursts and aspiration, and the resonances of the vocal tract. Only the three lowest resonances need to be variable for good modeling.

Speech may be produced from such a synthesizer by analyzing real speech to determine the appropriate parameter values needed to drive the synthesizer.

It is possible, given a specification of the sounds in an intended utterance, to algorithmically generate the parameters needed to drive the speech synthesizer. The target parameter values for all the sounds are stored in a table and a simple interpolation procedure is written to mimic variation from one sound target to the next. Appropriate sound energy source changes can also be computed.

8.4.2. Linear Prediction Speech Synthesis and Resynthesis

Linear prediction coding is an extremely effective formulation for synthetic speech and serves as the basis of many modern voice response systems. Linear prediction coding can be used to synthesize speech or to resynthesize natural speech. Variations of this form of analysis and resynthesis are commonly used for speech compression.

Robotic speech quality is obtained if the excitation signal is a synthetically generated pulse train or a random sequence. In the case of synthetic excitation it is easy to speed up or slow down the speech. This change in speed is accomplished simply by accessing the coefficient frames at a faster or slower rate. Since the voice pitch is controlled by the excitation function, the speech rate can be changed without producing a shift in pitch.

In the most faithful resynthesis approach, the residual difference signal between the original speech and the output of the linear prediction filter is used as the synthesis excitation signal. The residual signal approximates an uncorrelated noise for consonants and whispered vowels, and approximates a pulse train for voiced vowels. The linear prediction analysis and the residual together encode most of the information in the original speech. Resynthesized speech is highly intelligible and retains the original inflection and rhythm, yet it has a subtle synthetic quality that may be appropriate for computer animation.

8.4.3. Extending Synthesis to Include Faces

Voice sound changes result directly from movements of the vocal articulators including the tongue, lips, and jaw rotation which in turn cause changes in facial posture. As a result, programs for speech synthesis can be extended by adding information for each speech posture to control the relevant parameters for a face model.

In the approach described by Pearce et al. [PWWH86], the phoneme script is specified directly by the animator. For example, *Speak to me now bad kangaroo* would be input as the following phonetic sequence:

s p ee k t u m in ah uu b aa d k aa ng g uh r uu

The implementation reported by Hill et al. [HPW88] starts with input text for the desired speech segment and transforms it into a phoneme sequence.

It is difficult to achieve natural rhythm and articulation when speech is generated from a phoneme script. Synthetic speech quality can be improved somewhat by adding pitch, timing, and loudness annotations to the phoneme script.

Using synthesis by rule algorithms, the phoneme sequence is used to control the speech generation. The phoneme sequence is also used to control a parameterized facial model. The speech synthesis algorithms are extended to produce not only the varying parameters needed for acoustic synthesis, but also the varying parameters needed to control the visible articulation attributes of a rendered synthetic face. This joint production process guarantees perfect synchronization between the facial speech expressions and the generated speech. The synthetic speech and the corresponding facial image sequences are generated separately and then merged in a post-process to form the final speech animation.

The extended speech algorithm outputs 17 parameter values at successive two millisecond intervals. The speech parameters are sent directly to the speech synthesizer to produce synthetic speech output. Nine face parameters controlling the jaw and lips are used to drive a version of the Parke [Par74] parameterized face model. The parameters may be interactively edited until the desired speech is obtained. All of the parameters are available for editing.

The facial parameter data is converted from the once-per-two-millisecond sampling rate to a once-per-frame time sampling rate, based on the desired number of frames per second. This conversion is done by resampling linear interpolation of the parameters. Hill observed that some form of temporal anti-aliasing might seem desirable. In practice anti-aliasing does not appear to be needed. Indeed, the wrong kind of anti-aliasing could have a very negative effect, by suppressing facial movements altogether. It may be better to motion blur the images directly, rather than anti-aliasing the parameter track definitions.

The parameters used for speech articulation were those originally specified by Parke [Par74]. These parameters include jaw rotation, mouth width, mouth expression, lip protrusion, lower-lip tuck, upper-lip position, and mouth corner position offsets.

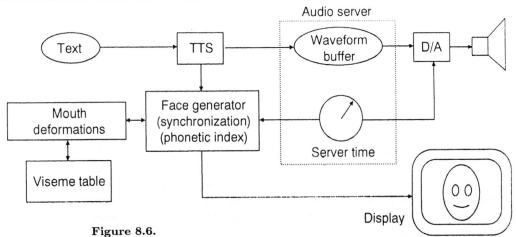

Figure 8.6.
Synchronized visual speech synthesis. (Adapted from [WL93].)

The tongue was not represented. High-quality speech animation requires that at least some parts of the mouth interior be included. At least the most visible part of the tongue and the more visible teeth should be included. Control of the tongue should be included in the low-level parameter set and reflected in the higher level phoneme parameterization.

8.4.4.   Waters' Real-Time Approach

Waters and Levergood developed a real-time synchronized visual speech system built around a software version of the DECtalk speech synthesizer [WL93]. In this system the text to be spoken was typed in and sent to the lexical analysis portion of the DECtalk synthesizer. This portion of the synthesizer produces a timed sequence of phonemes and control parameters that drive the speech output generation. Waters and Levergood intercept the timed phoneme information and use it to drive simultaneous real-time facial animation that is automatically synchronized with the generated speech. This process is illustrated in Figure 8.6.

8.5.   Speech-Driven Synchronization

If the desired speech track has already been recorded, then we would like automated techniques that analyze the speech track and produce the necessary timed control information to produce the synchronized facial animation. What we would like is a timed phoneme script that shows the sequence of speech phonemes and pauses along with timing information for each phoneme. This timing information would include when each phoneme begins and its duration. We would also like additional information about speech rhythm and intonation as well as indications of the speaker's emotional state. From the timed, and possibly annotated, phoneme script detailed low-level parameters are derived to control a face model. The generated facial image sequence is merged with the original speech recording to form the final speech animation.

Using recorded natural speech avoids many of the problems associated with synthetic speech such as the lack of natural speech rhythm, prosody, and emotional content. However, using recorded speech presents its own challenges.

8.5.1. Simple Volume Tracking

A very simple approach to speech synchronization is to simply open the mouth and rotate the jaw in proportion to the loudness of the speech. This approach requires only a very simple analysis of the speech track. Summing the absolute values of all digital samples in each interval will provide a measure of the speech loudness.

This approach is very limited. Real mouths don't just open and close. They assume a variety of visually distinct positions or postures during speech. This simple approach is not even approximately correct in all cases. For example, nasal *m* sounds can be loud even though the mouth is closed.

8.5.2. Speech Recognition Acoustic Preprocessor

Another analysis approach is to use the *front end* of a speech recognition system. Speech recognition involves transforming the speech into a representation in which the speech formant frequencies are emphasized and the pitch information is largely removed, and then parsing this representation to identify words. It is the parsing task that is most difficult. The acoustic preprocessing step is generally quite effective and fortunately is all that is required for deriving a phonetic script.

The first part of a speech recognition system is to analyze the speech waveform to identify speech components such as phonemes and pauses. If this analysis phase is augmented to tag these speech components with timing information, the result would be the phoneme script we need. However, most speech recognition systems do not provide output of this intermediate information. The acoustic analysis portion of a speech recognition system is probably overkill for the synchronization task. We really don't need the high level of speech component accuracy required for speech recognition.

What we really need is a system that will sample the speech waveform periodically and classify the current sample interval. This classification does not require the accuracy necessary for recognition. We just need to identify the viseme for each sample interval.

8.5.3. Linear Prediction Analysis

Lewis described such an automated method of analyzing recorded speech based on the *linear prediction* speech synthesis method [LP87] [Lew91]. In this approach, linear prediction is adapted to provide a fairly simple and reasonably accurate phoneme classification for each sample interval. The identified phonemes are then associated with mouth position parameters to produce synchronized speech animation.

This analysis approach uses the linear prediction speech synthesis model to obtain speech parameters that can be used to classify sample intervals into phoneme sets corresponding to visually distinctive mouth positions. This problem is considerably simpler than that of recognizing speech.

Linear-Prediction Speech Model

Linear prediction models a speech signal s_t as a broadband excitation signal ax_t input to a linear autoregressive filter. This filter uses a weighted sum of the input and past output of the filter:

$$s_t = \alpha x_t + \sum_{k=1}^{p} a_k s_{t-k}. \tag{8.3}$$

This is a fairly accurate model of speech production. The filter models the vocal tract including mouth, tongue, and lip positions. The excitation signal approximates the acoustic signal produced by the vocal cords. This model is useful, since both human speech production and human perception separate pitch (determined by vocal cord tension) from phonetic information (determined by the vocal tract filtering). This separation can be illustrated by sounding a fixed vowel while varying the pitch. The mouth position and vowel are entirely independent of pitch.

In linear prediction speech *resynthesis*, the excitation signal is approximated as either a pulse sequence, resulting in pitched vowel sounds, or as uncorrelated noise, resulting in consonants or whispered vowels depending on the filter. The filter coefficients a_k vary over time but are considered constant during the short time intervals used for analysis or synthesis. The analysis interval or frame time must be short enough to allow successive intervals to track perceptible speech events. However, the analysis interval needs to be longer than the voice pitch period. An analysis frame time of 15 to 20 milliseconds satisfies these conditions, and corresponds to 50 to 65 sample intervals or frames per second. The fact that this sampling rate works well suggests that sampling mouth movements at the standard 24 or

30 frame per second animation rates may not be sufficient to accurately represent many speech events.

For speech animation it is convenient to choose the analysis frame rate as twice the film or video playback frame rate. The resulting speech information can be reduced to the desired animation frame rate with a simple low-pass filter. Alternatively animation images may be generated at the higher sample rate (e.g., 60 frames per second) and filtered across image frames rather than across analysis frames. This supersampling approach reduces the temporal aliasing that can result from quantizing speech poses at the animation playback frame rate.

Solution Algorithm

Given an interval of digitized speech, the linear prediction coefficients a_k are determined by minimizing the squared error between the actual speech and predicted speech over some number of samples. Lewis points out that there are a number of approaches to determining this *least-squares* linear prediction.

References [RS79] [WI82] provide speech-oriented overviews of the autocorrelation approach and an additional covariance formulation, while [MG76] provides an exhaustive treatment of this subject.

Lewis uses the autocorrelation linear prediction method outlined below. This derivation views the speech signal as a random process that has stationary statistics over the analysis frame time. The expected squared estimation error

$$E = \mathbf{E}\{s_t - [\alpha x_t + \sum_{k=1}^{p} a_k s_{t-k}]\}^2 \qquad (8.4)$$

is minimized by setting

$$\partial \mathbf{E}/\partial a_k = 0.$$

Rewriting (8.4) in quadratic form leads to

$$\mathbf{E} = \{s_t s_{t-j} - (\alpha x_t s_{t-j} + \sum_{k=1}^{p} a_k s_{t-k} s_{t-j})\} = 0 \qquad (8.5)$$

for $1 \leq j \leq p$.

Since the excitation at time t is uncorrelated with the previous speech signal, the expectation of the product $\alpha x_t s_{t-j}$ is zero. The expectation of terms $s_{t-j} s_{t-k}$ are the $(j-k)$th values of the autocorrelation function. These substitutions result in the following equation:

$$\sum_{k=1}^{p} a_k R(j-k) = R(j) \qquad (8.6)$$

for $1 \leq j \leq p$, which can be solved for a_k given the analysis frame auto-correlation function R. The function R can be estimated directly from the sampled speech signal using

$$R(t) \approx (1/L) \sum_{t=0}^{L-\tau-1} s_t s_{t+t} \qquad (8.7)$$

for $0 \leq \tau \leq p$, where L is the length of the analysis interval in samples. The equations in (8.5) can be written in matrix form and solved using efficient numerical techniques. See [Lew91] for a more detailed treatment.

Classifying the Speech Sample

We don't need to know the exact phoneme, but just the visually distinct phoneme class. We do so by comparing the results of the analysis with similar results for a set of *reference phonemes* representing the visually distinct phoneme classes.

The coefficients a_k resulting from the linear prediction analysis describe the speech spectrum over the sample interval with the pitch information convolved out. A direct identification approach would be to compare the a_k coefficients for the interval with the a_k coefficients of the reference phonemes. However, least-squares identification directly on these coefficients performs poorly.

Lewis uses a classification scheme based on comparing the Euclidean distance of the interval spectrum with the spectra of the predetermined reference phonemes. This spectrum is obtained by evaluating the magnitude of the *z-transform* of (8.3) at N points on the complex z-plane. Lewis determined that a resolution of $N = 32$ is sufficient.

$$H(z) = \alpha / (1 - \sum_{k=1}^{p} a_k z^{-k}) \qquad (8.8)$$

where $z = e^{-j\pi k/N}$.

The value for p, the number of a_k coefficients used, is determined based on the maximum frequency of the sampled audio signal. One coefficient is used for each kHz of the audio digital sampling rate plus a few additional coefficients to model the overall spectrum shape.

Almost all of the semantically important information in speech lies below 5000 Hz, as demonstrated by the intelligibility of the telephone and AM radio. Therefore, if the signal has been low-pass filtered, an audio sampling

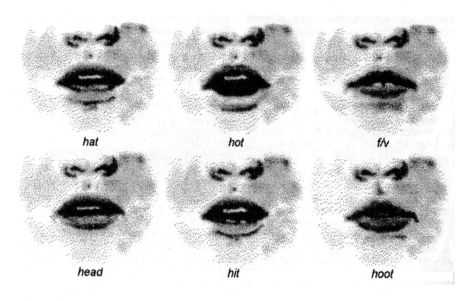

Figure 8.7.
Lip shapes for several of the reference phonemes.
(Adapted from [Lew91]).

rate of 10 kHz and a p of about 12 is sufficient for speech synchronization
analysis applications.

Reference Phonemes

There are more than 30 phonemes in spoken English [Fla65]. In most cases,
the visually distinctive mouth positions correspond to vowels; see Table 8.1
and Figure 8.2. The vowels are easily identified with the linear prediction
speech model. Lewis found that very accurate vowel identification is possible using the linear prediction approach with 12 reference phonemes. The
reference phoneme set he used consists of the vowels in the words *hate, hat,
hot, heed, head, hit, hoe, hug,* and *hoot* together with the consonant classes
m, s, and *f.* The mouth shapes for several of these reference phonemes are
shown in Figure 8.7.

Real-Time Implementations

In the system described by Lewis, the speech track analysis and the facial
image generation were implemented as separate nonreal-time tasks. The
timed phoneme information produced by the analysis task was saved and
used as input to the face animation system.

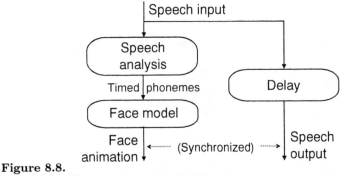

Figure 8.8.
Real-time synchronized speech animation.

With current high-end graphic workstations it is possible to analyze the speech and output synchronized facial animation essentially in real time. In this case, the speech analysis process feeds results directly into the facial animation process. The speech output is slightly delayed to compensate for the analysis processing time as shown in Figure 8.8.

8.6.   Expression Overlays

Complete communication between people takes place through the coordinated combination of spoken language, emotional voice qualities, facial expressions, and body language.

The face is an important and complex communication channel. While talking, a person is rarely still. The face changes expressions constantly. While talking, the lips move to help form the words, the eyebrows may raise, the eyes may move, the eyelids may blink, the head may turn, etc. Fully expressive automated character animation requires not only speech synchronization but also automatic generation of the characteristic facial movements such as expressions, prosodic nodding, and eye movements that occur during speech. The required expressions may be emotionally based or completely non emotional.

8.6.1.   Emotional Overlays

When people speak, there is almost always emotional information communicated along with the audible words. This emotional information is conveyed through multiple communication channels, including emotional qualities of the voice and visible facial expressions.

8.6.2.   Emotions

Emotion combines visceral and muscular physiological responses, autonomic
nervous system and brain responses, verbal responses, and facial expressions
[SLS84] [Ekm89]. Each emotion modifies physiology in particular ways. For
example, anger is characterized by muscle tension, a decrease of salivation,
a lowered brow, tense lips, and increased heart rate. Some of these physiological variations affect the vocal tract, while some muscle action variations
affect facial expressions.

Several universal facial expressions are linked to emotions and attitudes.
Anger, disgust, fear, happiness, sadness, and surprise are six emotions that
have universal facial expressions [EF75]. Three main areas of the face are
involved in visible expression changes: the upper part of the face with the
brows and forehead; the eyes; and the lower part of the face with the mouth.
Each emotion is characterized by specific facial changes. Fear is associated
with tense stretched lips with the eyebrows raised and drawn together. Sadness has the inner side of the brows drawn up, the upper eyelid inner corner
raised, and the corners of the lips down. The facial expressions of emotion
are called *affect displays* [Ekm89].

8.6.3.   Nonemotional Overlays

Not all facial expressions are the result of emotion. Some facial movements
are used as communication punctuation marks, similar to those used in
written text. For example, eyebrow motions can punctuate a conversation.
Ekman [Ekm89] divides nonemotional facial expression into the following
groups: *emblems, manipulators, conversational signals, punctuators,* and
regulators. The repertory of such movements is elaborate.

Emblems are movements whose meanings are well known and culturally
dependent. They are used to replace common verbal expressions. For example, instead of verbally agreeing, one can nod.

Manipulators correspond to the biological needs of the face, such as blinking the eyes to keep them wet and wetting the lips.

Conversational Signals

Conversational signals or *illustrators* are used to punctuate or emphasize
speech. Conversational signals may occur on an accented item within a
word or may stretch out over a portion of the sentence. These signals often
involve actions of the eyebrows. Raised eyebrows often accompany accented
vowels. Raised eyebrows can also signal a question. Head and eye motions
can illustrate a word. An accented word is often accompanied by a rapid
head movement [HSGR84] [BC85].

Conversational signals also depend on emotion. An angry or happy person will have more facial motions than a sad person. Emotion intensity affects the type and frequency of facial movements [Col85].

Punctuators

Punctuators are movements occurring at pauses. Punctuators appear at pauses due to hesitation or to signal the pauses associated with the commas or exclamation marks of written text [Dit74]. The number of pauses affects speech rate. The rate of occurrence and the type of punctuators are emotion dependent. A frightened person's speech seldom shows pauses even of short duration [Cah89]. A sad person's slow speech is partly due to a large number of long pauses. A happy person tends to punctuate speech by smiling.

Certain types of head movements occur during pauses. A boundary between intermediate phrases will often be indicated by slow movement while a final pause will often coincide with stillness [HSGR84]. Eye blinks can also occur during pauses [CO71].

Regulators

Regulators are movements that help control how people take speaking turns in conversation. Duncan [Dun74] enumerated the regulators as:

- *Speaker-Turn-Signal* is used when the speaker wants to give up her speaking turn. It is composed of several intonation, paralanguage, body movement, and syntax clues. At the end of the utterance, the speaker turns her head to the listener, takes a more relaxed position, and ends any hand gestures and body motions.

- *Speaker-State-Signal* is used at the beginning of a speaking turn. It usually consists of the speaker turning his head away from the listener and beginning a hand or arm gesture.

- *Speaker-Within-Turn* is used when the speaker wants to keep his speaking turn, and to assure himself that the listener is following. It occurs at the completion of a grammatical clause. The speaker turns his head toward the listener.

- *Speaker-Continuation-Signal* often follows a Speaker-Within-Turn signal. The speaker turns her head and eyes away from the listener.

When people talk to each other, the listener's head motions and facial expressions are synchronized with the speaker's voice. This synchronization plays an important role in effective conversation. These responses help regulate the flow of the conversation by providing feedback to the speaker.

8.6.4. Eye Actions

Eye actions include eye blinks, changes in eye gaze, and changes in pupil size.

Eye Blinks

Blinking is an important characteristic that should be included in synthetic face models used in conversational interface modes. Speaker eye blinks are an important part of speech response systems that include synchronized facial visualizations.

Eyes blink not only to accentuate speech but to address the physical need to keep the eyes wet. The eye blinks occur quite frequently. There is at least one eye blink per utterance.

The structure of an eye blink is synchronized with speech articulation. The eye might close over one syllable and start opening again over another word or syllable. Blinks can also occur on stressed vowels [CO71].

Blink occurrence is also emotion dependent. During fear, tension, anger, excitement, and lying, the amount of blinking increases while it decreases during concentrated thought [Col85].

Watanabe et al. [Wat93] proposed an eye blinking feedback model for synthetic faces. This model estimates eye blinks and head nodding responses based on the on-off characteristics of the speaker's voice.

Observations based on face-to-face human interaction indicate that there is synchronization between the speaker's voice and the speaker's eye blinks. Speaker's eye blinks follow pauses in the speech. There is a slight delay between speech pauses and the corresponding blinks. This delay is about 0.5 seconds. Experimental results indicate that this is a fairly strong effect occurring about 75 percent of the time.

Listener eye blinks and nods can be an important user feedback in speech recognition contexts. There is synchronization between the speaker's voice and the listener's eye blinks and also the listener's head nodding. Listener eye blinks also follow pauses in the speech. This effect is somewhat weaker, occurring about 50 percent of the time. The delay for the listener's blinks is about 0.4 seconds. Listener eye blinks frequently take place while nodding.

Eye Gaze

The eyes are almost always in motion. When looking at an object or person the eyes will scan it from the most important features to the least important in repeated cycles. When looking at a picture of a person the eyes spend about 60 percent of the time looking at the picture's eyes and about 15 percent of the time looking at the mouth [AC76]. In personal interactions eye gaze is modified by social and cultural context.

Eye contact is important nonverbal communication. The amount of allowed and expected eye contact is culturally dependent. Eye contact increases with the degree of intimacy and friendship. Eye contact decreases when a person is lying or having difficulty speaking. Aversion to eye contact can be a sign of shame or sorrow.

Gaze can be used to communicate intentions and to modify another person's behavior. Gaze can be a function of power, aggression, and domination especially when used contrary to normal cultural and social rules.

When a person is exasperated, or trying to solve a problem, or trying to remember something the eyes will look up.

Pupil Size

The pupils constrict in bright light and dilate in dim light. Pupil size also reflects a person's judgmental attitude. Large pupil size accompanies a positive attitude whereas constricted pupils are associated with negative judgments. Pupil dilation also changes during emotional experiences. Pupil dilation is followed by pupil constriction during happiness and anger and remains dilated during fear and sadness [Hes75].

8.7. Complete Speech Animation

As we have seen in the previous sections, complete speech animation of synthetic faces involves much more than simply manipulating the visible portions of the vocal tract. It involves the synchronized, coordination of many facial actions. Pelachaud [Pel91] has proposed an approach to computing the sequence of required facial poses that synchronizes and coordinates these many actions to produce complete speech animation.

This process is driven from an input script that contains the desired speech specified as phonemes along with emotion and intonation information. Based on the input script the following steps are applied to determine the complete facial posture for each phoneme of the animation. The computed complete postures are defined in terms of Ekman's facial action units [EF78].

1. Compute lip shapes by applying rules that transform phonemes into action units. Computing the lip shapes takes into account coarticulation of the phoneme sequences.

2. Determine the action units for the desired emotion.

3. Compute eyebrow actions based on speech intonation accents, pauses, and emphasis.

4. Compute eye blinks taking into account voluntary blinks associated with speech and emotion and the involuntary physiological eye blinks. Speech-related blinks are computed at the phoneme level

5. Compute head motion based on emotion, speech accents and pauses, and conversational turn-taking rules.

6. Compute eye movements to scan the listener's face and to follow head motion.

7. Compute eye pupil size.

8. Collect and reconcile the facial action units generated by the previous steps. Concurrent actions can occur. The final face posture is the summation of all applied actions modified to reconcile any conflicting actions.

9. Having computed the list of action units for each phoneme, in-between frames are obtained by spline interpolation of the phoneme values. Interpolation of the phoneme values takes into account the duration, onset, and offset characteristics of each action unit.

10. Generate the complete facial expression image for each frame based on the interpolated action unit information.

9

Performance Animation

9.1. Background

The creation of facial animation control parameters is a tedious process at best. Often dozens of parameters have to be specified and coordinated to create just a short animation sequence. For the face it is important to orchestrate the parameters carefully, since actions have to be timed and overlapped precisely to create believable facial expressions. For example, to create a believable expression of surprise, the onset and duration have to be correctly specified or else the motion will look more like a lazy yawn.

To alleviate the time-consuming activity of data collection, it is possible to capture the motion of live performers, or puppeteers, and translate their actions into animation control parameters. This process of motion capture has two fundamental approaches, in real time or nonreal time. Real-time systems, which are predominantly performance-based, record actions and play the results simultaneously. Nonreal-time systems typically record in real time with the animation subsequently animated by frame-by-frame slaving.

An early example of animation slaving, or *expression mapping*, was used to create the animated short film *Tony de Peltrie* by Bergeron and Lachapelle [BL85]. A person's face, onto which a polygon topology was painted, was photometrically digitized in a variety of expressions to create a database of facial postures. A mapping was then specified between the human's face to the very exaggerated "Tony" caricature face (see Figure 9.2). Consequently, shape changes from the database of digitized expressions were mapped onto the caricature face. A variation of expression slaving was developed by de-Graf and Wahrman [Par90]. Rather than slaving expressions, data collected from a series of laser scans were used directly and interpolated in real time.

Real-time systems offer an opportunity either for a live interactive performance or to combine computer graphics with traditional puppetry. This new art form presents many new possibilities in the realm of puppet character design and solves some of the nagging problems in computer animation.

Another powerful technique is to track the features of the face directly from live or video-recorded images. To date this method has been difficult; however, a number of emerging techniques, some manual and some automated, show great promise.

9.1.1. Basic Principles

The basic principles of performance-based animation are straightforward. Devices such as six-degrees-of-freedom trackers, DataGloves ^{TM} keyboards, joysticks, and video cameras capture the actions of a performer (see Figure 9.1). The actions are then processed and converted into time-varying control parameters. A computer-generated character is then animated in real time, or used to drive an animated character at a later date. An example of a real-time performance-based system is illustrated in Plate IX. The system, called System G, is a real-time 30-frames-a-second animation and texture mapper. The Kabuki mask originated as a flat image and was warped into a three-dimensional model and, by means of predefined macros, the face can be transitioned between a variety facial postures. To control the system a keyboard, connected to a PC, acts as a front-end device, as illustrated in Figure 9.1, such that when a key is depressed a facial posture is displayed. While the principles of performance-based animation are straightforward, the actual implementation details vary a great deal. Therefore the remainder of this chapter describes a variety of different performance-based animation techniques.

9.1.2. Animatronics

Animatronics is a mechanical precursor of computer-based performance animation. Animatronics frequently is used in special effects, especially when it is impossible for a puppeteer to insert a hand into the puppet. In such a situation the performer is placed off-camera and provided with a remote interface through which he can manipulate the character.

The most common animatronic puppets are radio controlled. Motors, mounted inside the puppet, move various features of the faces, such as opening and closing the mouth. The puppeteer is given a number of physical

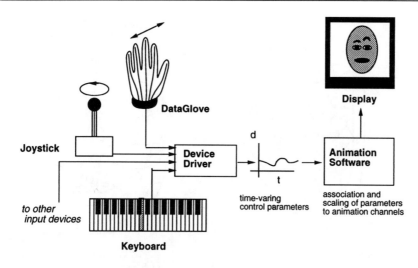

Figure 9.1.
The basic principles of performance-based animation control. In this
example one of the input device channels is associated with the raising
of an eyebrow. The animation software associates and scales the
parameters for the particular computer character.

controls which transmit radio signals to the motors mounted inside the puppet. As the puppeteer moves the controls, the puppet moves accordingly.
These interfaces often resemble the puppets they are designed to control,
and the manner in which the performer manipulates them is very similar
to the way he or she would manipulate the real puppet. A term commonly
used to refer to the skeleton type of interface is a *Waldo*.

A classic example of a Waldo is the bicycle scene from *The Muppet Movie*.
In this scene Kermit and Piggy are riding bicycles through a park while
singing a song. Lip-synching requires the puppeteer to have direct real-time
control. As one can imagine, it is difficult to hide a person on a bicycle
built for a three-foot puppet; hence the use of Waldos. Each Waldo consists
of a glove, much like the inside of a puppet, mounted on the end of a rod.
The performer places one hand in the glove and holds the end of the rod in
the other. Consequently, as the puppeteer's hand is opened and closed, the
mouth of the puppet opens and closes accordingly.

9.1.3. Computer-Aided Animatronics

The next logical development for animatronics involves replacing the mechanical puppet by an equivalent computer-generated model. Instead of
transmitting controls to a mechanical device, the parameters control a com-

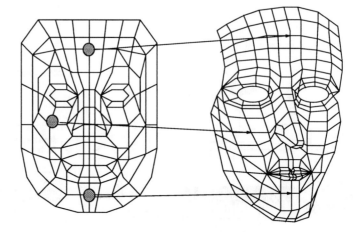

Figure 9.2.
A one-to-N correspondence mapping of the sampled face to a
computer-generated counterpart. The mapping can be specified as a
weighting function, which usually is specified by hand. However, a
weighting function can be specified as a proportion of distance d from
the center location. Such a function allows displacement fields to
interact and overlap.

puter-generated character directly. However, how does one integrate computer-
generated puppets with their real, physical counterparts?

9.1.4. Producing a Computer-Generated Waldo

Creating a scene with a computer-generated Waldo takes place in three
phases. The first phase involves a live session with an interactive wireframe
Waldo operating in concert with other characters (see Figure 9.3). This system outputs a low-resolution image of the character and, at the same time,
records its movements. This procedure is referred to as *interactive rotoscoping*. In the second phase of the production process, the recorded motion data
are input to an animation system. Within the animation system secondary
motion can be added, for example, a pseudodynamic simulation to generate
a flexible motion of the body and appendages. In the final phase, a fully
rendered version of the Waldo is composited with the live-action puppets,
and special effects are added and recorded to tape.

Phase 1: Interactive Rotoscoping

Interactive rotoscoping, which captures the Waldo's movements, is based on
an electromechanical armature. The armature itself, resembling an upside-

down luxo lamp, with optical encoders mounted at the joints and "clamshell" gloves mounted at one end, record the movements of the puppeteer (see Figure 9.3). The output of the animated character subsequently is fed to the regular video system used to record the performance of the handmade puppets. Waldo's performer places his hand in the glove and in real time can manipulate a low-resolution image of Waldo on the screen. This image is then composited on top of the regular puppet's performance [Gra89].

The fact that the live performance of Waldo can be seen on the same screen as that for the regular puppets is significant. When puppeteers perform they do not gauge their performance by looking at the puppets above their heads but rather by looking at the monitors that display the image being recorded by the camera. Thus from the performer's point of view, seeing Waldo on the screen is the same as having him float around in front of the camera. This means that in terms of eye contact, lip sync, and blocking, a Waldo can interact with the other characters as they interact with each other.

Phase 2: Secondary Action

The second phase creates the high-resolution images of the Waldo. It principly involves building any new models required for the Waldo's costumes, designing any secondary animation needed to affect Waldo's transformations, and finally specifying the parameters for the pseudodynamic simulation system.

Most of this work is done with a standard animation system. Models are constructed from primitives and reused as much as possible, so much so that modeling on the Waldo project is referred to as "wardrobe." Secondary animation is kept to a minimum, and the bulk of the character's personality is brought out through dynamics.

The pseudodynamic simulation is performed by examining the motion of an object and, based on a description of its flexibility, deforming its shape accordingly. An object can be made to appear flexible and dynamic.

It was decided that Waldo's face, tail, and upper body were to remain stiff, while his flippers, belly, nose, and hat get flexed towards their extremes. One successful use of this technique has been the automatic generation of effective squash-and-stretch and follow-through motions.

Phase 3: Compositing

In the final step the high-resolution animation is recomposited on top of the image of the puppets as performed. Careful consideration has to be given to ensure that the animation is perfectly synchronized with the original performance. The slightest deviation will cause glaring problems in lip sync, eye contact, and simple blocking.

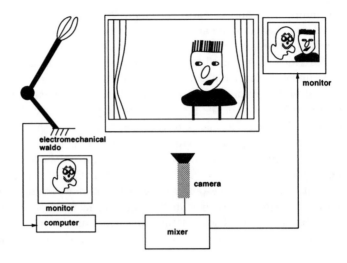

Figure 9.3.
The production of a computer-generated Waldo. The camera captures
the live action of the puppeteer, which is then mixed with a
computer-generated image for display on a monitor for both the
Waldo operator and the real puppeteer.

9.2. Virtual Actors

Virtual actors, as the name suggests, are computer-generated characters
whose movements are controlled by actors, or puppeteers, in real time. Mike
Normal, developed by deGraf and Wahrman [DW88], is an example of a
virtual actor.

9.2.1. Constructing Mike Normal

Mike Normal was constructed from a series of Cyberware^{TM} laser scans of
an actor Mike Gribble. In addition to a static pose, two dozen or so key postures were captured, including round- and close-mouth postures for speech
mapping. Each scan was subsequently resampled to reduce the resolution
from forty thousand polygons to approximately two thousand.

9.2.2. Animating Mike

Having all digitized postures topologically equivalent was the key to animating Mike because any intermediate postures could be simply generated by
interpolation functions.

In addition to interpolating the whole face configuration, regions of the face could be harnessed to particular actions. For example, the eyebrow region could be extracted from one scan and blended onto another. By grouping specific regions of the face to particular actions, a variety of channels could control the facial model. Each face unit was controlled by a single channel in real time, allowing the layering of new animation with predefined animation clips. The fundamental creation of a new face posture could be described by the following shorthand notation:

$$NewFace = ChannelA * FaceUnit1 + ChannelB * FaceUnit2 + ... \quad (9.1)$$

Some channels could be driven automatically, akin to the human nervous system, such as nostril flares, blinking, breathing, and babbling. Alternatively, units could be associated such that the brows rose when the mouth opened beyond a certain point.

Skilled puppeteers simultaneously controlled a number of Mike's degrees of freedom, allowing them to transparently translate their refined hand-eye coordination. It was crucial that the interface provided an interactive performance (10-12 Hz) to allow the puppeteer to observe the actions of the Waldo with the real puppets. The first puppeteer to use the system embedded amazing life into Mike in his first hour of use.

9.3. Advanced Techniques

The techniques described so far all require mechanical or electromechanical devices to translate the motions of puppeteers into time-varying control parameters. Although the results are satisfactory, there is growing interest in the development of noninvasive techniques to track a face over time and extract time-varying parameters automatically.

9.4. Automated Spot Tracking

The simplest approach to tracking the face and its features is to track markers placed directly on the subject's face. This technique is appropriate for one-time performances in which the actor is placed in an artificial environment with spots painted on his or her face. By recording the actions on videotape, an off-line process can then be applied to extract the location of the markers in the image plane. The resulting displacements of these spots then can be used to control a facial texture map [Wil90b].

The process involves sticking retroreflective markers directly onto the performer's face. A beam-splitter (a plate glass), set at 45 degrees between the

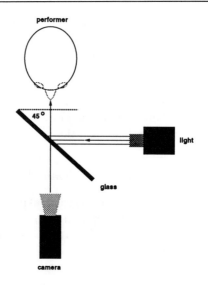

Figure 9.4.
The configuration of the camera, light, and glass plate during the video
recording process. This configuration ensures that the light and camera
are coaxial.

camera and the performer, and a slide projector, set at right angles to the
camera position, ensures that the direction of the light and the camera are
coaxial (see Figure 9.4). By adjusting the light intensity and camera aperture it is possible to generate views on which the retroreflective markers —
and little else — are visible.

The problem of digitizing the actor's performance now becomes one of
tracking a set of bright spots in a dark field. By placing the markers carefully
to avoid occlusion and by ignoring global head translation and rotation, the
problem reduces to a planar x, y-tracking problem.

The basis of the spot tracking algorithm is solved as follows. (1) The
centroid of a marker is selected manually from the first video frame. (2) A
window a few pixels larger than the spot, is positioned around the selected
pixel. (3) The x, y coordinates of each pixel are multiplied by the intensity
of the current pixel. (4) The window's center of gravity (c_x, c_y), based on
light intensity, is then calculated using the following equations:

$$S = \sum_x \sum_y I(x, y). \qquad (9.2)$$

$$C_x = \sum_y \sum_x x * I(x, y)/S. \qquad (9.3)$$

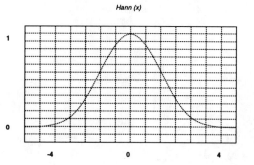

Figure 9.5.
Hann window.

$$c_y = \sum_y \sum_x y * I(x,y)/S. \qquad (9.4)$$

(5) To refine the location of the pixel intensities first moment, the process is iterated a few times.

Finally, the next frame and the subsequent motion of the spot are introduced, and the process is repeated using the old window position as a starting point. The result is a new center of gravity, and the window moves accordingly.

To apply the locator displacements to the facial model, a varation of a Hanning function was used [Wol91]. A Hanning function is specified as follows:

$$Hann(x) = \begin{cases} \alpha + (1-\alpha)\cos\frac{2\Pi x}{N-1}, & x < \frac{N-1}{2} \\ 0 & \text{otherwise.} \end{cases}$$

In three dimensions the Hanning function is described to be radially symmetric and is scaled to 1.0 in the center, diminishing smoothly to 0.0 at the edges with no negative values.

The technique of spot tracking is effective provided that there are discrete markers to track and that they remain in view at all times. More recently, there have been some commercializations of this type of approach. Adaptive Optics developed a device that the user wears on his or her head in combination with reflective markers placed on the face (see Figure 9.4.(a)). When the person moves, the head-mounted camera moves in unison (see Figure 9.4.(b)); as a result the markers remain in view at all times and obviates the need to compensate for head rotation, tilting, and looming. By tracking components of the face, it then becomes possible for a computer puppet to mimic the facial actions of the performer.

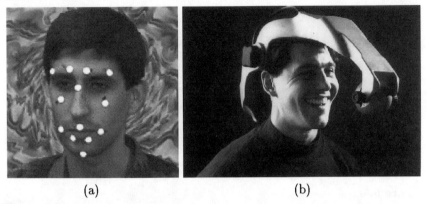

(a)   (b)

Figure 9.6.
A head-mounted optical face tracker (Courtesy of Adaptive Optics).
(a) illustrates the placement of reflective marker on the face, and
(b) shows the head-mounted device, without markers on the face.

The obvious limitations of this approach are that it requires a subject to wear head attire and to have his or her face marked or painted. While these limitation are fine in many situations, the ability to capture facial motion in an unconstrained environment is a more significant problem.

9.4.1. Image Analysis

The concept of automatically tracking the face and its features has drawn the attention of the computer vision community over the past few years. Much of this attention has been focused on the general problem of tracking the face in everyday environments under general lighting conditions. To *reliably* perform these tasks is hard.

Despite the complexity of the problem, there has been some success in both model-based and image-based analysis. Model-based analysis assumes that there is an underlying geometry to which the image can be matched. This method is in contrast to image-based approaches that deal with fundamental transformations of the image or parts of the image. Several examples follow.

9.4.2. Deformable Templates

A deformable template makes the assumption that the face consists of features (such as the eyes, nose, and mouth) that are uniquely identifiable in the image under analysis. Therefore, a model, called a *template*, can define the shape under observation by modifying the parameters that describe the geometry of the template. An example of a eye deformable template was developed by Yuille [YCH89]. The template, as illustrated in Figure 9.7, consists of the following features:

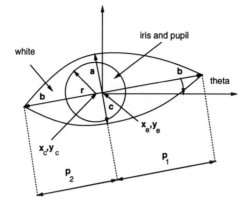

Figure 9.7.
A deformable template for an archetypal human eye.

- A circle of radius r, centered on a point $\vec{x}_c$. This circle corresponds to the boundary between the iris and the whites of the eye.

- A bounding contour of the eye attracted to edges. This contour is modeled by two parabolic sections representing the upper and lower parts of the boundary. It has a center $\vec{x}_e$, with eye width $2b$, maximum height c for the boundary below the center, and an angle of orientation θ.

- Two points, corresponding to the centers of the whites of the eyes, which are attracted to peaks in the image intensity. These points are specified by $\vec{x}_e + p_1(\cos\theta, \sin\theta)$ and $\vec{x}_e + p_2(\cos\theta, \sin\theta)$, where $p_1 \geq 0$ and $p_2 \leq 0$. The point $\vec{x}_e$ lies at the center of the eye, and θ corresponds to the orientation of the eye.

- The regions between the bounding contour and the iris also correspond to the whites of the eyes. These regions will be assosicated with large values in the image intensity function. These components are linked together by three types of forces: (i) forces that encourage $\vec{x}_c$ and $\vec{x}_e$ to be close together, (ii) forces that make the width $2b$ of the eye roughly four times the radius r of the iris, and (iii) forces that encourage the centers of the whites of the eyes to be roughly midway from the center of the eye to the boundary.

In total, the eye template has 11 parameters represented by

$$\vec{g} = (\vec{x}_c, \vec{x}_e, p_1, p_2, r, a, b, c, \theta).$$

All of these parameters are allowed to vary during matching.

Image Intensities

The deformable template acts on the representation of the image. The representation is chosen to extract properties of the image, such as peaks or troughs in the image intensity. In turn, the intensities act as potential fields, attracting components of the template. An image edge Φ_e, valley Φ_v, and peak Φ_p potential functions can be computed as follows:

$$\Phi_e(x,y) = e^{-\rho(x^2+y^2)^{1/2}} * \Psi_e(x,y),$$

$$\Phi_v(x,y) = e^{-\rho(x^2+y^2)^{1/2}} * \Psi_v(x,y),$$

$$\Phi_p(x,y) = e^{-\rho(x^2+y^2)^{1/2}} * \Psi_p(x,y), \tag{9.5}$$

where $-\rho(x^2+y^2)^{1/2}$ is an exponent smoothing function that enables interactions to be effective over longer distances.

Energy Function

At the heart of the algorithm is a potential energy function for the image which is minimized as a function of the parameters of the template. The complete energy function is given as a combination of terms due to valley, edge, peak, image, and internal potentials:

$$E_c = E_v + E_e + E_i + E_p + E_{prior}. \tag{9.6}$$

As an example, the edge potentials E_e are given by the integrals over the boundaries of the circle divided by its length and over the parabola divided by their lengths:

$$E_e = -\frac{c_2}{|\partial R_w|} \int_{\partial R_w} \Phi_e(\vec{x})ds - \frac{c_3}{|\partial R_w|} \int_{\partial R_w} \Phi_e(\vec{x})ds. \tag{9.7}$$

For the complete set of edge potentials described in Equation 9.6, the reader is referred to the original paper [YCH89].

One of the limitations of this approach is that the template can become brittle and unstable. For instance, the feature has to be apparent in the image under observation; if not, the template will continue to fit to the data with which it is presented, even though the feature may not be present. Another limitation is that although eyes usually appear to have an iris, a pupil, and distinct boundaries, under variable lighting conditions and observation angles the features can be misinterpreted.

9.4.3. Snakes or Active Contour Models

By relaxing the feature-based template constraint to a single two-dimensional curve or spline, it becomes possible to track feature lines and boundaries in the image. This ability is particularly interesting because the face has many such features such as brows, furrows, and lip margins. A technique commonly referred to as *active contour* or *snake* can be used to track features over time [KWT88].

9.4.4. A Discrete Deformable Contour

A discrete deformable contour is defined as a set of nodes indexed by $i = 1, \ldots, n$ that are connected in series by springs [TW90]. Associated with these nodes are time-varying positions $\vec{x}_i(t) = [x_i(t), y_i(t)]'$ in the image plane. An interactive deformable contour results from numerically simulating the first-order dynamical system

$$\gamma \frac{d\vec{x}_i}{dt} + \boldsymbol{\alpha}_i + \boldsymbol{\beta}_i = \vec{f}_i; \qquad i = 1, \ldots, n, \tag{9.8}$$

where γ is a velocity-dependent damping constant, $\boldsymbol{\alpha}_i$ and $\boldsymbol{\beta}_i(t)$ are "tension" and "rigidity" forces internal to the contour, and $\vec{f}_i(t)$ are external forces acting in the image plane.

By following the formulation of a basic spring lattice as described in Chapter 7, Equation 7.9, we can describe a chain of nodes connected together by springs where l_i is the natural length of the spring connecting node i to node $i+1$. Let $\vec{r}_i = \vec{x}_{i+1} - \vec{x}_i$ be the separation of the nodes, and let $e_i = ||\vec{r}_i|| - l_i$ be the deformation. Hence,

$$\boldsymbol{\alpha}_i = \frac{a_i e_i}{||\vec{r}_i||} \vec{r}_i, \tag{9.9}$$

where $a_i(t)$ is a tension variable. A viscoelastic contour may be obtained by letting $dl_i/dt = \nu_i e_i$, where ν_i is a coefficient of viscoelasticity. Next,

$$\boldsymbol{\beta}_i = b_{i+1}(\vec{x}_{i+2} - 2\vec{x}_{i+1} + \vec{x}_i) - 2b_i(\vec{x}_{i+1} - 2\vec{x}_i + \vec{x}_{i-1}) + b_{i-1}(\vec{x}_i - 2\vec{x}_{i-1} + \vec{x}_{i-2}), \tag{9.10}$$

where b_i are rigidity variables. Tension, rigidity, and viscoelasticity are locally adjustable though the a_i, b_i, and ν_i variables.

The deformable contour is responsive to a force field, derived from the image, that influences its shape and motion. It is convenient to express the force field though a time-varying potential function $P(x, y, t)$:

$$\vec{f}_i = p\nabla P(\vec{x}_i), \tag{9.11}$$

where p is the strength of the image forces and $\nabla = [\partial/\partial x, \partial/\partial y]'$ is the gradient operator in the image plane.

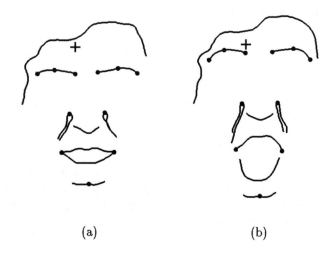

(a)   (b)

Figure 9.8.
Snakes and control points used for muscle contraction estimation on two
key frames: (a) a relaxed face and (b) a surprised expression.

9.4.5. Active Contours and Faces

The human face has many feature lines and feature boundaries that an active
contour can track. By placing the contours on or close to specific features,
such as an eyebrow or a lip boundary, it is possible not only to track the
feature but also to estimate face muscle contraction parameters from image
sequences. In turn these parameters can be used to drive a facial animation
model [TW93].

9.4.6. Image Processing and Facial Feature Tracking

To apply deformable contours to facial image analysis, the image intensity
function $I(x, y, t)$ at time t is transformed into a planar force field using
image processing techniques. The procedure is illustrated in Figure 9.8.
From the facial image in Figure 9.8(a), a 2D potential function $P(x, y, t)$ is
created whose ravines (extended local minima) coincide with the significant
intensity changes associated with facial features such as the eyebrows, mouth,
and chin. This action is accomplished by computing the magnitude of the
gradient of the image intensity:

$$P(x, y, t) = -||\nabla G_\sigma * I(x, y, t)||, \qquad (9.12)$$

where $G_\sigma *$ denotes convolution with a Gaussian smoothing filter of width σ
that broadens the ravines so that they attract the contours from a distance.

Figure 9.9(b) shows the negative of $P(x, y)$ computed from the frame in Figure 9.9(a).

The contours "slide downhill" in $P(x, y, t)$ (for fixed t) and come to equilibrium at the bottoms of the nearest ravines, thus conforming to the shapes of the facial features of interest. Once the contours have settled into ravines of the current image, the next image is introduced, and the contours again slide into the displaced ravines so long as the movement of facial features is small. This procedure is repeated on subsequent frames to track the nonrigid motions of the facial features. As the deformable contours evolve, their dynamic-state variables $\vec{x}_i^t$ provide quantitative information about the nonrigid shapes and motions of the facial features.

9.4.7. A Facial Image Analysis Example

Figure 9.9 illustrates the analysis of one of the frames in the sequence, showing nine deformable contours (black curves in Figure 9.9(a), white curves in Figure 9.9(b)) in their final equilibrium positions locked onto the left and right eyebrows, the left and right nasolabial furrows, the tip of the nose, the upper and lower lips, and the chin boss. Highlighter, applied to the brows and lips, enhanced the image feature boundary contrasts making them easier to track from frame to frame. From the state variables of the deformable contours, the following are automatically estimated:

- Head reference point from the average position of the hairline contour;

- Contractions of the left and right zygomaticus major from the position of the endpoints of the upper-lip contour;

- Contraction of the left and right levator labii superioris alaeque nasi from the positions of the uppermost points of the associated nasolabial furrow contours;

- Contractions of the left and right inner, major, and outer occipito-frontalis, respectively, from the positions of the innermost, center, and outermost points of the associated eyebrow contours; and

- Jaw rotation from the average position of the chin boss contour.

The estimated muscle contractions may be converted to dynamic contraction factors and input to the face model to reconstruct the expression. A sequence of frames from the reconstructed motion of surprise is illustrated in Figure 9.9(c).

Recently the spline-based approach to tracking facial features in images was improved by [BI94]. In their model the snake was a B-spline with time-varying control points. The most significant enhancement was the ability to sensitize the spline to various affine transformations, in particular zooming,

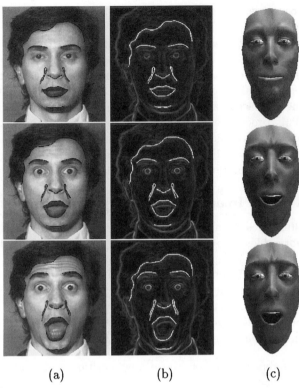

(a)   (b)   (c)

Figure 9.9.
Dynamic facial image analysis using deformable contours (a) and (b),
and the resulting facial mimic (c) from muscle contraction estimates.

translation, and rotation. This ability was achieved with a slightly modified steady-state Kalman filter [PFTV86]. This basic rigid motion tracker
was further enhanced to capture nonrigid motions such as the shape of the
lips during speaking. To achieve a profile lip tracker, as illustrated in Figure 9.10, additional lip posture key frames were added to the fundamental
matrix formulation (see [BI94] for details) such that nonrigid motion and
rigid motion could be monitored independently.

9.4.8. Local Parametric Models of Facial Image Motion

More recently it has been shown that it is possible to recover image motion
parameters that correspond to various facial expressions, which is achieved
by exploiting both the template-based and optic flow-based approaches (See
[MP91] [BY95] [EP94].)

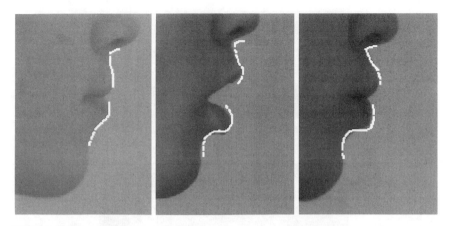

Figure 9.10.
Three example tracked key-frame lip postures. (Courtesy of A. Blake
and M. Isard.) A weighted sum of these key frames are added to the
formulation of the basic rigid motion tracker.

Optic-flow computations rely on a sequence of images at a pixel level of
detail [Sin91]. Essentially, flow can be estimated by tracking the motion of
pixels or of a small group of pixels from frame to frame. To be effective,
optical flow requires as much textural detail as possible to be present in the
region of interest; otherwise it becomes hard to determine where a group of
pixels move.

An example of an image flow field can be seen in Figure 9.11(d), where
flow vectors have been overlayed on the face image [EP94]. The resulting
facial image flow patterns makes it possible to estimate muscle activation
and subsequently classify facial expressions. This ability to capture the
dynamic characteristics of facial expression is particularly significant because facial coding systems, such as FACS, ignore the temporal aspects of
an expression that undoubtedly plays a significant role in the recognition of
emotions [Dar72]. Furthermore, it is being argued that the dynamics of expressions, rather than the detailed spatial deformations, are more significant
for facial expression recognition [Bas87]. By generating patterns of motion
energy (see Figure 9.11(c)) from optical flow examples of facial expression,
Essa and Pentland were able to construct a simple expression detector which
identifies motion energy associated with a particular facial expression [EP95].

In more general terms, two principle motions for the head and face have
to be accounted for if we are to track and identify expressions on the face:
rigid head motions and nonrigid motions associated with the facial features
(see Figure 9.12). Figure 9.13 illustrates the various parameters that can
be used to represent the motion of image regions [BY95]. The first two,

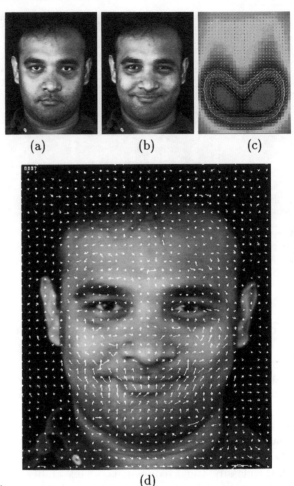

(a)   (b)   (c)

(d)

Figure 9.11.
Optic flow estimation images. (Courtesy of I. Essa.) (a) and (b) are two
poses of the face, static and smiling. (d) illustrates the flow estimates of
the face for the transition between (a) and (b) while (c) shows the
pattern of motion energy for the expression.

divergence and deformation, are affine transformations; the last, curl, is a
bending of the image. This type of parameterization can be captured in a
low-order polynomial:

$$u(x,y) = a_0 + a_1 x + a_2 y,$$

$$v(x,y) = a_3 + a_4 x + a_5 y, \tag{9.13}$$

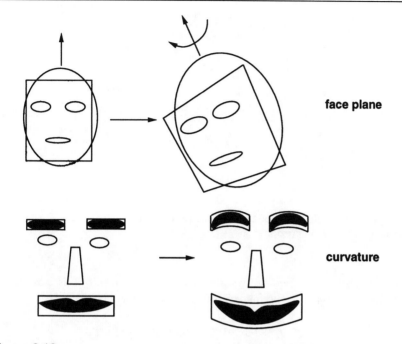

face plane

curvature

Figure 9.12.
The top row illustrates the basic affine transformations: divergence,
deformation, and curl. The principle assumption is that the face is a
planar surface. The bottom row illustrates the curvature
transformations for the face, the brows, and the lips.

where a_i are constants and where $u(x, y)$ and $v(x, y)$ are the horizontal and
vertical components of the flow at an image point $\mathbf{x} = (x, y)$.

The parameters a_i have simple interpretations in terms of image motion
(as illustrated in Figure 9.13). For example, a_0 and a_3 represent horizontal and vertical translation, respectively. These parameters take care of the
planar motions. Divergence (isotropic expansion), curl (rotation), and deformation (squashing) can be created by the following combinations:

$$divergence = a_1 - a_5$$

$$curl = -a_2 + a_4$$

$$deformation = a_1 - a_3. \qquad (9.14)$$

The affine transformations are not sufficient to capture the motion of
a face when it occupies a significant proportion of the field of view. To
accommodate these characteristics the face can be approximated as a single

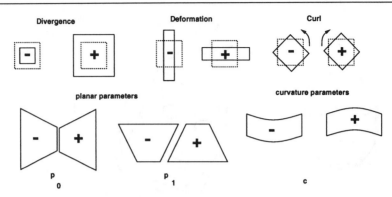

Figure 9.13.
A graphical representation of the motions captured by the various
parameters or various regions.

plane viewed under perspective projection. As a result it is possible to
describe the image by the following eight-parameter model:

$$u(x, y) = a_0 + a_1 x + a_2 y + p_0 x^2 + p_1 xy,$$

$$v(x, y) = a_3 + a_4 x + a_5 y + p_0 xy + p_1 y^2. \tag{9.15}$$

The two additional terms p_0 and p_1 are added to correspond to "yaw" and
"pitch."

The nonrigid motions of facial features such as the eyebrows and mouth
cannot be captured by the affine transformations. The basic curvature characteristics can be captured by the addition of a parameter c to the affine
transformation:

$$u(x, y) = a_0 + a_1 x + a_2 y,$$

$$v(x, y) = a_3 + a_4 x + a_5 y + c x^2. \tag{9.16}$$

The c parameter captures the gross curvature of the features. In combination with the basic affine transformation, the seven parameters can capture
the essential image motion of the mouth and eyebrows.

9.5. Future Work

In this chapter we can clearly see that animation and puppetry are very different disciplines: computer animation is planned, puppetry is spontaneous.
Spontaneity provides a Waldo vitality and expressiveness that would require

laborious efforts in a standard computer animation system. As a result, Waldos are a valuable tool in the animation process. However, the possibilities for Waldos are relatively unexplored, and there remain a number of areas that require additional invesigation:

- Editing systems. Given that we can capture live performance, what kinds of editing tools are appropriate for refining these performances?

- At what point should performance be abandoned in favor of more script-oriented animation systems?

- The puppet interfaces have to meet the requirements of puppeteer. In particular the interface must have a sense of the neutral and a sense of programmed control resistance, or force feedback.

The ability to track an actor's actions has enormous potential for performance-based animation. For facial animation this is particularly relevant because we are highly tuned to subtle facial actions that are extremely difficult to mimic using traditional script-based techniques. In the case of one-time performances in a studio, invasive markers can be tolerated. However, in situations where the actions are not known in advance, such as an avatar on the internet, head-mounted devices or markers cannot be effectively worn all the time.

The difficult task of automatically tracking heads and facial motion without invasive markers or special lighting conditions remains an active, and rapidly changing, area of research. As a result what has been covered in this chapter is neither inclusive nor complete, but provides an insight into current trends; no doubt we will see the most rapid development in the areas that will have commercial impact, for example, face tracking for video teleconferencing or the ability to develop synthetic agents capable of responding visually and audibly to our behavior. The latter offers a unique opportunity to break the traditional mold of human-computer interaction.

10

Modeling and Animating Hair

Realistic synthetic human images need realistic hair models and realistic hair motion. Such representations of human hair present challenges to all aspects of computer graphics including shape modeling, animation, and rendering.

10.1. Hair Characteristics

There are typically about 100,000 individual hair strands on the average person's head. The diameter of a human hair is from 40 to 120 microns. The shape of each of these thin hair strands can be quite complex.

Hair has complex dynamic and optical properties. Friction, static, strand-to-strand interactions, and hair-to-head interactions contribute to its dynamic complexity. Hair can have a wide variety of colors and mixtures of colors. It has anisotropic reflection properties. It is self-shadowing. Its color, optical, and dynamic properties may be altered by a variety of cosmetic products. Producing realistic renderings of the back lighting effects commonly seen on natural hair is also a challenge.

Accurately simulating the motion of hair is even more difficult. As the head moves or as the wind blows the hair, there are complex interactions of the strands with the head and even more complex strand-to-strand interactions. Friction, static charge, and various cosmetic products may also affect the way hair moves.

When the head moves or the winds blows, each individual hair moves, creating a complex changing of shape and appearance. The effects of hair strand collisions and air flow around the strands, make hair motion complex. Thus to accurately simulate hair, we need hair models that include collision and air flow dynamics.

Modeling, animating, and rendering hair is difficult primarily because of the very large number of hair strands on the head. Conventional polygon-based modeling methods require an enormous number of small polygons to realistically represent even simple hairstyles. The computer animation of realistic hair requires a great deal of computation.

We want hair models that allow realistic rendering, easy specification of hairstyles, and natural hair motion due to head movements and air flow. Modeling simplicity, controllability, realistic motion, realistic rendered images, and reasonable computational demands are the goal. Various simplifications have been made to produce effective results within the limitations of current computing technology.

10.2. Polygon-Based Hair

The simplest, and also probably the least satisfying, approach to approximating hair is to assign the desired hair color to some of the polygons on the existing head or face surfaces. This method is reasonably effective for facial hair. The shape of these colored polygons should of course approximate the shape of the desired hair areas. Parke [Par74] used this technique to include eyebrows and eyelashes, as shown in Figure 6.14.

10.2.1. Polygon Hair Shapes

The next level of complexity is to explicitly model the overall shape of hair areas with polygon surfaces and then render these polygons with the desired hair color. Of course this approach is not necessarily limited to polygonal surfaces. Other surface description primitives such as bicubic patches could be used to model the hair shapes.

DiPaola [DiP89] modeled facial hair (eyebrows, mustaches, and beards) using what he called *hair globs*. These globs were small irregular polygonally modeled shapes. A mustache, for example, was modeled as an overlapping collection of these globs arranged along an *attachment path* above the upper lip. The globs were flexibly *attached* to the face at defined points. When the surface of the face changed shape, these attachment points moved along with the shape changes. As the attachment points moved, the path through the points also changed. The globs were procedurally repositioned along the changed path. As a result, the mustache moved with the upper-lip surface.

Figure 10.1.
Use of hair globs. (Courtesy S. DiPaola.)

Similar glob collections may be used to form eyebrows and even beards. Facial hair created using this technique is shown in Figure 10.1.

Csuri et al. [CS79] used a massive number of polygons to form static representations of hair.

Another approach would be to model the hair using a set of polygon *ribbons* with or without texture mapping.

10.2.2. Surface Textures

An obvious extension to colored polygon hair shapes is to map hair textures onto hair-shaped surfaces. This technique can produce considerable static realism but lacks the dynamics of real hair and does not faithfully mimic the reflective properties of real hair.

Yamana and Suenaga [YS87] used a hair model that treated hair as a texture with anisotropic reflection mapped on the head surface. This approach assumes that adjacent hair strands are nearly parallel to each other and have anisotropic reflectance properties. It also assumes that precise rendering of each hair is not necessary. Their rendering was based on ray tracing that incorporated an anisotropic reflection table. Hair images created with this technique have a somewhat metallic appearance.

10.3. Special Shading and Special Shapes

Miller [Mil88] used anisotropic shading of multiple hair *sticks* to create images with hair and fur. A *pseudoreflectance map* was used to efficiently compute the reflection intensities of the anisotropically shaded sticks. This implementation was limited to relatively thick, straight hairs.

Perlin and Hoffert's *hypertexture* [Per89] used generalized Boolean shape operators and volume rendering to create visually realistic representations of shape and texture phenomena such as glass, fluid flow, erosion effects, *and hair*. Specification and control of dynamic hair based on hypertextures seems very difficult. And, this approach requires a great deal of computation.

Kajiya and Kay [KK89] used three-dimensional texture elements called *texels* to created a photorealistic, furry teddy bear image. This method, however, requires truly huge amounts of computation.

10.4. Strand-Based Hair Models

The creation of individual computer-modeled hair strands can be fairly simple. A strand of hair can be viewed as just a thin string-like three-dimensional object with cylindrical cross section. The major difficulties are to control and realistically render a large collection of such thin objects. Three *strand*-based approaches to modeling and animating hair have been reported [RCI91] [AUK92] [WS92]. These approaches vary in many details, but have much in common.

They all model the hair as a large collection of thin hair strands, each strand being approximated as a connected set of straight segments. If each hair-like strand is modeled with 32 linear cylinders, each cylinder approximated by a 16-sided prism (32 triangles), then the 100,000 hair strands would require over 100,000,000 triangles. For current technology, this amount is an unreasonable number of triangles to render for animation sequences. Therefore various simplifications have been used to reduce the necessary computation to reasonable levels.

All three approaches include techniques to approximate real hair motion based on reasonably simple dynamics and control parameters. And each approach takes into account the special problems of rendering hair, including hair lighting effects. Each of these approaches includes techniques for specifying and controlling hair shape and hairstyles.

These approaches can also be effective for modeling and rendering facial hair such as eyebrows, eyelashes, beards, and mustaches.

10.4.1. Strand Modeling

Watanabe and Suenaga [WS92] developed a hair model in which each hair strand is approximated as a connected series of short cylinders. However, to minimize the number of polygons to be rendered, each of these cylinders is represented as a prism with only three sides, referred to as a *trigonal* prism. These are the simplest possible prism approximations to the hair segment cylinders. Figure 10.2(a) shows a single segment of a *trigonal* hair

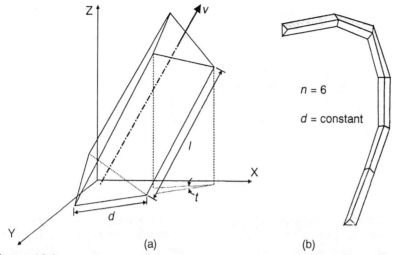

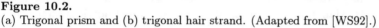

Figure 10.2.
(a) Trigonal prism and (b) trigonal hair strand. (Adapted from [WS92].)

strand, while Figure 10.2(b) shows an example trigonal hair strand made up of six prisms. Strand characteristics are defined by controlling the length l, direction vector v, thickness d, and twist angel t of each trigonal prism, while n represents the number of trigonal prisms per strand. In this example the hair strand segments have constant thickness. Straight, wavy, or curly hair strand types can be specified by controlling these segment parameters.

Anjyo et al. [AUK92] and Rosenblum et al. [RCI91] geometrically model each hair strand simply as a linearly connected point set. Anjyo et al. also developed a method for modeling hair dynamics, which employs the simple ordinary differential equations used to describe cantilever beam deformation along with appropriate simplifying heuristics. Rather than emphasizing a rigorous physical model, several simple and intuitive ideas are employed to speed computations, while producing visually satisfactory results. Simple differential equations of one-dimensional angular momenta are used for describing the dynamic behavior of the hair strands. Collision detection of hair strands with the head is also incorporated.

Rosenblum et al. used a mass-spring-hinge system to control each strand's position and orientation. This technique is simple in concept, but produces fairly realistic hair motion simulations. This implementation also included an interactive system for defining the position of hair strands on the head. Special attention was paid to self-shadowing of the hair strands.

10.4.2. Hairstyling

Many techniques are used to shape real hair such as combing, cutting, and cosmetic preparations for making hair more attractive. Important physical properties of hair include hair color, strand width, and pliability.

A necessary condition for a hair modeling method is that it represent the intrinsic properties of hair. This representation may be partially achieved through rendering techniques. However, efficient and effective techniques are desired for modeling the shape of hair.

10.5. Wisp-Based Hair

Watanabe and Suenaga [WS92] introduced the concept of hair *wisps*. Using wisps is one approach to forming and controlling hairstyles. In this approach, a head of hair contains many wisps, where wisps are groups of individual hair strands. Hairstyles are not created by controlling individual hairs, but by cutting and forming wisps or sets of hair strands.

Wisps are used as template units to efficiently create and control the total hair set. Wisps consist of many instances of the same string-like hair model. Using wisps drastically reduces the number of control parameters needed to obtain complete hair images. The details of each wisp are controlled by its own parameters.

The wisp model is illustrated in Figure 10.3 where each hair is defined as a connected sequence of trigonal prisms. In addition to the parameters controlling each strand, wisps are defined by the randomness, r, in their initial direction vectors and the density of strands, m. Figure 10.4(a) shows a wisp model defined by a large r, while Figure 10.4(b) shows a wisp model defined by almost parallel vectors, a small r. The hair density is typically 100 hairs per wisp.

Hairstyles are created by controlling a small number of additional parameters including hair color, the total number of wisps, and the kind of wisps. Different kinds of wisps may be used to vary hair shape on the forehead, side, and back of the head. Specifying more wisps produces heavier hair, and using more hairs per wisp produces denser hair. Eyebrows and eyelashes have also been created using the trigonal prism-based wisp model.

10.5.1. Animation Based on Wisps

Real hair motion is determined by the physical characteristics of each hair and the hair environment. When hair flows in the wind, each hair moves individually. When the head moves, the hair also moves.

In the wisp approach, hairstyle is determined by controlling the shape and characteristics of the wisps. Control of individual wisp shapes and motions

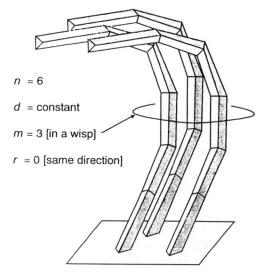

$n = 6$

d = constant

$m = 3$ [in a wisp]

$r = 0$ [same direction]

Figure 10.3.
Wisp model hair strands. (Adapted from [WS92].)

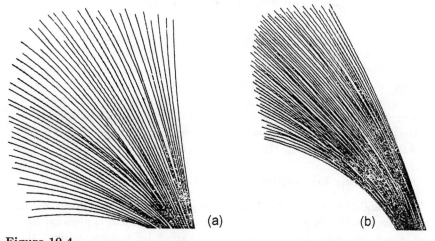

(a)   (b)

Figure 10.4.
Effect of wisp randomness: (a) large r, (b) small r.
(Adapted from [WS92].)

was also used to approximate realistic hair motion. Generating the hair
motion requires controlling only a small number of wisp parameters. For
example, as the head turns rapidly from a profile view to a full face view,
the hair first flies out, continues to move as the head stops, and then slowly
settles back down.

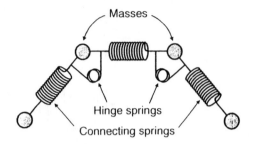

Figure 10.5.
Mass-spring-hinge model. (Adapted from [RCT91].)

An approximating parabolic trajectory is used to control the motion of each wisp. These wisp trajectories are determined using initial velocity vectors and acceleration vectors such as the acceleration of gravity.

10.6. Mass-Spring-Hinge Hair Model

In the Rosenblum et al. approach [RCI91], each strand of hair is represented as a series of connected straight strand segments. The position of each strand segment is determined by simple dynamic simulation. Each strand is modeled as a linearly connected series of point masses, springs, and hinges. The strand point masses have direct correspondence with the segment end-points used in rendering. Stiff connecting springs maintain relatively constant distances between the masses. Spring hinges placed between the strand segments allow the hair strands to bend.

10.6.1. Hair Dynamics

Each strand of hair is modeled as a series of interconnected masses, springs, and hinges as shown in Figure 10.5. Each strand segment is modeled as two point masses held a nearly fixed distance apart by a strong spring. Since hair does not stretch very much, this spring is stiff. A hinge spring is located between segments at the point mass locations. These hinges apply forces to the outlying masses. In this implementation, the hair strands do not interact.

Forces applied to each point mass by the *interconnecting* springs are determined from Hooke's law

$$F_s = k_s d \tag{10.1}$$

where F_s is the magnitude of the force, k_s is the spring constant, and d is the displacement of the spring. The direction of this force is always along the line connecting the two point masses. If the spring is stretched, the force vectors at each mass point towards each other. If the spring is compressed, the forces point away from each other. When simple damping is included the equation becomes

$$F_s = (1 - D_s)(k_s d) \qquad (10.2)$$

where D_s is the spring damping constant.

Similarly, a force is applied to each mass by its associated hinge spring

$$F_h = (1 - D_h)(k_h \alpha) \qquad (10.3)$$

where F_h is the hinge force magnitude, α is the hinge angular displacement, k_h is the hinge spring constant, and D_h is the hinge damping constant. This force is applied in three places. It is applied at the two outlying masses in the direction necessary to cause the strand to straighten. The negative sum of these two is also applied to the mass at the hinge location.

The force of gravity is included in the form

$$F_g = mg \qquad (10.4)$$

where F_g is the force of gravity, m is the mass of the point, and g is the acceleration of gravity.

Finally, an *aerodynamic* drag force is determined as

$$F_d = v * D_d \qquad (10.5)$$

where v is the current velocity of the mass and D_d is an aerodynamic drag coefficient.

All of the force components are summed and used to compute the acceleration of the mass based on Newton's second law:

$$a = F_{sum}/m \qquad (10.6)$$

where

$$F_{sum} = F_s + F_h + F_g + F_d.$$

The acceleration a is used to update the mass velocity, which in turn is used to compute the new mass position.

To calculate the motion for a single animation frame, the frame time is subdivided into smaller time steps. For each of these small time steps, the kinematic equations are used to compute new mass positions based on the sum of forces applied to each mass point.

Figure 10.6.
Two views of the dynamic hair. (From [RCT91].)

Strand-to-Head Collisions

Simple strand-to-head collision detection and response is supported as follows. The head is modeled as a sphere. Whenever a strand point mass lies inside the radius of this sphere, an outward spring force is applied to the mass. This force is applied only when the mass is moving closer to the head, and not when the mass is moving away from the head. This simulates inelastic collisions and allows strands to rest on the surface of the head.

Dynamic Simplifications

This model makes several simplifying assumptions. The aerodynamic drag does not take into account strand orientation relative to the current velocity vectors. The hinge model does not calculate torque, which would take into account the distance of the outlying masses from the hinge in the force calculations. And, the damping coefficients are entirely *ad hoc*. The simplified drag, damping, and hinge force calculations reduce the computational load. Figure 10.6 shows an animation frame with two views of the same hair. For this animation about 1100 hair strands were used, each strand having 14 segments. The first segment of each strand is embedded in the scalp and moves with the head. As Figure 10.7 shows, the head was initially tilted forward and then quickly flipped back. The simulation was calculated at 60 steps per second.

These simulations are subject to oscillations and instabilities. Reducing the time step size and increasing the number of steps per frame reduced these problems. These simulations also required experimentation to empirically

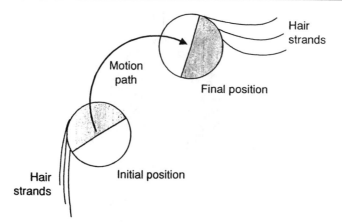

Figure 10.7.
Motion used to flip the hair. (Adapted from [RCT91].)

determine the mass, spring, and damping constant values that produce the desired results.

10.7. Beam Bending Hair

Anjyo et al. [AUK92] developed a hair modeling approach that consists of the following:

1. Define an ellipsoid that roughly approximates the desired three-dimensional head model (see Figure 10.8).

2. On this ellipsoid, specify the desired hair follicle regions. One hair strand will originate from each follicle location.

3. For each strand, calculate its bent shape based on a simplified cantilever beam simulation. This shape calculation includes collision detection between each hair and the approximating head ellipsoid.

4. Adjust or cut hair strand lengths for various follicle regions and apply shaping forces to achieve the desired overall hair shape.

While the head ellipsoid is not a completely accurate representation of the head, follicle positions are more easily specified on it than on a polygonal head model. A polar coordinate system is used for explicit follicle positioning on the ellipsoid. Collision detection between the approximating ellipsoid and the hair strands has lower computational cost than between a polygonal head model and the strands.

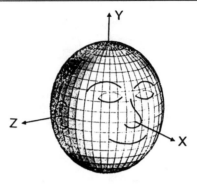

Figure 10.8.
Ellipsoid model for the head. (Adapted from [AUK92].)

In a physically faithful simulation, the number of functions appearing in the derived differential equations will be very large. In particular, it would be very difficult to numerically treat self-interaction or collision detection for the very large number of hair strands. The desire is for techniques that are physically faithful to the true dynamics of hair that are also computationally tractable. This model uses a differential equation-based approach that employs easy to solve equations that are approximately faithful to many physical aspects of the hair.

10.7.1. Cantilever Beam Simulation for Hair Bending

This hair modeling method involves a process to bend the hair, which is based on the numerical simulation of cantilever beam deformation. To describe the simulation technique, the simpler two-dimensional case is treated first.

Suppose that the two-dimensional cantilever beam is in an initial state as shown in Figure 10.9(a), where one end of the beam is fixed. This fixed end corresponds to the follicle end of a hair. In a typical case, the beam is loaded by an external force such as gravity uniformly distributed along the length of the beam. Two types of deformation actually occur; one caused by the bending momentum and one caused by the shearing force. Only the bending moment deformation is considered. The x axis is defined to be along the initial beam direction, and the y axis is perpendicular to this direction. The beam deflection y is in the y axis direction. Assuming elastic materials, the following equation describes this deformation:

$$d^2y/dx^2 = -M/(EI) \qquad (10.7)$$

where M is the bending moment, E is Young's modulus for the hair material, and I denotes the cross-sectional second moment of inertia about the neutral

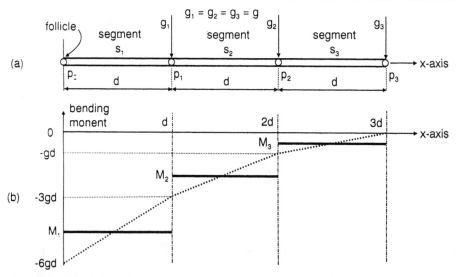

Figure 10.9.
(a) Cantilever beam hair model load distribution. (b) Beam bending moment diagram. (Adapted from [AUK92].)

axis of the beam. The term EI usually is referred to as the *flexural rigidity* and depends on the beam material properties. This equation is actually only valid for small deformations. It is considered valid for this model since the deflection of each segment is relatively small. The calculation method for the bending moment M is illustrated in Figure 10.9(b).

In this simulation, the distributed load $\mathbf{g}$ is approximated by the sum of segmentally averaged concentrated segment loads. The cantilever beam is considered to consist of a number of linear segments each with the same length. Let $\mathbf{p}_0, \mathbf{p}_1, \ldots, \mathbf{p}_k$ be the node vectors of the segments, where $\mathbf{p}_0$ is the follicle end and $\mathbf{p}_k$ is the free end of the beam. The simplified beam shown in Figure 10.9(a) consists of three segments s_1, s_2, and s_3, such that s_i corresponds to the vector $\mathbf{p}_{i-1}\mathbf{p}_i$ and the length of each segment $\parallel \mathbf{p}_{i-1}\mathbf{p}_i \parallel$ is d, for $1 \leq i \leq 3$. Let $\mathbf{g}_1, \mathbf{g}_2$, and $\mathbf{g}_3$ be the node forces, where $\mathbf{g}_i$ is a concentrated load at the node $\mathbf{p}_i$. The bending moment at point x on the beam is represented by the dotted line shown in Fig. 10.9(b). For simplicity, the bending moment is assumed constant on each segment. The constant bending moment values M_i for the segments s_i are defined as:

$$M_i = -\parallel \mathbf{g} \parallel d(\sum_{n=1}^{k-i+1} n + \sum_{n=1}^{k-i} n)/2 = -\parallel \mathbf{g} \parallel d(k-i+1)^2/2. \quad (10.8)$$

The displacement y_i of the node $\mathbf{p}_i$ can be determined using the following equation:

$$y_i = -((M_i/EI)d^2)/2, \tag{10.9}$$

which is derived from Equation (10.7). Suppose that node positions $\mathbf{p}_{i-2}$ and $\mathbf{p}_{i-1}$ have been computed. Then we can obtain the new position of the node $\mathbf{p}_i$. To do so, we determine the vector $\mathbf{e}_i$ such that

$$\mathbf{e}_i = \mathbf{p}_{i-2}\mathbf{p}_{i-1} + \mathbf{y}_i \tag{10.10}$$

where the x axis for this calculation is defined as being along the segment vector $\mathbf{p}_{i-2}\mathbf{p}_{i-1}$, and the vector $\mathbf{y}_i$ is in the deflection direction with its magnitude being equal to y_i in (10.9). The new node position $\mathbf{p}_i$ is defined as

$$\mathbf{p}_i = \mathbf{p}_{i-1} + (d/\parallel \mathbf{e}_i \parallel)\mathbf{e}_i \tag{10.11}$$

where $d = \parallel \mathbf{p}_{i-1}\mathbf{p}_i \parallel$. The deflection vectors and node positions are calculated successively working from $\mathbf{p}_1$ to $\mathbf{p}_k$.

Deflection in Three Dimensions

The deflection calculation is extended to three dimensions as follows. First a suitable coordinate system is defined. The $a0$ axis in Figure 10.10 corresponds to the x axis used in the two-dimensional case. The $a0$ axis is defined as being along the segment vector $\mathbf{p}_{i-2}\mathbf{p}_{i-1}$. Let $\mathbf{p}_i^*$ be a point which is a distance d from $\mathbf{p}_{i-1}$ along the $a0$ axis. Also let $\mathbf{p}_{i-1}^*$ denote a point which is positioned relative to $\mathbf{p}_{i-1}$ such that the three points $\mathbf{p}_{i-1}, \mathbf{p}_{i-1}^*$, and $\mathbf{p}_i^*$ define a plane. The $a1$ axis is perpendicular to the $a0$ axis and on the defined plane. The $a2$ axis is orthogonal to both the $a0$ and $a1$ axes. The two-dimensional method is applied to obtain the deflection component y_1 along the $a1$ axis and the deflection component y_2 along the $a2$ axis, using the respective components of the applied force. Assuming no compression of the beam, the composite deflection vector is $y_1\mathbf{a}_1 + y_2\mathbf{a}_2$, where $\mathbf{a}_1$ and $\mathbf{a}_2$ are unit vectors parallel to the $a1$ and $a2$ axes. As in the two-dimensional case, the new beam node positions are obtained by working sequentially from the follicle end to the free end, successively applying the computed deflection vectors.

Collision Detection

As in the previously described models, hair-to-hair strand collisions are ignored. A simplified collision detection is used to prevent the hair strands from intersecting the head. Collision detection is limited to checking for intersections between the approximating head ellipsoid and the hair strand

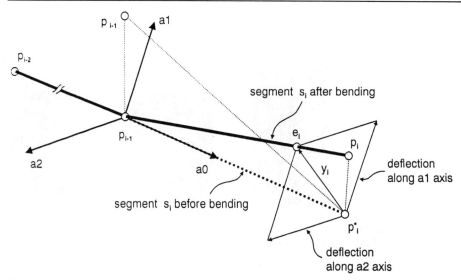

Figure 10.10.
Three-dimensional beam deflection. (Adapted from [AUK92].)

segments. Collision detection and avoidance is performed as part of computing the deflected positions of the $\mathbf{p}_i$ nodes. Suppose that two deflected beam nodes $\mathbf{p}_{i-2}, \mathbf{p}_{i-1}$ have been computed. Then, it is easy to determine whether the next node $\mathbf{p}_i$, computed using the beam deflection simulation, intersects the ellipsoid. This determination is done by checking the signature of the quadric equation $E(\mathbf{p}_i)$, which defines the ellipsoid: $E(\mathbf{p}) = 0$. If the node $\mathbf{p}_i$ is inside the ellipsoid, it is moved outside the ellipsoid such that it is near the original computed position $\mathbf{p}_i$ and lies on the plane formed by the points $\mathbf{p}_{i-2}, \mathbf{p}_{i-1}$, and $\mathbf{p}_i$.

Examples

Typically 10,000 to 20,000 individual hair strands are used to model the hair, each hair strand having less than 20 segments. The initial state of the hair strands is as shown in Figure 10.11(a), where the follicle positions and the initial length of the hair are specified. Since there are no external forces or gravity applied to the initial hair strands, they stand straight out radially. By adding gravity, the hair strands are bent down, as illustrated in Fig. 10.11(b). The hair strands near the top of the head are not bent much because these strands are essentially parallel to the gravity vector and their bending moments are small. Undulations of the hair in front of the face shown in Figure 10.11(b) are caused by the collision avoidance calculations. Cutting, combing, or brushing makes real hair more attractive.

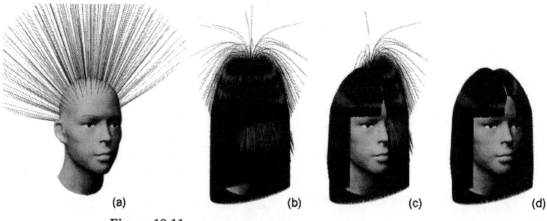

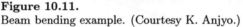

Figure 10.11.
Beam bending example. (Courtesy K. Anjyo.)

These techniques can be used to give short bangs, parting of the hair at the middle of the head, and so on. Instead of using shears and a brush or comb, in this approach cutting operations and the addition of external forces to the bending calculations are used for hairstyle modeling. Specification of the hair strands to be cut is performed using the polar coordinate system of the head ellipsoid and length thresholds. For instance, the follicle positions of the hair strands to be cut are specified using ranges of azimuth ϕ and elevation θ angles such as $\phi_0 < \phi < \phi_1$ and $\theta < \theta_0$.

The segments of hair strands whose follicles are within the specified ranges are displayed only if the distance from the follicle, along the strand, of their nodes is less than the designated length threshold. This cutting is done as a postprocess after the beam bending calculations. Each hair strand is displayed as a polyline connecting the strand segment nodes.

To create various hairstyles, different external forces may be applied to selected regions of the head. Hair strand length may also vary based on follicle location. To *comb* or shape the hair, external forces in addition to gravity are specified. To illustrate, the external force field shown in Fig. 10.12(a) is applied to the hair segments that are located higher than the eyes. Fig. 10.11(c) shows the result of using the external force field to simulate the hair segments in the positive z-region. The hair shown in Fig. 10.11(d) is obtained by using the external forces for hair in both the positive and negative z-regions. By cutting the back hair in Fig. 10.11(d), the hairstyle shown in Fig. 10.12(b) is created.

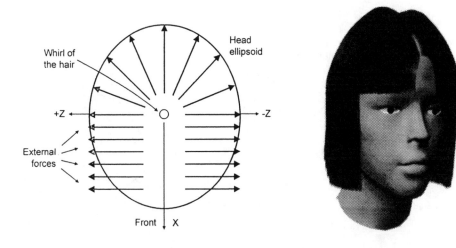

Figure 10.12.
(a) Top view of additional forces. (Adapted from [AUK92].)
(b) Resulting hairstyle. (Courtesy K. Anjyo.)

10.7.2. Dynamic Behavior of Bending Beam Hair

One aesthetic feature of hair motion occurs where long hair is gently blowing in the wind or is swaying according to head movements. Animating each individual strand of hair is not difficult. However, to create truly realistic motion requires that the hair strands interact with each other and with the head, and that physical properties such as friction and static charge are included. Heuristic techniques are used to roughly approximate solutions to this difficult problem.

Some aspects of hair motion are the result of inertia and applied forces. The motion equations used should at least include the inertial properties of hair. To do so, simple ordinary differential equations were used as follows.

One-Dimensional Projective Equations for Hair Dynamics

As described above, each hair strand is represented as a deformed beam composed of linked linear segments. The technique used for the dynamic behavior of the hair is based on solving simple one-dimensional differential equations of angular momentum for each hair. Collision and interaction of the hair strands with themselves and with the head are not explicitly considered. However, heuristic techniques are used in conjunction with the solution of these differential equations to give approximate solutions to these difficult problems. One heuristic is to use a pseudoforce field, described

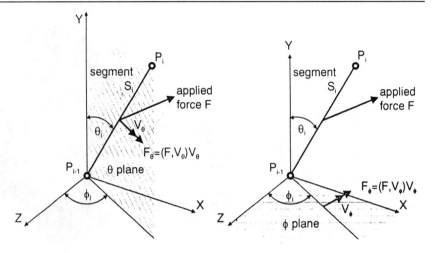

Figure 10.13.
Hair dynamics coordinate systems. (Adapted from [AUK92].)

below, in solving the differential equations. In addition, pliability of the hair
is included using a parameter for limiting the angles between adjacent hair
segments.

Consider the dynamics of a single hair. Using the polar coordinate system
as shown in Fig. 10.13, the behavior of the zenith angle θ_i and the azimuth
ϕ_i of the i-th segment s_i of the hair are observed. Particular consideration
is given to the projections of the segment on the θ and ϕ planes which are
defined as shown in Fig. 10.13. The θ plane is the plane spanned by the
y axis and the segment s_i. If s_i is almost parallel to the y axis, then the
θ plane is defined using the y axis and the applied force $\mathbf{F}$ instead of s_i.
The ϕ plane is defined as the xz-plane. On these planes, the variables $\theta_i(t)$
and $\phi_i(t)$ as functions of time, t, are governed by the ordinary differential
equations

$$d^2\theta_i/dt^2 = c_i u_i F_\theta \qquad (10.12)$$

$$d^2\phi_i/dt^2 = c_i v_i F_\phi, \qquad (10.13)$$

where c_i corresponds to the reciprocal of the inertia moment of s_i, $u_i = (1/2) \parallel s_i \parallel$, v_i is half the length of the projection of s_i onto the ϕ plane,
and F_θ and F_ϕ are the components of the applied force $\mathbf{F}$ in the respective
planes as shown in Fig 10.13.

The idea is to use the *one-dimensional projective equations*, (10.12) and
(10.13) for describing hair dynamics, even though these equations originally
described the *projective* behaviors of the hair model.

The component F_θ of the applied force field $\mathbf{F}$ is the scalar value defined by the inner product $(\mathbf{F}, \mathbf{V}_\theta) = \parallel \mathbf{F}_\theta \parallel = F_\theta$, where $\mathbf{V}_\theta$ is the unit vector on the θ plane that is perpendicular to the segment s_i. Similarly the F_ϕ component is defined by $(\mathbf{F}, \mathbf{V}_\phi) = \parallel \mathbf{F}_\phi \parallel = F_\phi$, where $\mathbf{V}_\phi$ is the unit vector on the ϕ plane that is perpendicular to the projection segment of s_i onto the ϕ plane.

For numerical simulation, these equations are the basis for simple second order recurrence formulas shown below. Using the known values $\theta_i^{n-1}, \theta_i^n, \phi_i^{n-1}$ and ϕ_i^n the new values $\theta_i^{n+1}, \phi_i^{n+1}$ at time $(n+1)\Delta t$ are obtained from:

$$\theta_i^{n+1} - 2\theta_i^n + \theta_i^{n-1} = (\Delta t)2c_i u_i F_\theta \qquad (10.14)$$

$$\phi_i^{n+1} - 2\phi_i^n + \phi_i^{n-1} = (\Delta t)2c_i v_i F_\phi. \qquad (10.15)$$

The calculation starts with segment s_1, and the new position of each s_i is successively determined using (10.14) and (10.15).

10.7.3. Inertia Moments and Heuristic Modifications

Consider a straight stick S with length kd and density ρ. Then its inertia moment I_s is given by $I_s = (1/3)\rho(kd)^2$. For this hair model, the terms $c_i v_i$ and $c_i u_i$ in (10.14) and (10.15) are closely related to I_s. For example, suppose that the inertia moment I_i of s_i is proportional to $1/i$ $(1 \le i \le k)$ and that I_k is equal to I_s. Then I_i is given as $I_i = (\rho/3i)k^3 d^2$. The term $(\Delta t)^2 c_i u_i$ in (10.14) may be rewritten as $(3(\Delta t)^2 i)/(2k_3\rho d)$. A similar expression may be obtained for the term $(\Delta t)^2 c_i v_i$ in (10.15). These expressions may be used for numerically estimating the magnitude of the right-hand side of the equations (10.14) and (10.15).

Strand-to-strand interaction effects can be approximated by modifying the c_i values actually used. For example, if the c_i values used are relatively small for the segments near the top of the head, then the hair near the top will move relatively slowly, when affected by an applied force field. This reault can be thought of as a rough approximation of frictional hair effects. Therefore, the c_i coefficients are heuristically modified to achieve the desired results.

Pseudoforce Field

Another conceptually simple technique is used for avoiding hair collisions with the head. The technique consists of using a heuristically determined pseudoforce field, instead of the specified force field. The pseudoforce field is based on $\mathbf{F}$, the force field specified by a user.

A segment direction $\mathbf{D}_i$ for each hair segment s_i is obtained using the head defining ellipsoid equation $E(\mathbf{p})$. $\mathbf{D}_i = (E_x(\mathbf{p}_i), E_y(\mathbf{p}_i), E_z(\mathbf{p}_i))$ where $E_x, E_y,$ and E_z are partial derivatives of the ellipsoid polynomial. The inner product $(\mathbf{D}_i, \mathbf{F})$ is compared with $\alpha \parallel \mathbf{D}_i \parallel \parallel \mathbf{F} \parallel$ where α is a selected value such that $\mid \alpha \mid \leq 1$. If the inner product is smaller it means that the segment direction is roughly opposite the direction of $\mathbf{F}$. If the segment is near the head, then $\mathbf{F}$ is replaced by the pseudoforce $\epsilon_i \mathbf{F}$, where $0 \leq \epsilon_i \leq 1$. The pseudoforce constants ϵ_i for the segments near the follicle are usually assigned smaller values, whereas those for the segments near the endpoint p_k are equal to one. The pseudoforce $\epsilon_i \mathbf{F}$ near the follicle can be viewed as the simplification of compositing the force $\mathbf{F}$ with an opposite repulsive force away from the head.

Joint Angle Adjustment

The joint angle ν_i at the node $\mathbf{p}_i$ is the angle between $\mathbf{p}_i \mathbf{p}_{i-1}$ and $\mathbf{p}_i \mathbf{p}_{i+1}$. Then the *stiffness* of the hair strand is determined by the parameters $\sigma_i (0 \leq \sigma_i \leq \pi)$. The i-th stiffness parameter σ_i is applied after the new $\mathbf{p}_{i+1}$ is determined using the recurrence formulas (10.14) and (10.15). If ν_i is greater than σ_i, the node $\mathbf{p}_{i+1}$ is adjusted such that the joint angle is equal to σ_i. Usually the stiffness parameters for nodes near a follicle are set at 180 degrees so that no adjustments of the nodes are done. For smooth curved hair strands, the parameters σ_i would be small, 10 to 15 degrees, for nodes far from the follicle.

Randomness

Small hair strand fluctuates were created using uniform random numbers. The random perturbations were applied after calculating the new node positions. Then, using the stiffness parameters, the hair strand nodes were adjusted to maintain smooth strand curvature.

Figure 10.14 illustrates the effectiveness of the bending beam approach to hair dynamics.

10.8. Interactive Hair Modeling Tools

This section describes the interactive hair modeling tools developed to support the wisp model and the Rosenblum et al. model.

10.8.1. The Wisp Model

Watanabe and Suenaga [WS92] described an interactive hair-modeling system. Their system had two modes; a wisp-modeling mode and a hair-drawing mode. Wisps were controlled by interactively selecting the desired parameter values in the wisp-modeling mode. Then hair images using these wisps were created in the hair-drawing mode. This system provided a number of default

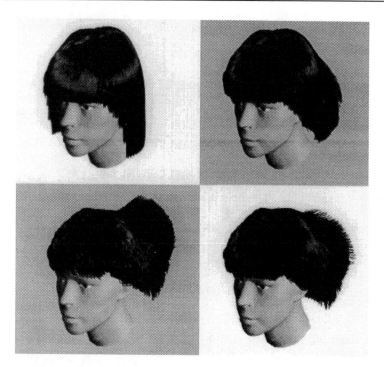

Figure 10.14.
Results of beam bending hair dynamics. (Courtesy K. Anjyo.)

wisp types which could be selected from a hairstyle menu. When selected, the 12 wisp-modeling parameters were set as a group. These parameters included angle, bend, ratio, thickness, length, fold, density, direction randomness, color, and two wave control values. A screen window was used to show the wisp shape and location generated by the selected parameters. The simplified wisps were shown in real time superimposed on the human head model. An overall hairstyle menu was used to specify the set of wisps types to be used.

In the hair-drawing mode, all the hair strands in the specified wisps were drawn on a human head model. The head model consisted of about 800 triangles. The hair strand root positions were located within about 300 triangles of the head model that formed the scalp area. In these triangles, several positions are selected as the hair orientation points for the wisps. Representing the hair strands required about 700,000 trigonal prisms.

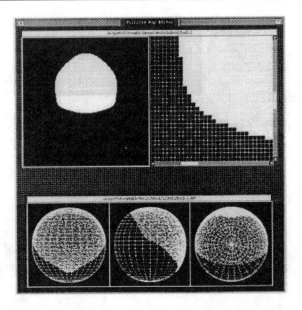

Figure 10.15.
Follicle map editor. (From [RCT91].)

10.8.2.   The Mass-Spring-Hinge Model

Rosenblum et al. [RCI91] described the development of an interactive graphical *follicle map editor*, used to place hair follicles onto a polygonally defined
head model. In their system, the user interactively draws the follicle positions in two dimensions. These positions were then spherically mapped onto
the head object. Several additional screen windows were used to display
orthogonal views of the resulting three-dimensional follicle placement. The
follicle editor also had an option to randomly jitter the follicle placement to
remove patterns caused by the mapping process. See Figure 10.15.

10.9.   Strand Rendering

Hair has complex optical properties. It is not completely opaque and the
strands actually have two specular highlights. One is reflected directly off
the surface of the strand while the other is a reflection of transmitted light
off the strand's back wall. The surface of hair is not smooth, but is covered
with layers of scales. The properties of these scales strongly influence light
reflection. The optical and dynamic properties of hair are also influenced by
oil on the hair and various cosmetic hair products.

Techniques for rendering cylinders are well known. However, the very small diameter of human hair makes it difficult to realistically render using traditional rendering techniques. Because of small size and the very large number of strands to be rendered, several specialized strand rendering techniques have been developed.

10.9.1. Mass and Spring Hair Rendering

Rosenblum et al. [RCI91] used z-buffer-based techniques for efficient rendering of these high complexity scenes. The very thin hair strand segments make anti-aliased rendering especially important, therefore stochastic supersampling [Cro81] [Coo86] was used. See Section 5.5.

A polygon mesh could be used to approximate each segment cylinder, however this would not be very efficient for cylinders that are at most a few pixels wide. Also, the lack of spatial coherence in stochastic sampling does not support incremental scan conversion of polygonal approximations. The fact that each strand segment has a small rectangular profile after transformation into screen space can be exploited. Containment within the projected strand segment can be determined by testing the distance between a sample point and the center line of the strand.

The total number of samples used to scan convert each segment should be minimized. This reduction is done by only sampling the immediate region containing the segment. To test if a sample falls within a segment, the distance from the sample point to the center line of the segment is compared to the strand width.

If P_1 and P_2 are the two endpoints that define the segment in screen space, then the parametric form of the line that passes through these points is

$$P(t) = P_1 - (P_2 - P_1)t. \qquad (10.16)$$

The parameter t for the point on $P(t)$ that has minimum distance to a given sample point P_0 is given by

$$t = (\Delta x(x_1 - x_0) + \Delta y(y_1 - y_0))/(\Delta x^2 + \Delta y^2). \qquad (10.17)$$

If this t value is between 0.0 and 1.0, it is used to calculate x and y of the nearest point. If the square of the distance between P_0 and $P(t)$ is less than or equal to half the strand width then the sample is inside the segment.

For each segment, the Δx and Δy values are constant and only need to be computed once. Rewriting this equation results in a computationally efficient form for t:

$$t = AC + BD \qquad (10.18)$$

where $C = x_1 - x_0$, and $D = y_1 - y_0$.

The square of the distance between $P(t)$ and P_0 becomes

$$(C + \Delta x t)^2 + (D + \Delta y t)^2. \qquad (10.19)$$

An estimate of the segment z depth at the sample point can be computed as

$$z = z_1 + (z_2 - z_1)t \qquad (10.20)$$

where z_1 and z_2 are the depths of P_1 and P_2 in screen space. This z depth value is used by the supersampled z-buffer to determine sample visibility.

An approximate *ad hoc* shading technique for small cylinders as reported by Kajiya [KK89] was used for shading the strand segments. The shading components are defined as

$$diffuse = k_d sin\theta_{vi}$$

$$specular = k_s cos^p \phi_{ee}, \qquad (10.21)$$

where k_d is the diffuse coefficient, k_s is the specular coefficient, θ_{vi} is the angle between the tangent vector at the sample and the light vector, ϕ_{ee} is the angle between the eye vector and the specular reflection vector, and p is an exponent to control highlight sharpness.

For each segment, the tangent vector is parallel to the line defined by its endpoints. For adjacent segments, a vertex tangent vector is the vector sum of the adjacent tangent vectors. These vertex tangent vectors are interpolated to smoothly shade along the length of the strand.

Since for this approximate shading, the tangent vector is the basis for the calculations, shading will change as the tangent vector is interpolated along the length of the strand. Shading changes across the width of the strand are ignored. The net result is that the strands are rendered as anti-aliased lines with smooth interpolated shading along their lengths.

Shadows were used to enhance perceived depth and realism and to minimize unwanted lighting effects. Without the use of shadows, unwanted specular highlights appear causing the hair to *glow* [KK89]. A high resolution shadow depth buffer [Wil78] was used to determine shadows. In the shadow algorithm a small experimentally determined bias value was added to the depth values to avoid incorrect self shadowing caused by precision problems. This bias was adjusted to eliminate incorrect self-shadowing while still allowing strands to shadow each other.

10.9.2. Backlighting Effects

In backlit situations the silhouette hair strands seems to shine. Reproducing this effect is important for realistic hair images. Watanabe and Suenaga [WS92] used an extension to the conventional z-buffer approach to include

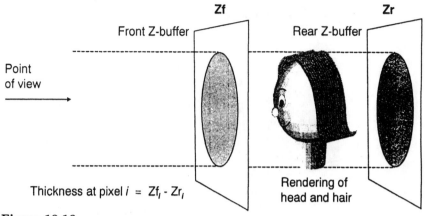

Figure 10.16.
Use of double z-buffer. (Adapted from [WS92].)

this effect. This method identifies the areas for the backlighting effect, during image generation, using a *double z*-buffer.

A z-buffer is generally used to determine which portions of an object are visible from a particular viewpoint. The contents of the z-buffer are the depth values for pixels from that viewpoint. Depth values can also be used to compute object thickness. The difference between front surface and rear surface depth values defines object thickness. See Figure 10.16.

The pixel-by-pixel z depth difference corresponds to object thickness at each pixel. Using these depth differences, thin areas can easily be identified. Backlighting effects are obtained by giving higher shading intensities to pixels in *thin* areas.

10.9.3. Anisotropic Reflection Model for a Three-Dimensional Curve

At the rendering stage, the geometry of the bent strand hair model [AUK92] is a collection of piecewise-linear three-dimensional curves, drawn as polylines. A standard illumination equation involves ambient, diffuse, and specular components. The hair treated by this approach was mainly straight, relatively dark, and glossy. For this hair, the specular component seemed dominant. The diffuse term was eliminated for simplicity. The resulting hair shading was based on the sum of an ambient constant and specular components. When hair strands are represented as polylines with no volume, they have ill-defined normal vectors. For shading purposes, each hair strand segment is modeled as a cylinder with a very small radius. An accurate calculation of the specular reflection would involve integration around the circumference of the hair. However, a simple approximate technique for

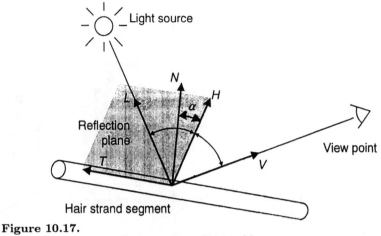

Figure 10.17.
Anisotropic reflection. (Adapted from [AUK92].)

calculating the specular shading term was developed. Referring to Figure 10.17, we see the specular term ϕ_s at the point $\mathbf{P}$ on a surface is defined by

$$\phi_s = k_s(\mathbf{N}, \mathbf{H})^n, \tag{10.22}$$

where k_s is the specular reflection coefficient, $\mathbf{N}$ is the surface normal at point $\mathbf{P}$, $\mathbf{H}$ is the vector halfway between the light vector $\mathbf{L}$ and the vector $\mathbf{V}$ toward the eye, and n is the exponent indicating the sharpness of the specular highlight. The normal $\mathbf{N}$ used lies in the plane defined by the vector $\mathbf{H}$ and the hair direction vector $\mathbf{T}$ at point $\mathbf{P}$. The inner product $(\mathbf{N}, \mathbf{H})$ can be rewritten as

$$(\mathbf{N}, \mathbf{H}) = cos\alpha = (1 - (\mathbf{T}, \mathbf{H})^2)^{1/2}. \tag{10.23}$$

The total shading intensity at a point $\mathbf{P}$ on the hair strand is then

$$I(\mathbf{P}) = I_a k_a + I_s \phi_s(\mathbf{P}), \tag{10.24}$$

where I_a is the intensity of the ambient light, k_a is the ambient reflection coefficient, and I_s is the intensity of the light source. The ambient reflection coefficient k_a is a hair material property that plays an important role. In this model, the k_a values have a normal random distribution. That is, k_a has the same value for each segment in a given hair strand, but randomly differs between strands.

Let $\mathbf{p}_0, \mathbf{p}_1, \ldots$, and $\mathbf{p}_k$ be the nodes of the hair segments $s_1, s_2, \ldots$, and s_k. The shading value or color at each node $\mathbf{p}_i$ is defined by $I(\mathbf{p}_i)$ as in Equation (10.22), where the direction vector $\mathbf{T}$ is defined as $\mathbf{p}_{i-1}\mathbf{p}_i / \parallel \mathbf{p}_{i-1}\mathbf{p}_i \parallel$. Then

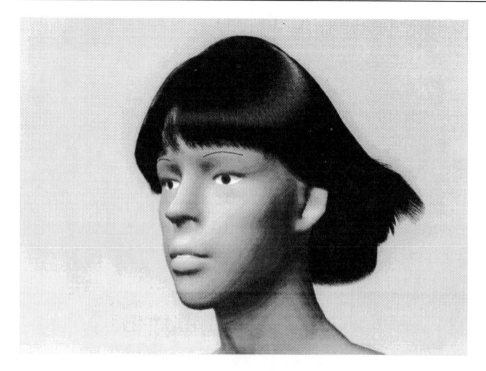

Figure 10.18.
"Wind-blown" beam bending hair with anisotropic shading.
(Courtesy K. Anjyo.)

the color at each point on the segment is linearly interpolated between the
node colors.

This approach can take advantage of the hardware z-buffer, anti-aliased
line drawing, and linear color interpolation support of high-end graphics
workstations. Anti-aliasing is needed since the hair strands are typically
about 1/4 of a pixel wide when transformed into screen space. The anti-
aliasing can be done by supersampling. Figure 10.18 illustrates the effectiveness of this shading approach, about 50,000 hair strands were used whose
screen width is about 1/4 pixel size.

A

A Face Model

This appendix briefly outlines a program that constructs a face model from three input data files, articulates the face geometry with muscles, and displays the results. The underlying muscle model algorithms are described in Chapter 6 and represent the code used to generate some of the illustrations in this book. The code should be viewed as a basic boiler plate for muscle modeling with the distinct advantage that the muscles are not "hard-wired"into a specific facial geometry. Therefore, with a little effort, it is possible to use your favorite facial geometry with this version of the muscle model.

This version of the code uses simple keyboard bindings to drive the face and was written in "C" using OpenGL display commands. The data structures are more complex than necessary; however they do provide a certain amount of design flexiblity and scope for further developement. The geometry is based on a discrete triangle representation documented in the header files. Once you have understood this simple geometry configuration it should be straightforward to convert your face data into this representation. As a final step, the muscle geometry file will have to be adapted to the face geoemtry you provide. This step simply involves the specification of the head and tail of each muscle as a pair of three-space vectors. A copy of the code can be obtained at the following URL and FTP sites:

http://www.research.digital.com/CRL/books/facebook
ftp://ftp.digital.com/pub/digital/CRL/books/facebook
ftp://crl.dec.com/pub/books/facebook

A.1.   The Data Files

There are three basic input files: **faceline.dat**, **index.dat**, and **muscle.dat**. The polygon index list provides unique indexes into the three-dimensional node list file which constructs the facial geometry as a collection of triangular polygons that can be displayed and rendered. In addition predetermined indices are defined for the jaw and eyelid pointers so they can be opened and closed.

The muscle data file contains a list of muscle descriptions in the form of a head and tail three-space vector, two zones of influence, an angular zone, and a muscle bias factor. In this version there are 18 paired muscle types: the zygomatic majors, depressor anguli oris, inner portion of the frontalis majors, mid portion of the frontalis majors, outer portion of the frontalis majors, levator labii superioris alaeque nasi, levator anguli oris, and the corrugators supercilli.

A.2.   Control

Simple keyboard bindings are used to control the face. The principle controls are for individual muscle activation. For example, the "**a**" key will progressively increment the activation of the current muscle, while "**A**" progressively decrements the current muscle activation. To select another muscle the "**n**" key is used, which cycles through the muscle list. The full listing of the binds are in the readme file provided with the source code.

B

Simple Parameterized Face Program

The following is brief documentation for a simple interactive parameterized three-dimensional face model implemented in the C language. It runs on systems using the GL graphics programming interface. Input to the model consists of three data files and user keyboard commands. Output consists of facial images in a GL screen window.

This version uses a very simple keyboard-driven user interface. This simple command interface was used to avoid as much GL-specific code as possible, which should make it relatively easy to port to your favorite system and your favorite user interface.

This program is a fairly primitive direct descendent of the original Parke parameterized face model developed at the University of Utah. It and its associated data files should be viewed as a *starter kit* for direct parameterized facial modeling. You will undoubtedly find many ways to improve and enhance the model, its user interface, and its associated data files.

B.1. Input Data

The input data files consist of two three-dimensional vertices data files and one polygon topology file. The two vertices files describe the basic face and extreme position values for those points that are computed using interpolation. The program asks for the two vertex file names. The standard topology file name is assumed. The standard files used are:

st1.pts The first vertex data set.

st2.pts The second vertex data set.

stt.top The face topology file.

The face topology used is shown in Figure B.1.

You are certainly free to construct and use your own data files. Brief study of these standard files will give you the required file formats.

Warning: The face polygon topology, as specified in the topology file, is intimately related to the parameterized manipulation of the face. Changes in this topology will usually require corresponding changes in the *points* procedure of the program.

Hints: In the topology file, vertices specified in the following form $n.m$ have the following interpretation. n refers to the vertex number, and m refers to the normal number to be used for this instance. Multiple normals are used for vertices along creases.

The first value on each line is a surface attribute (primarily color) index for that polygon.

In the first vertices file, points not specified are part of the eyelid and are computed by the program.

For vertices 184 through 221, which form most of the eyelid, the first value is a radius value used to fit the eyelid to the eyeball.

In the second vertices file, points not specified are at the same position as in the first vertices file.

Positions consist of X, Y, Z values in the face coordinate system – X is forward, Y is to the face's left, and Z is up.

B.2. Running the Program

The program first asks for the vertices data file names and reads in the desired data. It then prompts with a ">". At the prompt it is expecting a command. Commands consist of single characters followed by a "carriage return." The following commands are valid:

"p" Change a parameter value.

> The program asks for a parameter number and then the new parameter value. The valid parameters and their initial values are indicated in the source code.

"d" Display a new face image.

"r" Read and output a current parameter value.

"q" Quit and exit the program.

B.3.   Source and Data File Listings

These files are slight modifications of those included in the SIGGRAPH '90
State of the Art in Facial Animation tutorial notes [Par90].

A copy of the code, the topology data file, and the two vertices data files
can be obtained at the following URL and FTP sites:

http://www.research.digital.com/CRL/books/facebook
ftp://ftp.digital.com/pub/digital/CRL/books/facebook
ftp://crl.dec.com/pub/books/facebook

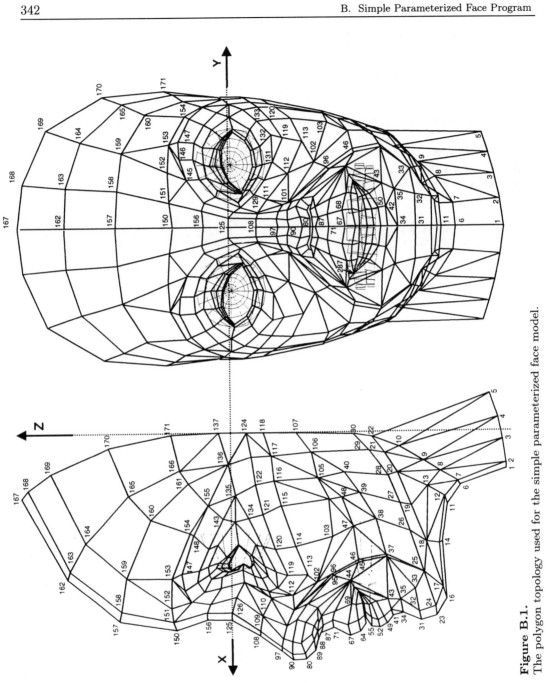

Figure B.1.
The polygon topology used for the simple parameterized face model.

Bibliography

[AC76] M. Argyle and M. Cook. *Gaze and Mutual Gaze.* Cambridge University Press, Cambridge, UK, 1976.

[AHK87] J. Allen, M. S. Hunnicutt, and D. Klatt. *From text to speech: The MITalk system.* Cambridge University Press, Cambridge, UK, 1987.

[App67] A. Appel. The notion of quantitative invisibility and the machine rendering of solids. In *Proc. ACM National Conference,* Volume 14, pages 387–393. ACM, New York, August 1967.

[AUK92] K. Anjyo, Y. Usami, and T. Kurihara. A simple method for extracting the natural beauty of hair. *Computer Graphics (SIGGRAPH '92),* 26(2):111–120, July 1992.

[AWW89] J. B. Allan, B. Wyvill, and I. H. Witten. A methodology for direct manipulation of polygon meshes. In *Proc. CG International 89,* pages 451–469. 1989.

[Atk80] R. J. Atkin. *An Introduction to the Theory of Elasticity.* Longman Group, London, 1980.

[Bas87] J. N. Bassili. Facial motions in the perception of faces and of emotional expression. *Journal of Experimental Psychology,* 4:373–379, 1987.

[Bat82] K. J. Bathe. *Finite Element Procedures in Engineering Analysis.* Prentice-Hall, Englewood Cliffs, NJ, 1982.

[Bau72] B. G. Baumgart. Winged edge polyhedron representation. Technical Report STAN-CS-320, Stanford University, Stanford, CA, 1972.

[BBB87] R. Bartles, J. Beatty, and B. Barsky. *Introduction to Splines for Use in Computer Graphics and Geometric Modeling.* Morgan Kaufmann, Los Altos, CA, 1987.

[BC85] P. Bull and G. Connelly. Body movement and emphasis in speech. *Journal of Nonverbal Behavior*, 9(3), 1985.

[BCH82] E. Bizzi, W. Chapple, and N. Hogan. Mechanical properties of muscles. *TINS*, 5(11):395–398, November 1982.

[BG76] B. G. Breitmeyer and L. Ganz. Implications of sustained and transient channels for theories of visual pattern masking, saccadic suppression, and information processing. *Psychological Review*, 23(1):1–36, 1976.

[BGP83] R. H. Bates, K. L. Garden, and T. M. Peters. Overview of computerized tomography with emphasis on future developments. *Proc. IEEE*, 71(3):356–372, March 1983.

[BI94] A. Blake and M. Isard. 3D position, attitude and shape input using video tracking of hands and lips. *Computer Graphics (SIGGRAPH '94)*, 28:185–192, July 1994.

[Bie88] M. Bierling. Displacement estimation by hierarchical block matching. In *SPIE Conf. Visual Communications and Image Processing.* SPIE, Bellingham, WA, 1988.

[BK70] W. Bouknight and K. Kelley. An algorithm for producing half-tone computer graphics presentations with shadows and movable light sources. In *Proc. AFIPS Spring Joint Computer Conf.*, Volume 36, pages 1–10. 1970.

[BL85] P. Bergeron and P. Lachapelle. Controlling facial expressions and body movements. In *Advanced Computer Animation, SIGGRAPH '85 Tutorials*, Volume 2, pages 61–79. ACM, New York, 1985.

[Bla49] P. Blair. *Animation: Learning How to Draw Animated Cartoons.* Walter T. Foster Art Books, Laguna Beach, CA, 1949.

[Bli78] J. Blinn. Simulation of wrinkled surfaces. *Computer Graphics (SIGGRAPH '78)*, 12(3):286–292, 1978.

[Bli82] J. F. Blinn. A generalization of algebraic surface drawing. *ACM Trans. on Graphics*, 1(3):235–256, July 1982.

[BN76] J. F. Blinn and M. E. Newell. Texture and reflection in computer generated images. *CACM*, 19(10):542–547, October 1976.

[Bou70] W. Bouknight. A procedure for generation of three-dimensional half-tone computer graphics presentations. *CACM*, 9(3):527–536, September 1970.

[Bou73] G. H. Bourne. Structure and function of muscle. In *Physiology and Biochemistry, Second edition*, Volume III. Academic Press, New York, 1973.

[Bre82] S. E. Brennan. Caricature generator. Master's thesis, Massachusetts Institute of Technology, Cambridge, MA, 1982.

[BT75] P. Bui-Tuong. Illumination for computer generated pictures. *CACM*, 18(6):311–17, June 1975.

[BTTU84] L. J. Brewster, S. S. Trivedi, H. K. Tut, and J. K. Udupa. Interactive surgical planning. *IEEE Computer Graphics and Applications*, 4(3):31–40, March 1984.

[Bul48] J. Bulwer. *Philocopus, or the Deaf and Dumbe Mans Friend*. Humphrey and Moseley, London, 1648.

[Bul49] J. Bulwer. *Pathomyotamia, or, A dissection of the significtive muscles of the affections of the minde*. Humphrey and Moseley, London, 1649.

[BW93] J. Bloomenthal and B. Wyvill. Interactive techniques for implicit modeling. In *Modeling, Visualizing and Animating Implicit Surfaces, SIGGRAPH '93 Course Notes # 25*. ACM, New York, August 1993.

[BY95] M. J. Black and Y. Yacoob. Tracking and recognizing rigid and non-rigid facial motions using local parametric models of image motion. In *IEEE International Conference on Computer Vision*, pages 374–381. IEEE Computer Society Press, Los Alamitos, CA, June 1995.

[Cah89] J. Cahn. Generating expression in synthesized speech. Master's thesis, Massachusetts Institute of Technology, Cambridge, MA, 1989.

[Car84] L. Carpenter. The a-buffer, an antialiased hidden surface method. *Computer Graphics (SIGGRAPH '84)*, 18(3):103–108, July 1984.

[Cat74] E. Catmull. A Subdivision Algorithm for Computer Display of Curved Surfaces. PhD thesis, University of Utah, Salt Lake City, UT, December 1974.

[Cat78] E. Catmull. A hidden-surface algorithm with anti-aliasing. *Computer Graphics (SIGGRAPH '78)*, 12(3):6–11, August 1978.

[CDL+87] H. E. Cline, C. L. Dumoulin, W. E. Lorensen, H. R. Hart, and S. Ludke. 3D reconstruction of the brain from magnetic resonance images using a connectivity algorithm. *Magnetic Resonance Imaging*, 5(5):345–352, 1987.

[Che92] D. Chen. Pump It Up: Computer Graphics System to Analyze and Design Musculoskeletal Reconstructions of the Lower Limb. PhD thesis, Massachusetts Institute of Technology, Cambridge, MA, 1992.

[Che71] H. Chernoff. The use of faces to represent points in n-dimensional space graphically. Technical Report Project NR-042-993, Office of Naval Research, Washington, DC, December 1971.

[CHP89] J. Chadwick, D. Haumann, and R. Parent. Layered construction for deformable animated characters. *Computer Graphics*, 23(3):234–243, 1989.

[CHT90] C. S. Choi, H. Harashima, and T. Takebe. Highly accurate estimation of head motion and facial action information on knowledge-based image coding. *IEICEJ*, PRU90-68:1–8, October 1990.

[CK80]   W. Cheney and D. Kincaid. *Numerical Mathematics and Computing*. Brooks-Cole, Monterey, CA, 1980.

[Cla92] M. Clayton. *Leonardo da Vinci, The Anatomy of Man*. Bulfinch Press, Boston, 1992.

[CM90]   M. Cohen and D. Massaro. Synthesis of visible speech. *Behavioral Research Methods and Instrumentation*, 22(2):260–263, 1990.

[CM93]   M. Cohen and D. Massaro. Modeling coarticulation in synthetic visual speech. In N. M. Thalmann and D. Thalmann, editors, *Models and Techniques in Computer Animation*, pages 141–155. Springer-Verlag, Tokyo, 1993.

[CM94]   M. Cohen and D. Massaro. Development and experimentation with synthetic visual speech. *Behavioral Research Methods, Instrumentation, and Computers*, 26:260–265, 1994.

[CO71]   W. S. Condon and W. D. Osgton. Speech and body motion synchrony of the speaker-hearer. In *The Perception of Language*. Horton and Jenkins, 1971.

[Coo86] R. Cook. Stochastic sampling in computer graphics. *ACM Transactions on Graphics*, 5(1):51–72, January 1986.

[Coq90] S. Coquillart. Extended free-form deformation: A sculpturing tool for 3D geometric modeling. *Computer Graphics*, 24(4):187–196, 1990.

[Col85] G. Collier. *Emotional Expression*. L. Erlbaum Associates, Ltd., Hillsdale, NJ, 1985.

[CPC84] R. Cook, T. Porter, and L. Carpenter. Distributed ray tracing. *Computer Graphics (SIGGRAPH '84)*, 18(3):137–145, 1984.

[CR74]   E. Catmull and R. Rom. A class of local interpolating splines. In *Computer Aided Geometric Design*, pages 317–326. Academic Press, San Francisco, 1974.

[Cro76] F. C. Crow. The Aliasing Problem in Computer Synthesized Images. PhD thesis, University of Utah, Salt Lake City, UT, 1976. Technical Report, UTEC-CSc-76-015.

[Cro81] F. Crow. A comparison of anti aliasing techniques. *IEEE Computer Graphics and Animation*, 1(1):40–48, January 1981.

[CS79]   C. Csuri, R. Hackathorn, R. Parent, W. Carlson, and M. Howard. Towards an interactive high visual complexity animation system. *Computer Graphics*, 13(2):289–299, August 1979.

[Cyb90] Cyberware Laboratory Inc. *4020/RGB 3D Scanner with Color Digitizer*. Monterey, CA, 1990.

[Dar72] C. Darwin. *Expression of the Emotions in Man and Animals*. John Murray, London, 1872.

[DB88] T. DeRose and B. Barsky, editors. *Geometric Splines*. Morgan Kaufmann, San Mateo, CA, 1988.

[deG89] B. deGraf. Notes on facial animation. In *State of the Art in Facial Animation, SIGGRAPH '89 Tutorials*, Volume 22, pages 10–11. ACM, New York, 1989.

[Den88] X. Q. Deng. A Finite Element Analysis of Surgery of the Human Facial Tissue. PhD thesis, Columbia University, New York, 1988.

[DiP89] S. DiPaola. Implementation and use of a 3D parameterized facial modeling and animation system. In *State of the Art in Facial Animation, SIGGRAPH '89 Tutorials*, Volume 22. ACM, New York, NY, 1989.

[DiP91] S. DiPaola. Extending the range of facial types. *J. of Visualization and Computer Animation*, 2(4):129–131, October-December 1991.

[Dit74] A. T. Dittman. The body movement-speech rhythm relationship as a cue to speech encoding. In *Nonverbal Communications*. Oxford University Press, Oxford, 1974.

[Duc62] G. B. Duchenne. *The Mechanism of Human Facial Expression*. Jules Renard, Paris, 1862.

[Duc90] G. B. Duchenne. *The Mechanism of Human Facial Expression*. Cambridge University Press, New York, 1990.

[Dun74] S. Duncan. On the structure of Speaker-Auditor interaction during speaking turns. *Language in Society*, 3:161–180, 1974.

[DW88] B. DeGraph and M. Wahrman. Mike, the talking head. *Computer Graphics World*, 11(7):15–17, July 1988.

[EF75] P. Ekman and W. V. Friesen. *Unmasking the Face*. Consulting Psychologists Press, Inc., Palo Alto, CA, 1975.

[EF78] P. Ekman and W. V. Friesen. *Manual for the Facial Action Coding System*. Consulting Psychologists Press, Inc., Palo Alto, CA, 1978.

[EFE72] P. Ekman, W. V. Friesen, and P. Ellsworth. *Emotion in the Human Face: Guidelines for Research and a Review of Findings*. Pergamon Press, New York, 1972.

[Ekm73] P. Ekman. *Darwin and Facial Expressions*. Academic Press, New York, 1973.

[Ekm77] P. Ekman. Facial signs: fact, fantasies, and possibilities. In T. Seboek, editor, *Sight, Sound, and Sense.* Indiana University Press, Bloomington, IN, 1977.

[Ekm89] P. Ekman. The argument and evidence about universals in facial expressions of emotion. In H. Wagner and A. Monstead, editors, *Handbook of Social Psychophysiology*, pages 143-146. John Wiley, Chichester, 1989.

[Els90] M. Elson. Displacement facial animation techniques. In *State of the Art in Facial Animation, SIGGRAPH Course Notes #26*, pages 21–42. ACM, New York, August 1990.

[EP94] I. Essa and A. Pentland. A vision system for observing and extracting facial action parameters. Technical Report 247, MassachusettsInstitute of Technology, Perceptual Computing Section, Cambridge, MA, 1994.

[EP95] I. Essa and A. Pentland. Facial expression recognition using a dynamic model and motion energy. In *Proc. International Conference on Computer Vision*, pages 360–367. IEEE Computer Society Press, Los Alamitos, CA, 1995.

[FAG83] H. Fuchs, G. Abram, and E. Grant. Near real-time shaded display of rigid objects. *Computer Graphics (SIGGRAPH '83)*, 17(3):65–72, July 1983.

[Fai90] G. Faigin. *The Artist's Complete Guide to Facial Expressions.* Watson-Guptill, New York, 1990.

[FB88] D. R. Forsey and R. H. Bartels. Hierarchical B-spline refinement. In *Computer Graphics (SIGGRAPH '88)*, 22(4):205–212, August, 1988.

[FKN80] H. Fuchs, Z. Kedem, and B. Naylor. On visible surface generation by a priori tree structures. *Computer Graphics, (SIGGRAPH '80)*, 14(3):124–133, July 1980.

[FKU77] H. Fuchs, Z. Kedem, and S. Uselton. Optimal surface reconstruction from planar contours. *CACM*, 20(10):693–702, October 1977.

[Fla65] J. Flanagan. *Speech Analysis, Synthesis, and Perception.* Springer-Verlag, New York, 1965.

[FPC63] Famous Photographers School, Inc. *Famous Photographers Course*, Lesson 10. Westport, CT, 1963.

[Fri76] L. A. Fried. *Anatomy of the Head, Neck, Face, and Jaws.* Lea and Febiger, Philadelphia, 1976.

[FS83] H. Ferner and J. Staubesand. *Sobotta Atlas of Human Anatomy, Volume 1: Head, Neck, Upper Extremities.* Urban and Schwarzenberg, Munich, 1983.

[FvDFH90] J. Foley, A. van Dam, S. Feiner, and J Hughes. *Computer Graphics: Principles and Practice, Second edition.* Addison-Wesley, Reading, MA, 1990.

[FZY84] E. J. Farrell, R. Zappulla, and W. C. Yang. Color 3D imaging of normal and pathological intracranial structures. *IEEE Computer Graphics and
Applications*, 4(7):5–17, September 1984.

[GGB85] W. E. Glenn, K. G. Glenn, and C. J. Bastian. Imaging system designed based on psychophysical data. *Proc. Society of Information Display*,
26(1):71–78, 1985.

[GH24] H. S. Gasser and A. V. Hill. The dynamics of muscular contraction. *Royal
Society of London Proceedings*, 96:398–437, 1924.

[Gil74] M. L. Gillenson. The Interactive Generation of Facial Images on a CRT
Using a Heuristic Strategy. PhD thesis, Ohio State University, Computer
Graphics Research Group, Columbus, OH, March 1974.

[Gla84] A. Glassner. Space subdivision for fast ray tracing. *IEEE Computer Graphics and Applications*, 4(10):15–22, October 1984.

[Gla89] A. Glassner, editor. *An Introduction to Ray Tracing*. Academic Press, London, 1989.

[GMAB94] T. Guiard-Marigny, A. Adjoudani, and C. Benoit. A 3D model of the
lips for visual speech synthesis. In *Proc. 2nd ETRW on Speech Synthesis*,
pages 49–52. New Platz, New York, 1994.

[Gou71] H. Gouraud. Continuous shading of curved surfaces. *IEEE Trans on Computers*, 20(6): 623–629, June 1971.

[Gra88] C. W. Grant. Introduction to image synthesis. In *Image Synthesis, SIG-
GRAPH '88 Tutorials*, Volume 9, pages 1–12. ACM, New York, August
1988.

[Gra89] G. Graves. The dynamics of waldo. *The IRIS Universe*, 6–9, August 1989.

[Gre73] D. Greenspan. *Discrete Models*. Addison-Wesley, Reading, MA, 1973.

[GTG84] C. Goral, K. Tottance, and D. Greenberg. Modeling the interaction
of light between diffuse surfaces. *Computer Graphics (SIGGRAPH '84)*,
18(3):213–222, 1984.

[GuF65] M. Gonzalez-Ulloa and S. E. Flores. Senility of the face: Basic study
to understand its causes and effects. *Plastic and Reconstructive Surgery*,
36(2):239–246, 1965.

[GW87] R. C. Gonzales and P. Wintz. *Digital Image Processing, Second edition*.
Addison-Wesley, Reading, MA, 1987.

[GWJS86] M. D. Grabb, C. William, W. James, and M. D. Smith. *Plastic Surgery*.
Little, Brown and Company, Boston, 1986.

[Hal65] R.G. Halton. *Figure Drawing*. Dover Publishing, New York, 1965.

[Har77] R. D. Harkness. *Mechanical Properties of Skin in Relation to its Biological Function and its Chemical Components*. Wiley-Interscience, New York, 1977.

[HDH83] D. C. Hemmy, D. J. David, and G. T. Herman. Three-dimensional reconstruction of cranial deformity using computed tomography. *Neurosurgery*, 13(5):534–541, November 1983.

[Hes75] E. H. Hess. The role of pupil size in communication. *Scientific American*, 113–119, November 1975.

[Hjo70] C.-H. Hjortsjo. *Man's Face and Mimic Language*. Studentliterature, Lund, Sweden, 1970.

[HL83] W. S. Hinshaw and A. H. Lent. An introduction to NMR imaging from the bloch equation to the imaging equation. *Proc. IEEE*, 71(3):338–350, March 1983.

[HN54] A. F. Huxley and R. Niedergerke. Structural changes in muscle during contraction. *Nature*, 173:971–973, 1954.

[Hog81] B. Hogarth. *Drawing the Human Head*. Watson-Guptill, New York, 1981.

[HPW88] D. R. Hill, A. Pearce, and B. Wyvill. Animating speech: An automated approach using speech synthesis by rules. *The Visual Computer*, 3:277–289, 1988.

[HSGR84] U. Hadar, T. J. Steiner, E. C. Grant, and F. C. Rose. The timing of shifts in head postures during conversation. *Human Movement Science*, 3:237–245, 1984.

[HS85] P. Hanrahan and D. Sturman. Interactive animation of parametric models. *The Visual Computer*, 1(4):260–266, 1985.

[HVW85] J. D. Hale, P. E. Valk, and J. C. Watts. MR imaging of blood vessels using three-dimensional reconstruction methodology. *Radiology*, 157(3):727–733, December 1985.

[Inc93] Bright Star Technologies Inc. *Beginning Reading Software*. Sierra On-Line, Inc., 1993.

[IYT93] T. Ishii, T. Yasuda, and J. Toriwaki. A generation model for human skin texture. In N. M. Thalmann and D. Thalmann, editors, *Proc. CG International '93: Communicating with Virtual Worlds*, pages 139–150. Springer-Verlag, Tokyo, 1993.

[Joy88] K. Joy, C. Grant, and N. Max, editors. *Image Synthesis, SIGGRAPH '88 Course Notes #9*. ACM, New York, August 1988.

[KA91] T. Kurihara and K. Arai. A transformation method for modeling and animation of the human face from photographs. In N. Magnenat-Thalmann and D. Thalmann, editors, *Computer Animation '91*, pages 45–58. Springer-Verlag, Tokyo, 1991.

[Kau88] A. Kaufman. Tsl — a texture synthesis language. *Visual Computer*, 4(3):148–158, 1988.

[Kay79] D. Kay. Transparency, reflection and ray tracing for computer synthesized images. Master's thesis, Cornell University, Ithaca, NY, January 1979.

[KB84] H. D. Kochanek and R. H. Bartels. Interpolating splines with local tension, continuity and bias control. *Computer Graphics*, 3(18):33–41, 1984.

[KGEB75] R. M. Kenedi, T. Gibson, J. H. Evans, and J. C. Barbenel. Tissue mechanics. *Physics in Medicine and Biology*, 20(5):699–717, February 1975.

[KK86] T. Kay and J. Kajiya. Ray tracing complex scenes. *Computer Graphics (SIGGRAPH '86)*, 20(4):269–278, 1986.

[KK89] J. T. Kajiya and T. L. Kay. Rendering fur with three-dimensional textures. *Computer Graphics*, 3(23):138–145, August 1989.

[Kle88] Kleiser-Walczak. *Sextone for President*, Short Animated Film. Hollywood, CA, 1988.

[Kle89a] J. Kleiser. A fast, efficient, accurate way to represent the human face. In *State of the Art in Facial Animation, SIGGRAPH '89 Tutorials*, Volume 22, pages 37–40. ACM, New York, 1989.

[Kle89b] Kleiser-Walczak, Hollywood, CA. *Don't Touch Me*, Short Animated Film. Hollywood, CA, 1989.

[KM77] R. D. Kent and F. D. Minifie. Coarticulation in recent speech production models. *Journal of Phonetics*, 5:115–135, 1977.

[KMMTT91] P. Kalra, A. Mangili, N. Magnenat-Thalmann, and D. Thalmann. SMILE: a multi layered facial animation system. In *IFIP WG 5.10*, pages 189–198. Tokyo, 1991.

[KMMTT92] P. Kalra, A. Mangili, N. Magnenat-Thalmann, and D. Thalmann. Simulation of facial muscle actions based on rational free form deformations. In *Proc. Eurographics 92*, pages 59–69. Cambridge, 1992.

[KMT94] P. Kalra and N. Magnenat-Thalmann. Modeling vascular expressions in facial animation. In *Computer Animation '94*, pages 50–58. IEEE Computer Society Press, Los Alamitos, CA, May 1994.

[Knu69] D. Knuth. *The Art of Computer Programming, Volume 2: Seminumerical Algorithms*. Addison-Wesley, Reading, MA, 1969.

[Kod61] Eastman Kodak Co. *Studio Techniques for Portrait Photography*. Kodak Publication No. O-4., Rochester, NY, 1961.

[KT73] J. J. Kulikowski and D. J. Tolhurst. Psychophysical evidence for sustained and transient detectors in human vision. *Journal of Physiology*, 232:149–162, 1973.

[Kun89] J. Kunz. Painting portraits in watercolor: Part 1 — facial features. *The Artist's Magazine*, 6(6):62–71, 1989.

[KWT88] M. Kass, A. Witkin, and D. Terzopoulos. Snakes: Active contour models. *International Journal of Computer Vision*, 1(4):321–331, January 1988.

[Lar86] W. Larrabee. A finite element model of skin deformation. I. Biomechanics of skin and soft tissue: A review. *Laryngoscope*, 96:399–405, 1986.

[Las87] J. Lassiter. Principles of traditional animation applied to 3D computer animation. *SIGGRAPH '87 Tutorials*, Volume 21, pages 35–44. ACM, New York, 1987.

[LC87] W. E. Lorensen and H. E. Cline. Marching Cubes: High resolution 3D surface construction algorithm. *Computer Graphics*, 21(4):163–169, 1987.

[Len80] P. Lennie. Parallel visual pathways; a review. *Vision Research*, 20:561–594, 1980.

[Lew89] J. P. Lewis. Algorithms for solid noise synthesis. *Computer Graphics (SIGGRAPH '86)*, 23(3):263–270, 1989.

[Lew91] J. P. Lewis. Automated lip-sync: Background and techniques. *J. of Visualization and Computer Animation*, 2(4):118–122, October-December 1991.

[LGMCB94] B. LeGoff, T. Guiard-Marigny, M. Cohen, and C. Benoit. Real-time analysis-synthesis and intelligibility of talking faces. In *Proc. 2nd ETRW on Speech Synthesis*, pages 53–56. New Platz, New York, 1994.

[LKMT91] A. LeBlanc, P. Kalra, and N. Magnenat-Thalmann. Sculpting with the ball and mouse metaphor. In *Proc. Graphics Interface '91*, pages 152–159. Canadian Information Processing Society, Calgary, 1991.

[Lof90] A. Löfqvist. Speech as audible gestures. In W.J. Hardcastle and A. Marchal, editors, *Speech Production and Speech Modeling*, pages 289–322. Kluwer Academic Publishers, Dordrecht, 1990.

[LP87] J. P. Lewis and F. I. Parke. Automatic lip-synch and speech synthesis for character animation. In *Proc. Graphics Interface '87 CHI+CG '87*, pages 143–147. Canadian Information Processing Society, Calgary, 1987.

[LSS85] D. R. Ladd, K. Scherer, and K. E. Silverman. An integrated approach to studying intonation and attitude. In C. Johns-Lewis, editor, *Intonation in Discourse*. Croome Helm, London-Sydney, 1985.

[LTW93] Y. Lee, D. Terzopoulos, and K. Waters. Constructing physics-based facial models of individuals. In *Proc. Graphics Interface '93*, pages 1–8. Canadian Information Processing Society, May 1993.

[LTW95] Y. Lee, D. Terzopoulos, and K. Waters. Realistic modeling for facial animation. *Computer Graphics*, 29(4):55–62, August 1995.

[Mad69] R. Madsen. *Animated Film: Concepts, Methods, Uses.* Interland, New York, 1969.

[MAH89] S. Morishima, K. Aiwaza, and H. Harashima. An intelligent facial image coding driven by speech and phoneme. In *Proc. IEEE ICASSP89*, pages 1795–1798. IEEE Computer Society Press, Los Alamitos, 1989.

[MG76] J. Markel and A. Gray. *Linear Prediction of Speech.* Springer-Verlag, New York, 1976.

[MH93] S. Morishima and H. Harashima. Facial animation synthesis for human-machine communication system. In *Proc. 5th International Conf. on Human-Computer Interaction*, Volume II, pages 1085–1090. ACM, New York, August 1993.

[Mil88] G. Miller. The motion dynamics of snakes and worms. *Computer Graphics*, 22(4):169–178, 1988.

[MTMdT89] N. Magnenat-Thalmann, H. Minh, M. deAngelis, and D. Thalmann. Design, transformation and animation of human faces. *The Visual Computer*, 5:32–39, 1989.

[MTPT88] N. Magnenat-Thalmann, N. E. Primeau, and D. Thalmann. Abstract muscle actions procedures for human face animation. *Visual Computer*, 3(5):290–297, 1988.

[MTT87] N. Magnenat-Thalmann and D. Thalmann, editors. *Synthetic Actors in Computer-Generated 3D Films.* Springer-Verlag, Tokyo, 1987.

[MP91] K. Mase and A. Pentland. Automatic lipreading by optical-flow analysis. *Systems and Computers in Japan*, 22:6, 1991.

[Nag72] M. Nagao. Picture recognition and data structure. In Nake and Rosenfeld, editors, *Graphics Languages*. Elsevier Science, North-Holland, Amsterdam, 1972.

[NDW93] J. Neider, T. Davis, and M. Woo. *OpenGL Programming Guide: The Official Guide to Learning OpenGL.* Addison-Wesley, Reading, MA, 1993.

[NHK+85] H. Nishimura, A. Hirai, T. Kawai, T. Kawata, I. Shirakawa, and K. Omura. Object modeling by distribution function and method of image generation. In *Electronic Communications Conf.*, J68-D(4):718-725, 1985. (In Japanese.)

[NHRD90] M. Nahas, H. Huitric, M. Rioux, and J. Domey. Facial image synthesis using texture recording. *The Visual Computer*, 6(6):337–343, 1990.

[NHS88] M. Nahas, H. Huitric, and M. Sanintourens. Animation of a B-spline figure. *The Visual Computer*, 3(5):272–276, March 1988.

[NN85] T. Nishita and E. Nakamae. Continuous tone representation of three-dimensional objects taking account of shadows and interreflection. *Computer Graphics (SIGGRAPH '85)*, 19(3):23–30, 1985.

[Nit79] E. B. Nitchie. *How to Read Lips for Fun and Profit*. Hawthorne Books, New York, 1979.

[NNS72] M. Newell, R. Newell, and T. Sancha. A new approach to the shaded picture problem. In *Proc. ACM National Conf.*, pages 443–450. ACM, New York, 1972.

[NS79] W. Newman and R. Sproull. *Principles of Interactive Computer Graphics, Second edition*. McGraw-Hill, Auckland, Australia, 1979.

[Par72] F. I. Parke. Computer generated animation of faces. Master's thesis, University of Utah, Salt Lake City, UT, June 1972. UTEC-CSc-72-120.

[Par74] F. I. Parke. A Parameteric Model for Human Faces. PhD thesis, University of Utah, Salt Lake City, UT, December 1974. UTEC-CSc-75-047.

[Par82] F. I. Parke. Parameterized models for facial animation. *IEEE Computer Graphics and Applications*, 2(9):61–68, November 1982.

[Par90] F. I. Parke, editor. *State of the Art in Facial Animation, SIGGRAPH '90 Course Notes #26*. ACM, New York, August 1990.

[Par91a] F. I. Parke. Perception-based animation rendering. *Journal of Visualization and Computer Animation*, 2:44–51, 1991.

[Par91b] F. I. Parke. Techniques for facial animation. In N. Magnenat-Thalmann and D. Thalmann, editors, *New Trends in Animation and Visualization*, pages 229–241. John Wiley, Chichester, 1991.

[Pat95] M. Patel. Colouration issues in computer generated facial animation. *Computer Graphics Forum (UK)*, 14(2):117–126, June 1995.

[PB81] S. M. Platt and N. I. Badler. Animating facial expressions. *Computer Graphics*, 15(3):245–252, 1981.

[Pea85] D. Peachey. Solid texturing of complex surfaces. *Computer Graphics (SIGGRAPH '85)*, 19(3):279–286, July 1985.

[Pel91] C. Pelachaud. Communication and Coarticulation in Facial Animation. PhD thesis, University of Pennsylvania, Philadelphia, October 1991. Technical Report MS-CIS-91-77.

[Per85] K. Perlin. An image synthesizer. *Computer Graphics (SIGGRAPH '85)*, 19(3):287–296, July 1985.

[Per89] K. Perlin. Hypertexture. *Computer Graphics*, 23(3):253–262, August 1989.

[PFTV86] W. Press, B. Flanney, S. Teukolsky, and W. Verttering. *Numerical Recipes: The Art of Scientific Computing*. Cambridge University Press, Cambridge, UK, 1986.

[Pie89] S. D. Pieper. More than skin deep: Physical modeling of facial tissue. Master's thesis, Massachusetts Institute of Technology, Media Arts and Sciences, Cambridge, MA, 1989.

[Pie91] S. D. Pieper. CAPS: Computer-Aided Plastic Surgery. PhD thesis, Massachusetts Institute of Technology, Media Arts and Sciences, Cambridge, MA, September 1991.

[Pix88] PIXAR. *Tin Toy*, Short Animated Film. San Rafael, CA, 1988.

[Pla80] S. M. Platt. A system for computer simulation of the human face. Master's thesis, The Moore School, University of Pennsylvania, Philadelphia, 1980.

[PMTT91] A. Paouri, N. Magnenat-Thalmann, and D. Thalmann. Creating realistic three-dimensional human shape characters for computer generated films. In N. Magnenat-Thalmann and D. Thalmann, editors, *Proc. Computer Animation '91*, pages 89–99. Springer-Verlag, Geneva, 1991.

[Pol87] Polhemus Navigations Sciences. *3Space Isotrack Users Manual*. Colchester, VT, 1987.

[Por83] T. Porter. Spherical shading. *Computer Graphics (SIGGRAPH '83)*, 17(3):282–285, July 1983.

[PR85] D. Pearson and J. Robinson. Visual communication at very low data rates. *Proc. IEEE*, 73:795–812, April 1985.

[PWWH86] A. Pearce, B. Wyvill, G. Wyvill, and D. Hill. Speech and expression: A computer solution to face animation. In *Proc. Graphics Interface '86*, pages 136–140. Canadian Information Processing Society, Calgary, 1986.

[RCI91] R. Rosenblum, W. Carlson, and E. Tripp III. Simulating the structure and dynamics of human hair: Modelling, rendering and animation. *J. Visualization and Computer Animation*, 2(4):141–148, October-December 1991.

[Ree90] W. T. Reeves. Simple and complex facial animation: Case studies. In *State of the Art in Facial Animation, SIGGRAPH '90 Course Notes #26*, pages 88–106. ACM, New York, August 1990.

[Ric73] A. A. Ricci. A constructive geometry for computer graphics. *The Computer Journal*, 16(2):157–160, May 1973.

[Rob63] L. Roberts. Machine perception of three dimensional solids. Technical Report TR 315, Massachusetts Institute of Technology, Cambridge, MA, 1963.

[Rom67] G. J. Romanes. *Cunningham's Manual of Practical Anatomy, Volume 3: Head, Neck, and Brain*. Oxford Medical Publications, Oxford, 1967.

[RS79] L. Rabiner and R. Schafer. *Digital Processing of Speech Signals*. Prentice-Hall, Englewood Cliffs, NJ, 1979.

[RVK78] E. H. Rose, L. M. Vistnes, and G. A. Ksander. A microarchitectural model of regional variations in hypodermal mobility in porcine and human skin. *Annals of Plastic Surgery*, 1(3):252–266, 1978.

[RWE69] G. Romney, G. Watkins, and D. Evans. Real time display of computer generated half-tone perspective pictures. In *Proc. 1968 IFIP Congress*, pages 973–978. Elsevier Science, North-Holland, Amsterdam, 1969.

[SBGS69] R. Schumacker, B. Brand, M. Gilliland, and W. Sharp. Study for applying computer generated images to visual simulation. Technical Report AFHRL-TR-69-14, U. S. Air Force Human Resources Lab., 1969. NTIS AD 700 375.

[SBMH94] M. A. Sagar, D. Bullivant, G. D. Mallinson, and P. J. Hunter. A virtual environment and model of the eye for surgical simulation. *Computer Graphics (SIGGRAPH '94)*, 28(4):205–212, July 1994.

[Sib78] R. Sibson. Locally equiangular triangulations. *The Computer Journal*, 21(3):243–245, 1978.

[Sin91] A.Singh. *Optical Flow Computation: A Unified Perspective*. IEEE Computer Society Press, Los Alamitos, CA, 1991.

[SLS84] K. Scherer, D. R. Ladd, and K. Silverman. Vocal cues to speaker affect: Testing two models. *Journal Acoustical Society of America*, 76:1346–1356, November 1984.

[Smi78] A. Smith. Color gamut transform pairs. *Computer Graphics (SIGGRAPH '78)*, 12(1):12–19, 1978.

[SP86] T. W. Sederberg and S. R. Parry. Free-form deformation of solid geometry models. *Computer Graphics (SIGGRAPH '86)*, 20(4):151–160, 1986.

[SSS74] I. Sutherland, R. Sproull, and R. Schumacker. A characterization of ten hidden-surface algorithms. *Computing Surveys*, 6(1):1–55, 1974.

[Sut74] I. E. Sutherland. Three-dimensional data input by tablet. *Proceedings of the IEEE*, 62:453–461, 1974.

[Ter88] D. Terzopoulos. The computation of visible-surface representations. *IEEE Trans. on Pattern Analysis and Machine Intelligence*, PAMI-10(4):417–438, 1988.

[TF88a] D. Terzopoulos and K. Fleischer. Deformable models. *The Visual Computer*, 4(6):306–331, 1988.

[TF88b] D. Terzopoulos and K. Fleischer. Viscoelasticity, plasticity and fracture. *Computer Graphics*, 22(4):269–278, 1988.

[TJ81] F. Thomas and O. Johnson. *Disney Animation: The Illusion of Life.* Abbeville Press, New York, 1981.

[TLSP80] J. T. Todd, S. M. Leonard, R. E. Shaw, and J. B. Pittenger. The perception of human growth. *Scientific American*, 242:106–114, 1980.

[Tod80] J. T. Todd. Private communication. 1980.

[Tol75] D. J. Tolhurst. Sustained and transient channels in human vision. *Vision Research*, 15:1151–1155, 1975.

[TST87] Y. Takashima, H. Shimazu, and M. Tomono. Story driven animation. In *CHI+CG '87*, pages 149–153. ACM, New York, 1987.

[TW90] D. Terzopoulos and K. Waters. Physically-based facial modeling, analysis, and animation. *J. of Visualization and Computer Animation*, 1(4):73–80, March 1990.

[TW91] D. Terzopoulous and K. Waters. Techniques for realistic facial modeling and animation. In N. Magnenat-Thalmann and D. Thalmann, editors, *Computer Animation '91*, pages 59–74. Springer-Verlag, Tokyo, 1991.

[TW93] D. Terzopoulos and K. Waters. Analysis and synthesis of facial image sequences using physical and anatomical models. *IEEE Transactions on Pattern Analysis and Machine Intelligence*, 15(6):569–579, 1993.

[Vie93] Viewpoint. *Viewpoint Data Catalog.* 1993.

[VMW83] M. W. Vannier, J. F. Marsh, and J. O. Warren. Three-dimensional computer graphics for craniofacial surgical planning and evaluation. *Computer Graphics*, 17(3):263–273, 1983.

[WA77] K. Weiler and P. Atherton. Hidden surface removal using polygon sorting. *Computer Graphics* (SIGGRAPH '77), 11(2):214–222, 1977.

[Wai89] C. T. Waite. The Facial Action Control Editor, FACE: A parametric facial expression editor for computer generated animation. Master's thesis, Massachusetts Institute of Technology, Media Arts and Sciences, Cambridge, MA, February 1989.

[Wan93] C. L. Wang. Langwidere: Hierarchical spline based facial animation system with simulated muscles. Master's thesis, University of Calgary, Calgary, October 1993.

[War69] J. Warnock. A hidden line algorithm for halftone picture representation. Technical Report TR 4-15, University of Utah, Salt Lake City, UT, 1969.

[War73] R. Warwick. *Grey's Anatomy, 35th Edition.* Longman Group, London, 1973.

[Waf73] J. H. Warfel. *The Head, Neck and Trunk.* Lea and Febiger, Philadelphia, 1973.

[Wal82] E. F. Walther. *Lipreading*. Nelson-Hall Inc, Chicago, 1982.

[Wat70] G. Watkins. A Real Time Hidden Surface Algorithm. PhD thesis, University of Utah, Salt Lake City, UT, June 1970. Technical Report UTEC-CSc-70-101.

[Wat87] K. Waters. A muscle model for animating three-dimensional facial expressions. *Computer Graphics (SIGGRAPH '87)*, 21(4):17–24, July 1987.

[Wat92] K.Waters. A physical model of facial tissue and muscle articulation derived from computer tomography data. In *SPIE Conf. Visualization in Biomedical Computing*, Volume 1808, pages 574–583. SPIE, Bellingham, WA, 1992.

[Wat93] T. Watanabe. Voice-responsive eye-blinking feedback for improved human-to-machine speech input. In *Proc. 5th International Conf. on Human-Computer Interaction*, Volume II, pages 1091–1096. ACM, New York, August 1993.

[Wed87] C. Wedge. Balloon guy. *SIGGRAPH Animation Film Show*, August 1987.

[Wei82] P. Weil. About face. Master's thesis, Massachusetts Institute of Technology, Architecture Group, Cambridge, MA, August 1982.

[Wel91] W. Welsh. Model-Based Coding of Images. PhD thesis, Essex University, Electronic System Engineering, Colchester, UK, 1991.

[Whi80] T. Whitted. An improved illumimation model for shaded display. *CACM*, 23(6):343–349, June 1980.

[WHP88] B. Wyvill, D. R. Hill, and A. Pearce. Animating speech: An automated approach using speech synthesized by rules. *The Visual Computer*, 3(5):277–289, March 1988.

[WI82] I. I. Witten. *Principles of Computer Speech*. Academic Press, London, 1982.

[Wil78] L. Williams. Casting curved shadows on curved surfaces. *Computer Graphics (SIGGRAPH '78)*, 12(3):270–274, 1978.

[Wil83] L. Williams. Pyramidal parametrics. In *Computer Graphics (SIGGRAPH '83)*, 17(1):1–11, 1983.

[Wil90a] L. Williams. 3D paint. *Computer Graphics*, 24(2):225–233, March 1990.

[Wil90b] L. Williams. Performance driven facial animation. *Computer Graphics*, 24(4):235–242, 1990.

[WL93] K. Waters and T. M. Levergood. DECface: an automatic lip synchronization algorithm for synthetic faces. Technical Report CRL 93/4, DEC Cambridge Research Laboratory, Cambridge, MA, September 1993.

[WMW86] B. Wyvill, C. McPheeters, and G. Wyvill. Animating soft objects. *Visual Computer*, 2(4):235–242, August 1986.

[Wol91] G. Wolberg. *Digital Image Warping*. IEEE Computer Society Press, Los Alamitos, CA, 1991.

[Woo86] J. R. Woodwark. Blends in geometric modeling. In *Proc. 2nd IMA Conf. on the Mathematics of Surfaces*. September 1986.

[Wri77] V. Wright. Elasticity and deformation of the skin. In H. R. Elden, editor, *Biophysical Properties of Skin*. Wiley-Interscience, New York, 1977.

[WR88] B. W. Peterson and F. J. Richmond. *Control of Head Movement*. Oxford University Press, Oxford, 1988.

[WREE67] C. Wylie, G. Romney, D. Evans, and A. Erdahl. Halftone perspective drawing by computer. In *Proc. Fall Joint Computer Conf.*, pages 49–58. 1967.

[WS92] Y. Watanabe and Y. Suenaga. A trigonal prism-based method for hair image generation. *IEEE Computer Graphics and Applications*, 12(1):47–53, January 1992.

[WSW90] W. Welsh, S. Searby, and J. Waite. Nodel-base image coding. *British Telecom Technology Journal*, 8(3):94–106, July 1990.

[WT91] K. Waters and D. Terzopoulos. Modeling and animating faces using scanned data. *J. of Visualization and Computer Animation*, 2(4):123–128, October-December 1991.

[WW90] J. Waite and W. Welsh. Head boundary location using snakes. *British Telecom Technology Journal*, 8(3):127–136, July 1990.

[WWDB89] P. L. Williams, R. Warwick, M. Dyson, and L. H. Bannister. *Grey's Anatomy, 37th Edition*. Churchill Livingstone, London, 1989.

[WS81] C. Williams and K. Stevens. Vocal correlates of emotional states. In *Speech Evaluation in Psychiatry*. Grune and Stratton, New York, 1981.

[YS87] T. Yamana and Y. Suenaga A Method of Hair Representation Using Anisotropic Reflection. *IECEJ Technical Report*, PRU87-3:15–20, May 1987. (In Japanese.)

[YCH89] A. L. Yuille, D. S. Cohen, and P. W. Hallinan. Feature extraction from faces using deformable templates. In *IEEE Computer Society Conference on Computer Vision and Pattern Recognition (CVPR'89)*, pages 104–109. IEEE Computer Society Press, Los Alamitos, CA, June 1989.

Index